The Bible Speaks Today
Series editors: Alec Motyer (OT)
John Stott (NT)
Derek Tidball (Bible Themes)

The Message of
the Church

The Bible Speaks Today: Bible Themes series

The Message of the Church

Assemble the people before me

Chris Green

Oak Hill Theological College, London

Inter-Varsity Press

InterVarsity Press
P.O. Box 1400, Downers Grove, IL 60515-1426
Internet: www.ivpress.com
Email: email@ivpress.com

ISBN 978-0-8308-2415-1 (print)
ISBN 978-0-8308-7964-9 (digital)

Printed in the United States of America ∞

Library of Congress Cataloging-in-Publication Data
Green, Christopher, 1958-
  The message of the church / Chris Green.
    pages cm.—(The Bible speaks today: Bible themes series)
  Includes bibliographical references.
  ISBN 978-0-8308-2415-1 (pbk. : alk. paper)
  1. Church—Biblical teaching. 2. Bible—Theology. I. Title.
BV600.3.G725 2014
262—dc23

                                                                    2013042804

P	22	21	20	19	18	17	16	15	14	13	12	11	10	9	8	7	6	5	4	3	2	1
Y	32	31	30	29	28	27	26	25	24	23	22	21	20	19	18	17	16	15	14			

*Gracious Father, I humbly pray thee for thy Holy Catholic
Church; fill it with all truth, in all truth with all peace;
where it is corrupt, purge it; where it is in error, direct it;
where it is superstitious, rectify it; where anything is amiss,
reform it; where it is right, strengthen and confirm it;
where is want, furnish it; where it is divided and rent asunder,
make up the breaches of it; O Thou Holy One of Israel.*

A prayer written by William Laud, first published in
A Summarie of Devotion in 1677 (cited in T. George, *Galatians*
[NAC Nashville: Broadman & Holman, 1994], p. 283).

For Sharon, Edward and Alex

Contents

BST | The Bible Speaks Today

GENERAL PREFACE

THE BIBLE SPEAKS TODAY describes three series of expositions, based on the books of the Old and New Testaments, and on Bible themes that run through the whole of Scripture. Each series is characterized by a threefold ideal:

- to expound the biblical text with accuracy
- to relate it to contemporary life, and
- to be readable.

These books are, therefore, not 'commentaries', for the commentary seeks rather to elucidate the text than to apply it, and tends to be a work rather of reference than of literature. Nor, on the other hand, do they contain the kinds of 'sermons' that attempt to be contemporary and readable without taking Scripture seriously enough. The contributors to *The Bible Speaks Today* series are all united in their convictions that God still speaks through what he has spoken, and that nothing is more necessary for the life, health and growth of Christians than that they should hear what the Spirit is saying to them through his ancient – yet ever modern – Word.

ALEC MOTYER
JOHN STOTT
DEREK TIDBALL
Series editors

Author's preface

I am so grateful for being part of the experiment of Grace Church, Highlands, and for working at Oak Hill Theological College among many young people preparing to serve Christ's church. Wendy Bell, the librarian, has found me everything I ever wanted, and Adam Stewart, George Crowder, Andrew Sach and Andrew Towner have been more useful conversation partners than they realized. Philip Duce at Inter-Varsity Press and Derek Tidball the series editor have been consistently patient and encouraging. Many churches have listened as I have had this project on my heart, and my dear wife and children must at times have thought I love the church more than them.

One cannot write on the church without being aware of 'the communion of the saints', the crowd of believers across time and space. My great predecessor at Oak Hill, Alan Stibbs, is little known today, but his two short books on the church published half a century ago have sat on my desk as masterpieces of robust, succinct evangelical thought.[1] It is sometimes alleged that evangelicals lack a doctrine of the church; Stibbs alone disproves that.

The other 'saint' is the presiding genius of this series, the late John Stott, who died as I was working on the manuscript. All contributors to 'The Bible Speaks Today' hear Stott's meticulous phrasing as they write, and are rightly daunted by his passionate devotion to clear exposition of Scripture.

With gratitude for two such great saints, we are aware once again of God's permanent kindness to his church in never failing to give us such gifts.

CHRIS GREEN
Oak Hill College, London
Easter 2013

---

[1] A. M. Stibbs, *The Church Universal and Local* (London: Church Book-Room Press, 1948) and *God's Church* (London: IVP, 1959).

Abbreviations

Bibles

ASV	American Standard Version
ESV	English Standard Version
HCSB	Holman Christian Study Bible
KJV	King James Version
LXX	Septuagint
NASB	New American Standard Bible (Chicago: Moody, 1977)
NIV	New International Version
NKJV	New King James Bible (Nashville: Thomas Nelson, 1982)
NLT	New Living Translation (Carol Stream: Tyndale, 2004)
NRSV	New Revised Standard Version (Cambridge: Cambridge University Press, 1989)

Commentary series

AB	Anchor Bible
BECNT	Baker Exegetical Commentary on the New Testament
BST	The Bible Speaks Today
CBC	Cornerstone Biblical Commentary
CGTC	Cambridge Greek Testament Commentary
CNTC	Calvin's New Testament Commentaries
EBC	Expositors' Bible Commentary
ECNT	Expositors' Commentary on the New Testament
ICC	International Critical Commentary
IVPNTC	IVP New Testament Commentary
NAC	New American Commentary
NIBC	New International Biblical Commentary

NICNT	New International Commentary on the New Testament
NIGTC	New International Greek Testament Commentary
NIVAC	New International Version Application Commentary
PNTC	The Pillar New Testament Commentary
TNTC	Tyndale New Testament Commentary
WBC	Word Biblical Commentary

Other works

BGD	*A Greek-English Lexicon of the New Testament and Other Early Christian Literature*, rev. and augmented F. Walter Gingrich and Frederick W. Danker from Walter Bauer's 5th ed. 1958 (2nd ed., Chicago and London: University of Chicago Press, 1979)
DLNTD	*Dictionary of the Later New Testament and its Developments*, eds. Ralph P. Martin and Peter H. Davids (Downers Grove and Leicester: IVP, 1997)
DPL	*Dictionary of Paul and His Letters*, eds. Gerald F. Hawthorne, Ralph P. Martin and Daniel G. Reid (Downers Grove and Leicester: IVP, 2003)
EQ	*Evangelical Quarterly*
JETS	*Journal of the Evangelical Theological Society*
JSOTSS	*Journal for the Study of The Old Testament Supplement Series*
LS	*A Greek-English Lexicon*, H. G. Liddell and R. Scott, new ed. H. S. Jones and R. McKenzie (Oxford: Oxford University Press, 1925)
NIDPCM	*New International Dictionary of Pentecostal and Charismatic Movements*, eds. Stanley M. Burgess and Eduard M. van der Maas (Grand Rapids: Zondervan, 2002–03)
NPNF	Nicene and Post-Nicene Fathers (http://ecmarsh.com/fathers/index.html)
NSBT	*New Studies in Biblical Theology*
RTR	*Reformed Theological Review*
SOED	*Shorter Oxford English Dictionary* (Oxford: Clarendon 1978)
SNTSMS	*Society for New Testament Studies Monograph Series*
TDNT	*Theological Dictionary of the New Testament*, eds. G. Kittel, G. Friedrich and G. Bromiley (Grand Rapids: Eerdmans, 1965)

1. Introducing the church

1. I have a dream . . .

I have been with fifteen thousand people singing to stunning contemporary rock, and with two people praying in silence. I have heard how Christ transforms lives, and how Christian friends encourage each other along. I have prayed the Lord's Prayer with people from thirty-five nations, each in our own language, and discussed with them how the gospel impacts the differences that so recently have led to war. I have met people from countries I could not place on a map, and we have treated each other as we truly are – closer than blood relatives in Christ. Time after time I have thought, 'I wish every church could be like this'. Often I have thought, 'I wish *our* church could be like this'. Perhaps you share that dream as well.

Church is made up of people, and God's people at that. Indeed, the English word, 'church' comes from the Greek word, *kyriakon*, meaning 'the Lord's'.[1] The Bible begins and ends with God dwelling with his people, from Adam and Eve in the garden, to untold billions in the great city garden in Revelation. And at each step, God gathered his people together, to speak to them, hear from them, and change them to be more like him.[2] Jesus came to *gather* his reluctant people,[3] and one day he will send his angels to *gather* us all.[4] God gathering his people is what the Bible calls 'church'.

The awful opposite of being gathered as one of God's people is to be scattered as one of his enemies, lonely, loveless and lost, for ever.[5]

---

[1] 1 Cor. 11:20; Rev. 1:10.
[2] See Moses' daily prayer: Num. 10:35–36; Deut. 31:12–13.
[3] Matt. 23:37.
[4] Matt. 24:31.
[5] Lev. 26:33; Deut. 4:27; 28:64–65.

After people built Babel, 'the LORD scattered them from there over all the earth, and they stopped building the city. That is why it was called Babel – because there the LORD confused the language of the whole world. From there the LORD scattered them over the face of the whole earth'.[6] On the Last Day, Jesus will gather one group, 'Come, you who are blessed by my Father', but scatter the other, 'Depart from me, you who are cursed'.[7]

God loves his gathered people. It was only to form his church that the Father sent the Son, that the Son went to the cross, and that the Father and Son sent the Spirit.[8] God wrote the Bible solely to speak to us and bring us to salvation. He warns our leaders that we are 'the church of God' (say this slowly) 'which he bought with his own blood'.[9]

Whether your church is purpose-driven, Jesus-driven, deliberate or intentional, whether it is contagious, irresistible, unstoppable or provocative, whether it has been recently rediscovered or is only just emerging, whether it is five-star or 'come as you are', deep, wide, healthy, organic, equipping, connecting or even unleashed,[10] you trust God's unshakeable plan to make a people for his own possession. Church – a group of vibrant, loving, risk-everything people who are passionately committed to living out the values of God's word and looking forward to the new creation – that is a plan worthy of God himself.

2. . . . and I have a nightmare

But you and I have also endured the nightmare of dreadful services, deadly meetings, bitter power struggles and lingering hurts. It is easy to agree with our savage critic Friedrich Nietzsche, that 'They would have to sing better songs to make me believe in their Redeemer; his disciples would have to look more redeemed!'[11] Those charged with teaching truth have spread lies, those charged with sharing ministry have hoarded it, the broken have stayed broken and – worst of all – the lost have stayed lost.

Some of us share responsibility for that nightmare. If a church is not functioning properly, and we are that church's leadership, we know where to begin to place the blame. Repeated surveys report

---

[6] Gen. 11:8–9, NIV.

[7] Matt. 25:34, 41, NIV.

[8] John 14 – 17.

[9] Acts 20:28, NIV.

[10] All titles of recent books about the church.

[11] *Thus Spake Zarathustra* II 4, quoted by H. Küng, *The Church* (Tunbridge Wells: Search Press, 1968), p. 150.

that church is boring, irrelevant and bigoted, and that Christians yearn for what C. S. Lewis called 'Deep Church': passionately God-honouring, intimate, truthful, connected around the world and across the centuries.[12]

We can address all those things if we truly want to, but cheap solutions are as flawed as the problems themselves. Some have insisted on staying comfortably boring because change is painful – and then hinted that those who do adapt have trivialized the faith. A growing church *must be* a compromised church. Other churches try to make God interesting by making church entertaining, or intellectually relevant, or spiritual, and so the space is filled with lights and smoke machines, or is dark and candlelit, or is empty and Zen-cool – but the Bible is never opened and humbly taught. And so the church remains ignorant about itself.

That is critical. William Gladstone, British prime minister under Queen Victoria, said of his evangelical youth, 'I had been brought up with no notion of the Church as the Church or body of Christ'.[13] He was not the first or last to move to a different tradition of the church because of Evangelical silence on this theme, and was certainly not the last to complain about it.

3. The task

This series studies themes from the central biblical passages which bear upon them, for individual Christians, study groups, a leadership team, or the pastor preparing a sermon. Different churches must apply what they learn in different ways, but God wrote the Bible with your church in mind, and so this book contains an 'Action and Study Guide', to encourage your leaders in obedient practice.

But we need to ask whether 'church' is the right place to start. Many contemporary writers assume a different perspective, which is that because God is a missionary God, we should begin with his mission, and let our doctrine and practice of the church follow. Michael Frost and Alan Hirsch have argued strongly that we think as in the following diagram:[14]

---

[12] C. S. Lewis, 'Mere Christians', *Church Times* 135 (1952). See J. Belcher, *Deep Church: A Third Way Beyond Emerging and Traditional* (Downers Grove: IVP, 2009), p. 13.

[13] Quoted in B. M. G. Reardon, *From Coleridge to Gore: A Century of Religious Thought in Britain* (London: Longman, 1971), p. 31.

[14] M. Frost and A. Hirsch, *The Shaping of Things to Come: Innovation and Mission for the 21st-Century Church* (Peabody: Henderson/Erina/Strand, 2003), p. 209.

This is attractive in many ways, and I share much of that passion. But two aspects trouble me. First, Frost and Hirsch are right that God is a missionary God; but he is simultaneously a Trinity of love, expressed in assembling his saved people around him. Since God is not at war with himself, mission and church are not competing for primacy.[15] Secondly, where does the Bible fit? How are we to find out the right content of those three boxes? I suggest an alternative might be:

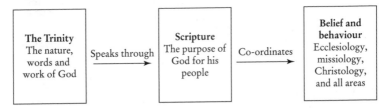

This diagram privileges one God speaking through the Bible, producing a coordinated result among believers. So a biblical theology of mission should shape the form and function of the church – and in the same way a biblical theology of church should shape the form and function of mission.[16] For instance, we can say that mission is temporary, but church is eternal. Or, mission is a means, not an end, but church is both means and end. To rephrase John Piper, mission only exists because church doesn't.[17] God coordinates his one truth, so getting one aspect right means getting the others right as well – provided we sit humbly under his word.

---

[15] He is also a Trinity of truth, so truth and love similarly align. So will justice, holiness and so on.

[16] We must distinguish Christology from Christ: it is not our Christology which produces our missiology and our ecclesiology, but the reigning Son, a member of the Trinity, who speaks through the Scriptures about himself and his work. This guarantees the truth of our Christology, and coordinates it with missiology and ecclesiology.

[17] Piper says, 'Mission is not the ultimate goal of the church. Worship is. Missions exist because worship doesn't. Worship is ultimate.' It is the opening sentence of *Let the Nations be Glad: A Biblical Theology of Missions* (Leicester: IVP, 1994).

4. The plan

God is eternally and infinitely wise, so every doctrine is endless, and interacts with all others ceaselessly. There are almost one hundred biblical images of the church,[18] feeding into the doctrinal questions of the past. And the doctrine of the church is not academic: pastors who lead churches, and the churches they lead, need what the Bible says about who they are and what they are to do. And differing publications, conferences, blogs and websites aim to equip pastors to be better at their roles (preachers, leaders, pioneers, prophets, managers, visionaries . . .), and to equip church members to exercise their ministries (gifts, callings, graces, discipleship . . .) in their particular kind of church (emerging, emergent, fresh expression, body-life, paleo-orthodox – you get the idea). Every debate *in* the church touches on some aspect of the doctrine *of* the church, yet any study has to draw the line somewhere.

One pastor advised me, 'Whatever you talk about most is your gospel.' And a scholar said, 'Students don't get what you teach, they catch your enthusiasms.' So we need to agree at the start, that however much we talk about it, and however highly we esteem it, the church is not the gospel. It may be evidence, proof, plausibility, manifestation, physical or cultural expression of the gospel, but it is not the gospel.[19] So 'The Message of the Church', means, or at least I am going to take it to mean, that first, the church *has* a message, which is that God has saved his people through Christ; second, that the church is the created and saved *result* of that message, we are a 'creature of the Word' as Luther famously put it;[20] and finally the church *is* a message, which is that God has saved broken people like us, and by belonging to his people we are trying to respond to him in the ways he requires. Theologically, believing comes first, because we cannot be members of Christ's saved people except by faith, but many people encounter the reality of God's new community (belonging on a human level) before they have saving faith and living discipleship (believing and belonging on a supernatural level, leading to behaving).

This study describes the main contours of the Bible's teaching about the church. Sometimes there is a tight focus, occasionally we

[18] Paul Minear's classic list contains ninety-six. Removing thirty-two 'minor images' the remainder cluster under four headings: 'The people of God', 'new creation', 'fellowship in faith' and 'body of Christ'. P. Minear, *Images of the Church in the New Testament* (London: Lutterworth, 1961), p. 268f.

[19] This is what Lesslie Newbigin meant in his famous summary that the congregation is 'the hermeneutic of the gospel'. L. Newbigin, *The Gospel in a Pluralistic Society* (London: SPCK, 1989), pp. 222–233.

[20] See M. Chandler, E. Geiger and J. Patterson, *Creature of the Word: The Jesus-Centered Church* (Nashville: Broadman and Holman, 2012).

move around to establish patterns. When choosing 'key' passages, the alternatives are usually footnoted. And on some debates I have had to say 'here is a problem, and you may these books helpful'.[21] I have used three principal translations: the ESV, the Holman Christian Standard Bible and the NIV (2011 1st ed.), although other translations appear occasionally as well.

God's plan for his church should give every congregation its purpose and direction. God said to Moses, 'Assemble the people before me, to hear my words, so that they may learn to revere me.'[22] And our prayer and praises echo back: 'Let the assembled peoples gather round you, while you sit enthroned over them on high.'[23]

---

[21] A useful complement to this book is therefore David Peterson, *Encountering God Together: Biblical Patterns for Ministry and Worship* (Nottingham: IVP, 2013). Peterson takes a similar theological position but approaches 'church' more systematically.

[22] Deut. 4:10, NIV.

[23] Ps. 7:7, NIV.

Ephesians
2. The church from eternity to Eden

To begin to understand the church we need a well-read Bible, and a long timescale. The word 'church' can be quite loose,[1] but the biblical equivalent is precise. It did not suddenly appear from nowhere at Pentecost, or in Jesus' teaching about 'my church'. God had successively shaped his people through the Old Testament plotline, and the Hebrew word *qāhāl*, 'assembly', repeatedly described his solemn gathering of those people; above all, it summarized the Sinai meeting and anticipated a future gathering from exile.[2] In its Greek translation, *ekklēsia*, it therefore became the term Christians reached for to describe their meetings, which were the fulfilment of those promises. But 'church' did not really start at Sinai, nor even with sinless people enjoying God's presence in Eden.[3] We must travel into eternity, where God drew his plans, examined the cost, and determined that his church would be his treasure. Ephesians is the book to take us there.

Many early copies of Ephesians have left the destination blank, and perhaps Paul intended his letter to have a wide readership; yet this letter to no-church-in-particular has 'church' as its unifying theme. In it, Paul four times describes 'church' in the most dazzling language, exploring his vision of its heavenly aspect, which is

[1] But so are 'église', 'iglesia', 'kirche', 'chiese' and 'kirk', for example.
[2] See ch. 5. Another word, *'ēdâh*, was more informal, and could also be used of God's people when they were not meeting. *Ekklēsia* is constructed from two words which mean 'called out', but it was always used to mean 'called together'; usage is always more important than etymology. The idea of 'meeting' (assembly, congregation, gathering) is critical, because it was not a simple synonym for 'the nation of Israel', or 'the people of God' generally. *Qāhāl* / *ekklēsia* both mean, 'God's people in their gathered state'.
[3] Doctrinally we would begin with the Trinity, but that is not the format of these expositions. See below, 'Additional Note: The Church and the Trinity', p. 36.

sometimes called the 'cosmic' or 'invisible' church. Those four references will give this chapter its structure, and along the way we shall pause to admire Paul's images of the relationship between Christ and his church. Keep in mind, though, that in among those images and metaphors, 'church' stands out because it alone is not a metaphor: the word means what it says, 'a gathering'.

Paul's thinking in Ephesians stretches from before the creation of the world (1:4) until when the times will have reached their fulfilment (1:10), and reaches from the lower, earthly realms (4:9) up into the heavenly realms (1:3), and then even higher than all the heavens (4:10). He is painting on a vast canvas, but like all great artists, he relates everything to his one central subject: the Lord Jesus Christ.[4] Nineteen times Paul says we are in Christ,[5] three times that we are with Christ (2:5, 6, 20); everything exists under Christ (1:10), and we relate to God through Christ (1:5). Our actions show our reverence for Christ (5:21) and we should live and love as Christ did, and does (5:2, 25, 29). Otherwise, we are separate from Christ (2:12).

With Christ established as the dramatic centre, Paul can afford to direct our gaze elsewhere. Why did God launch this extraordinary salvation plan? *For the church* (1:22).[6] How will he display his wisdom to his enemies? *Through the church* (3:10). Where is his glory to be found? *In the church* (3:21). Where is his love experienced? When Christians love each other *as Christ does the church* (5:29). Those are the four phrases about the church for us to study.

1. God's power was exerted for the church (1:1–23)

Paul's opening sentence contains over two hundred words, so to anchor us, he repeats that Christ is the consistent centre of God's action: God *blessed us in Christ* (1:3), and *predestined us . . . through Christ* (1:5), by *making known to us* his plans that he purposed *in Christ* (1:9). He also emphasizes our response: *Blessed be the God and Father of our Lord Jesus Christ, who has blessed us in Christ with every spiritual blessing in the heavenly places* (1:3).[7] God has *blessed us* in and through Christ, so we bless him. We can follow the trail of Paul's logic by asking questions.

---

[4] W. Liefeld, *Ephesians*, IVPNTC (Downers Grove and Leicester: IVP, 1997), p. 29.
[5] *In Christ* occurs at 1:1, 3, 12, 20; 2:6, 7, 10, 13; 3:6, 11, 21; 4:32; and *in him* (i.e. Christ) at 1:4, 7, 10, 11, 13; 2:21, 22; 3:12.
[6] NIV is smoother than ESV's *to the church*. See below.
[7] NIV translates the first 'blessed' as 'praise'.

a. What has God done? Gathered his people

God *chose* (1:4) and *predestined us* (1:5) from eternity,[8] to *be holy and blameless before him* (1:4) for eternity; in the present he applies Christ's death to his chosen people, in *redemption* and *forgiveness* (1:7) Those combined benefits are *the gospel of salvation* (1:13): *In him you also, when you heard the word of truth, the gospel of your salvation, and believed in him, were sealed with the promised Holy Spirit, who is the guarantee of our inheritance until we acquire possession of it, to the praise of his glory* (1:13–14).

Now, although each of us have *heard* and *believed* individually, at that point we became one of God's people: so in that sentence Paul's words *you* and *your*, like *our* and *we*, are all plural. God's people are the visible result of his *guarantee* that Jesus' work was effective, his reign is secure, his Spirit is given, and his word can be trusted for *our* (joint) *inheritance*. God's eternal plan was to have a chosen, redeemed, forgiven people gathered around him, for ever. That heavenly gathering of his people, is his heavenly church.

b. When was this planned? Before creation

God's time-frame begins *before the foundation of the world* (1:4), moves through our appropriation of Christ's death, when *we have redemption* (1:7), and climaxes in his *plan for the fullness of time* (1:10), which is *to unite all things in him, things in heaven and things on earth* (1:10). So today every conversion, every church plant, every prayer and every act of mercy, is *according to the purpose of him who works all things according to the counsel of his will* (1:11). God's eternal plan for the world was always that Jesus should rule for ever.

c. Where was this achieved? In the heavenly places

The heavenly places (1:3) are the supernatural power-rooms where God has his throne – where too are the malicious forces which enslave and blind people. Paul returns to those shortly, but notice that in this decisive spiritual battleground, God has already won his victory *when he raised [Christ] from the dead and seated him at his right hand in the heavenly places, far above all rule and authority and power and dominion, and above every name that is named, not only in this age but also in the one to come* (1:20–22). The *heavenly places* are the most important place to be blessed, and God in his loving wisdom has done that.

---

[8] Rom. 8:29–30; Col. 3:12; 1 Thess. 1:4; 2 Thess. 2:13.

d. Who has done this? Father, Son and Holy Spirit

When Paul writes 'God' he usually means *the God and Father of our Lord Jesus Christ* (1:3). Throughout the Old Testament, *Lord* is God's personal name,[9] but Paul uses it for *Jesus Christ, our Lord*. Furthermore, the one who brings us to believe in God, to grow in our knowledge of him, to pray to him and to live in a way that pleases him, is *the promised Holy Spirit* (1:13–14). Only God is *holy* in himself, so the *Holy Spirit* is also fully, characteristically, God. In other words, the God who accomplished this plan is Father, Son and Holy Spirit. There is no other God, and he has no other plan, or church. We are the beloved focus of this God's purpose.

e. So who is the most important person in the cosmos? Christ

The Lord Jesus Christ has no rival. He is enthroned at his Father's

> *right hand in the heavenly places, far above all rule and authority and power and dominion, and above every name that is named, not only in this age but also in the one to come. [The Father] put all things under [Jesus'] feet and gave him as head over all things* (1:20–22).[10]

No-one is excluded from his rule, nor can anyone ever supplement him, or replace him in his Father's affection. So now comes the critical question.

f. Why has God done all this?

From one angle, God has done it for the reason he does anything: *to the praise of his glorious grace* (1:6). More precisely, there are now Jewish Christians *to the praise of his glory* (1:12) and Gentile Christians *to the praise of his glory* (1:14). Paul continues in verse 6, *to the praise of his glorious grace, with which he has blessed* (literally, 'graced') *us in the Beloved*.

But that does not fully capture Paul's thought. Until now I have deleted three words from verse 22; replace them and there is a dizzying change of perspective: God raised Jesus

> *from the dead and seated him at his right hand in the heavenly realms, far above all rule and authority, power and dominion, and*

---

[9] E.g. Gen. 15:7; Exod. 6:2; Lev. 11:44–45; Num. 3:13; Deut. 5:6.
[10] Paul uses Ps. 110 and quotes Ps. 8:6; both expand Gen. 1:26–28.

every title that can be given, not only in the present age but also in the one to come. And God placed all things under his feet and appointed him to be head over everything **for the church** (1:20–22).[11]

Those words, *for the church*, govern each of the four acts of God in this passage. God raised Jesus *for the church*; he seated him at his right hand *for the church*; he placed all things under Jesus' feet *for the church*; and appointed him head over everything *for the church*.[12]

In many parts of the world Christians are insignificant, and church is ridiculed. Their future is apparently inevitable decline, with buildings emptying by the week, and the few remaining leaders becoming increasingly shrill or accommodating to keep people coming. Other parts of the world see Christians being murdered into extinction. But neither is the ultimate truth. God has not only organized the whole universe to establish his plan of making a church, and then engineered the path of history and the patterns of billions of individual human hearts, but he eternally purposed that his Son, *the Beloved* (1:6) should die to achieve that plan. And day by day, across the world, he applies it to those *he chose . . . in [Christ] before the foundation of the world, that we should be holy and blameless before him* and *predestined . . . for adoption through Jesus Christ, according to the purpose of his will* (1:4–5). There is nothing in the whole of creation which has any significance outside of God's plan *for the church*.

g. Pause and wonder

(i) The church is God's inheritance

Paul longs for Christians to grasp *the riches of his glorious inheritance in the saints* (1:18), and *inheritance* means that there is a glorious future yet to be entered. But although in verse 14 Paul talks of *our inheritance*, meaning all that Christ has won for us, here he means Christ's *inheritance*, the final and complete gathering of his chosen people that he has won for himself. We are his prize.

(ii) The church are saints

Saints simply means 'the holy people', a holy God's possession, who reflect his holy character.[13] All Christians are saints (1:1, 18), because

---

[11] NIV runs more smoothly than ESV's 'to the church'.
[12] Jesus is *head over everything*, which is not the same as *head of the church* (5:23). Paul wants to establish that nothing, anywhere in the universe, is outside Jesus' rule.
[13] Dan 7:18, 26–27.

they are *holy and blameless in his sight* (1:4, NIV), and members of his perfect, heavenly people. As perfect as him.

(iii) The church is Christ's body

In 1 Corinthians, Paul used 'body' language for the relationships within a single, local congregation,[14] but here he switches scale, and just as in Ephesians 'church' means not one, local assembly but the all-embracing cosmic one, so too *body* means not the local but the cosmic. This is all Christians seen from heaven's perspective. We are Christ's body that he rules and directs as he sees fit, for his own ends. Just as with the word 'church', though, 'body' cannot be used of anything other than either a local or a heavenly gathering.

Is Christ in some way incomplete without the church? The phrase *the fullness of him who fills all in all* (1:23) is complicated,[15] but it surely cannot mean that. Such confusion might come from combining 'head' and 'body' into one image, not keeping them separate.[16] Rather than think of the church as 'completing' Christ, we should think of his filling of the church with his presence, by his Spirit.

We certainly should not think the church as Christ's body in the sense that he cannot act without us, or is indistinguishable from us. Catholic and Orthodox theology has often applied the doctrine of the incarnation to the church as Christ's body, and in such thinking, the church continues Christ's incarnation. Liberal theology, both Catholic and Protestant, can speak similarly, but there the incarnation is a metaphor, as true for us as it was for Jesus. Both produce a 'high' ecclesiology, but Mark Saucy has shown that both are confusing and dangerous.[17] Taking the descriptions of Christ as prophet, priest and king, he insists that none of those describes the church. Unlike Christ, the church is not a prophet of new truth but merely a witness; not the sacrifice for others, but the sinful recipient of his work; not the King, but rather his willing subject. Saucy argues that the alleged 'high' view of the church actually replaces Christ, because only one may be the prophet, priest and king, and if it is to be the church, it cannot be Christ.

That warning is helpful, because some evangelical churches also use those three terms to describe their predominant character: some

---

[14] 1 Cor. 1:2; 12:1 – 14:40.

[15] For a summary see H. W. Hoehner, *Ephesians* (Grand Rapids: Baker, 2002), pp. 294–301, but for solutions see P. T. O'Brien, *The Letter to the Ephesians*, PNTC (Grand Rapids: Eerdmans and Leicester: Apollos, 1999), pp. 149–152 and A. T. Lincoln, *Ephesians*, WBC 42 (Dallas: Word, 1990), pp. 72–78.

[16] See below (p. 33) on Christ as the church's head.

[17] M. Saucy, 'Evangelicals, Catholics, and Orthodox together: Is the church the extension of the incarnation?', *JETS* (June 2000), pp. 193–212.

are prophetic, teaching-based churches; some kingdom-based, justice churches; some priestly, experience-rich churches. If we do that, we should take care to insist, first, that such characteristics are only ever the pale counterpart of Christ's work, second, that Christ holds those three together so we should not dare choose between them, and third, that they are at best a doctrinal summary of several of Christ's offices, never a direct, complete biblical model of church. We are certainly not taught to see church leaders as prophets, priests or kings.

Christ's incarnation was and remains a physical reality, so language about the church being Christ's body is metaphorical, just like our being the vine, the bride, the stones, sheep and so on. That does not mean it is not true, but that we should not push it beyond its intended limits. We are Christ's flock, but that does not mean we have wool and bleat. Similarly, we are Christ's body, but we have not replaced or completed him.

I am therefore uneasy about saying that a church has an 'incarnational' mission, even though the idea has rightly challenged Christians to be compassionate in potentially dangerous situations. The New Testament uses a number of arguments to provoke us to act compassionately, but the similarity between the incarnate Christ and the church as the body of Christ is not one. Equally, the New Testament has a number of conclusions about the church being the body of Christ, but social action is not one. The uniqueness of Christ's incarnation, and its glorious enthronement in heaven today, is a treasure too easily lost.[18] We are dependent on Christ's care, exercised from his heavenly throne, *for the church*. Equally, compassion is too important to build on flimsy exegesis.[19]

2. God's wisdom is demonstrated through the church (2:1 – 3:13)

In the second main section of Ephesians, Paul says that God's intent was that that *through the church the manifold wisdom of God might **now** be made known to the rulers and authorities in the heavenly places. This was according to the **eternal** purpose that he has realized in Christ Jesus our Lord* (3:10–11). God's eternal plan has an outworking now. Again, asking questions shows Paul's thinking.

---

[18] On 'As the Father has sent me, even so I am sending you' (John 20:21), see Andreas Köstenberger, who argues persuasively that Jesus' point is that 'Just as the Father had authority to send me, so I have the authority to send you'. A. Köstenberger, *The Missions of Jesus and the Disciples According to the Fourth Gospel* (Grand Rapids: Eerdmans, 1998).

[19] See ch. 7.

a. How is God's manifold wisdom displayed? Christian unity

The fundamental human division lies between Jew and Gentile. Addressing Gentiles like me, Paul says that *you were dead in your transgressions and sins, in which you used to live when you followed the ways of this world and of the ruler of the kingdom of the air, the spirit who is now at work in those who are disobedient* (2:1–2, NIV). Remember before you became a Christian, and remember that at that time *you were separate from Christ, excluded from citizenship in Israel and foreigners to the covenants of the promise, without hope and without God in the world* (2:12, NIV). We were Christless, homeless, friendless, hopeless and Godless.

Not that Jews were in any better condition. As Paul points out, *we **all** once lived in the passions of our flesh, carrying out the desires of the body and the mind, and were by nature children of wrath, **like the rest** of mankind* (2:3). Jews were, as regards salvation, no better off than the Gentiles, except that God had covenanted he would save them. God made no similar covenant with Gentiles.

But here is the wonder of Christ's work:

> *Remember that formerly you who are Gentiles by birth and called 'uncircumcised' by those who call themselves 'the circumcision' (which is done in the body by human hands) – remember that at that time you were separate from Christ, excluded from citizenship in Israel and foreigners to the covenants of the promise, without hope and without God in the world. **But now in Christ Jesus you who once were far away have been brought near through the blood of Christ*** (2:11–13, NIV).

God has permitted Gentiles to enter into the blessings which he promised to Israel. In fact, this was what God had eternally planned, and Abraham had been circumcised for this very reason.[20]

This was Paul's concern as a *prisoner for Christ Jesus on behalf of you Gentiles* (3:1). He now knew God's age-long plan, and our joint place in it. *This mystery is that the Gentiles are fellow heirs, members of the same body, and partakers of the promise in Christ Jesus through the gospel* (3:6). No longer stateless, but heirs. No longer hopeless, but sharing in the same promise. No longer Christless and Godless, but in Christ. No longer friendless strangers, but heirs together, members together, sharers together.[21] Christ came and *preached peace to you who were far off and peace to those who were near. For through*

[20] Gen. 18:18–19. See ch. 4.
[21] My translation for emphasis: the prefix *syn-* (with) is embedded in three Greek words: *synklēronoma*, *syssōma* and *symmetōga*.

him we both have access in one Spirit to the Father. So then you are no longer strangers and aliens, but you are fellow citizens with the saints and members of the household of God (2:17–19).

Obviously this insight treats racism with contempt. It must make us passionate for Jews and Gentiles both to become believers. But first, we must pause to adore God's wisdom, that his promises to one man eventually blessed every nation, and in his great mercy, those to whom he has made absolutely no covenant promise at all become his people. *But God, being rich in mercy, because of the great love with which he loved us, even when we were dead in our trespasses, made us alive together with Christ – by grace you have been saved* (2:4–5). God owed us nothing, yet he saved us.

b. Before whom is God's manifold wisdom displayed? The heavenly rulers

Now hear the wonder in Paul's voice as he reveals what the church has to do with this.

> *To me … this grace was given, to preach to the Gentiles the unsearchable riches of Christ, and to bring to light for everyone what is the plan of the mystery hidden for ages in God who created all things, so that **through the church** the manifold wisdom of God might now be made known to the rulers and authorities in the heavenly places. This was according to the eternal purpose that he has realized in Christ Jesus our Lord* (3:8–11).

The *rulers and authorities* are those personal forces in the heavenly realms, most likely the malevolent ones led by Satan, the *prince of the power of the air* (2:2). Paul calls them later, *the rulers, … the authorities, … the cosmic powers over this present darkness, … the spiritual forces of evil in the heavenly places* (6:12).

Here is Paul's extraordinary thought. The mere existence of the church demonstrates that Christ has been victorious and is enthroned. The mere existence of a Gentile believer as a full member of God's people displays God's wisdom, and the malevolent beings who hate and defy God are forced to see the evidence of his might and their destruction every time they see the church. Which is permanently before their eyes, because they are *in the heavenly places* (6:12) where God has seated Christ *at his right hand in the heavenly places,* and *raised us up with him and seated us with him in the heavenly places in Christ Jesus* (1:20; 2:6). How wonderful that *through the church the manifold wisdom of God might now be made known to the rulers and authorities in the heavenly places* (3:10).

c. Pause and wonder

(i) The church as a temple

When Paul said we are together becoming a *holy temple*, he brought a central Old Testament motif through Christ to us. The Jerusalem temple, like the tabernacle before it, presented several truths simultaneously. Most obviously, it was the place where God dwelt, and its construction climaxed when his glory arrived, making the mountain, the city and the people his holy possession.[22]

But it simultaneously taught separation. The constant sacrifices exposed the sin which God had not yet removed. Only priests could sacrifice, and only the high priest could enter the Holy of Holies. There he encountered curtains embroidered like a garden and statues of two cherubim, reminders that glorious as the temple was, the way back to Eden was barred.

The temple also demarcated Israel. Solomon prayed that Gentiles would be able to pray towards, but not in, the temple.[23] Ezekiel later reported God's revulsion that Israel had not noticed their privileged status:

> Thus says the Lord GOD: O house of Israel, enough of all your abominations, in admitting foreigners, uncircumcised in heart and flesh, to be in my sanctuary, profaning my temple ... Thus says the Lord GOD: No foreigner, uncircumcised in heart and flesh, of all the foreigners who are among the people of Israel, shall enter my sanctuary.[24]

That corruption led God to withdraw, and Ezekiel's opening describes the terrifying reversal of God's arrival. His judgment was that the temple should be destroyed, desecrated by the presence of *foreigners*.[25] But God promised a new temple, with sin and guilt removed, and all nations welcomed. Isaiah prophesied that the destroying Gentile armies would be removed, and 'there shall no more come into you the uncircumcised and the unclean'.[26] Instead, believing Gentiles would be welcomed:

> And the foreigners who join themselves to the LORD,
> to minister to him, to love the name of the LORD,

---

[22] 2 Chr. 7:1–4.
[23] 2 Chr. 6:32–33.
[24] Ezek. 44:7, 9.
[25] Jer. 51:51; Lam. 5:2.
[26] Isa. 52:1.

and to be his servants,
everyone who keeps the Sabbath and does not profane it,
and holds fast my covenant—
these I will bring to my holy mountain,
and make them joyful in my house of prayer;
their burnt offerings and their sacrifices
will be accepted on my altar;
for my house shall be called a house of prayer
for all peoples. [27]

So calling the church *a temple* says we are what the prophets foretold,[28] and the answer to Solomon's prayers. God is truly among us. That is how the inclusion of the Gentiles in the salvation plan for Jews demonstrates God's wisdom.

(ii) The church as a building

Paul's other image in this section is a growing *building*,[29] with the apostles and prophets as the *foundation*, and Jesus the *cornerstone* (2:21).[30]

In most industrialized countries, large buildings go up with dizzying speed, but once they took decades or even generations to complete, and the image of a building 'growing' would have been entirely natural. More importantly, the picture of a new, expanding temple was another way of describing God's increasing reign over the nations, until 'the whole earth be filled with his glory'.[31] The church is a building which grows because God's glory is among us, and attracts his people; it grows *from Christ* our Lord (4:16) and *to Christ* our goal (4:15). It is ironic that in common use 'church' means the very kind of physical building which cannot grow at all.

3. God's glory is shared in the church (3:14–21)

We have so far explored two of Paul's four sections about the church in Ephesians, and they have both been quite long and complex. The other two are much briefer. This third section about the church is a prayer. If the church is God's temple, then we can see why he prays that *Christ may dwell in your hearts through faith* and that we *may be filled with all the fullness of God* (3:17, 19). That is another way

[27] Isa. 56:6–7.
[28] See G. K. Beale *The Temple and the Church's Mission*, NSBT (Downers Grove: IVP and Leicester: Apollos, 2004), pp. 123–167.
[29] NIV.
[30] Ps. 118:22; Isa. 8:14; 28:16.
[31] Ps. 72:19. See Beale, *Temple*, throughout.

of saying that God's infinite and eternal glory dwells in us, and Paul prays that we may *comprehend with all the saints what is the breadth and length and height and depth, and to know the love of Christ that surpasses knowledge* (3:18–19). He dwells in us, and we dwell in him. We are that temple which God promised to Solomon.

This prayer is that God will *strengthen* us *with power*, and that we may *have strength* to grasp all that he has done, is doing and will do in and for the church. The church has *his power . . . at work within us* (3:20), and the result of God's powerful action will be the presence of his *glory in the church and in Christ Jesus . . . for ever* (3:21). This is not a day to be pessimistic about the church.

But if we have the wrong idea of God's glory and power being in and among us, then we will turn up to church with quite the wrong expectations, and we shall become pessimistic and cynical very quickly. Paul does not mean that churches deserve any kind of necessary visible success because of this. Instead, God's glory is shown as we slowly become more like Jesus, at church, and therefore at home and at work (5:15 – 6:9).

a. Pause and wonder: the church as God's household

The idea of the church as a *family* is perhaps so familiar to us, it is a shock to realize that 3:15 is the only time Paul uses the *family* concept, and he is not even referring to the church. God is the *Father*, and there is wordplay between 'Father' (*pater*) and 'family' (*patria*) to keep in mind. But the word *patria* means more properly *line* or *people*.[32] It is a broad word, and the majority of commentators and Bible translations prefer something like, *from whom every family in heaven and on earth derives its name*, referring to every possible grouping and allegiance. God is the supreme *Father* over every other. We cannot take *family* as a particular synonym for the church here, and the phrase 'the church family' probably ought to be played down.[33]

Instead the images from 2:19–22 show the privileges of being *members of the household of God*. Six words share the Greek word *oikos* (*house*). Gentile believers are no longer *aliens* (*paroikoi*) but *members of the household* (*oikeioi*), *built on* (*epoikodomēthentes*) a sure foundation, where the *building*[34] (*oikodomē*) is being *built together* (*synoikodomeisthe*) to become a *dwelling* (*katoikētērion*).

---

[32] Luke 2:4; Acts 3:25. It 'can denote a family, one's father's house, a clan, a tribe or even a nation' (Lincoln, *Ephesians*, p. 202).

[33] NLT unhelpfully also uses 'family' in 2:19.

[34] NIV.

The emphasis falls on the privilege of being allowed to belong to God when we are, by nature, foreigners with no claim on him.

It has its roots in the idea that God's *house* is another way of describing his global reign. At the precise moment that David began to plan a temple (a *house*) for God, God promised:

> When your days are fulfilled and you lie down with your fathers, I will raise up your offspring after you, who shall come from your body, and I will establish his kingdom. He shall build a house (Gk, **oikodomēsei**) for my name, and I will establish the throne of his kingdom forever.[35]

That is the *house* God is building today.

4. God's love is expressed between Christ and the church (5:22–33)

Having described God's power exerted *for the church*, his wisdom demonstrated *through the church*, and his glory displayed *in the church*, Paul's fourth and final insight is the relationship between Christ *and the church*, modelled by the way a husband loves his wife *as Christ loved the church* (5:25).

Notice the past tense. Obviously Christ *loves us*,[36] but Paul insists twice in Ephesians that Christ *loved* us, and in almost identical words, he means on the cross (5:2, 25). On that second occasion, Paul is moving through his instructions to various groups in the church, and it looks initially as though he is digressing from marriage to talk about the church. A closer look, though, reveals that for him marriage is a picture of Christ's relationship with the church, not the other way round. That order is important. If Christ loved the church as a bridegroom loves his bride, that would open up areas of delight, affection and romance. But if bridegrooms love their brides as Christ loved the church when he died for it, that opens up areas of loving sacrifice. Similarly if brides are to love their husbands as they love Christ, that infuses romantic love with something quite different.

Above all, as a marriage, this is a covenanted unity that Christ will not break. Paul takes the most intimate relationship between a husband and wife, and says, that is how closely Christ has become one with us. In an almost shockingly graphic way he takes the Genesis pattern for marriage and transforms it: '*Therefore a man shall leave his father and mother and hold fast to his wife, and the*

---

[35] 2 Sam. 7:12–13.
[36] Rev. 1:5b.

two shall become one flesh.' This mystery is profound, and I am saying that it refers to Christ and the church (5:31–32). The *mystery* is that physical union in marriage shows how closely bonded we are with Christ. That great phrase, *in Christ,* could not be more clearly explained, because we have become *one flesh* with Christ, and we are *members of the same body* (3:6; 4:25; 5:30). Listen again to the care that Christ shows us: *In the same way husbands should love their wives as their own bodies. He who loves his wife loves himself. For no one ever hated his own flesh, but nourishes and cherishes it, just as Christ does the church, because we are members of his body* (5:28–30). We are so closely identified with Christ, that in caring for us it is almost as though he is caring for himself.

a. Pause and wonder

(i) The church as a bride

In the Old Testament marriage described God's persistent faithfulness, despite his people's unfaithfulness.[37] So sin is *adultery.*[38] Jesus described himself as a bridegroom planning his wedding,[39] and Paul's concern for the doctrinal purity of the Corinthians was because he 'betrothed you to one husband, to present you as a pure virgin to Christ'.[40]

Paul uses these ideas here, without using 'wife' or 'bride' for the church. This is the work of Christ portrayed as a wedding ceremony:

> *Husbands, love your wives, as Christ loved the church and gave himself up for her, that he might sanctify her, having cleansed her by the washing of water with the word, so that he might present the church to himself in splendour, without spot or wrinkle or any such thing, that she might be holy and without blemish (5:25–27).*

Normally it is the family which takes pride in the bride's beauty on her wedding day. Here, though, it is Christ who has taken all that trouble, and showered on us not transient glamour, but a *radiant beauty*[41] we neither possessed nor deserved. Our perfection is not found in the rapture of a dazzled groom, nor the magic of make-up, but the straight gaze of a holy God who can say, because *Christ loved the church and gave himself up for her that he might sanctify her,* she is indeed *holy and without blemish.*

---

[37] Most shockingly Ezek. 23 and Hos. 1 – 3.
[38] Jas 2:11; 4:4; 2 Pet. 2:14; Rev. 2:22.
[39] E.g. Matt. 9:15; 25:1–13; Rev. 19:6–9; 21:9.
[40] 2 Cor. 11:2.
[41] NIV.

(ii) Christ as the church's head

Of all the descriptions of the church this is the one which causes most contemporary anxiety, because of the implications for the relationships of husbands and wives. It has generated enormous literature in which both sides have claimed victory several times.[42] We need first to understand the concept as it relates to Christ and the church, and then to draw two lines of conclusion, one for marriage and a second for ministry.

Ephesians 1:22 combines three similar but quite distinct images: *And he put all things under his feet and gave him as head over all things to the church, which is his body, the fullness of him who fills all in all.* We have seen that in Ephesians head refers to Christ's position of royal supremacy, but body is a separate expression of our intimate relationship of being one with him and each other.[43] Feet draws on Psalm 8:

> Yet you have made him a little lower than the heavenly beings
> and crowned him with glory and honour.
> You have given him dominion over the works of your hands;
> you have put all things under his feet.[44]

The victory of God's king (*crowned, dominion*) is summarized by *all things under his feet* – as Ephesians says. Both *head* and *feet* are therefore political terms, both describing the position of the exalted Lord Jesus over the whole cosmos, for the church. The alternative proposed translation for *head, source,* cannot work here because the motif is of a victory won and enemies defeated. Christ's headship here is not a position which he occupies as the eternal creator, but one he was appointed to on the basis of his resurrection victory, over an already existing cosmos.[45] Paul then transfers that idea to Christ's particular and loving headship over the church. He is our absolute Lord and Saviour, or Head, and our proper response to him is to *submit* (5:24).

It lies outside our study to explore what loving headship means for marriage, although Paul must mean that the husband is in some sense 'in authority over' his wife. That needs to be explored with

---

[42] See, supporting 'source', C. C. Kroeger, 'Head', *DPL* (pp. 375–377), and the critical review by W. Grudem, 'The meaning of *kephalē* ("HEAD"): An Evaluation of New Evidence, Real and Alleged', *JETS* 44/1 (2001), pp. 25–65. In addition, see the literature in ch. 12. I think it is hard to make the translation 'source' coherent in this passage.

[43] And Col. 1. Elsewhere 'body' describes our relationships with each other.

[44] Ps. 8:5–6.

[45] Deut. 28:13; Judg. 10:18; 11:11; 2 Sam. 22:44; Isa. 7:8–9.

cultural sensitivity – and above all with *love* – but I cannot see that the text will bend in any other direction. It might even be said to be a mark of how willing we are to *submit* to Christ that we accept this.

Second, we should notice that the term *head* is used for the Lord Jesus in his relation to the church, but for no-one else. Since the Lord Jesus is not an absent master but exercises his active headship by continually giving gifts to the church,[46] it makes sense to keep that title for him alone. Evangelicals are unlikely to describe a pope or archbishop as the 'head' of their churches, but we should still be wary. For instance, in many debates over the respective roles of men and women in ministry[47] the issue is frequently described as a 'headship' issue – but that is to confuse categories. The relationship between Christ and the church is one of headship, and the marriage relationship is like that. But the relationship between a pastor and a congregation is *not* like that, because if it were it would imply that the pastor has replaced the Lord Jesus. No, the pastor works under the active and present headship of the Lord Jesus Christ.[48]

5. The church, both local and cosmic

'Church' means 'gathering', and in Ephesians we have seen it means all Christians in permanent heavenly assembly, around the eternally enthroned Jesus. You might be reading this at home, or during your lunch break, but at this moment you are, as always, a member of that heavenly gathering. You are in cosmic church. So, why bother about the local church you turn up to?

Paul does not explain exactly how, but our 'local gatherings . . . are earthly manifestations of that heavenly gathering around the risen Christ'.[49] When a city or province contained more than one gathering, the New Testament always uses the plural, church*es* of Galatia, church*es* in Syria and Cilicia, church*es* of Asia, church*es* of Macedonia, church*es* of Judea, even though it would never talk of Christ having 'brides', 'flocks', 'temples' or 'peoples'.[50] To use the singular word 'church' for something that never met would stretch the word impossibly. In English, to use the word 'gathering' for something that never 'gathered' would be equally odd.

---

[46] 4:7–13, see ch. 13.

[47] See ch. 13.

[48] I suspect this happened with the transfer of models from the household to the congregation (see ch. 12), but that was not on the basis of 'headship'.

[49] O'Brien, *Ephesians*, p. 147.

[50] Galatia (Gal. 1:2; 1 Cor. 16:1); Syria and Cilicia (Acts 15:41); Asia (1 Cor. 16:19; Rev. 1:4, 11); Macedonia (2 Cor. 8:1); Judea (Gal. 1:22).

It is worth grasping this at the outset, because we must let the Bible teach us how to speak. Consider the unconverted Paul's determination:

> And there arose on that day a great persecution against the church in Jerusalem, and they were all scattered throughout the regions of Judea and Samaria, except the apostles. Devout men buried Stephen and made great lamentation over him. But Saul was ravaging the church, and entering house after house, he dragged off men and women and committed them to prison. Now those who were scattered went about preaching the word.[51]

The impact of Paul's destruction shows it was the undoing of a meeting: 'they were all *scattered* . . . Now those who were *scattered* went about preaching the word.'

That explains the only apparent exception. Once only, Luke uses the singular phrase 'the church' to describe what was happening in several locations: 'So the church throughout all Judea and Galilee and Samaria had peace and was being built up. And walking in the fear of the Lord and in the comfort of the Holy Spirit, it multiplied.'[52] The key is that this occurs when a concerned reader would wonder what had happened to the Jerusalem 'gathering' which Paul had *scattered* all around the countryside? Luke's answer is 'the church' (that is, that very Jerusalem 'gathering', which Paul had 'scattered through the regions of Judea and Samaria') 'had peace' and 'it multiplied'. Luke consistently uses 'church' to describe a local meeting, even though, on this unusual occasion, it was scattered. It immediately 'multiplied'– became plural.

So the New Testament never used 'church' to describe all earthly believers, except in those very early days when they all met together and none had died. It was not used for all the Christians in one city who never met all together.[53] It is not a synonym for 'the people of God'. It was certainly never used to describe a sub-group of believers, as when we describe denominations as 'churches'. There are biblical words for ties between local churches, but 'church' is not one of them. And to use 'church' for a denomination places a wrong emphasis on such structures, and encourages us to misread and overplay them. Similarly, it is unhelpful to use 'church' to mean all living Christians, as when the phrase 'the church visible' contrasts with 'the church invisible'. But the 'church invisible' is the cosmic

---

[51] Acts 8:1–4.

[52] Acts 9:31.

[53] Paul wrote to *all those in Rome* (1:7), but only the localized gathering is called *the church* (16:5).

church we have seen in Ephesians, and it includes us. The 'church visible' is where that appears as a meeting of believers.

One common element that all churches share today is the historic creeds: the Apostles' Creed, the Nicene Creed and the much longer Athanasian Creed. Together, they teach that the church is 'one, holy, catholic and apostolic', and all four of those terms have been defined in Ephesians. The church's unity is our membership of one body under one head; the church's holiness comes from being God's prized possession; the church's catholicity (meaning, its variety) is in the bridging of the Jew/Gentile division; and the church's apostolicity is our foundation, from which we cannot shift, in this apostolic teaching (2:20). This is the church which exists *to the praise of his glorious grace* (1:6).

Additional note: The church and the Trinity

Some chapters have 'Additional Notes' at the end. These address issues relevant to many, but not all, readers, and this one addresses the relationship between the church and the Trinity.

Contemporary theologians normally begin their theology of the church with a theology of the Trinity, tracing God's eternally loving community onto ours. Kevin Giles writes that the Trinity is the 'model on which ecclesiology should be formulated. On this premise, the inner life of the divine Trinity provides a pattern, a model, an echo, or an icon of the Christian communal existence in the world'.[54] This is part of a much larger renewal of the doctrine of the Trinity, which lies outside our scope,[55] although it is surprisingly hard to find one clear biblical passage which makes Giles' precise point and which could have formed a chapter for this book. Perhaps, although theologians present it as a starting point, they might be better to present it as a conclusion. But one aspect of that debate does concern us, and is one which Ephesians addresses.

Part of the renewal of Trinitarian doctrine has been to describe the internal life of the Trinity. Stanley Grenz puts it well: 'God's triune nature means that God is social or relational – God is the "social Trinity". And for this reason, we can say that God is "community". God is the community of the Father, Son and Spirit, who enjoy perfect and eternal fellowship.'[56] And this takes us to the

---

[54] K. Giles, *What on Earth is the Church?* (London: SPCK: 1995), p. 222.

[55] For this series, see B. Edgar, *The Message of the Trinity* (Leicester, IVP: 2004).

[56] S. Grenz, *Created for Community* (Grand Rapids: Baker Books, 1998), p. 52. See too M. Volf, *After Our Likeness: The Church as the Image of the Trinity* (Grand Rapids: Eerdmans, 1998).

heart of one of the hottest debates of today – what doctrine of the Trinity do we map onto the church?

Much contemporary writing insists that within the Trinity there is absolutely no hierarchy between the three persons, and therefore there should be no hierarchy within any church. Giles insists, 'Nothing in scripture indicates that the Father-Son-Spirit are eternally hierarchically ordered in being, work/function, or authority',[57] and more broadly, 'Historic orthodoxy has never accepted hierarchical ordering in the Trinity'.[58] Gilbert Bilezikian agrees: 'The notion of such a relationship of submission in the Godhead is completely foreign to Scripture. Indeed, its content teaches exactly the opposite.'[59] The words 'hierarchy' and 'submission' mean that this obviously spills into our leadership and gender debates, and Frank Viola agrees: 'The Trinity is the paradigm informing us on how the church should function. It shows us that the church is a loving, egalitarian, reciprocal, cooperative, non-hierarchical community.'[60] Again, 'Within this divine dance of love, there exists no hierarchy. There exists no control. There exists no authoritarianism. There exists no conflict of interests. Instead there's mutual love, mutual fellowship, and mutual subjection.'[61]

These authors together insist that the biblical language of Jesus' obedience applies only to his incarnate, historic nature. Addressing several of those passages, Viola says they 'refer to [Jesus'] temporal relationship as a human being who voluntarily submitted Himself to His Father's will. In the Godhead, the Father and the son experience communality and mutual submission through the Spirit'.[62]

The common allegation is clear: contemporary Christians who claim that the Bible teaches a hierarchy within the Trinity which should be modelled onto the church, particularly but not only in male/female roles, have imposed that on the Trinity. Giles even goes so far as to identify that teaching as a new version of an ancient heresy that the creeds were formulated to deny, that the Son is not as fully God as the Father.[63]

Naturally this has been hotly denied, because the allegation that much contemporary evangelical thought is fundamentally heretical

[57] K. Giles, *Jesus and the Father: Modern Evangelicals Reinvent the Trinity* (Grand Rapids: Zondervan, 2006), p. 127.

[58] Ibid., p. 9, pp. 38–39.

[59] G. Bilezikian, *Community 101* (Grand Rapids: Zondervan, 1997), p. 200.

[60] F. Viola, *Reimagining Church: Pursuing the Dream of Organic Christianity* (Colorado Springs: David C. Cook, 2008), p. 41.

[61] Ibid., p. 225.

[62] Ibid., p. 295.

[63] K. Giles, *The Trinity and Subordinationism: The Doctrine of God and the Contemporary Gender Debate* (Downers Grove: IVP, 2002).

is a strong one. Steven Holmes has surveyed the field as thoroughly as Giles, and insists that it is the social, complementarian view which is the imposition.[64] Although this debate is technical and difficult, it is obviously hugely important, and both scholars and pastors need to be informed.[65]

Ephesians contributes by using a phrase which occurs in all three of the great creeds that every church affirms: the Father *raised Christ from the dead and seated him at his right hand in the heavenly realms* (1:20). That phrase *at his right hand* is a widely used biblical description. In the Old Testament it describes a place of royal honour, favour, victory and power.[66] Psalm 110:1 describes it as the place occupied by the coming, victorious Son of David:

> The LORD said to my lord:
>   'Sit at my right hand
>   until I make your enemies your footstool.'

Jesus himself anticipated that this would be the position he would occupy for eternity.[67] So New Testament writers take up the idea, and either explicitly quoting Psalm 110 (which is the most frequently quoted psalm) or more generally using the thought, state that Jesus is, now and for ever 'at the right hand of the Majesty in heaven'.[68]

What does this language mean? Commenting on Acts 2, David Peterson says it 'suggests that a king who rules in Jerusalem is the Lord's earthly vicegerent. God rules his people through his chosen representative (his "anointed")'[69] – 'vicegerent' means a monarch who reigns in the presence and under the authority of another, like Solomon who was crowned while David was still alive.[70] Commenting on Hebrews 1:3, Peter O'Brien says Christ's 'enthronement "at the right hand of the divine Majesty" shows that the rank and rule of God the Father is not compromised in any way'.[71] In other words,

---

[64] S. R. Holmes, *The Holy Trinity: Understanding God's Life* (Milton Keynes: Paternoster, 2012).

[65] See too, R. Letham, *The Holy Trinity: In Scripture, History, Theology and Worship* (Augsburg: Presbyterian and Reformed, 2012).

[66] Honour: 1 Kgs 2:19; favour: Ps. 80:15; Jer. 22:24; victory: Pss 20:6; 44:3; Isa. 41:10; power: Exod. 15:6; Ps. 89:13; Isa. 48:13.

[67] Matt. 22:44; 26:64; Mark 12:36; 14:62; Luke 20:41–44; 22:69.

[68] Heb. 1:3. See Acts 2:33–34; 5:31; 7:55; Rom. 8:34; Phil. 2:9; 1 Pet. 3:21–22; Rev. 3:21; 22:1.

[69] D. G. Peterson, *The Acts of the Apostles*, PNTC (Grand Rapids/Cambridge: Eerdmans and Nottingham: Apollos, 2010), p. 151.

[70] 1 Kgs 1 – 2. A vice-regent, by contrast, reigns as a substitute for a monarch.

[71] P. T. O'Brien, *The Letter to the Hebrews*, PNTC (Grand Rapids/Cambridge: Eerdmans and Nottingham: Apollos, 2010), pp. 59–60.

this image shows us that Christ's enthronement still places him, for eternity, as subordinate to the Father.

Notice too that this is not a reversible image: the Father is never seated at the Son's right hand. So Michael Horton concludes:

> From his incarnation to his reign at the Father's right hand, Jesus is not only the Lord who became the servant, but the servant who is Lord and *continues even in this exalted state to serve his Father's will and his people's good. From eternity to eternity, he offers his 'Here I am' to the Father on behalf of those who have gone their own way.*[72]

That imagery is decisive for me. Yes, the Son is fully and eternally divine, from and for eternity, and yes, he is seated on and shares his Father's throne and glory.[73] But he is at his Father's right hand for eternity, and that is what is meant by the eternal subordination of the Son. We may map that onto the church.

---

[72] Michael Horton, *The Christian Faith* (Grand Rapids: Zondervan, 2011), p. 533, emphasis added.
[73] Rev. 5:11–14.

Genesis 17:1–27; Galatians 3:15–29; Colossians 2:11–18
3. The church from Eden to exodus

Every Christian church practices baptism,[1] and it marks us out from our Jewish forbears and our pagan contemporaries. It is the public doorway to church membership. But it is no mere rite of passage. It connects us with God's eternal plan for his church and humanity, and takes us to the next stage in our Bible timeline of church, which now moves from eternity to Eden, and beyond.

1. The garden and the garden-city

The story moves fast. Adam's royal task was to 'fill . . . and subdue . . . and have dominion in the world', and to 'work . . . and . . . keep' the garden,[2] a phrase that connects him to the later priests.[3] Eden's rich minerals and plants were echoed in those priests' robes,[4] and in the tabernacle[5] and temple.[6] God was 'in the garden',[7] foreshadowing his later presence in the Holy of Holies.[8] So Adam and Eve are the first hints of what will become church, worshipping God as they obeyed his word. Christians too are 'a royal priesthood',[9] with those same privileges of God's presence, and obedient service.

But disobedience scattered those hints. After their banishment, Eden was guarded by cherubim to prevent re-entry, and the ark containing God's word in the Holy of Holies was guarded by golden

---

[1] Except the Salvation Army, who stress that personal faith, not baptism, is essential.
[2] Gen. 1:28; 2:15.
[3] E.g. Num. 3:7–8; 1 Chr. 23:32; Ezek. 44:14.
[4] Exod. 28:6–34.
[5] Exod. 26:1–37.
[6] 1 Chr. 29:2; 1 Kgs 6 – 7.
[7] Gen. 3:8.
[8] Lev. 26:12; Deut. 23:14; 2 Sam. 7:6–7.
[9] 1 Pet. 2:9.

cherubim.[10] But rather than rejecting humankind, God patiently prepared his plan so that the story which began with a marriage in a garden would end with a marriage in a garden-city. In the new heavens and the new earth, God's exuberant generosity will be seen in the new Jerusalem, filled with gold and precious stones, trees and fruit, and inhabited by obedient people from every nation.

In the next scene, the flood (Gen. 6 – 9), eight survivors were saved because they believed God's promise of rescue. Peter later identified them with the church: 'God's patience waited in the days of Noah, while the ark was being prepared, in which a few, that is, eight persons, were brought safely through water. Baptism, which corresponds to this, now saves you.'[11] Christians are another group of people, with obedient faith in God's saving promises, living differently from our sinful culture, and with baptism (getting wet but not drowning) as evidence of that faith. The ark is a second miniature hint at church, this time with baptism.

Human attempts to live without God collapsed at Babel, but where Genesis chapters 3 to 11 recounts our failure to build a city, Genesis 12 to the end of Revelation recounts God building one for us, beginning with Genesis 12 – 25, and his dealings with Abraham. We join Abram (as he was then still called) in Genesis 17, but we shall also follow Paul's footsteps as he twice explicitly connected God's promises to Abram with our baptism.

2. The God who makes promises to his people (Gen. 17)

Genesis 17 is rich, but simply shaped: God covenanted that Abram would become the father of nations and kings (1–8), and introduced circumcision (9–14); he promised that Sarah would become the mother of nations and kings (15–22), and the males were circumcised (23–27). God spoke five times (1–2, 4–8, 9–14, 15–16, 19–21), and the central themes (*circumcision*, *flesh*) are underlined. Abram is named fourteen times,[12] addressed in each speech. The central subject emerges as, ten times, God promised a *covenant*.[13]

This was not news. On three previous meetings (12:1–3; 13:14–17; 15:1–21), God had 'covenanted' land, descendants and blessing (15:18), but something changes here, marked by subtly different names for both the man and his wife, and a sign for their heirs. The 'covenant' became *an everlasting covenant* (7).

[10] Exod. 25:17–22; 26:1.
[11] 1 Pet. 3:20–21. See Heb. 11:7.
[12] As Abram: 17:1 (twice), 3, 5a; as Abraham: 17:5b, 9, 15, 17, 18, 22, 23 (twice), 24, 26.
[13] 17:2, 4, 7 (twice), 9, 10, 11, 13 (twice), 14.

Each element of God's vow intensified. The initial promise of 'this land' (12:7), then 'all the land that you see' (13:15), was finally named *the land of Canaan, for an everlasting possession* (8). Numerous descendants (13:16; 15:5) became here *nations, kings of peoples* (16), but also one, miraculous descendant. The promise of protection (12:3), particularly during Egyptian slavery (15:13–14), became an intimate promise *to be God to you and to your offspring after you* (7).

God's promises of place, people and protection, form the 'covenant'. God's covenant with his people flows through Noah,[14] Abraham, Sinai,[15] the covenant with David,[16] to the new covenant,[17] which Jesus inaugurated with his death.[18] Those promises are why 'covenant' is foundational to 'church', and to baptism.

3. The promise of a royal dynasty (Gen. 17:1–21)

Royal families capture worldwide attention. Their weddings promise the monarchy a future, and their funerals, with a sovereign entombed among the ancestors, embody stability. Queen Victoria was nicknamed 'the grandmother of Europe' because of the spread of her dynasty. But no contemporary royal family comes close to the significance of Abram's dynasty.

a. Many descendants

Abram's people would be miraculously fruitful (2, 3, 4, 5). God explains the numbers using mathematics (*multiply*) and biology (*seed*), astronomy ('stars'),[19] and geology ('dust'),[20] and later, he invited Abram to count the sand grains trickling through his fingers (22:17). Abram's descendants will number billions.

Abram and Sarah were well beyond child-bearing, so they could only have a child if God took the miraculous initiative. His promise that they would be *exceedingly fruitful* (6) echoes his original command to Adam, 'be fruitful',[21] but now he promises *I will make you exceedingly fruitful*. The continuity with that command means

---

[14] Gen. 8:20 – 9:17. Many theologians conclude God made a covenant with Adam (also see Hos. 6:7, but translating the verse is difficult).
[15] Exod. 19 – 31.
[16] 2 Sam. 7:1–16.
[17] Isa. 40 – 66; Jer. 31 – 33; Ezek. 40 – 48.
[18] Matt. 26:28.
[19] Gen. 15:5.
[20] Gen. 13:16.
[21] Gen. 1:28; 9:1, 7.

that God's blessing of Abram will be the way humanity's created purpose will be reached. Church is why God made people.

This covenant would not become increasingly remote as time passed. God stated five times that his promise was to *you* (Abram) *and your offspring* (7 twice, 8, 9, 10). This was both once-made and yet a constant promise, made to each spreading and successively circumcised generation.

b. Many nations

Second, God promised Abram an international family. He will be *the father of a multitude of nations* (4, 5, 6), and Sarah *shall become nations* (16). So from now on Abram is consistently 'Abr*a*ham', marking his new role.

Abraham never saw this fulfilled. His first son, Ishmael, was given a wonderful promise by God, that *He shall father twelve princes, and I will make him into a great nation* (20)[22] but (because Ishmael was not Sarah's son, born only because Abraham did not trust God) *I will establish my covenant with Isaac, whom Sarah shall bear to you next year* (21). Ishmael did not carry the promise. Isaac in his turn had two sons: deceitful Jacob (later renamed 'Israel' and promised a nation, 35:9–13) and his dangerous rival Esau, given a nickname that would carry to his descendants, the rival Edomites (25:30).

To number two nations among your descendants should be a privilege, but it seems quite paltry given God's extravagant promises. Two is hardly *a multitude*. Jacob himself knew that the promise had an ultimate, international, fulfilment, because on his deathbed he prophesied that Joseph would in turn become 'a company of peoples'.[23] God's promise waited.

c. Many kings, one land

Third, God promised Abraham a royal family: *kings shall come from you* (6), and to Sarai: *kings of peoples shall come from her* (16). She is promised a number of royal families. Like her husband, from here on she is renamed, 'Sarah'. There is little difference in meaning, and both names are to do with royal families: they both mean, 'Princess'.

Fourth, God promised them *Canaan* (8). The land is a major biblical topic, but as these expositions concern the people rather than the place, we will not explore it.

[22] See Gen. 21:18; 25:13–16.
[23] Gen. 48:4.

4. The promised royal dynasty: baptism (Gal. 3:15–29)

Thousands of years later, a church in Galatia (today's Turkey), was furiously split between Christians with a Jewish background, and those who were Gentiles. To what extent was the Old Testament law binding on Christians? Should Gentiles be circumcised? Should Jewish Christians eat separately? The church was being torn apart by the law.

Paul had to address this visibly broken unity, but also the underlying question of how Christians see each other. The central question of this section, as of the letter, is, 'Who is a true heir of Abraham?' 'Who belongs?' Paul's answer will be that Christians are deeply interrelated, and that Genesis 17 speaks about all those who have been *baptized* (27).

a. The promise – to whom was it made?

God's covenant can be summarized as *promises* (plural, 16), or *the promise* (singular, 17). But the content of Genesis 17 is seemingly unrecognizable. Land, descendants and protection have become the experience of justification by faith (Gal. 3:8–9), the gift of the Holy Spirit (3:10–14), and of sonship (3:26–29). What has happened?

(i) The promise was made to Abraham, and to Christ

Paul first asks, to whom God made his promise? We might expect the answer, 'to all the multiple descendants of Abraham', but instead Paul notices that the Hebrew in Genesis 17 is not plural, *seeds* (or *heirs*, or *descendants* depending on the version), but singular. That seems at first sight rather petty. Does not Paul see that in the context, God must be talking about multiple descendants in the singular word, 'seed' or 'offspring'?

Of course he knows that. The promise was made repeatedly to and about multiple descendants,[24] and Paul uses 'seed' in that sense in Romans 4:14–16. But Genesis emphasizes one descendant, embodying all future descendants.[25] Genesis 3:15 promised one 'seed' of Adam who would crush the serpent: '*He* shall bruise your head, and you shall bruise *his* heel.' Cain killed Abel, but Eve was optimistic about her third son: 'God has appointed me another offspring [seed] instead of Abel, for Cain killed him.'[26] Genesis uses 'seed' both ways, and the expectation of the one serpent-crusher drives the story.

[24] Gen. 12:1–3; 13:16; 15:1–5; 17:4–8; 18:18; 22:17–18; 26:4.
[25] Isaac: 21:12; 26:3–4; Jacob: 28:13–14; 35:12–13.
[26] Gen. 4:25.

Therefore, says Paul, God's promise to Abraham was *referring to one, 'And to your offspring', who is Christ* (17); *the offspring . . . to whom the promise had been made* (19). God had not merely made promises 'about' Christ, but *to* Christ. But if all God's promises were to Christ, what is there for us?

(ii) The promise was made to all those in Christ
Jesus is the means by which God's promises to bless the Gentiles would be kept. Paul has already argued that Jesus' death is the basis for being right with God (Gal. 3:10–14); here he aligns that with the promise to Abraham. Our access to all Christ's blessings is by *faith*, emphasized some fifteen times in this chapter. Everything has happened *so that the promise by faith in Jesus Christ might be given to those who believe* (22).

This is where the singular/plural meanings of 'seed' contain a third concept. Not only does 'seed' mean both multiple descendants, and one descendant, but in addition God has so identified Christians with Christ, that the phrase used of us is that we are *in Christ* (26). It is central to Paul's thinking that Christians share Christ' destiny and status.[27] We are so wrapped up in him, that God treats us as he treats Christ because we are *in Christ*.

That idea has a particular edge here. If Christ is the descendant, and we are in him, then because he is the heir, the offspring, *then you are Abraham's offspring, heirs according to promise* (29). Christians are the result of God keeping his promise to Abraham. If we imagine history as a giant capital X, all those apparent plural promises to Abraham flow down to Christ as the sole heir. But now they spread out across every tribe and tongue and language, as an international membership inherits those blessings. We are what God meant, when he told Abraham to count the stars.

There has never been a time when the number of disciples has been larger or grown faster than today, and that is widely known. So there is no excuse for us to think of ourselves individually as the centre of God's plan. That plan has always been for innumerable individuals, each one known, loved and won, but together demonstrating the greatness of God's victory.

b. The law – what time is it?[28]

The problem in Galatia was that some believers, like bewildered tourists, had set their watches to the wrong time zone. In this case,

---

[27] See ch. 2.
[28] The 'central question of the entire Galatian letter is *what time is it?*', T. George, *Galatians*, NAC (Nashville: Broadman & Holman, 1994), p. 255.

they were not out by an hour, or a day, but by an entire covenant. They behaved as if they lived BC. But in 3:19–25 Paul identifies a tension between the way the Galatians should have understood the promise given to Abraham, and the way they had mis-understood the law given through Moses. Because the law came later than *the promise* (17), they thought it overrode it, but Paul responds that the law was only ever a temporary measure until Christ came. God, having once covenanted that his people should relate to him on the basis of promises, did not change his mind when he gave the law. It *does not annul a covenant previously ratified by God so as to make the promise void* (17). The promise came first.

Furthermore, Abraham did not make equal, balanced promises back. This was an unbreakable one-way agreement, its binding promises made by only one party. Abraham and his seed would not be able to break the promise, and because God had made this binding promise, even his law could not overwrite it. *For if the inheritance comes by the law, it no longer comes by a promise; but God gave it to Abraham by a promise* (18).

Time markers run through verses 19–25: *until . . . now . . . until . . . before . . . no longer . . .* showing Paul's answer to the Galatians' dilemma. The law was to cover God's people only *until* the arrival of the promised heir, who has now come. So the Old Covenant law can be safely retired. It ruled from Mount Sinai to Mount Calvary, but it is *no longer* needed.

Setting their watches by the wrong time zone, and imposing the outdated food and circumcision laws, ripped this church apart (2:11–14). But the temporary laws that separated Jews from Gentiles have no place in church, and obeying them wrecked fellowship, as they will today.

c. Baptism – what is the difference?

Into the middle of this, Paul slips in a reference to baptism. *For as many of you as were baptised into Christ have put on Christ* (27). To keep this in perspective, this is the only reference to baptism in Galatians, and by comparison there are fifteen references to *faith* in this chapter alone. Nevertheless Paul finds this a natural place to mention baptism.

That is embarrassing today, because what Paul lightly mentions as a point of unity is perhaps the most visible point of difference between churches. Significant, Bible-honouring scholars still dis-pute whether it is permissible to baptise the children of believers, or whether sprinkling, pouring or immersing someone in water is most authentic.[29] Because we have no direct evidence of what New Testament believers practiced with their children, we have to draw reasonable inferences. Those who believe in the permissibility of infant baptism draw parallels with circumcision, and tend to use the language of 'covenant'; those who believe in the rightness of adult-only baptism insist on faith, and tend to use the language of 'conversion'. Both have biblical language, but standing back from the debate, we can see it is a question of biblical theology. If our fundamental model is continuity across Scripture, that will incline us towards the possibility of infant baptism; if it is contrast, that will incline us towards its impossibility. And since every Christian believes in both continuity and contrast, where do we put baptism?

Paul does not solve that question. Rather, his point is that baptism identifies us with Christ. It is a baptism *into Christ* (27), so we share his destiny and privileges. Both infant and adult baptism can become a mere ceremony, expected by family and church, but here is an understanding that is far richer.

(i) Baptism is about Christ, not the person being baptized

The person being baptized *into Christ* has *put on Christ*. Although we do not know whether these earliest Christians gave new clothes to the baptized, as later churches did,[30] the Old Testament language about God clothing himself in his holy character, his people clothing themselves in righteousness, and even God clothing his people,[31] combined with the idea that we are *in Christ*, produced the language of clothing ourselves spiritually.[32] Paul repeats that we are 'in Christ', *in Christ Jesus* and 'in the Lord'.[33]

(ii) Baptism is about God's promises, not ours

Promises are central to baptism, whether those of a new convert, or of believing parents for their child. But rooting baptism biblically means that the fundamental promise is God's to Abraham, fulfilled in Christ, by which we are *heirs according to promise* (29). That is critical for the many times when we fail, because our standing before God will only, ever, be on the basis of being 'in Christ', and he will not break that promise.

[29] See D. Bridge and D. Phypers, *The Water that Divides* (rev. ed., Ross-shire: Christian Focus, 2008) or with a wider range of views, P. E. Engle and J. H. Armstrong (eds.), *Understanding Four Views on Baptism* (Grand Rapids: Zondervan, 2007).

[30] S. McKnight, *Galatians*, NIVAC (Grand Rapids: Zondervan, 1995), p. 198.

[31] God clothes himself: Job 29:14; Isa. 51:9; 59:17. His people clothe themselves: 2 Chr. 6:41; Ps. 132:9; Prov. 31:25; Isa. 52:1. God clothes his people: Isa. 61:10; Zech. 3:3–5.

[32] Rom. 13:12; 1 Cor. 15:53–54; Eph. 6:11–17; Col. 3:12; 1 Thess. 5:8.

[33] 1:22; 2:17; 2:4; 3:14, 26; 5:6; 5:10.

(iii) Baptism is about the church, not the individual

Unsurprisingly, therefore, this part of Galatians is consistently plural, underlining both *we/our* and *you*. And even the reference to baptism is plural: *as many of you as were baptised* (27). We are *all sons of God* and *all one in Christ* (26, 28). This is Paul's counter-blast to their selfish divisions. Circumcision and food laws divided, but baptism unites us, not because we use the same formula or share the same practice, but because it expresses that we are all *in Christ*, the foundational unity of all Christians.

The Nicene Creed includes the phrase 'one baptism for the forgiveness of sins'. Under the intense persecution of the Emperor Diocletian in AD 303-305, many Christians 'handed over' their scriptures as proof that they had rejected Christianity. The Latin word for 'handing over' was *traditores*, giving us the word 'traitor'.[34] Some Christians saw these 'traitors' as weaker sisters and brothers, but others insisted they had broken their vows to Christ, and that nothing done by treacherous clergy could ever be spiritually valid. Bishop Donatus in North Africa insisted that any person baptized by such a minister would have to be re-baptized. The 'one baptism' clause was inserted to reject that purist 'Donatism', because it became obvious that if ministers have to be sinless for their ministry to have an effect, no ministry would ever be valid. Instead, reflecting Paul, all churches were to recognize all baptisms, no matter how flawed the baptizer. That is why we are not re-baptized after every sin, nor re-baptized whenever we move church.

d. The royal family

Paul identifies three areas where human beings divide: racial religion (Jew/Gentile), status (slave/free) and gender (male/female). Paul has a triple negation, insisting that these divisions no longer apply within the new royal family in Christ.

(i) Neither Jew nor Greek

This was the most obvious division affecting the Galatian church, and its successful obliteration was critical for Paul. There are many implications, but two are particularly relevant today.

First, this distinction, introduced by God, is now over. Jews have been the objects of particular prejudice over many centuries, reaching a ghastly peak in the Holocaust. One understandable consequence of our revulsion at that prejudice, is that Christians now find it hard to express the gospel to their Jewish friends. North London, where

---

[34] In a quite different sense, it gives us 'tradition' – something handed on.

I live, contains a sizeable Jewish community, and by and large the churches respect Jewish people by honouring a sense of distance. But that, although understandable, will not do. The gospel is for all non-Christians, not just Gentile ones. We need to address carefully how we approach evangelism in a Jewish context. And, it must be underlined, anti-Semitism within the church is grotesque.

Second, if this was the only racial separation that God permitted, and he has now erased it, it follows that no other racial separation is ever permissible within the church. I have been in churches in multi-racial towns where the only non-white people were cleaners: that must stop. Those of us who live in such multicultural contexts have a duty to address this. It exposes how we see our sisters and brothers in Christ.

Again, our history can hinder us. In 2011, a Norwegian terrorist exploded a bomb in the centre of Oslo, and gunned down dozens of teenagers in a holiday camp, both to advance a self-styled 'Christian' ideology – by which he meant a racially pure Aryan ideology, harking back to Nazism. The vicious far-right in the UK, while denying such violence, similarly claim to identify a 'Christian' England. Those of us who carry the name 'Christian' must ensure no-one thinks that such ignorance or hatred has any similarity to the Lord Jesus, whose death ends any racial supremacism.

Also near where I live is a sizeable Cypriot community: some are Greek Cypriots, and others Turkish Cypriots. The tensions run deep. If we had two non-Christian enquirers, one from each community, would we put them in the same evangelistic Bible study? My hunch is that we might not; racial hatred is only one of the many sins that need to be repented of at conversion. But as they emerge from the baptism waters, they should embrace each other, one *in Christ*.

(ii) Neither slave nor free
Those of us who live in countries which have abolished slavery need to understand the chasm between these two groups, which was a long way from an employer and an employee. Across the Roman Empire, one owned the other, much as we might own a saucepan, and with as little compassion.

The Old Testament permitted some slavery, principally as a temporary action for someone trapped in poverty to provide for his family.[35] But even someone captured in war or bought in trade, was to be adopted into God's people. God instructed Abraham, 'both he

---

[35] Lev. 25:25–28; Deut. 15:12–18.

who is born in your house and he who is bought with your money, shall surely be circumcised'.[36]

The New Testament grappled with this, as when Paul wrote to Philemon, sending back a runaway slave who had subsequently been converted. The New Testament assumes the continuation of slavery: there was no realistic alternative, even though they had slaves and masters sitting together in church. But alongside that, the New Testament contains deep criticism of the slave trade itself. Paul criticized those acting contrary to the gospel, including 'enslavers' in his list, just after 'men who practice homosexuality'.[37] And in Revelation, the climax of the trade that supported Rome/Babylon is 'slaves, that is, human souls'.[38] Now, if Christians taught that the slave trade was itself sinful and under God's judgment, they had begun to destroy the machinery that made slaves. Rather than suggest that Christians have changed their mind over slavery, it might be truer to say that even some senior Christians in history have found it hard to live by the truths clearly taught in the New Testament. No Christian should ever have condoned any slave trade. Those who wish to use the abolition of slavery as a template for a moral change over time, must notice how culturally radical the New Testament itself was over human trafficking.

Few people in the contemporary West are slaves, and those that are, are so illegally. So perhaps the contemporary expression of the judgment criticized by Paul takes a different form. For example, the British judge people by their background. Was the school they went to state or private? Did they attend university? And if so, which one? Does their accent betray where they come from, or does it betray that they are hiding where they come from? In a word, 'class' is the equivalent British expression of status. One recent study, limited to English people's habits, did not contain a chapter on 'class', and the author explained that this was not because it was unimportant; rather it was so pervasive, it was impossible to isolate.[39] Christians outside Britain might find this hard to believe, but even so small a thing as which teenage summer camp someone attended can affect which church they pastor.

(iii) No male and female
This is the most famous pairing, and in many churches and denominations it is either the most welcome, or the most notorious. Later,

[36] Gen. 17:13.
[37] 1 Tim. 1:10.
[38] Rev. 18:13.
[39] K. Fox, *Watching the English* (London: Hodder & Stoughton, 2005).

we consider the question of women and ministry from a direct passage,[40] but here we must attend to exactly what Paul is saying.

First, Paul breaks his rhythm. The *neither/nor* pattern is replaced by *no male and female*,[41] possibly under the influence of Genesis 2:27: 'male and female he created them'. Second, Paul does not say 'man and woman', or 'husband and wife', as if he were reinterpreting marriage. This is a general principle, applying to all men and women in the church. Third, Paul does not think that all aspects of these three distinctives have been obliterated. For instance, elsewhere he addresses each category of people here with different instructions. In 1 Corinthians 7 we not only find single, engaged, married and widowed women, but single, engaged and married men, each subset being given its own advice. Furthermore, in verses 17–19, he addresses circumcised Christians and uncircumcised Christians, and then in verses 21–23 he addresses slaves and free. So Paul still used those categories, and where necessary, drew differing patterns of behaviour for them.

This leaves two truths to be held together. First, each of these three pairings is truly radical, and would have stretched the understanding and obedience of the Galatian Christians. We can imagine them poring over the letter. Does that really mean that Jews and Gentiles could eat together? That slaves and slave-owners should treat each other as brothers and sisters? That men and women should sit together, learn together and pray together? What an awesome idea!

We need to hear, teach and act upon this radical insight. We need to know that men and women are utterly equal before God, and to be convinced that this is our truth, and not one we have stolen, or had imposed upon us by a secular culture. It was, and remains, the New Testament's understanding that Christian believers are *sisters* and *brothers*, and together we are 'the children of God'.[42]

Nevertheless, Paul does not think that this radical insight removes all distinctions based on gender. In fact, even here in Galatians he has consistently said something hard, but important. Because our fundamental relationship with God is that we are *in Christ*, and Christ is 'the Son of God who loved me, and gave himself for me',[43] how then, does God see us? *(I)n Christ Jesus you are all sons of God, through faith* (26). Paul sees all Christians as *sons*, not as the

[40] Ch. 12.
[41] This translation is ASV. Neither ESV nor HCSB observe the change; NIV does, but does not reference Genesis.
[42] On 'sisters' and 'brothers': e.g. Rom. 16:1; 1 Cor. 7:15; Phlm. 2; 'children' e.g. Rom. 8:16.
[43] Gal. 2:20.

remains of an unconverted misogyny, but as a critical insight into how God sees us: 'because you are sons, God has sent the Spirit of his Son into our hearts, crying "Abba, Father!".'[44] That any Christian, male or female, is a son of God is an extraordinary privilege, not a demeaning of one gender's rights. In the context of Galatians, to say that we are 'sons and daughters of God', or more neutrally that we are 'children of God' misses this truth, and runs the risk of suggesting we have a relationship with God outside the relationship of being in his Son. With increasing frequency through Galatians, Paul called them *brothers* (1:11; 4:12, 28, 31; 5:11, 13; 6:1, 18). He drew this church closer together, closer to him and closer to Christ, by using this language, once we see it as our privilege to use.

So this second insight is as radical as the first, but perhaps today less welcome. In Paul's mind, even in the very letter that he teaches *there is no male and female*, he still insists that the terms are not interchangeable.

e. The Messiah and his people

Before returning to Abraham and God's promises, consider once again the glorious, expansive greatness of God's plan. God promised that old man a global multitude, growing daily, of people who call him 'Father'. *(I)f you are Christ's, then you are Abraham's offspring, heirs according to promise* (29). Calvin writes, 'Abram . . . was not called the father of many nations, because his seed was to be divided into many nations; but rather because many nations were to be gathered together into him.'[45] The glory of that promise is that we cannot think of it without seeing its fulfilment in Christ; we cannot think of Christ as the Son, without seeing that we are sons in him; and we cannot think of him as the heir without seeing that we are heirs in him. We are men and women, from every race and language, completely united in him. We are the heirs that Abraham was promised.

5. The sign of the promise (Gen. 17:9–14, 22–27)

So we must return to Abraham. We noticed that while the triple theme of people, place and protection climax here, they are not new; the news is that the males should be circumcised.

---

[44] Gal. 4.6.
[45] J. Calvin, *A Commentary on Genesis*, transl. and ed. John King (London: Banner of Truth, 1965 [1578]), p. 447.

a. Circumcision

Circumcision would already have been on Abraham's mind. Ishmael was born when Abraham was eighty-six (16:16), and the old man was now ninety-nine (17:1). Ishmael was thirteen, on the brink of puberty, and it was the custom in many cultures of the time that, as the boys became young men, they should be circumcised.

What would not have occurred to Abraham was that it was him, not the lad, who should be circumcised (11), at the age of ninety-nine. This circumcision is not the move from youth to adulthood, but of bearing the sign that Abraham belongs inside the covenant. All God's previous promises were made to him in his uncircumcised state, of course, so this does not mark the moment when Abraham suddenly belonged to God. As Paul later argued in Romans 4, Abraham had a real, living, saving faith before he was circumcised (Rom. 4:11), making him a valid father to Christians who also believe without being circumcised. But that is to look ahead. Here circumcision becomes the sign that all males belonging to Israel should carry, whether they were born or brought into the people (17:12–13, 23, 27). Again this is reinforced by God's repetition, as in one speech both 'covenant' and 'circumcision'/'uncircumcision' are mentioned six times.[46]

Circumcision carries a number of meanings:

1. *It marks God's prior grace.* This people belong to God not because of any obedience on their part, but solely by God's grace; it is given eight days after birth, not on the brink of adulthood (12).
2. *It marks God's permanent promise.* God promised to *be God to you, and to you and to your offspring after you* (7), and *made a covenant . . . between me and you and your offspring after you* (10). God could have made a promise only to Abraham, and then only Abraham would have had the privilege of carrying the sign of the promise. But God made a promise to each successive generation, and so each successive generation carried the sign.
3. *It marks the responsibility of belonging to God*, and so being '*un*circumcised' is the same as being 'unclean'.
4. Furthermore, *it was a sign of a deeper issue.* Centuries later, Jeremiah warned his stubborn hearers to 'circumcise yourselves to the LORD; remove the foreskin of your hearts'.[47] They were

---

[46] *Covenant:* vv. 9, 10, 11, 13 (twice), 14; *circumcision/uncircumcision:* vv. 10, 11, 12, 13, 14 (twice).
[47] Jer. 4:4.

internally unconverted, despite their physical circumcision. Because they no longer loved to listen to God's law, 'their ears are uncircumcised'.[48] The physical sign identified a great problem.

5. Obviously, *it was connected with blood*. God's covenant with Abraham was first mentioned in the context of blood sacrifice,[49] and when the covenants with Noah and Moses were inaugurated, animals were sacrificed. Solomon slaughtered 22,000 oxen and 120,000 sheep.[50] So Jesus described the wine at the Last Supper as 'my blood of the covenant'.[51] As we shall see, Paul can talk of Jesus' bloody death as a form of circumcision.

b. 'Flesh'

This is another significant repetition. The males were to *be circumcised in the flesh of your foreskins . . . in your flesh . . . in the flesh of his foreskin* (11, 13, 14); and Abraham *circumcised the flesh of their foreskins* (23). Abraham was *circumcised in the flesh of his foreskin*, and Ishmael was *circumcised in the flesh of his foreskin*' (24, 25). *Flesh* is central to this covenant. As God summarized, *So shall my covenant be in your flesh an everlasting covenant* (13).

6. The promise kept: circumcision (Col. 2:11–18)

Travel forward to the New Testament. Like the Galatian church, the Colossians were confused over the law, but this time the issues of membership, status and elites were followed to their ruthless conclusion. If circumcision, food laws and festivals identify who is 'in', then in the spiritual realm it is even more devastating, because the issue becomes one of spiritual status, and who is *really* 'in'. Are some Christians closer to Christ than others?

We join Paul in mid-discussion, where the heart of his argument lies in the position won for Christians 'in Christ';[52] all four references to *you* are plural, and there are two references to *us* as well.[53] These are insights for the church as whole, centred again on *baptism* (11). Paul draws five contrasts, which we will pull slightly out of order to see them clearly, and move quickly through the first few to consider the last in more detail.

---

[48] Jer. 6:10; Acts 7:51.
[49] Gen. 15:7–18.
[50] Noah: Gen. 8:20 – 9:17; Moses: Exod. 24:1–8; Solomon: 2 Chr. 7:4–22.
[51] Matt. 26:28.
[52] The key verses are 2:6–7, but see 1:14–22; 2:3–15; 3:18; 4:7, 17.
[53] *You were circumcised* (11) and *you were . . . raised* (12) are plural, as are 'you' and 'your' in v. 13.

a. The defeaters defeated

The Colossian Christians were being distracted by silly talk about whether different spiritual beings could grant or hinder access to God. Paul calls this 'empty deceit' about 'the elemental spirits of the world'.[54] These beings are under Christ, *the head of all rule and authority* (10), and by raising him from the dead, God *disarmed the rulers and authorities and put them to open shame, by triumphing over them in him* (15). There is no need to be distracted by a defeated enemy.

b. The trespasses forgiven

Our access to God had been barred by *trespasses* (13).[55] Imagine the demarcation line between two hostile countries, bristling with weapons across a strip of land, only metres wide. Any soldier who placed one boot on the ground risks being shot immediately. The other side would interpret it as an act of war.

That 'boot on the ground' is a trespass, an act of defiance with dreadful consequences, turning our loving God into an enemy, with right on his side, authority to do what is right, and power to accomplish it. But what God chose to do was erect a cross, on which he himself, in the person of his Son, bore the penalty of that 'boot on the ground', and so he has *forgiven us all our trespasses* (13).

c. The debts cancelled

Another image for our plight is financial. Perhaps you know the worry of an unpayable credit card, and if not, on a vaster scale, we all see countries struggling with national debt, rewriting budgets, and borrowing mind-boggling amounts to repay the loans.

Consider, then, our unpayable debt to God. And consider too what God has done. As Jesus hung on the cross, he was *cancelling the record of debt that stood against us with its legal demands. This he set aside, nailing it to the cross* (14). Our unpayable bill has been paid.

d. The dead raised

The physical consequence of our disobedience and debt is *death*.[56] Paul combines them in his phrase, *you were dead in your trespasses*

[54] 2:8, 20.
[55] *Paraptōma*, a false step.
[56] Gen. 2:17; 3:6; Rom. 5:12; 6:23; 1 Cor. 15:21–22.

(13). Corpses are inert. But Christians have been so identified with Christ that we have been *raised with him through faith in the powerful working of God, who raised him from the dead* (12). The worst enemy we could face, the consequence of our debt and trespass, has been destroyed – not just in the resurrection of Christ, but in that we have been raised in him. Death has done its worst, and failed.

e. The uncircumcised circumcised

Those previous four aspects of Christ's victory are familiar, but the last is unusual, and has no exact parallel in Paul.[57] He brings God's promises to Abraham to the fore, and again insists they are about us and our baptism. If we separate the different concepts, they make more sense when they are reassembled.

(i) Our uncircumcision

We have seen that because everyone has sinned, everyone is spiritually uncircumcised. Genesis 17 emphasized 'flesh', and that informs Paul's expression: *the uncircumcision of your flesh* (13). That odd phrase only makes sense if the term *flesh* has Paul's usual sense of 'our sinful nature'. Combining that with *uncircumcision* is a highly compact way of saying that because of our sin we are alienated from God and not part of his people. He is using *flesh* in conjunction with *circumcision* to drive us back to Genesis 17, and the issue of how sin has taken humankind out of a right relationship with God.

(ii) Christ's circumcision

There is a translation question to be solved before we can move on. 'The circumcision of Christ' could mean either, 'the circumcision *done by* Christ', or 'the circumcision *performed on* Christ'. The nearby references to our being circumcised in Christ (11), and to baptism (12), leads some to suggest that the former translation is correct: that there is a spiritual counterpart to baptism, and as someone is baptized, there is a 'circumcision made without hands' that Christ performs, in the heavenly places. The NIV translates with this interpretation in mind: 'you were circumcised by Christ, having been buried with him in baptism'.

But if we retained the ambiguity, as ESV and HCSB do, to what might Paul be referring? On its own, it might refer to Christ's circumcision as a baby on the eighth day, exactly as God had instructed Abraham.[58] But it is hard to fit that into Colossians, where centre

---

[57] See Phil. 3:3 where Christians are *the circumcision*, and Rom. 2:28–29.
[58] Luke 2:21; Gen. 17:12.

stage stands the cross. This leads most commentators to suggest that this is a particular way of talking about Christ's bloody death.[59] This unusual language brings covenant, people and promise under the effect of the cross, where the promises to Abraham focus, and where the Messiah begins to build his international and eternal kingdom.

(iii) Circumcised in and with Christ

So, if in our sinful state we were 'uncircumcised', and on the cross Christ was 'circumcised', at what point was a Christian 'circumcised'? Paul is clear that we were so circumcised: *In him also you were circumcised with a circumcision made without hands* (11). So when did it occur?[60]

Paul's answer is, at the cross. If Christ's death and burial story can be summarized as his circumcision, and we travelled that journey 'with him', then that was our circumcision too, when each believer, Jewish or Gentile, became a member of God's people. Paul therefore does not say that the circumcision is performed 'by' Christ; it is performed on Christ and those who are *buried with him in baptism* (12), which is exactly what we would expect from Genesis 17. But instead of a mere physical symbol, sin and *flesh* are eradicated, and our uncircumcised hearts are circumcised forever.

7. The promise kept: baptism (Col. 2:11–15)

Once again, an unusual reference to circumcision is connected with baptism, but Paul is not saying that baptism is like circumcision as a rite of entry or a covenantal requirement. This truth is more fascinating than that.

a. Baptism is about Christ's story, not my story

It is beautiful when someone tells the church of their unique conversion, and they are baptized. But baptism points us to an even more beautiful story, and one which is the same for each of us. Look again at verse 12: *having been buried with him in baptism, in which you were also raised with him through faith in the powerful working of God.* Baptism identifies us with Christ, so his story becomes our

---

[59] NIV makes this less obvious: 'Your whole self ruled by the flesh was put off when you were circumcised by Christ' runs neatly, but has made both clauses about us ('your' and 'you' have been inserted). HCSB is almost unrecognizable as the same passage: 'by putting off the body of flesh, in the circumcision of the Messiah'. It is tougher to understand, but closer to what Paul wrote.

[60] *Made without hands* means 'made by God'; e.g. Mark 14:58; Acts 7:48; 2 Cor. 5:1; Heb. 9:11.

story, and all those *with Christ*, and *in Christ* phrases show their true meaning. I remember one preacher explaining dying and rising with Christ, and the link with baptism. He showed a clip of a baptism, and as the man was plunged under the water he said 'Stop the movie!' As the preacher explained baptism and dying with Christ, the screens showed a man being held under water, for something over fifteen minutes. At last the preacher relented. 'Now, let me explain the connection between resurrection and baptism. Start the movie!' And as the man rose out of the water, we all understood. I do not know the man's name, his address, nor how he was converted. But that is not important, because baptism is about Christ's story, not ours.

That makes baptism quite different to circumcision. Circumcision stood for promises made, but baptism stands for promises kept; circumcision stood for true circumcision being needed, but baptism stands for the spiritual circumcision having occurred; circumcision marked the waiting for the true heir, but baptism marks believers as true heirs in the heir who has arrived. It is so tempting to connect the two that we must first underscore the differences. In the Old Testament, there is physical circumcision but no spiritual circumcision; in the New Testament there is spiritual circumcision, and therefore no physical circumcision. That is why I am reluctant to draw a connection between circumcision and baptism, as equivalent marks of the two covenants. Every Christian was spiritually circumcised, but not at their baptism. Nor was it at their conversion. No, you were spiritually circumcised in Christ, with Christ, on the cross and in his tomb.

b. Baptism, the Messiah and his people

So far we have said little about the church in this chapter, but there are two reasons.

First, we need to be jolted out of our individualism. God's plan was always to win billions of people through the work of Christ. Those who receive that lavish love see God's promises from our perspective. Paul himself wrote to the Galatians about 'the Son of God, who loved *me* and gave himself for *me*'.[61] But circumcision shows us God's promises from his side, a promise which, despite appearances, narrowed to one man on a cross, and then exploded into the incredibly rich, multinational people of God of today, and which will not stop there. The greatest acts of the church lie in the future.

This might need some fresh thinking. For instance, the first question in the Westminster Shorter Catechism of 1647, still used

---

[61] Gal. 2:20.

by many churches today, is, 'What is the chief end of Man?' Answer: 'Man's chief end is to glorify God and enjoy him forever.' Today we might be shocked by their English, and want a gender-neutral replacement for 'Man'; the original drafters might be as startled by our assumption that 'Man' means one male. Perhaps we might redraft it: 'What is our chief end?' 'Our chief end is to glorify God and enjoy him *together* forever.'[62]

Secondly, we need to move on. The church is people, but billions of Christians are not a church. 'Christians' and 'church' are not synonyms. For 'Christians' to become 'church' they must do something.

---

[62] A suggestion made, I am told, by Broughton Knox.

Exodus 19; Hebrews 12:18–29
4. The church from exodus to exile

Church /*church*/ *n.* a building set apart for public worship, *esp.* that of a parish, and *esp.* that of an established or once established form of the Christian religion.[1]

We have seen enough to recognize that such dictionary definitions put the emphasis in quite the wrong place. Although we habitually refer to bricks, cement and glass as 'a church', that is not the Bible's way: the place where we meet, shiny or ancient, cathedral or hut, is just a convenience.

But as we have focused on the people, it has become obvious that God has never been content to leave us as a rabble. And so we become curious. 'Why are we supposed to meet? Who called the meeting? And what is on the agenda?' Which is where we stop next on our biblical journey.

Stephen's sermon in Acts 7 recalled God's giving of the law at Sinai; an event Stephen called 'the assembly in the wilderness'.[2] The word behind '*assembly*' is that familiar word *ekklēsia*, such an everyday Greek word that Acts could use it as easily for a riot (19:32), a citizens' assembly (19:39) or a gathering of Christians (20:28). But its Old Testament use gave it theological seriousness, with the backdrop of one particular meeting with a purpose. To understand it we need to go back to the 'assembly in the wilderness' in Exodus 19, and then to Hebrews 12, which contrasts that meeting with Christian church.

[1] *The Chambers Dictionary* (9th ed., Edinburgh: Chambers Harrap, 2003), p. 273.
[2] Acts 7:38, NIV.

1. The first church (Exod. 19)

Moses initially questioned God's ability to rescue the people from Egypt, and asked for a sign. God graciously replied, 'I will be with you, and this shall be the sign for you, that I have sent you: when you have brought the people out of Egypt, you shall serve God on this mountain.'[3] Emboldened, Moses instructed Pharaoh: 'Thus says the LORD, the God of Israel, "Let my people go, that they may hold a feast to me in the wilderness."'[4] He insisted, 'The LORD, the God of the Hebrews, sent me to you, saying, 'Let my people go, that they may serve me in the wilderness. But so far, you have not obeyed.''[5]

This drives the Exodus story. Salvation is not just from Egypt, but for meeting and serving God at that mountain. The first sign that God gives Moses, then, is not one he can hold, like his miraculous staff, or show, like his miraculously healed hand,[6] but one that he must believe, a promise. A promise that when God has saved his people he will take them to church.

The gathering of God's people at Sinai defined their relationship: both how God saw them as his people, and how they were to respond. As they renewed their commitment over the centuries, it came to be seen as normative.

a. God called his saved people together (19:1–3)

Words like 'meeting' or 'assembly' capture the humanly visible elements of church, but they must not obscure God's initiative. He saved his people, brought them safely through sea and desert, and kept his promise that they would worship him right there, on Sinai.

> On the third new moon after the people of Israel had gone out of the land of Egypt, on that day they came into the wilderness of **Sinai**. They set out from Rephidim and came into the wilderness of **Sinai**, and they encamped in the wilderness. **There** Israel encamped before the mountain, while Moses went up to God (1–3).

God called the assembly, and he alone decides what happens. In business language, he is in the chair and he sets the agenda. In biblical

[3] Exod. 3:12. For 'serve', NIV has 'worship'.
[4] Exod. 5:1.
[5] Exod. 7:16. For 'serve', NIV has 'worship'.
[6] Later called 'signs', Exod. 4:8.

language, he is on the throne, and he gives the commandments. So it is with church today. We do not have any right to insist on certain ways of meeting, whether traditional or innovative. God rules the church, and he tells it what to do.

b. God addressed his people (19:3)

God's saved people gather to hear: *The LORD called to him out of the mountain, saying, 'Thus you shall say to the house of Jacob, and tell the people of Israel'* (3). Notice, they do not come first to sing, or pray, or adore, or any of the other activities we might normally expect to associate with 'serving' or 'worshipping' God. They come first to listen.

God's promise to Moses makes sense of this: 'you shall *serve* God on this mountain.'[7] What else do servants do, but carry out instructions and wishes? And how do they know what those instructions are unless they first pay attention? This is the origin of calling our meetings a 'service'; we are servants, come to hear our Master's commands.

So the lesson for us is the same. Of course we pray and sing and celebrate – but we must first attend closely to God's word. How else do we know how or whom to serve, or what we are to sing or celebrate? Gathering God's people to listen was the great cause of the assembly on Sinai.

c. God established his covenant with his people (19:3–5)

God's words were simple:

> *Thus you shall say to the house of Jacob, and tell the people of Israel: You yourselves have seen what I did to the Egyptians, and how I bore you on eagles' wings and brought you to myself. Now therefore, if you will indeed obey my voice and keep my covenant, you shall be my treasured possession among all peoples, for all the earth is mine* (3–5).

That covenant promise of land and descendants to Abraham, Isaac and Jacob, had looked under threat to a people fearing genocide. But God heard their groaning and remembered his covenant with Abraham, with Isaac and with Jacob. He saw the people of Israel and he knew.[8] He explicitly underlined that covenant from the

---

[7] Exod. 3:12, emphasis added.
[8] Exod. 2:24.

burning bush: 'I am the God of your father, the God of Abraham, the God of Isaac and the God of Jacob.'[9]

No longer, though, was it ratified with just one person; the whole nation in solemn assembly heard. Previously they had been promised a land, but now they would be told how to live there; they had been promised descendants, but now they will be told how to guard that land as a blessing for future generations.

Once again, God promised his commitment to his people, demonstrated by their deliverance from Egypt, and now being brought into his presence. What is required of them is therefore inevitable: *obey my voice and keep my covenant* (5). The full commands and terms, as well as the punishments which flow from breaking them, come in chapters 20 – 31, but the nature of the relationship between God and his people is in place. God sovereignly saves to keep his loving promises, and he expects his people to obey him.

d. God reminded his people of his wonderful promises (19:5–6)

Now therefore, if you will indeed obey my voice and keep my covenant, you shall be my treasured possession among all peoples, for all the earth is mine; and you shall be to me a kingdom of priests and a holy nation (5–6). Israel was to have a rich relationship with God. They were his treasured possession, his delight among every nation on earth. As a kingdom of priests they would rule under him, and serve him, like thousands of Adams in the new Eden they would shortly inherit. This would be a holy nation, set apart for God's purposes, and privileged to be so.

The tabernacle's splendour reminded Israel of that unique status; every fork and tong associated with the sacrifices would be ceremonially distinctive, the richness of the priests' robes would remind them of their privileges. But just as surely their history would teach that these promises were only partly fulfilled. Was a kingdom of priests the same as a few corrupt priests and a divided monarchy? Did their ruinous exile in Babylon represent the death of their status as *my treasured possession among all peoples . . . a holy nation?* These promises require greater fulfilment.

e. God's people respond with a commitment to serve him (19:7–9)

So Moses came and called the elders of the people and set before them all these words that the LORD *had commanded him. All the people answered together and said, 'All that the* LORD *has spoken*

---

[9] Exod. 3:6.

we will do.' And Moses reported the words of the people to the
LORD. And the LORD said to Moses, 'Behold, I am coming to you
in a thick cloud, that the people may hear when I speak with
you, and may also believe you forever.'

The people's side of the covenant is clear, and they agree. They are
to obey. This has been a motif throughout this section, but this scene
is formative for the development of the doctrine of God's people in
assembly. When Stephen spoke of the 'assembly in the wilderness'
it was this pattern he had in mind; when Jesus talked of 'my church'
he meant 'my assembly of my people whom I have saved, who will
do what I say and bind themselves unconditionally to me'; and when
Paul, John, Peter and the other New Testament writers wrote to and
about 'churches' this is what they meant. Not just meetings of
people, but meetings with the clear purpose of discovering from
God's word how to serve him. Meetings to discover why it is that
Christians should pray and praise, but not engage in idolatry or
drunkenness. Rather, they break bread and drink wine in obedience
to the instructions of their covenant-making God.

f. God's people fail, but the covenant stands (19:9)

Idolatrous, drunken assemblies were temptations for Israel too. They
knew the repeated reality of the relationship they were entering:
'Behold, I am coming to you [Moses] *in a thick cloud, that the people*
may hear when I speak with you, and may also believe you forever.'
Fire and smoke, thunder and lightning bolts engulfed the whole
event, which went on for forty days.

Yet down the mountain the people quickly lost faith in those
promises and broke their word. In a grim parody of Sinai, the people
constructed their own god and their own pattern of worship.

When the people saw that Moses delayed to come down from the
mountain, the people gathered themselves together to Aaron and
said to him, 'Up, make us gods who shall go before us. As for this
Moses, the man who brought us up out of the land of Egypt, we
do not know what has become of him.' So Aaron said to them,
'Take off the rings of gold that are in the ears of your wives, your
sons, and your daughters, and bring them to me.' So all the people
took off the rings of gold that were in their ears and brought them
to Aaron. And he received the gold from their hand and fashioned
it with a graving tool and made a golden calf. And they said, 'These
are your gods, O Israel, who brought you up out of the land of
Egypt!' When Aaron saw this, he built an altar before it. And

Aaron made proclamation and said, 'Tomorrow shall be a feast to the LORD.' And they rose up early the next day and offered burnt offerings and brought peace offerings. And the people sat down to eat and drink and rose up to play.[10]

God's saved people found another god who saved them; they came to the mountain for a sacred 'feast'[11] but instead had a rebellious one; and while Moses was being told to fashion their gold into the vessels and furniture for the tabernacle, they melted it into an idol. God's word, central to their covenantal relationship, had been smashed by their actions, and when Moses saw what had been done he showed the physical equivalent of their spiritual lawlessness, and smashed the Ten Commandments.

The heart of this story is alternative worship. They decided which gods they wanted to serve, and on what terms. Aaron tried to rectify the problem by reclaiming it as an authentic 'feast to the LORD'. But it was not. A fig-leaf of theological orthodoxy will not cover religious rebellion. God is only pleased by our serving him in ways he has laid down. DIY worship is a contradiction, and the people had 'sinned a great sin'.[12]

For the sake of later generations, Moses ensured that the fate of those who rebelled was burned into the memories of those who would enter the Promised Land, on the border of their new home. He taught specifically about that 'day of the assembly', and recalled why God had assembled his people together:

On the day that you stood before the LORD your God at Horeb, the LORD said to me, 'Gather the people to me, that I may let them hear my words, so that they may learn to fear me all the days that they live on the earth, and that they may teach their children so.'[13]

And the LORD gave me the two tablets of stone written with the finger of God, and on them were all the words that the LORD had spoken with you on the mountain out of the midst of the fire on the day of the assembly.[14]

And [God] wrote on the tablets, in the same writing as before, the Ten Commandments that the LORD had spoken to you on

[10] Exod. 32:1–6.
[11] Exod. 5:1.
[12] Exod. 32:30.
[13] Deut. 4:10.
[14] Deut. 9:10.

the mountain out of the midst of the fire on the day of the assembly. And the LORD gave them to me.[15]

The LORD your God will raise up for you a prophet like me from among you, from your brothers – it is to him you shall listen – just as you desired of the LORD your God at Horeb on the day of the assembly, when you said, 'Let me not hear again the voice of the LORD my God or see this great fire any more, lest I die.'[16]

Two features stand out. First, 'the day of the assembly' became a recognized title for the Sinai events. The Old Testament alludes back to it in that way, and uses identical or similar words to describe later meetings, underlining that they shared its contours.

Secondly, the principal event of the assembly was the giving of the Law. God promised he would not change his mind, and the significance of this for the tabernacle and temple is clear. They were not human inventions designed to please or placate God, but his own design blueprint. Israel's obedience in the construction and use of the tabernacle was therefore service, but only one aspect of it. God wanted obedience to all the law, and that complete service by the entire nation across the whole of life was what God called 'worship'.[17] Part of Israel's later failure was to shrivel 'worship' down to the temple activities, so the rest of life could be lived without regard to their Lord.

This has relevance for our church. We cannot assume that we know what appropriate 'worship' is, but must listen to God telling us. We cannot unthinkingly transfer patterns of 'worship' from our culture or history, lest we fall into the golden calf trap – and we cannot assume that Old Testament models can be a pattern either. The path is surrounded by thorns: we behave as if it is obvious that animal sacrifices do not have a place in our gatherings, but unless we know why, how do we know whether psalms do? What about renewing the covenant, or circumcision, or trumpets, or incense? What about singing, or preaching, or images, or silence? God needs to tell us.

2. What church do you attend? (Heb. 12:18–24)

a. The church you don't attend (12:18–21)

Sinai must have been stunning. Moses recalled it on his deathbed:

[15] Deut. 10:4.
[16] Deut. 18:16.
[17] Exod. 3:12.

The LORD came from Sinai
and dawned from Seir upon us;
he shone forth from Mount Paran;
he came from the ten thousands of holy ones,
with flaming fire at his right hand.[18]

The author of Hebrews agrees. His terrifying description summarizes it in seven tangible experiences:

For you have not come to (1) what may be touched, (2) a blazing fire and (3) darkness and (4) gloom and (5) a tempest and (6) the sound of a trumpet and (7) a voice whose words made the hearers beg that no further messages be spoken to them. For they could not endure the order that was given, 'If even a beast touches the mountain, it shall be stoned.' Indeed, so terrifying was the sight that Moses said, 'I tremble with fear.' (18–20)

Each of these dreadful experiences occurred at Sinai.[19] *But you* [that is, we Christians] *have not* come to that kind of church, or assembly, or meeting. So where have we come?

b. The church you do attend (12:22–24)

The two churches are compared. The phrase *you have not come* (18) is echoed by *but you have come* (22), and the contrasts are stark.[20] Gloomy Mount Sinai was the meeting place of the old covenant, glorious *Mount Zion* is the meeting place of the new; the first was visible, temporary, imperfect and legal, the second is invisible, permanent, perfect and based on the gospel. Fear is replaced by joy, Moses by Jesus. Mount Sinai is past, Mount Zion is present, and there is a future *kingdom* yet to come (28).

But *come* is used throughout Hebrews to mean 'coming before God'.[21] This church is not one we attend on Sundays and leave two hours later: it is the continual, heavenly gathering which contains all Christians permanently, relating to God through Christ. The contrast is not between the experience of the Israelites at Sinai and our

[18] Deut. 33:2.
[19] Touch (Exod. 19:12); fire (Exod. 19:18; Deut. 4:11–12; 5:22–27); darkness (Deut. 4:11; 5:23); gloom (Deut. 4:11); storm (Deut. 4:11); trumpet blast (Exod. 19:19); voice speaking words (Exod. 20:19; Deut. 5:23). They appear throughout the OT as aspects of God's presence.
[20] See 2:1–3; 3:5–6; 7:11–28; 8:1–13; 9:11–28; 10:1–4; 11:1–14. Both 3:1 – 4:11 and 11:27–30 compare the Sinai generation with Christians.
[21] 4:16; 7:25; 10:1, 22; 11:6. Only 12:18 and 10:1 use it of old covenant assembling, both negatively.

experience on Sundays, but between their meeting God on earth, and our meeting him in heaven.[22] That is reinforced by the perfect tense of the verb, which 'indicates arrival at some point in the past with continued enjoyment of the results of that arrival in the present'.[23] So we should be careful in drawing patterns from Sinai to govern our congregational lives today, even (or especially) when the points it teaches seem obvious.

There are seven marks of this meeting too:

> *But you have come (1) to Mount Zion and to the city of the living God, the heavenly Jerusalem, and (2) to innumerable angels in festal gathering, and (3) to the assembly of the firstborn who are enrolled in heaven, and (4) to God, the judge of all, and (5) to the spirits of the righteous made perfect, and (6) to Jesus, the mediator of a new covenant, and (7) to the sprinkled blood that speaks a better word than the blood of Abel.*

(i) Mount Zion, the city of the living God, the heavenly Jerusalem (22)

Zion, the mount in Jerusalem, was where God's dwelt, his throne-room,[24] and the city and its temple were so closely allied they could be seen as identical.[25] God said he had laid the foundations of the temple-city himself,[26] enfolding the Sinai experience:

> The chariots of God are twice ten thousand,
> thousands upon thousands;
> the Lord is among them; Sinai is now in the sanctuary.[27]

The ransack of that temple-city by Babylon was a spiritual disaster, and the prophets continually promised its rebuilding.[28] Hebrews promises that Christians *have come* to that rebuilt city-temple, the *heavenly Jerusalem*[29] where even Abraham was 'looking forward' to being a member.[30] By faith in Christ, being in the presence of God is our permanent right.

---

[22] D. G. Peterson, *Hebrews and Perfection*, SNTSMS (Cambridge: Cambridge University Press, 1982), p. 160.

[23] D. A. Hagner, *Hebrews*, NIBC (Carlisle: Paternoster, 1995), p. 225.

[24] Isa. 2:2, etc.

[25] E.g. 2 Sam. 5:6–7; 2 Kgs 19:21; Ps. 2:6; Mic. 4:1–2.

[26] E.g. Ps. 48; Isa. 14:32.

[27] Ps. 68:17.

[28] Isa. 24:23; Mic. 4:7; Zeph. 3:14–20; Zech. 1:16; Jer. 31:38; Joel 3:17.

[29] Gal. 4:26; Rev. 3:12; 21:2.

[30] Heb. 11:10, 16; 13:14.

(ii) Thousands upon thousands of angels in joyful assembly (22)[31]
'Tens of thousands of holy ones' had attended the first, temporary church,[32] and *assembly*[33] became the term for the great festivals of Passover, Pentecost and Tabernacles,[34] overflowing with celebration and happiness.

But Daniel reported seeing that 'a thousand thousands served him, and ten thousand times ten thousand stood before him';[35] in heaven – and that is where we meet. Once again, Hebrews contrasts the temporary nature of those annual festivals with the permanent and continual celebration in heaven, which we cannot see, but *have come* to and take part in by faith.

(iii) The church of the firstborn, whose names are written in heaven (23)
Israel was God's 'firstborn', as Moses told Pharaoh,[36] and he had ordered that they all be counted and recorded by name.[37] The first *assembly of the firstborn* would seem, once again, to be Sinai.[38]

But Hebrews reserves the word *assembly* for its permanent heavenly expression,[39] and here the phrase reinforces our family right to belong in that assembly. Jesus is the uncreated *firstborn* (1:5–6), but because of his cross-work he has many 'brothers and sisters'[40] in the heavenly congregation, whose names have been recorded in heaven.[41]

(iv) God, the judge of all (23)
At Sinai the encounter with God was terrifying, but here we meet in gospel unity. The contrast with Sinai is once again stark: then they heard *a voice whose words made the hearers beg that no further messages be spoken to them* (19), but today 'a Christian believer

---

[31] See the commentaries for the punctuation here; I think NIV is correct.
[32] Deut. 33:2.
[33] *Panēgyris.*
[34] Ezek. 46:11; Hos. 9:5; Amos 5:21.
[35] Dan. 7:10.
[36] Exod. 4:22.
[37] Num. 3:40.
[38] The word 'firstborn' has also been taken to mean: the patriarchs, the apostles, dead Christians, martyrs, the first converts and even angels. The nature of the argument, which deliberately includes the readers in the assembly, seems to preclude all but the interpretation above.
[39] See too 2:12.
[40] Heb. 2:10–11, NIV. The more literal *brothers* might seem less inclusive, but more accurately captures that it is Christ's first-born inheritance rights that we share.
[41] Luke 10:20; Phil. 4:3; Rev 3:5; 13:8; 17:8; 20:12, 15. This is a blessing which only believers, and not angels, share (see fn. 44).

comes gladly and with confidence, knowing that what is for others a throne of judgment, is for [us] a throne of grace'.[42]

(v) The spirits of righteous people made perfect (23)

Hebrews has consistently stressed that the work of Christ has made us eternally perfect: 'For by a single offering he has perfected for all time those who are being sanctified.'[43] This verse is therefore describing God's inclusive heavenly assembly in which we on earth are involved, so there is no need to restrict it to dead Christians, or Old Testament believers. This heavenly assembly is not our final destination, and ahead of us lies our resurrection (11:10, 13–16; 13:14) and *a kingdom that cannot be shaken* (12:28) – but being perfect now is the application of Christ's work to us now, and so we all participate now. As David Peterson says, 'in contrast to the traditions about Sinai, every aspect of this vision provides encouragement for the recipients to approach God boldly'.[44]

(vi) Jesus the mediator of a new covenant (24)[45]

Even Moses the mediator said *I tremble with fear* (21) when he introduced the covenant, yet it was one which the prophets said would need to be replaced.[46] Jesus has a *new*[47] and *better*[48] covenant of which he is *the mediator*, inaugurated by his death.[49] Once again, the cross is central to our appearance in the heavenly church.

(vii) The sprinkled blood that speaks a better word than the blood of Abel (24)

As many pastors have noticed, Abel was murdered during an argument about worship.[50] Both his meat and Cain's fruit were acceptable forms of sacrifice, so the problem probably lies more with the casual nature of Cain's offering, compared to the valuable nature of Abel's *firstborn* offering. That aside, the consequence is shocking.

---

[42] P. E. Hughes *A Commentary on the Epistle to the Hebrews* (Grand Rapids; Eerdmans, 1977), p. 549, citing Heb. 4:16; 10:22. This concerns ultimate judgment, not God's disciplining of Christians.

[43] Heb. 10:14.

[44] Peterson, *Hebrews*, p. 160.

[45] 'This verse forms the climax of vv18-24, and thus rhetorically of the whole Epistle', P. Ellingworth, *The Epistle to the Hebrews*, NIGTC (Grand Rapids: Eerdmans, 1996), p. 681.

[46] Jer. 31:31; Ezek. 11:19.

[47] Heb. 8:8, 13; 9:15. See Luke 22:20; 1 Cor. 11:25; 2 Cor. 3:6.

[48] Heb 7:22; 8:6.

[49] 10:29.

[50] Gen 4:3–10.

Abel's spattered blood flowed from his corpse,[51] and was 'crying' for justice, punishment and revenge; it was a witness to the foul nature of sin and its consequence. Cain was banished from God's presence, and so are all sinners; which is why the Sinai story shows the Israelites and their elders keeping their distance from God, and even Moses trembling with fear.[52]

The contrast with our heavenly church appears once again. Cain 'went away from the presence of the Lord',[53] but we *have come* into it; a different corpse, and being sprinkled by different blood, means that we are not marked as excluded sinners, but gathered as those who have been made righteous. Hebrews has repeatedly underlined that it is Jesus' bloody death which has made the change, his 'blood . . . securing an eternal redemption'; he 'appeared once for all at the end of the ages to put away sin by the sacrifice of himself'; we 'have been sanctified through the offering of the body of Jesus Christ once for all', 'for by a single offering he has perfected for all time those who are being sanctified'.[54] Which is why we should never, ever, assume we are part of the heavenly assembly by any right of our own, but only, permanently, because of Christ's death for us.

3. Spectacular, sensational worship (Heb. 12:21–24)

Perhaps the most remarkable contrast between the two churches was that Sinai was an assault on the senses: sight, hearing, touch, taste and smell were all evoked by the loud fiery mountain. Hebrews summarizes the whole terrifying event as a *sight* (21), translating the unusual word *phantazomenon*. By contrast, the present, heavenly church is spectacular and sensational – but only when seen from heaven. Here and now, we see it only through the eyes of faith.

All through Christian history, believers have found this hard, and have sought to do what Hebrews warns against, which is to replicate the sensational, spectacular impact of the worship of Sinai. Surely, they argue, if Sinai was like that, and what we have is better, then we must be even more sensational and spectacular. So Christians built Chartres cathedral with its dazzling stained glass and mysterious mazes; St Paul's Cathedral in London offers spine-tingling acoustics; eastern Orthodoxy offers golden icons and the scent of incense as windows into heaven.

---

[51] Gen. 4:10.
[52] Exod. 19.
[53] Gen. 4:16.
[54] 9:12, 26; 10:10, 14. W. L. Lane, *Hebrews 9–13*, WBC 47B (Dallas: Word, 1991), p. 473.

This is not just a temptation for traditional churches. Dan Kimball has argued that contemporary churches should move in this direction too. Noticing that 'In many contemporary worship settings, well meaning leaders and designers have removed the sense of awe, wonder and transcendence', he says that by contrast 'Emerging generations are very visual. They crave a sense of mystery and wonder of God as they worship. They desire a spiritual environment for worship.' So what should our meetings be like? 'Multisensory worship involves seeing, tasting, smelling, touching, and experiencing.'[55]

This calls for careful thought. Of course, we are sensory beings – in fact it is impossible to be a human being in any context without the involvement of the senses. Our physical context has undeniable impact: some songs are upbeat and uplifting, others are downbeat and sorrowful. Either kind played badly is depressing. Bright, light auditoriums create one physical response; damp, dark Victorian Gothic quite another. Wine which makes you wince and typefaces you cannot read make a sensual impact. These choices are not irrelevant.

Nevertheless, it is striking to compare Kimball's call for 'multi-sensory worship' with the call from Hebrews 12, where *you have not come* contrasts with where *you have come*, and where earthly multisensory overload contrasts with the heavenly reality. The hard lesson is that the invisible and intangible church in heaven is *better* (24) than Sinai. The awe, wonder, transcendence and mystery that we crave is not produced by candles, medieval architecture, Latin chants and incense; nor by echoing the emotional impact of a contemporary music festival, such as Glastonbury or Burning Man. Instead, it is produced by the gospel, by the awareness that, by faith, we participate in this heavenly assembly. That means we must deliberately refuse to do anything which might seem to produce an 'effect' of mystery, awe and so on. The lights go on, the windows are opened, and it is an ordinary meeting – because it is in the heavenly church that the encounter with God takes place.

4. Make sure you attend the right church (Heb. 12:25–28)

For all the contrasts between the two churches, Sinai and Zion, there is one point of similarity: at Sinai there was *a voice speaking words* (19),[56] and now the writer warns us, *See that you do not refuse him who is speaking. For if they did not escape when they refused him who warned them on earth, much less will we escape if we reject him*

[55] D. Kimball, *Emerging Worship* (Grand Rapids: Zondervan, 2004), pp. 78–81.
[56] NIV.

who warns from heaven (25). Notice that at Sinai God spoke to them *on earth*, but now he speaks to us *from heaven*.[57] The encouragement to pay attention to the present, speaking God has been continually emphasized in Hebrews:

Long ago, at many times and in many ways, God spoke to our fathers by the prophets, but in these last days he has spoken to us by his Son, whom he appointed the heir of all things, through whom also he created the world.[58]

Therefore we must pay much closer attention to what we have heard, lest we drift away from it. For since the message declared by angels proved to be reliable and every transgression or disobedience received a just retribution, how shall we escape if we neglect such a great salvation?[59]

Anyone who has set aside the law of Moses dies without mercy on the evidence of two or three witnesses. How much worse punishment, do you think, will be deserved by the one who has spurned the Son of God, and has profaned the blood of the covenant by which he was sanctified, and has outraged the Spirit of grace?[60]

We should *not refuse* this God.[61]

Hebrews underlines that the word God speaks is the Scriptures: Psalm 8 is described emphatically as speaking 'today'; and the Ten Commandments are 'living and active'.[62] The covenant, the blood, the assembly and so on are now located in the heavenly Jerusalem, but the point of similarity between the two churches, and the point of contact between heaven and earth, is an attentiveness to the God who speaks in Scripture.

Moreover, God *has promised, 'Yet once more I will shake not only the earth but also the heavens.' This phrase, 'Yet once more,' indicates the removal of things that are shaken – that is, things that have been made – in order that the things that cannot be shaken may remain* (26–27). The quotation is from Haggai 2:6, where the prophet promises the returned exiles from Babylon that God will remove their temporary foreign monarch and replace him with a king

[57] It is probably Jesus who speaks, from the preceding verse.
[58] 1:1–2.
[59] 2:1–3.
[60] 10:28–29.
[61] 2:1–4; 3:7–19; 5:11 – 6:12; 10:19–39; 12:14–29.
[62] 4:7–8, 12.

infinitely more splendid. Hebrews takes that promise further: Sinai's earthquakes will be repeated on a cosmic scale. Everything, even in the heavenly realms, that is not gospel-based will be removed, and only God's new unshakeable[63] *kingdom* (28) will remain. It is a mark of how seriously we attend to this speaking God that we take his warning to heart.

5. Acceptable worship (Heb. 12:28–29)

The promise to Moses before Egypt was, 'I will be with you, and this will be the sign to you, that it is I who have sent you: When you have brought the people out of Egypt, you will worship God on this mountain.'[64] At the heart of the golden calf episode lay God's right to determine how he should be worshipped. And it is a critical question for our author too: *Therefore let us be grateful for receiving a kingdom that cannot be shaken, and thus let us offer to God acceptable worship, with reverence and awe* (28). He is quoting Deuteronomy 4:24[65] where Moses explicitly recalled the Sinai event to impress its seriousness on the next generation, and here Hebrews repeats it for us. More than repeats, in fact, because this is a 'how much more' argument: if God at Sinai was a consuming fire, how much more should we treat him with reverence and awe, and offer acceptable worship. This is the third time that Hebrews has warned Christian readers of God's fiery holiness (6:8; 10:27).

So the living God demands *acceptable worship*, and for that we need worship which is better than spectacular, and better than sensational. What would such worship look like? That is where Hebrews 13 takes us, and in a quite radical direction. In fact, what we are about to discover is probably the most radical thought in this entire book.[66]

We use the word 'worship' routinely and easily. 'Let's have a time of worship.' 'John's going to lead us in worship.' 'We have our worship service at 6.30.' 'I worship at Highlands Community Church.' Here is the radical thought. No New Testament writer wrote those sentences, or anything like them. In fact, they might not have understood what we are talking about.

So that we keep clear minds, we need to focus properly. There is of course a range of New Testament words to describe delighting in God (praise, glory, extol, magnify, for instance) and the activities we

[63] Ps. 102:25; Isa. 66:2; Zech. 14:10.
[64] Exod. 3:12, NIV.
[65] See too Deut. 9:9; 10:4; 18:16.
[66] See I. H. Marshall, 'How far did the early Christians "worship" Jesus?', *Churchman* 99 (1985), pp. 216–229.

engage in to do that (sing, pray, teach, for instance). But the word 'worship' does not fit in either of those lists, in its New Testament usage. Instead, it was used in three ways.

a. Worship was a proper activity in the temple

There are myriad references to temple worship in the Old Testament, both to its appropriateness, and to the judgment on those who worship in any other way.[67] The God-given law, the God-required sacrifices, the God-ordained priesthood, and the God-designed tabernacle/temple itself, all led people to worship. They worshipped God with a passion. Kings, prophets and priests engaged in daily, weekly monthly, annual and one-off acts of worship. Psalms encouraged them to worship, prophets rebuked them for the half-hearted worship, David and Solomon provided for their worship. This was a direct encounter with the living God, located at the Mount Sinai, the tabernacle or the Temple Mount, expressed in ritual, improvisation, activity and song. In any concordance, the overwhelming majority of the uses of the word *worship* are in that context.

This is one fundamental starting point: God decides what is acceptable worship, not us. Just 'making up' how we worship God leads us into dangerous territory:

> Now Nadab and Abihu, the sons of Aaron, each took his censer and put fire in it and laid incense on it and offered *unauthorized* fire before the LORD, *which he had not commanded them.* And fire came out from before the LORD and consumed them, and they died before the LORD.[68]

Notice, their disobedience lay not in breaking a law, but in being creative.

Now although obedience to God's commands is always required in every field, the reason why worshipping God acceptably was so important was that God was physically present among them.[69] He noticed what they did when they came near to him, and they had to behave in particular ways.

These ideas remain as the New Testament opens. Mary, Joseph Simeon and Anna all rightly gather in the temple at the time of Jesus' circumcision, as the law, the prophets, and the temple all point to

---

[67] Deut. 4:15–18.
[68] Lev. 10:1–2. See too 1 Sam. 13:1–14.
[69] See Lev. 26:1–45.

him.[70] But as the Gospels unfurl, a strange transfer begins. People begin to worship Jesus, from the wise men confronted with the baby to the disciples confronted with their risen Lord.[71] Jesus replaced the temple as the appropriate place for worship, because when people met him they encountered God, physically present.[72]

b. Worship is a proper activity in the heavenly assembly

So when Jesus was physically relocated from earth to his heavenly throne, he became there the proper object of heavenly worship, and the book of Revelation is therefore the most consistent user of the word *worship*.[73] As all creation sees him as the Lamb, Lion, Bridegroom and Conqueror, their continual, heavenly cry is one of *worship*. But we should remember where that takes place: once again, it is in his visible, physical presence. There he fulfils and surpasses all the earthly role of the temple, just as at the cross he fulfilled and surpassed the sacrificial system by being both victim and priest. As Hebrews earlier explained, there Jesus is eternally our 'high priest, one who is seated at the right hand of the throne of the Majesty in heaven, a minister in the holy places, in the true tent that the Lord set up, not man'.[74]

This is the second way the New Testament uses the word 'worship', and it is obviously an extension of the first. But it is so radical we must force ourselves to see the amazing nature of what Christ has done. It is a very common human habit to see our religious activities as things we do to come into the presence of a god. And even in well-taught churches we encourage each other to 'enter into God's presence', when we should really be encouraging each other to delight that because of Christ's victory we are permanently in God's presence – in the heavenly places, where it really matters. More seriously, we call the people who write our songs, lead our singing, and verbalize our praises, our 'worship leaders'. But look again at the phrase Hebrews uses about Jesus: *a minister in the holy places*. *Minister* (*leitourgos*) means 'someone who leads us in God's worship', and gives us our word 'liturgy'. Jesus is our permanent, glorious, irreplaceable, and final worship leader.

Many churches rightly embrace the teachings brought to light at the Reformation. They would never call their pastor a 'priest', they

[70] Luke 2:22–39.
[71] See Matt. 2:11; 14:33; 28:9, 17.
[72] John 1:14–18; 2:14–19.
[73] Rev. 4:10; 5:14; 7:11; 9:20; 11:1, 16; 13:4, 8, 12, 15; 14:7, 9, 11; 15:4; 16:2; 19:4, 10, 20; 20:4; 22:3, 8–9.
[74] Heb. 8:1–2.

would never call the Lord's Supper 'a sacrifice', they would never call the table 'an altar'. So why do we call the person who leads the band, directs the prayers or preaches the sermon, 'a worship leader'?

c. Worship for Christians?

It is only when you search the Bible for yourself that you will dare to believe the third meaning of the word 'worship'. Because you will first discover how shockingly few references we have left. There is just one reference to a local church 'worshipping'.[75] Despite the section headings that editors put in Bibles, the chapters of 1 Corinthians flow past without the word ever appearing.

Instead, the word now comes to mean the entirety of our lives lived in God's presence. The *acceptable worship* of Hebrews 12 is explained as activities like caring for the poor and maintaining a faithful marriage in chapter 13. The whole of our lives, minds and bodies, is what Paul claimed is our 'spiritual worship'.[76] Now we must not misunderstand this truth: it is not that worship is everything we do with the sole exception of our time together as a church; that would be foolish. We shall see later that 'praise' and 'thanksgiving', 'praying' and 'singing' are utterly appropriate activities for Christians to engage in at church – in fact, not to engage in them is disobedience.[77] But there is no biblical warrant for referring to our time together uniquely as 'worship'. Some churches describe their meetings as 'corporate worship', which I think is valid if it serves to reinforce the fact that everything else we do, outside the meeting, is also worship. We worship God by basing our whole lives on the wonder of the gospel; that is what he wants us to do. He tells us to sing, so we obey him; and he tells us to pay our taxes, so we do that too. Neither has a privileged status. Both are equally worship.[78]

[75] Acts 13:2. See ch. 16.
[76] Rom. 12:1–2. See ch. 13.
[77] See ch. 9.
[78] See D. G. Peterson, *Engaging with God* (Leicester: IVP, 1992) and V. Roberts, *True Worship* (Carlisle: Paternoster, 2002). D. A. Carson (ed.), *Worship by the Book* (Grand Rapids: Zondervan, 2002) and J. Frame, *Worship in Spirit and Truth* (Phillipsburg: Presbyterian and Reformed, 1996) cover similar ground excellently, but both are strangely unwilling to follow to conclusion how we use the word 'worship' (despite Carson's co-authors).

Matthew 16:13–20
5. The church from exile to eternity

So God loved his people from eternity, and through his dealings with Israel established the pattern of a people gathered around his word. 'Church' is written on his heart, and throughout history.

1. Did Jesus mean to start a 'church'?

But 'church' has its critics. The radical French Catholic, Alfred Loisy, famously wrote, 'Jesus foretold the kingdom, and it was the church which came'.[1] Many today blame the consequences of the conversion of the Roman Emperor Constantine when, as William Beckham puts it, the church became 'trapped in an *institutional*, rather than *incarnational* wineskin'.[2] Christianity became a political system, professional bureaucrats developed church structures, spiritual power gave way to political ambition, servant leadership was replaced with authoritarianism, the church became defensive rather than offensive, and the small-group context of the church was made suspect. The results, he writes, are still with us: 'people go to a building (cathedral) on a special day of the week (Sunday) and someone (a priest, or today, a pastor) does something to them (teaching, preaching, absolution or healing) or for them (ritual or entertainment) for a price (offerings).' In a phrase that many have quoted, and more have echoed, 'the changes

---

[1] *The Gospel and the Church* (Philadelphia: Fortress, 1976), p. 166. Excommunicated by the Vatican in 1908, Loisy thought that Jesus did intend to form some sort of society. It was the aping of state government which he questioned.
[2] W. A. Beckham, *The Second Reformation* (Houston: TOUCH Publications, 1995), p. 42, emphasis added.

grew out of new ways of thinking about God's church as an *organization* rather than as an *organism*.[3] So it is common to talk of the need to 'rediscover' the real meaning of church after centuries of its being obscured. Its advocates frequently compare the need to the great changes of the sixteenth century: cell groups are 'the Second Reformation', and unleashing spiritual gifts is a 'New Reformation'.[4]

Other streams of discontent are more cultural. Contemporary culture values youth, informality, spontaneity, experience, creativity and authenticity in relationships – which churches seem reluctant to provide; it distrusts hierarchies, dogmatism, authoritarianism and words – all of which churches provide. Put simply, churches are said to be losing members because we are unreal. Erwin McManus describes the stark decision many churches have made, 'we kept our traditions and lost our children'.[5] In reaching today's non-Christians, discipling them and developing them into godly leaders for the future, we must recognize that the 'church' culture erects an almost insurmountable barrier in the way. Dan Kimball makes this point strongly, and encourages us to return to more ancient, pre-modern, spirituality. But, as Erwin McManus points out, 'The key to regaining an ancient faith is not the reclamation of the icons and rituals of pre-modern medieval Western Christianity. We must go back further than this. It is essential we return to the origins of the church and re-establish the elemental faith of the first disciples.'[6] If we stop the clock 600 years ago, we will only reintroduce their errors, and lose the Reformation's discoveries. Equally, those who react to this by wanting to stop the clock 500 years ago and resurrect the music and aesthetics of Calvin's Geneva can make the same mistake. Such things are treasured because they are old, but their problem is that they are not old enough.

But for some critics,[7] Constantine's legacy produced Christendom, and thus the West, the Reformation, and modernity; so we

---

[3] Beckham, *Reformation*, pp. 42–43, emphasis original.

[4] The full title of Beckham, *Reformation*. See: C. George, *Prepare your Church for the Future* (Grand Rapids: Revell, 1991), and subsequently B. Donohue and R. Robinson, *Building a Church of Small Groups* (Grand Rapids: Zondervan, 2001); T. Chester and S.Timmis, *Total Church* (Leicester: IVP, 2007). *The New Reformation* was the 1995 title of G. Ogden, *Unfinished Business* (Grand Rapids: Zondervan, 2003).

[5] E. McManus, *An Unstoppable Force* (Loveland: Group, 2001), p. 6.

[6] McManus, *Unstoppable*, p. 206.

[7] For instance, L. Sweet, *Post-Modern Pilgrims* (Nashville: Broadman & Holman, 2000); D. Kimball, *The Emerging Church* (Grand Rapids: Zondervan, 2003).

need radically to reinvent church in a postmodern world.[8] Were the Reformation, and its contemporary heirs, evangelicalism, a cultural construct, not as biblical as we think?

There is a good example of this dilemma in a report for the Church of England, called *Mission-Shaped Church*.[9] Passionate for evangelism, and crammed with experiment, the report's definition of church comes from the Nicene Creed, 'the One, Holy, Catholic and Apostolic Church'. Those are four classic signs of a church, and we shall revisit them in chapters 12–15; but if we had asked any of the Reformers, 'What are the marks of the church?' they would have replied in a different vein. Calvin famously defined it, 'Wherever we see the Word of God purely preached and heard, and the sacraments administered according to Christ's institutes, there, it is not to be doubted, a church of God exists'.[10] Sometimes the Reformers added a third mark, 'discipline', as in the Belgic Confession of 1560:

The marks, by which the true Church is known, are these: if the pure doctrine of the gospel is preached therein; if she maintains the pure administration of the sacraments as instituted by Christ; if church discipline is exercised in punishing of sin: in short, if all things are managed according to the pure Word of God, all things contrary thereto rejected, and Jesus Christ acknowledged as the only Head of the Church.

But always they insisted that word and sacrament define a church. Consider the difference: the Reformation marks are visible, and the creedal marks are invisible. There is nothing wrong with either description, but *Mission-Shaped Church* has taken the invisible marks and made them the definition of a visible community. So,

[8] For the charge, see B. McLaren and T. Compolo, *Adventures in Missing the Point* (Grand Rapids: Zondervan/Youth Specialties, 2006); S. Chalke and A. Watkis, *Intelligent Church* (Grand Rapids: Zondervan, 2006); M. Williams, *Church after Christendom* (Carlisle: Paternoster, 2005). For sympathetic surveys of the subject see E. Gibbs and I. Coffey, *Church Next* (Leicester: IVP, 2001), and E. Gibbs and R. K. Bolger, *Emerging Churches* (London: SPCK, 2006); for a more critical one see D. A. Carson, *Becoming Conversant with the Emerging Church* (Grand Rapids: Zondervan, 2005); for a critical insider's view see Mark Driscoll, *Confessions of a Reformission Rev.: Hard Lessons from an Emerging Missional Church* (rev. ed., Grand Rapids: Zondervan, 2006). On the point that our understanding of church is a product of Christendom, see the introduction to ch. 11.

[9] London: The Archbishops' Council, 2004.

[10] *Institutes* 4.1.9. The Church of England's 39 Articles were therefore typically Reformed: 'The visible Church of Christ is a congregation of faithful [people], in the which the pure Word of God is preached, and the Sacraments be duly ministered.' Article XIX (changing 'men' to 'people').

is a group of Christians meeting to chat over a cup of coffee a church? *Mission-Shaped Church* can argue, 'yes'. The Reformers would not answer that question unless they had first discovered whether the Bible was opened and obeyed,[11] and that is controversial precisely because of the suggestion that such a classic Evangelical emphasis on Scripture is itself a product of culture, not the gospel.

Some have found the decay even within the first Christian churches. The seminal missiologist David Bosch explicitly finds those elements he dislikes within the New Testament churches, sees them as an inherent distraction from the primary task of mission, and calls the patterns for congregational life in 1 Corinthians, 1 Timothy and 3 John a 'failure': the church 'ceased to be a movement and turned into an institution'.[12]

Indeed, the New Testament scholar C. K. Barrett also quoted Loisy, and said that 'beyond the time of his suffering [Jesus] envisaged no period of continuing history, in which a Church organized in this world would find a place, but an apocalyptic era of vindication'.[13]

All these contemporary tensions show the pressing need to return to the beginning of the church, to where Jesus' new gathering begins, and consider what he intended to do.

2. Who is Jesus?

Now when Jesus came into the district of Caesarea Philippi, he asked his disciples, 'Who do people say that the Son of Man is?' And they said, 'Some say John the Baptist, others say Elijah, and others Jeremiah or one of the prophets.' He said to them, 'But who do you say that I am?' Simon Peter replied, 'You are the Christ, the Son of the living God.' And Jesus answered him, 'Blessed are you, Simon Bar-Jonah! For flesh and blood has not revealed this to you, but my Father who is in heaven. And I tell you, you are Peter, and on this rock I will build my church, and the gates of hell shall not prevail against it. I will give you the keys of the kingdom of heaven, and whatever you bind on earth shall be bound in heaven, and whatever you loose on earth shall be loosed in heaven.' Then he strictly charged the disciples to tell no one that he was the Christ.

---

[11] Baptism and the Lord's Supper (and church discipline) happen because the Bible says we are to do them, therefore opening the Bible is logically prior.

[12] D. Bosch, *Transforming Mission: Paradigm Shifts in Theology of Mission* (New York: Orbis, 1991), p. 50.

[13] C. K. Barrett, *Jesus and the Gospel Tradition* (London: SPCK, 1967), p. 87.

The question of Jesus' identity runs through Matthew's Gospel, and this passage stands as the climax of the first half.[14] On the positive side, John the Baptist's recognition of Jesus as his superior (Matt. 3:14) and Peter and Andrew's decision to follow him (4:18–20) move through to the centurion's recognition that Jesus was 'the Son of God' (27:54), but there is mounting hostility from the mob (11:16–19) and the leadership (12:9–14, 22–32, 38–42; 15:1–20) which climaxes with their whipping up the crowd to bay for Jesus' death (27:20–24) because he allegedly claimed 'I am the Son of God' (27:43). Up to this passage, John the Baptist, his family, the mob, King Herod and others have all been in settings where people question Jesus' identity,[15] and it is into this barrage of questions that this conversation is placed, with its emphasis on Jesus' death and resurrection, followed by God's verdict at the transfiguration (17:1–13). Jesus, faced with rejection, forms a new community which correctly identifies him, relies on his death and resurrection, and will be the focus of God's saving activity for the rest of history.

3. Peter identifies Jesus

Jesus took his disciples away from the spotlight to Caesarea Philippi, where he makes them review his identity. Even his question shows the importance of the matter, because by asking them first *'Who do people say the Son of Man is?'* and then *'who do you say that I am?'* he is starting to give them the answer – he is the mysterious Son of Man of Daniel 7. Peter, their representative (the *you* is plural), replies to the first question with four responses. Some of the crowd and Herod think Jesus is *John the Baptist* (11:9–14; 14:2) and some *Elijah* (11:14; 27:45–49). *Jeremiah* was opposed and persecuted, so maybe he is the correct identity.[16] Or perhaps, more generally, Jesus was a *prophet* (21:11, 46). All four answers share the prophecy theme, and of course Jesus was a prophet (11:21–24; 24:2–31), but he was so much more than that as Peter's answers show.[17]

---

[14] See C. Caragounis, *Peter and the Rock* (Berlin/New York: Walter de Gruyter, 1990), pp. 76–81.

[15] John (11:2–3); family (12:46–50); mob (12:23); Herod the tetrarch (14:1–2); Pharisees (12:24); teachers of the law (12:38), etc.

[16] R. T. France, *Matthew*, TNTC (Leicester: IVP, 1985), p. 252; D. Turner, *The Gospel of Matthew*, CBC (Carol Stream: Tyndale House, 2005), p. 220.

[17] This theme is particularly prominent in John. See John 1:21, 25 (picking up Deut. 18:15–18); 6:14–15; 7:40; 9:17.

a. Jesus is the Christ

Matthew has consistently taught that Jesus is the Christ, from the opening verses (1:1, 16), through the stories of his birth (1:18; 2:4) and his ministry (11:2), and it now becomes a title that Jesus will use, carefully, of himself (22:42; 23:10; 24:5, 23). It becomes key at his trial (26:63, 68) and execution (27:17, 22).

Christ means 'one who is anointed', and although to Gentile ears it would have sounded weird ('the smeared one'),[18] to a Jew with Old Testament ears it would have sounded rich. Prophets were anointed,[19] and so were priests[20] and kings.[21] But it has a particular significance for looking at 'the church', because none of those titles can exist without other people. A prophet implies people to whom to speak, a priest implies people for whom to intercede, and a king implies people over whom to rule. The three make up the title *Christ*, and as is frequently noted, 'A Messiah requires and comes for *a people* – Messiah and People of God are reciprocal ideas',[22] and 'A Messiah without a Messianic Community would be unthinkable to any Jew'.[23]

Nor is this limited to *Christ*. The title *Son of Man* is unthinkable without the people whom he embodies;[24] the Servant is unthinkable without the people for whom he is both representative and substitute.[25] It should have been, and should be, obvious that if Jesus is the Christ, he creates a people.

b. Jesus is the Son of the living God

The second part of Peter's answer raises the stakes even higher. The title *Son of God* was a royal title,[26] used of both David and his successors.[27] It was also used of Israel's unique relationship with God,[28] and that underlines again the intimate relationship between Jesus and his people: a royal Son of God without other sons of God

[18] P. Barnett, *Jesus and the Rise of Early Christianity* (Downers Grove: IVP, 1999), p. 26.

[19] Ps. 105:15.

[20] Exod. 28:41.

[21] 2 Sam. 1:14. See M. J. Wilkins, *Matthew*, NIVAC (Grand Rapids: Zondervan, 2004), p. 558.

[22] O. Cullman, *Peter: Disciple-Apostle-Martyr* (London: SCM Press, 1953), p. 106.

[23] W. F. Albright and C. S. Mann, *Matthew*, AB, vol. 26 (Garden City: Doubleday, 1971), p. 195.

[24] Dan. 7:13–14, 27.

[25] Isa. 42:1–4; 49:1–6; 50:4–9; 52:13 – 53:12.

[26] Although it is used of angels in Gen. 6:2; Job 1:6 and Dan. 3:25.

[27] 2 Sam. 7:14; Pss 2:7; 89:26–27.

[28] Exod. 4:22–23; Hos. 11:1; Mal. 2:10.

(his people) was also unthinkable. Matthew has drawn particular attention to this title, using it repeatedly on the lips of others (27:40, 43, 54), demons (4:3, 6; 8:29), the disciples (14:33), as a fulfilment of Old Testament themes (1:21–23; 2:15) and as the ultimate climax to his Gospel (28:19). It is a title God the Father himself uses (3:17), and Jesus is obviously very comfortable talking about *my Father*.[29]

Two particular occasions in Matthew clarify this. In an earlier moment of high personal identity, Jesus had said 'All things have been handed over to me by my Father, and no one knows the Son except the Father, and no one knows the Father except the Son and anyone to whom the Son chooses to reveal him'.[30] That note seems to stretch forwards too: 'And Jesus came and said to them, "All authority in heaven and on earth has been given to me. Go therefore and make disciples of all nations, baptizing them in the name of the Father and of the Son and of the Holy Spirit." '[31]

The phrase *Son of God* seems to be both a straight synonym for Christ, but also more richly, a reference to Jesus' eternal sonship of *the living God*. But notice that both those passages have an explicit reference to the people that the Son of God will gather, those to whom Jesus will reveal the Father, and whom the disciples will reach, teach and baptize in his name. The Son of God is also unthinkable without his people.

It was particularly ironic, then, that the High Priest, interrogating Jesus, unwittingly paraphrased Peter's confession: 'I charge you under oath by the living God: Tell us if you are the Christ, the Son of God.'[32] Jesus was and is, and that was why he would die and be raised.

4. Jesus identifies Peter

Peter has identified Jesus by his title (*Christ*) and person (*Son of God*), and now Jesus does the same, using the same phrase[33] to identify a title (*Peter/Rock*) given to a person (*Simon, son of Jonah*). We can lay it out like this:

(1) *Blessed are you, Simon Bar-Jonah!*
For flesh and blood has not revealed this to you,
but my Father who is in heaven.

[29] Matt. 7:21; 10:32; 11:27; 12:50; 16:17; 18:10, 19; 20:23; 25:34; 26:39, 42, 53.
[30] Matt. 11:27.
[31] Matt. 28:18–19.
[32] Matt. 26:63, NIV.
[33] You are (*sy ei*) . . . You are (*sy ei*).

(2) *And I tell you, you are Peter,*
and on this rock I will build my church,
and the gates of hell shall not prevail against it.
(3) *I will give you the keys of the kingdom of heaven,*
and whatever you bind on earth shall be bound in heaven,
and whatever you loose on earth shall be loosed in heaven.[34]

a. Simon

Although Jesus had asked all the disciples the question of his identity (13, 15), he now turns to Simon, holding back from using 'Peter' until verse 18, where it has a new significance. Simon had some evident leadership role among the disciples,[35] and all four lists of the Twelve name him first,[36] but what unfolds now is not his representative role, but his destiny, for which he was *blessed*. Peter had confessed something which Jesus' *Father who is in heaven* had revealed, and now Jesus would do the same, unfolding Peter's significance for the church in the millennia which lay ahead.

b. Son of Jonah (Bar-Jonah)

What an odd little comment this is, tucked in here almost unnecessarily, almost as a throwaway comment. Except that it is the subtle balance to what Peter has just said: Jesus identifies Peter by reference to his father, just as Peter had done for him.

So it is perhaps too weak to use the word 'title' for *Son of God*, because that might imply it is not something that Jesus is, but merely a role or office he occupies. That crown had been waiting for the arrival of its wearer for many centuries, and Jesus did and does occupy the office of the Son of God, but that does not quite capture everything Matthew wants to say, which that little balanced echo here captures. Jesus is by nature God's Son, just as Peter is by nature Jonah's son. Notice how easily Jesus talked of what had been revealed *by my Father who is in heaven*, as if to say, 'Yes, Peter, I am the Son you have identified'. The passages from 11:27 and 28:18–19 suggest an intimacy between God the Father and the Son that seems to stretch back and forwards into eternity, and the phrase *Son of God* seems to be both a straight synonym for *Christ*, but also a reference to Jesus' eternal sonship of the *living God*. Throughout this section Peter seems constantly to confess more than he realizes.

[34] Wilkins, *Matthew*, p. 560.
[35] Matt. 10:2; 14:28–31; 15:15; 17:24–27; 18:21.
[36] Matt. 10:2–4; Mark 3:16–19; Luke 6:13–16; Acts 1:13.

Now, though, we move to what Jesus says of Peter's future, and as Davies and Allison warn, 'This verse is among the most controversial in all of scripture. The literature it has generated is immense, and not a little of it rather polemic.'[37]

c. You are Peter . . .

Peter is called 'Peter' on twenty-two other occasions in Matthew,[38] and since there is no obvious variation before or after this incident we should probably not see it as a significant renaming incident. Rather, Jesus has given him this name at some point, and now he explains its significance.[39] It certainly was not a nickname to describe his character, for Peter was anything but 'rock' like in his instability and unreliability. Indeed, the very next story has Jesus giving him another name: *Satan* (16:23).

d. Peter the rock

In Aramaic, Jesus would have called Simon 'Cephas', 'rock' and it became a name by which he was regularly identified.[40] The wordplay translates neatly into Greek: Peter/Petros. John recalled the actual naming moment itself, '"So you are Simon the son of John? You shall be called Cephas" (which means Peter)'.[41] Although here Jesus uses slightly different words for 'rock' (*petra*) and Peter (*petros*), there is no substantial difference between them, and attempts to find them are too subtle.[42] There are broadly five ways to understand what Jesus meant, and all five can claim support from both the Early Church and the present.

(i) Option 1: The rock is Peter himself as leader, and the church is the institution he founded

This is, of course, the classic position of the Roman Catholic

[37] W. D. Davies and D. C. Allison, *Matthew; vol. II, Commentary on Matthew VIII to XIII*, ICC (Edinburgh: T&T Clark, 1991), p. 623.
[38] Matt. 4:18; 10:2; 14:28–29; 15:15; 17:1, 4, 24–27; 18:21; 19:27; 26:33, 35, 37, 40, 58, 69, 73, 75.
[39] See Caragounis, *Peter*, pp. 17–25 for the evidence that 'Cephas' and 'Peter' were contemporary names.
[40] 1 Cor. 1:12; 3:22; 9:5; 15:5; Gal. 1:18; 2:9, 11, 14.
[41] John 1:42.
[42] 'The distinction is largely confined to poetry' (D. A. Carson, *Matthew*, in F. E. Gæbelein (ed.), EBC, vol. 8, *Matthew, Mark and Luke* [Grand Rapids: Zondervan, 1984], p. 368); and by 'Jesus' day the terms were usually interchangeable' (C. S. Keener, *A Commentary on the Gospel of Matthew* [Grand Rapids/Cambridge: Eerdmans, 1999], p. 426).

church.[43] Carved in stone around the massive marble dome of St Peter's in Rome is the Latin translation of Jesus' words: *Tu es Petrus, et super hanc petram aedificabo Ecclesiam meam*, and it is a significant claim that Peter, the first bishop of Rome, buried under that dome, initiated a church that still has his successor as its visible head, as Jesus intended. As the Second Vatican Council put it, Jesus intended that Peter would be 'a permanent and visible source and foundation of unity of faith and of fellowship ... The Roman Pontiff as the successor of Peter, is the perpetual and visible source and foundation of the unity of the bishops and of the multitude of the faithful'.[44]

There is a sequence of assumptions in this claim which call it into serious question, and in particular three: first, that Peter was the most senior of all the apostles, second that he was the first bishop of Rome and that Rome has a primacy over the other churches, and third that Jesus intended Peter to pass the role of bishop of Rome to his successors, and that he did so. It is quite plausible that Peter did die in Rome; his reference to 'Babylon' in 1 Peter 5:13 is normally taken to indicate that he wrote from there. But what he did, and whether he was the chief elder of the church there is unknown to us. Both the claim to Roman primacy and to Peter as the first bishop are third-century developments,[45] possibly natural in view of the political primacy of Rome, and the first pope to explicitly base his and his successor's authority on the verse seems to have been Leo the Great (440-461).[46] Luz claims it did not become a common piece of exegesis until the Counter Reformation.

In any case, Peter's primacy over the other apostles is far from clear in the New Testament. His serious mistakes in leading the Galatian church into error (Gal. 2:11-14) did not discount him from ministry, but even without that it is clear he saw himself as simply one of the apostles,[47] and accountable to the Jerusalem church.[48] There is nothing in Matthew 16 to indicate that Peter was supposed to pass on the 'rock' role to others, and the most natural reading is that Peter's role is unique and unrepeatable. So the idea that Peter himself is the 'rock' does not work with either what Jesus says, nor how the New Testament church treated him. In fact, as David Turner

[43] Upheld by Catholic commentators R. Brown, K. P. Donfried and J. Reumann (eds.), *Peter in the New Testament* (Augsburg: Paulist Press, 1973).

[44] *Dogmatic Constitution of the Church*, chs 18, 23. W. M. Abbott and J. Gallagher, *The Documents of Vatican II* (London/Dublin: Geoffrey Chapman, 1966), pp. 38, 44.

[45] See the thorough description in U. Luz, *Matthew 8-20*, Hermeneia (Augsburg: Fortress, 2001), pp. 369-377. On apostolic succession, see ch. 12.

[46] Sermon 3, NPNF 2, 12:117. See Luz, *Matthew*, p. 375.

[47] He and John are sent to Samaria by the others, Acts 8:14.

[48] Acts 11:1-18.

points out, 'In Peter's own words, Jesus himself is the chief shepherd, senior pastor or *pontifex maximus* of the church (1 Pet. 5:4)'.[49] Jesus is also, as we shall see in chapter 9, the only personal focus of our unity and as we saw in chapter 3, the permanently installed leader who needs no successor.

(ii) Option 2: The rock is Peter's confession

Chrys Caragounis has recently revived the view that *this rock* is the confession Peter makes about Jesus.[50] His argument is that Matthew (and Jesus) intend a distinction to be drawn between *Petros* and *this rock (petra)*, indicating that they point to different subjects. But Michael J. Wilkins has indicated such fundamental problems[51] that neither this, nor Luther's suggestion of 'Peter's faith'[52] really works here.

(iii) Option 3: The rock is Jesus' teaching

Robert Gundry argued that the *rock* in question is Jesus' teaching,[53] and he draws attention to what Jesus said in Matthew 7:24: 'Everyone then who hears these words of mine and does them will be like a wise man who built his house on the rock.' Although there are superficial similarities, the passage is a long way from Matthew 16, and makes a major assumption that the reader will pick up the cross-reference. David Turner is probably right that this suggestion is 'overly subtle'.[54]

(iv) Option 4: The rock is Jesus himself

Later in Matthew, Jesus uses similar language about himself:

Have you never read in the Scriptures:

'The stone that the builders rejected
has become the cornerstone;

---

[49] Turner, *Matthew*, p. 222. *Pontifex maximus*, Latin for 'High Priest', is usually translated by the title 'Supreme pontiff'. It was a title from ancient Rome, later used of the emperors. The first Pope to use it was Damasus 1 (366–383), and it is still in use today.

[50] Caragounis, *Peter*, pp. 88–119. See too J. Nolland, *The Gospel of Matthew: A Commentary on the Greek Text*, NIGTC (Grand Rapids: Eerdmans and Bletchley: Paternoster, 2005), p. 669.

[51] Jesus continues to address Peter as the subject; the connective *and* (*kai*) suggests identification rather than contrast between *Peter* and the *rock*; and *Peter* is the nearest antecedent for *this rock*. Wilkins, *Matthew*, pp. 563–564. Wilkins also suggests that the original Aramaic would argue against Caragounis' suggestion.

[52] Cullman, *Peter*, pp. 162–163.

[53] R. H. Gundry, *Matthew: A Commentary on his Handbook for a Mixed Church under Persecution* (Grand Rapids: Eerdmans, 1994), pp. 334–335.

[54] Turner, *Matthew*, p. 221.

> this was the Lord's doing,
> and it is marvellous in our eyes'? . . .

[T]he one who falls on this stone will be broken to pieces; and when it falls on anyone, it will crush him.[55]

This led many of the church Fathers to identify the rock in our passage as Jesus. They also claimed the support of Paul who, when explaining the exodus narrative said, 'they drank from the spiritual Rock that followed them, and the Rock was Christ',[56] and the numerous Old Testament passages where 'rock' is a title for God.[57]

This has failed to win widespread support today, largely because of the question, 'What did Jesus mean *here*?' Paul's interpretation is not relevant to that question, and the reference in chapter 21 is not only a long way from chapter 16, but uses a different Greek word, *lithos*, for *stone*. It is also a very odd way for Jesus to have said 'You are Peter, and on me as the rock . . . ' What would be the point of emphasizing the name, *Peter*?

(v) Option 5: The rock is Peter because he has just confessed Christ

The final option is the one that commands widest support, which is to identify the *rock* with Peter, because he has just confessed who Christ is.[58] It is the most natural sense, and as D. A. Carson observes, if 'it were not for Protestant reaction against extremes of Catholic interpretation, it is doubtful whether many would have taken "rock" to be anything or anyone other than Peter'.[59] The balance between Peter's identification of Jesus in 16:16 and Jesus' of Peter is too close to avoid here. Michael Wilkins helpfully comments that 'This was the interpretation of most of the early church fathers, although very early many fought against its use for establishing any kind of papacy (e.g., Ignatius, Justin, Origen, Tertullian, Cyprian, Firmilian)'.[60] What

---

[55] Matt. 21:42–44.

[56] 1 Cor. 10:4.

[57] See, for instance, Deut. 32: 4, 18, 30–31, 37; Pss 18:31; 28:1; Isa. 17:10; 26:4; 44:8; Hab. 1:12.

[58] Among Protestants see, for instance, C. L. Blomberg, *Matthew*, NAC (Nashville: Broadman, 1992); Carson, *Matthew*; France, *Matthew*; D. A. Hagner, *Matthew 14–28*, WBC 33B (Dallas: Word, 1995); Keener, *Matthew*; Nolland, *Matthew*; Turner, *Matthew*; Wilkins, *Matthew*. Exceptions include Caragounis, *Peter*; F. D. Bruner *The Churchbook: Matthew 13-28* (rev. and expanded ed., Grand Rapids: Eerdmans, 2004), p. 127; and Luz, *Matthew*.

[59] Carson, *Matthew*, p. 368. Similarly, France talks of a 'Protestant overreaction', France, *Matthew*, p. 254.

[60] Wilkins, *Matthew*, p. 563, fn. 27.

Peter's role would be as *rock* is explained in the rest of the verse, but he is clearly to have a foundational one.

e. I will build my church

The word *church* (Gk, *ekklēsia*) causes some controversy about whether this verse is authentically Jesus' words, and what he intended, but the basic biblical building blocks are clearly in place for this to be a major and necessary part of Jesus' thinking. We have seen it is the inevitable outworking of the titles *Christ*, *Son of Man* and *Son of God*. Even so, Jesus talks of 'my assembly', 'my meeting', *my church*, and this is a direct claim to divine status, and for his church to be as significant as Sinai.[61] The ease with which the New Testament writers talk of 'the churches of Christ' as much as 'the church of God'[62] should shock us at the extraordinarily high claim they are making.

Jesus would *build* this church on Peter. The precise idea of a *church* being something to *build* is only used on one other occasion in the New Testament, when Paul talks about someone who 'builds up the church',[63] but the idea of foundations and stones is used sufficiently frequently that it was obviously well understood. It stands at the meeting of two images, the church as an assembly which God calls, and the church as the temple building where God dwells. But how is this church built *on* Peter?

f. The gates of hell

The *gates of hell* (sometimes translated *Hades*)[64] is an Old Testament expression for the entrance to death,[65] but the stream of interpretations for this phrase[66] occurs because of a tension between the noun

---

[61] The useful preposition *epi* +dative is well known to mean 'positioned on'; Jesus intends to build 'on' the rock of Peter (see D. Wallace, *Greek Grammar beyond the Basics* [Grand Rapids: Zondervan, 1996], p. 376, who calls it one of the 'basic uses'). By contrast, the LXX of Deut. 4:10 uses *pros* + accusative to mean *before*, which would be needed to avoid identifying Peter as 'the Rock'.

[62] Churches of Christ: Rom. 16:16. See Gal. 1:22; Eph. 1:22–23; 5:23; 1 Thess. 1:1; 2:14. Church of God: 1 Cor. 1:2; 10:32; 11:22; 15:9; 2 Cor. 1:1.

[63] 1 Cor. 14:4; Eph. 4:12 uses it of a body being built, which seems a more obvious image.

[64] NIV.

[65] Job 17:16; 38:17; Pss 9:13; 107:18; Isa. 38:10. The NIV translates *Sheol* as *death*, but the word is a title for a place: e.g. Gen. 37:35; Num. 16:30; Deut. 32:22; 1 Sam. 2:6; 2 Sam. 22:6; 1 Kgs. 2:6, 9; Job 7:9; Ps. 6:5, etc.

[66] Davis and Allison list twelve (*Matthew*, pp. 630–632), and other commentators give additional options.

and the verb: how is that *gates* do not *prevail*? There are basically two options.

One is that the church is being assaulted by many enemies, including death, but that they will not win. The church cannot and will not die: her Lord, as the next verse says, died but was raised, so will individual Christians, so may the church in many lands, but overall the church will live because the gospel wins. That is the view which sees the church under pressure, and the *gates of hell* coming against her but never defeating her. This was the view taken by the Reformer Heinrich Bullinger, who said that this is 'a saying which is indeed a great comfort to the faithful in so many and so great persecutions intended to the utter destruction of the church'.[67] Martin Luther, in more flamboyant mood, said

if the church is to perish, the Christ, upon whom it is built upon a rock against the gates of hell . . . must perish first. If Christ is to perish, then God himself, who has established rock and foundations, must perish first. But who would have supposed these lords to have such great power that the church, together with Christ and God himself, should perish so easily before his threats . . . They must be far, far mightier than the gates of hell and all devils, against which the church has prevailed, and must prevail.[68]

The alternative sees the church here as much more on the offensive, taking the battle up to the enemy's *gates* and being unstoppable in her Christ-honouring rescue mission. In this case *prevail against* means something like 'will be unable to resist'. The Lord Jesus is risen, the gates of death have been rendered powerless, and the church's growth is unstoppable.

These are not necessarily alternative views, because the second necessarily encompasses the first. At the very least Jesus means that the church and its members will never die and the gospel will do its work, and to those churches under the hammer blows of persecution that is a necessary truth. Jesus ultimately wins. But the second view, in which the victory of the cross is shown in the rescue of men and women and their being added to the inevitably growing church, seems to be a fuller New Testament view. Take Peter's first Pentecost sermon:

'[Christ] was not abandoned to Hades, nor did his flesh see corruption. This Jesus God raised up, and of that we all are witnesses.

[67] Quoted in C. Brown, 'The Gates of Hell and the Church', in James E. Bradley and Richard R. Muller, *Church, Word and Spirit: Historical and Theological Essays in Honor of Geoffrey W. Bromiley* (Grand Rapids: Eerdmans, 1987), p. 15.

[68] Quoted in Brown, 'Gates', p. 16.

Being therefore exalted at the right hand of God, and having received from the Father the promise of the Holy Spirit, he has poured out this that you yourselves are seeing and hearing' . . . And with many other words he bore witness and continued to exhort them, saying, 'Save yourselves from this crooked generation.' So those who received his word were baptized, and there were added that day about three thousand souls.[69]

That is the first example of Peter's preaching: the risen Jesus calls men and women to be saved by him. It is Peter opening the door to the *kingdom of heaven*.[70]

g. The keys of the kingdom of heaven

And he opens that door by using *the keys* Jesus gave him. That is probably the cleanest way of understanding what Jesus meant by giving Peter *the keys of the kingdom of heaven*.[71] On the Day of Pentecost, then when the first Samaritans were converted, and finally when the first Gentiles were converted, Peter was critically involved.[72] Similarly when people were excluded, Peter was in charge.[73] And when the church faced decisions over who may or may not be included, or what behaviour was and was not acceptable, Peter was a central witness.[74]

Once those decisions had been taken, Peter fades from view in Acts. The keys which Jesus gave him have been used, and they do not need to be used again. Every door to the gospel has been flung open, and the keys disappear.[75]

h. Binding and loosing

That is probably the way in to the final knotty section of our section. D. A. Carson separates five questions which need to be un-tangled.[76] First, how should we translate and understand the verbs *will be bound* and *will be loosed*? Literally they should translated

---

[69] Acts 2:31–41. See ch. 4.

[70] From a heavenly perspective (see ch. 6) the *kingdom of heaven* is identical to the heavenly assembly which Jesus calls *my church*.

[71] Davis and Allison list thirteen options on this section (*Matthew*, pp. 636–639).

[72] Acts 2:14–41; 8:14–25; 10:1–48.

[73] Acts 5:1–10; 8:18–24.

[74] Acts 11:1–18.

[75] It lies quite outside the context to see the keys in the Roman Catholic sense of the sacraments, penance or absolution; the issue of forgives arises in the context of Matt. 18.

[76] Carson, *Matthew*, pp. 370–374.

'shall-have-been-bound/loosed',[77] and the question is, does Peter ratify a decision previously made in heaven, or does heaven ratify a decision (possibly on the Day of Judgment) previously made by Peter? Second, does *whatever* refer to some 'things' (which is what the neuter would suggest), or to some 'people' (which is what the similar phrase in 18:18 means)? Third, what do 'binding' and 'loosing' mean? Is it to do with forbidding and permitting behaviour,[78] or including and excluding people?[79] Fourth, is this responsibility given uniquely to Peter, to all the apostles, or as Matthew 18:19 seems to imply, to the church as a whole? Indeed, how are the two passages related? Finally, how should we connect *heaven* and *earth*? Is the connection spatial, so that what happens in the one simultaneously happens in the other, or is it temporal, so that what happens on the one subsequently happens in the other?

The answers to those questions must be determined by the context, with Peter himself as the *rock* in possession of the *keys of the kingdom*. Foreseeing both the inclusion of the Gentiles in the church and the lifestyle debates which would follow, Jesus confirmed to Peter that both have been foreseen and planned in heaven. That is, in the future Peter will make decisions about evangelism which he will at that point discover have already been made in heaven. Those decisions will be uniquely his. Since Peter's teaching on the inclusion of the Gentiles and the place of circumcision and food laws are so intimately connected, it would seem unnecessary to say that Jesus means one or the other, but there is an obvious contrast with the teaching of the Pharisees who in Matthew 23:13, 'shut the kingdom of heaven in people's faces. For you neither enter yourselves nor allow those who would enter to go in'. Peter's unique role is echoed in the decisions Christians have constantly had to make about belief and behaviour. That is the issue in Matthew 18:15–20, and the setting for Jesus' other use of the word *church*.[80]

5. A church built on Peter

What will it mean for a church to be built on this *rock*, of the Peter who confesses Christ? There is no need to hunt for a mythical historical connection to him, because that is not what Jesus intended. This *rock* would be the authentic foundation even of a church which was made up of people who were so isolated that had never met any other Christians, and became believers by reading a New Testament

[77] They are future perfect passive periphrastic.
[78] Luke 11:52.
[79] Acts 4:11–12.
[80] See ch. 15.

that washed up on the shore of a desert island. They would share the same three characteristics Peter displays.

a. It will be a Christ-centred church

We have seen that the context of Peter's confession is absolutely central to understanding our passage, and nothing can claim to be a church which does not share Peter's moment of revelation, that Jesus is not even the greatest of the great prophets, but God's anointed King and Son.

b. It will be a cross-centred church

The context, pointing forwards, also shows that to understand this Christ correctly we have to understand 'that he must go to Jerusalem and suffer many things from the elders and chief priests and scribes, and be killed, and on the third day be raised'. Our response to that must not be the immediately triumphalistic one of Peter, 'This shall never happen to you!'[81] but the mature one of his later years, 'And after you have suffered a little while, the God of all grace, who has called you to his eternal glory in Christ, will himself restore, confirm, strengthen, and establish you'.[82]

c. It will be an evangelistically-centred church

Thirdly, a church built on Peter will see how he flung open the gates, and have a passion for the lost that subsumes and drives everything else they do. Nothing will divert it from its desire to be that kind of church, one which resists all the onslaughts of Hades, and continues, unshakable, for ever.

[81] Matt. 16:21–22.
[82] 1 Pet. 5:10.

Acts 2:41–47
6. The church's life

I stood at the back of a vast building, one of the first constructed by William the Conqueror in England after 1066, and in continuous use by Christians ever since. The minister showed me a small table on which hymnbooks had been stacked. He asked me how old I thought it was. I said I had no idea, and he said it went back to the English Reformation; it was a cheap Tudor table, brought in to use for the Lord's Supper as a simple and flexible alternative to the stone medieval altar.

Those Reformers knew then what many churches continue to find today. Layers of centuries can get in the way of a direct experience of being Christ's people, and regularly we need to cut back to the original.

But it is too easy to romanticize the earliest churches, imagining their lives as simpler than ours. Far from it. Acts records how they oscillated between persecution and complex internal issues, and how even as they grew, they split. We might envy them the problems that come from life, but threats, internal and external, are their constant background. The first few decades of the church were turbulent and hazardous.

Nevertheless, our instinct to travel back is right. There is an appealing clarity to life in the early weeks of the church in Jerusalem, after Pentecost.[1]

1. The church's commitments

a. The believers devoted themselves . . . (42)

To be *devoted* indicates a serious commitment. Luke used it for the apostles '*devoting* themselves to prayer' after Jesus' ascension,[2] and

---

[1] See ch. 16.
[2] Acts 1:14.

later for their decision that 'we will *devote* ourselves to prayer and the ministry of the word'.[3] These are settled spiritual priorities.

It also indicates how Luke thought other churches should spend their time too. Within this section of Acts (2:1 – 6:7), which focuses exclusively on the Jerusalem church, he presents a series of summary passages, of which this is the first.[4] The intense spotlight on the Jerusalem church, and the way the summaries are often expanded in the surrounding narratives show that Luke intends this church to be seen as an ideal church: not idealized, because like any church it had weak as well as strong disciples (5:11), internal divisions and pressures (6:1), and external persecutions (5:17–18) as well as unity, courage and growth (5:41–42); but ideal in that its good decisions are commendable and normative.[5] Here is how the Jerusalem church kept to its decisions about four central priorities.

Some things we shall discover about the church from the Bible are invisible, or promises about the future, but these four are observable, objective, plannable, activities, to which we should be *devoted*. Each was so obvious that someone could say to members of the Jerusalem church, 'Where and when do I have to turn up to take part in this? It's obviously central' – and they could give the time, date, street and house. That means we should be able to respond in the same way when anyone asks the same question about our church. Perhaps our difficulty in doing so would not be that we do not practice these four, but that we do so many other things as well that they do not stand out. In the midst of music rehearsals, finance committees, policy planning and building projects, what do our diaries reveal about these activities to which we should be *devoted*?

b. The believers devoted themselves to the apostles' teaching (42)

The first commitment was to being taught by the apostles.[6] In addition to their three years with Jesus, the apostles had been given forty days of instruction after his resurrection (Acts 1:3); so now, as his Spirit-filled delegates, they spoke of him with authority. The first example

[3] *Proskarterein*, Acts 6:4.

[4] See too 4:32–35 and 5:12–16. 9:31 and 12:24 are possibly summaries too. B. Witherington, *The Acts of the Apostles* (Grand Rapids: Eerdmans and Carlisle: Paternoster, 1998), p. 159f.

[5] On the structure of Acts, see C. Green, *The Word of His Grace* (Leicester: IVP, 2005).

[6] 'The Greek indicates that they gave the apostolic teaching their constant attention'. D. J. Williams, *Acts*, NIBC (Peabody: Hendrickson and Carlisle: Paternoster, 1985/1990), p. 59. For OT background for apostles, see e.g. Isa. 61:1; Jer. 1:7; Ezek. 2:1–4; Dan. 10:11.

of their evangelistic teaching in Acts 2 summarized the life, teaching, death, resurrection, ascension, reign and return of Jesus, with a call to repent and believe in him. The pattern was informed by seeing Jesus as the centre and climax of the Old Testament, and his resurrection and the gift of the Spirit as the key to the present and the future. Luke's Gospel shows how Jesus taught those things, and Acts shows how the apostles taught them too. This opening section repeatedly stresses the teaching work of the apostles (2:42; 4:2, 18; 5:21, 25, 28, 42), and so this crowd of believers only exists because they had *accepted [Peter's] message* (2:41, NIV).

The first challenge for our churches then, is whether we share that devotion *to the apostles' teaching*. For us, their teaching was expanded and collected as the New Testament, containing within it the keys to the Old, but the challenge is still that every aspect of our church life should be marked by this same attentiveness to the whole of what they taught. When the preacher wants to talk about something more interesting than the apostles' teaching, or we want to do something other than listen, or understand, or remember, or the musicians want us to sing a song with powerful music but questionable lyrics, or the children's leaders want them to play and explore, or the small groups want to centre on personal experiences, who has the quiet voice which says, 'But we must *devote [ourselves] to the apostles' teaching*'?[7]

c. The believers devoted themselves to the fellowship (42)

The second commitment was to spend their time in *fellowship*. It is a word which we tend to use rather loosely, to include chatting after the service, or just being in each others' company. Although Luke only uses the Greek word (*koinōnia*) on this one occasion, he uses a related word[8] in 2:44, where the Christians had possessions *in common*, and in 4:32 where 'they had everything in common'.[9]

The word had two circles of meaning. Broadly, it meant being in a deep connection with someone: so John says we have '*fellowship* . . . with the Father and with his Son', and Paul says we have '*fellowship* with the Spirit'. Both underline that which links us with other believers. John wrote 'that which we have seen and heard we proclaim also to you, so that you too may have *fellowship* with us; and indeed our *fellowship* is with the Father and with his Son Jesus Christ',[10] and Paul wrote that

[7] On the place of teaching in the church see chs. 6, 9, 10 and 11.

[8] *Koinos* The related word *koinōnikos* means 'generous'.

[9] ESV, translated 'they shared everything they had' by the NIV.

[10] 1 John 1:3.

If there is any encouragement in Christ, if any consolation of love, if any *fellowship* with the Spirit, if any affection and mercy, fulfil my joy by thinking the same way, having the same love, sharing the same feelings, focusing on one goal. Do nothing out of rivalry or conceit, but in humility consider others as more important yourselves. Everyone should look out not only for his own interests, but also for the interests of others.[11]

So fellowship with God causes us to come into fellowship with other believers, giving each other 'the right hand of *fellowship*'[12] as we work together in the *'fellowship* in the gospel'.[13] So close is our relationship with Christ, we even have 'the *fellowship* of sharing in his sufferings, becoming like him in his death'.[14] But Paul warns that there is a stark choice for Christians: 'Do not be unequally yoked with unbelievers. For what partnership has righteousness with lawlessness? Or what *fellowship* has light with darkness? What accord has Christ with Belial? Or what portion does a believer share with an unbeliever?'[15] Fellowship with Christ and his people is the consequence of the gospel, and its opposite is fellowship with Satan and his world. So these 3,000 believers made a serious commitment to each other.

But there is a narrower meaning. Paul used it three times for the money he collected for the famine-stricken Palestinian Christians,[16] and he tells Timothy to tell the rich members of his church 'to do good, to be rich in good works, to be generous and ready to share *(koinōnikous)*'.[17] The author of Hebrews reminds us 'not to neglect to do good and to share *(koinōnias)* what you have, for such sacrifices are pleasing to God'.[18] The word has an inescapable financial meaning – rich Christians are supposed to share their money with poor Christians. That this is Luke's meaning is clear from the context in this section: *And all who believed were together and had all things in common. And they were selling their possessions and belongings and distributing the proceeds to all, as any had need* (44–45); and 'no one said that any of the things that belonged to him was his own, but they had everything in common'.[19] It is seen in the example of

[11] Phil. 2:1–4, HCSB.
[12] Gal. 2:9.
[13] Phil. 1:5, NKJV.
[14] Phil. 3:10, 1984 NIV.
[15] 2 Cor. 6:14–15.
[16] Rom. 15:26 (often translated *contribution*); 2 Cor. 8:4; 9:13 (NIV: *sharing*).
[17] 1 Tim. 6:18.
[18] Heb. 13:16.
[19] Acts 4:32.

Barnabas[20] that introduces the story of Ananias and Sapphira who die horribly because they lie to God about their supposed generosity (5:1–11).

Although superficially this might seem like early communism, with no private property and a common purse, that is not quite what is going on. That is clear even from Acts 2, where although verse 45 records their commitment to *selling their possessions and belongings*, verse 46 records that they broke bread *in their homes*. Clearly they did not sell everything and give it away. So here, the field belonged to Ananias (5:4), and Peter does not say either that he was wrong to have owned it, or that he would have been wrong to have kept some of the money for himself. His lie was presenting part of the money as if it were the whole, and he were as generous as Barnabas. This church valued generosity, and Ananias and Sapphira coveted that reputation.

Wealthy Christians like such subtle nuances, and we hide behind them. But the physical poverty of many of our brothers and sisters is a question mark against our affluence, and we are wise to squirm uncomfortably before a commitment such as this. I remember being driven round Hyderabad in India by a Christian man whose daily wage was less than I would spend on a coffee. Yet from that wage he was giving, because his family were the only Christians in the village, and he wanted to employ an evangelist to live there and reach his neighbours. That shocked me. Luke does not mean fellowship is only expressed financially, of course, and that aspect is not mentioned until verse 44. But it is still mentioned so often that unless it includes help to those who are poor, it is probably not true *fellowship* as Luke understands it.

The writer Tertullian, described part of a church meeting in his day, about 100 years later:

There is no buying and selling of any sort in the things of God. Though we have our treasure-chest, it is not made up of purchase-money, as of a religion that has its price. On the monthly day, if he likes, each puts in a small donation; but only if it be his pleasure, and only if he be able: for there is no compulsion; all is voluntary. These gifts are, as it were, piety's deposit fund. For they are not taken thence and spent on feasts, and drinking-bouts, and eating-houses, but to support and bury poor people, to supply the wants of boys and girls destitute of means and parents, and of old persons confined now to the house; such, too, as have suffered shipwreck; and if there happen to be any in the mines, or banished to the islands, or shut up in the prisons, for nothing but their fidelity to

[20] Acts 4:36–37.

the cause of God's Church, they become the nurslings of their confession. But it is mainly the deeds of a love so noble that lead many to put a brand upon us. *See, they say, how they love one another.*[21]

Would they say that of us, in our church?[22]

d. The believers devoted themselves to the breaking of bread (42)

The third commitment was eating together, which is a surprise compared to the other commitments in the list, which are more obviously 'spiritual'.

We might expect Luke to mean what we call 'the Lord's Supper', or 'Holy Communion', or whichever name we give to our formalized pattern of eating bread and drinking wine to remember Jesus' death.[23] But that is not quite what he does.

'Breaking of bread' is another phrase with two, concentric meanings. At its broadest it is the everyday phrase for having a meal together, as in Acts 20:11 and 27:35. It would be hard to read anything formal or liturgical into those events. They were meals eaten because people were hungry.

But, more narrowly, at the Last Supper, Jesus took bread, and when he had given thanks, he broke it and gave it to them, saying, 'This is my body, which is given for you. Do this in remembrance of me'.[24] Jesus wrapped the Passover, charged with meaning, around his own imminent death. He would be the Passover lamb, and his would be the spilt blood. From that moment on, it would become almost impossible to have the most ordinary meal without remembering Jesus' death, because every time the wine was opened or the bread was brought out, they automatically trigger the recollection that Jesus has died, was raised and will come again.[25]

So were the Jerusalem Christians meeting for the Lord's Supper? If we mean, were they holding a 'service' to receive a sip of wine or grape juice and a small piece of bread, as a token of a real meal, of course not. They were meeting for real meals. *They broke bread in their homes and ate together with glad and sincere hearts* (46, NIV), which 'implies a substantial meal'.[26] But every meal where bread is torn and wine poured now has an edge.

---

[21] Tertullian, *Apology* XXXIX.
[22] See ch. 7.
[23] 1 Cor. 11:26.
[24] Luke 22:19.
[25] Luke 24:30, 35.
[26] R. Longenecker, *The Acts of the Apostles*, EBC vol. 9: *John, Acts* (Grand Rapids: Zondervan, 1981), p. 291.

Perhaps we need to question how we celebrate the Lord's Supper. In many traditions its link with a real meal is slender, and we may need to remember that the Passover meal, for all that it had strongly liturgical elements to it, was a family occasion like Christmas or Thanksgiving. Such parties often have *glad hearts* (ESV) at them, but the solemnity of remembering Jesus' death as the basis for who we are together means that alongside that happiness goes being *sincere* (46). This is no paper hats and party poppers occasion, but an enjoyment of being in each other's company because we are in the Lord's – of *fellowship* in the broad sense.[27]

e. The believers devoted themselves to prayer (42)

The fourth commitment was to spend their time praying, and again Luke repeats this. They met 'constantly' (1:14),[28] but also when a special need arose (1:24–25). They took part in the temple prayers (3:1),[29] but also informally at home (4:24–31). They prayed spontaneously (3:1), but also define it as one of the two principal responsibilities of the apostles (6:4–6).

The rest of Acts fills out this pattern, and shows how inescapable prayer was in the early church. They prayed in prison (16:25), and for those in prison (12:5, 12). They prayed on their own (11:5) and together (12:5). They prayed indoors (12:12), outdoors (10:9), at midday (10:9) and midnight (16:25), in the Jerusalem temple (22:17) and in a Roman palace (26:29), at sea (27:29) and on a beach (20:36). They prayed for non-Christians to be converted (26:29), and confused Christians to be filled with the Spirit (8:15). They prayed when they ate (2:46–47) and when they fasted (14:23). They prayed for the sick to be healed (28:8) and the dead to be raised (9:40). They prayed when their leaders were initially commissioned (14:23) and when they were given final responsibility (20:36). They prayed when they had just become Christians (9:11) and when they were seconds from death (7:60). The early church *devoted themselves to prayer.*

The relevance for us is almost too obvious to be made, but we must face it. It is not just the range of things prayed for which is striking, but the frequency of their praying. They planned for it in their meetings *every day* (47), and they were disciplined about it, so when Peter is on his own, away from Jerusalem, he still prays (10:9).

More than that, they expected God to answer their prayers: 'And now, Lord, look upon their threats and grant to your servants to continue to speak your word with all boldness, while you stretch

[27] On the Lord's Supper see ch. 8.
[28] NIV.
[29] See too 22:17.

out your hand to heal, and signs and wonders are performed through the name of your holy servant Jesus.' And so he did: 'And when they had prayed, the place in which they were gathered together was shaken, and they were all filled with the Holy Spirit and continued to speak the word of God with boldness.'[30]

They would not be naïve of course. When James the brother of John was arrested no doubt they prayed for him, but Herod had him executed 'and when he saw that it pleased the Jews, he proceeded to arrest Peter also . . . intending after the Passover to bring him out to the people'.[31] But their bitter experience did not defeat the Christians' faith, because 'Peter was kept in prison but earnest prayer for him was made to God by the church'.[32] And the Lord brought him out of the prison (12:17).

Perhaps that is the main lesson to learn. Although the book is frequently called 'The Acts of the Apostles', it really is 'The Acts of God', and although he is sovereign and generates his own acts, he responds to the prayers of his people, and his people know that.

f. Meeting in the temple courts and homes (46)

Those were the four commitments of the Jerusalem church to which they were *devoted*. But none of them could have happened without the underlying commitment that *day by day* they would *meet together*, a phrase which John P. Wilson helpfully calls Luke's 'signature phrase for the gathered church'.[33] The Christians put an extraordinarily high value on their time together.

They met *in the temple courts*,[34] a thirty-five acre space which held 75,000 people at festival time.[35] Presumably a number of the initial converts at Pentecost were festival visitors who had subsequently returned to their homes, but Luke's comments on the continual growth of the church necessitated this larger meeting space.

Although Luke tells us that Peter and John joined in the temple prayers (3:1), there is no indication that they joined in the sacrifices.

---

[30] Acts 4:29–31.

[31] Acts 12:3–4.

[32] 12:5.

[33] J. Wilson, 'From House Church to Home Groups', *RTR* 63:1 (April 2004), pp. 1–15; p. 1. He notes that *Epi to auto* occurs in Acts 1:15; 2:1; 1 Cor. 11:20 and 14:23.

[34] NIV. ESV's *attending the temple* implies more than Luke says.

[35] See Schnabel for the dimensions, including huge water cisterns which could be used for mass baptisms: E. Schnabel, *Early Christian Mission, vol. 1: Jesus and the Twelve* (Leicester: Apollos and Downers Grove: IVP, 2004), p. 419. The Greek phrase translated 'temple courts' is singular, and does not prove that the early church held 'multi-site worship'.

Rather, it was simply a place where they could meet, as well as where they could meet a crowd of non-Christians. As the angel told the apostles: '"Go, stand in the temple courts," he said, "and tell the people the full message of this new life." At daybreak they entered the temple courts, as they had been told, and began to teach the people.'[36] Calvin is right to underline this evangelistic purpose: '[T]here was there a great concourse of godly men who laid aside their private cares, which might have distracted them more fully anywhere else, and sought the Lord. [The Christians] were continually in the temple that they might win such men for Christ.'[37]

Their second venue was *in their homes*, not meaning that each family went back to their own homes, but that they met 'from house to house'.[38] That habit stayed with them for many years, so when Paul, before his conversion, was seeking to strike at the heart of the Christian movement, he attacked these venues. 'Saul was ravaging the church, and entering house after house, he dragged off men and women and committed them to prison.'[39]

Presumably there they followed the same four commitments, but they would have discovered that each feels different when there are only a dozen people rather than many hundreds. Only in this home context was it possible that 'everyone could know everybody. Only here everybody could have contact with everyone. Only here . . . could they take care of each other's material needs'.[40] As thousands of churches have discovered when they run small groups alongside their large meetings, small groups give a sense of belonging, and of mutual care. John Stott says they are 'indispensable for our growth into spiritual maturity'.[41] Small groups make a big church small.[42]

Getting the relationship right between these two is critical. Had they overemphasized the small groups they could not have *devoted themselves to the apostles' teaching*, because there were a restricted number of apostles. The same danger applies today when overbalancing on the 'cell' level of meeting means an absence of authoritative teaching. Had they overemphasized the temple courts

---

[36] 5:20–21, NIV.

[37] John Calvin, *The Acts of the Apostles, 1–13*, transl. John W. Fraser and W. J. G. McDonald, CNTC (Grand Rapids: Eerdmans, 1996 [1552]), p. 88.

[38] Williams, *Acts*, p. 61.

[39] 8:3. Architecture suggests rooms which could accommodate about forty people; E. Schnabel, *Early Christian Mission, vol. 2: Paul and the Early Church* (Leicester: Apollos and Downers Grove: IVP, 2004), pp. 1305–1306.

[40] Werner Vogler, quoted by Schnabel, *Jesus*, p. 414.

[41] J. R. W. Stott, *The Living Church* (Nottingham: IVP, 2007), p. 93.

[42] R. Warren, *The Purpose Driven Church* (Grand Rapids: Zondervan, 1995), p. 325f.

then they would not have been able to eat in each other's homes, and the full range of *fellowship* would have been missing. Again, the danger applies to any church which treats its members as so many bodies on a Sunday, but does not expect, or plan for, its members to know people beyond their immediate circle. Just as the four commitments were deliberate decisions, so was the expectation that the Christians would meet frequently, and in this two-venue pattern.

2. God's actions

There is a beautiful balance in Luke's arrangement. Having reported what the disciples did *day by day* (46), he now reports what God was doing on a *day by day* basis (47).

a. Signs and wonders

God responded to their prayers with miracles of a wonderful range and number. It is what every church today longs for when the congregation prays for its sick members, its unconverted friends, its imprisoned brothers and sisters worldwide. Rightly so – God is a sovereign God who answers prayers.[43]

But we need to be careful, because Luke does not quite say that here. He draws our attention to the twelve: *And awe came upon every soul, and many wonders and signs were being done through the apostles* (43); 'Now many signs and wonders were regularly done among the people by the hands of the *apostles*'.[44] That is not to say that only the twelve perform miracles in Acts, because Luke draws our attention to Stephen (6:8), Philip (8:6) and Barnabas (15:12). But *wonders and signs* is a phrase associated overwhelmingly[45] with the signs which accompanied the exodus from Egypt.[46] A *sign and wonder* is not just an ordinary miracle, but one that points to an event in world history as significant as the Exodus. Moses led the Israelites 'performing wonders and signs in Egypt and at the Red Sea and in the wilderness for forty years'.[47]

Two events have added to that information. First, as Peter said at Pentecost, 'Jesus of Nazareth, a man attested to you by God with mighty works and wonders and signs that God did through him in

---

[43] See 1 Cor. 12:28; Jas. 5:14; and ch. 11.

[44] 5:12.

[45] For exceptions, e.g. Isa. 8:18 or Dan. 4:2–3.

[46] Exod. 7:3, etc.; Deut. 4:34, etc. For later reflection, see Neh. 9:10; Ps. 78:43, etc.; Jer. 32:20–21.

[47] Acts 7:36.

your midst'.[48] To underline the point, Peter is not just saying that Jesus was 'attested by God with mighty works', which would have been wonderful enough, but that there were *wonders and signs*, which means that Jesus is extraordinarily important, and God is drawing our attention to him.

Secondly, there were Old Testament promises that God would do more wonders and signs, and Peter claims that Jesus has fulfilled them in forming the church:

But this is what was uttered through the prophet Joel:

> 'And in the last days it shall be, God declares,
>   that I will pour out my Spirit on all flesh,
>   and your sons and your daughters shall prophesy,
> and your young men shall see visions,
>   and your old men shall dream dreams;
> even on my male servants and female servants
>   in those days I will pour out my Spirit,
>   and they shall prophesy.
> And I will show wonders in the heavens above
>   and signs on the earth below . . . '[49]

God promised the wonders (2:19), Jesus did wonders (2:22), and now the apostles do them too (43).

The early church had a wider category for 'miracles',[50] but it used the term 'wonders and signs' with care. Paul talks of his authority, that 'the signs of a true apostle were performed among you with utmost patience, with signs and wonders and mighty works',[51] and that Satan's work is marked by 'false signs and wonders'.[52] The writer to the Hebrews seems to think of the apostles in particular when he recalls that the gospel 'was declared at first by the Lord, and it was attested to us by those who heard, while God also bore witness by signs and wonders and various miracles and by gifts of the Holy Spirit distributed according to his will'.[53] No wonder the visitors were filled with *awe* (43).

Perhaps that care would be wise for us too. Every Christian who prays is asking for God to intervene, and that means asking for a miracle of some kind, even if it is through the agency of another

[48] 2:22.
[49] Acts 2:16–19.
[50] 5:16; 8:7; 9:34; 14:9; 28:8.
[51] 2 Cor. 12:12.
[52] 2 Thess. 2:9.
[53] Heb. 2:3–4.

person. Some answers to prayer are stunningly visible, and we rightly use the term 'miracle' for such kindness. They seem to accompany the growth of the church here in Acts. But just as we echo their enthusiasm and confidence, we should echo their care, and reserve 'signs and wonders' for those remarkable events by which God marked the start of the church age.

b. Growth

Numerical growth is another of the continual markers in Acts. It is not only the church which grows: 'The word of God continued to increase', 'increased and multiplied', and 'continued to increase and prevail mightily'.[54] Nor are conversions the only growth: 'miraculously unclean spirits came out of *many* who were possessed, crying with a loud voice, and *many* who were paralyzed or lame were healed'; strategically, they reached 'many' Samaritan villages; evangelistically, Jews visited Paul 'in greater numbers'.[55] But for all that we might say there are other ways to grow than by numbers, the careful monitoring of the numerical growth is one of Acts' key elements.

Luke holds together the eternal, invisible element of salvation with the temporal, visible element of church membership, which again can only be God's work: *the Lord added to their number day by day those who were being saved* (47). This is a feature of these chapters, because Luke gives a sequence of such numerical markers. In addition to that verse and the 3,000 of verse 41 (to which the daily converts would have been added, once the festival visitors had returned home), 'many of those who heard the word believed, and the number of the men came to about five thousand',[56] then 'more than ever believers were added to the Lord, multitudes of both men and women',[57] until finally Luke concludes: 'the word of God continued to increase, and the number of the disciples multiplied greatly in Jerusalem, and a great many of the priests became obedient to the faith'.[58]

The striking nature of this theme becomes apparent if the relevant verses[59] in the whole of Acts which have some kind of numerical marker are laid out in sequence.

[54] Acts 6:7; 12:24; 19:20.
[55] Acts 8:7, 25; 28:23.
[56] Acts 4:4.
[57] Acts 5:14.
[58] Acts 6:7. See too the introduction to the final story in the section, 'In those days when the disciples were increasing in number . . . ' (6:1).
[59] This is not a complete list (1:15 is the first numbering), and one might draw implications from, say, the cost of the scrolls burned in Ephesus (19:19) or the fact that Luke counts only the men in some of the verses.

Acts 2:41   So those who received his word were baptized, and there were added that day about *three thousand souls.*

Acts 2:47   And the Lord *added to their number* day by day those who were being saved.

Acts 4:4   But many of those who had heard the word believed, and the number of the men came to about *five thousand.*

Acts 5:14   And *more than ever* believers were *added* to the Lord, *multitudes* of both men and women.

Acts 6:1   Now in these days when the disciples were *increasing in number . . .*

Acts 6:7   The *number* of the disciples *multiplied greatly* in Jerusalem, and *a great many* of the priests became obedient to the faith.

Acts 9:31   So the church throughout all Judea and Galilee and Samaria had peace and was being built up. And walking in the fear of the Lord and in the comfort of the Holy Spirit, it *multiplied.*

Acts 9:42   And it became known throughout all Joppa, and *many* believed in the Lord.

Acts 11:21 And the hand of the Lord was with them, and *a great number* who believed turned to the Lord.

Acts 11:24 [Barnabas] was a good man, full of the Holy Spirit and of faith. And *a great many people* were added to the Lord.

Acts 11:26 For a whole year [Barnabas and Saul] met with the church and taught a *great many* people.

Acts 12:12 *. . . many* were gathered together and were praying.

Acts 13:43 *Many* Jews and devout converts to Judaism followed Paul and Barnabas.

Acts 13:45 But when the Jews saw the *crowds,* they were filled with jealousy . . .

Acts 14:1   [Paul and Barnabas] spoke in such a way that *a great number* of both Jews and Greeks believed.

Acts 14:21   When they had preached the gospel to that city and *had made many disciples*, they returned to Lystra and to Iconium and to Antioch.

Acts 16:5   So the churches were strengthened in the faith, and *they increased in numbers daily.*

Acts 17:4   And *some* of them were persuaded and joined Paul and Silas, as did *a great many* of the devout Greeks and not a few of the leading women.

Acts 17:12   *Many of them* therefore believed, with *not a few* Greek women of high standing as well as men.

Acts 18:8   Crispus, the ruler of the synagogue, believed in the Lord, together with his entire household. And *many* of the Corinthians hearing Paul believed and were baptized.

Acts 18:10   The Lord said . . . 'I am with you, and no one will attack you to harm you, for I have *many* in this city who are my people.'

Acts 21:20   [James and the elders said to Paul]: 'You see, brother, how many *thousands* [lit., *tens of thousands* – see below] there are among the Jews of those who have believed.'

Doubtless there are good reasons why churches do not grow, and Luke has emphasized that it is *the Lord*'s sovereign work anyway, so the responsibility is all his. Nevertheless, especially for those of us who live in the self-styled 'post-Christian' West, it is really important to grasp that God's plan is that churches should grow numerically.

That might be by individual congregations getting larger, as Luke shows in his careful charting of the growth of the Jerusalem church: a crowd of 'a hundred and twenty', then *three thousand*, then 'five thousand' and finally 'tens of thousands'.[60] That Greek word is *myriades*, from which the word 'myriad' comes, and one of its two meanings is 'numberless, countless, infinite'.[61] But the other meaning is quite precise: it meant, ten thousand, and was a number used in counting military units. Assuming that he was not saying that the Jerusalem church contained an infinite number, Luke is

---

[60] Acts 1:15; 2:41; 4:4; 21:20.
[61] LS 1154. Acts 21:20, NKJV: 'how many myriads of Jews there are who believed'.

unmistakeably saying that there were not just 'thousands', but *tens of thousands* – that is, at least twenty thousand.

The other kind of numerical growth is in the number of congregations being planted. David Pao tracks the phrase *the word of God* through Jerusalem, Judea and Samaria, Caesarea, Phoenicia, Cyprus, Syrian Antioch, Cyprus, Galatia, Pisidian Antioch, Lystra, Perga, Macedonia, Achaia, Philippi, Berea, Corinth, Ephesus and Miletus. Luke's final verse describes Paul 'proclaiming the kingdom of God and teaching about the Lord Jesus Christ with all boldness and without hindrance' to crowds in the great world capital, Rome.[62]

Have we started to believe the lie that this is a 'post-Christian' society, in which churches are doomed to dwindle, apart from a few that sell out to entertainment or a cheap gospel? Do we expect our churches to grow numerically, and are we aware of what we do which inhibits that growth? I put it that way, because if growth is natural, we do not ourselves produce it, but our spiritual inattention and love of congregational habits can cause it to be stifled. Do we expect our churches to plant, and are we taking the trouble to plan for, and provide for, that process?[63]

3. The 'church'

There is one striking omission: so far we have not met the word 'church'. There has been a range of terms, like *all who believed* (44), 'their friends', and 'your [God's] servants',[64] but 'church' has been missing.

There is a reason. Luke allows key ideas to be introduced slowly, and only when they are in place does he unveil them. He describes Christians constantly, but it is only at Antioch that people first used the title (11:26). A murderous persecutor is introduced under the name Saul – only later revealed as the well-known Paul (13:9). He likes describing something and then revealing its name.

This opening section has seen those four basic commitments worked out wonderfully, but also shockingly, and it has shown an outworking of the first summary: the *glad and generous hearts* of the disciples (46) as they were *praising God* (47) have been matched by the *awe* and *favour* of the watchers (43, 46). The counterpart of the wonderful generosity of the whole body of believers, and exemplified in Barnabas, is Ananias and Sapphira. And it is here that

[62] Acts 28:31. D. W. Pao, *Acts and the Isaianic New Exodus* (Grand Rapids: Baker, 2000), pp. 150–156.
[63] See ch. 16.
[64] 4:23, 29.

Luke reveals his hand. What is this group of believers, where there is such sharing, truth, love and fellowship, and where God is present in such awesome power that even its members are in awe? 'And great fear came upon *the whole church* and upon all who heard of these things.'[65] This is what church is like.

[65] Acts 6:11.

2 Corinthians 8 – 9
7. The church's compassion

Churches feel uncomfortable around money. Because of the temptation of manipulating vulnerable people, many preachers simply avoid the issue until there is a cash crisis. But we must look at it, because Paul insists that coordinating our giving is characteristic of being a church.

The reign of the Emperor Claudius (AD 41–54) saw frequent famine, and in 45–47 it devastated Judea. The Christians in Jerusalem were badly affected, enhanced by their economic isolation in a hostile city, and although many churches provided emergency relief,[1] a more structured response was needed. So around AD 55, Paul was tasked with organizing a collection to support 'the poor among the saints at Jerusalem',[2] recorded in Romans 15:25–32, 1 Corinthians 16:1–4, and here.[3] Gentile Christians from four Roman provinces[4] supported Jewish Christians, demonstrating Paul's desire for love between equal churches across a racial divide. It was time for the Gentiles to recognize their sisters and brothers in need.

Then the plan unravelled. The Corinthians, initially so keen that they had been a stimulus to other churches, and especially to the Macedonians from Philippi, Thessalonica and Berea who had suffered so greatly (9:1–5), did not deliver on their promises, and Paul wrote this section of 2 Corinthians as a tactful reminder to complete their gift. It was extraordinarily delicate, because Paul not only had to write as carefully as any fundraiser, he was himself

---

[1] Acts 11:27–30.

[2] Rom. 15:26; Gal. 2:10.

[3] For the chronology, see P. Barnett, *The Second Epistle to the Corinthians*, NICNT (Grand Rapids/Cambridge: Eerdmans, 1997), pp. 387–450 and S. McKnight, 'Collection for the Saints', *DPL*, pp. 143–147.

[4] Macedonia and Achaia (Rom. 15:26, etc.); Galatia (1 Cor. 16:1); Asia (Acts 20:4).

being portrayed as a financial charlatan by his opponents. The Corinthian church was closing its heart to him, and to any other congregation.

Paul highlights the role of churches. He contrasts the Corinthians to *the churches of Macedonia* (8:1),[5] and reports that one person responsible for the collection was *famous among all the churches* and *appointed by the churches* (8:18, 19). Money was handled by *messengers of the churches* (8:23) *to give proof before the churches* (8:24). Churches are not so spiritual that they should avoid thinking about cash, nor transparency.

Yet Paul writes without mentioning money itself. Instead, it is *grace* with which he opens (*we want you to know, brothers, about the grace of God that has been given among the churches of Macedonia,* 8:1) and closes (*the surpassing grace God upon you,* 9:14). But that is only the start. The word *charis* occurs ten times with perhaps six meanings: *grace,* meaning God's kindness (8:1, 9; 9:8, 14); *act of grace,* meaning the collection (8:6); *grace of giving,*[6] meaning the willingness to give (8:7); *the offering,* meaning the combined gift from all churches (8:19);[7] *favour* (8:4); and *thanks* (8:16; 9:15). Grace encapsulates God's initiative (*the grace of God*), their attitude (*grace of giving*), the action (*the offering*) and the response (*thanks be to God*). Grace was to flood their generosity.

1. Where do we give?

a. The poor

Although financial terms hardly figure here, the rich language of the gospel and its implications run throughout.

Love describes Paul's relationship with the Corinthians (8:7–8, 24). Verse 7 might mean the Corinthians' love for Paul, or his love for the Corinthians,[8] but verse 8 is clear that the Corinthians, who *excel in everything* which seems to build their own congregation, must demonstrate that their *love also is genuine,* by excelling in generosity to others. *Love* is affection made visible. The collection is the *proof . . . of your love* (8:24), meaning the *proof* of their love for the Jerusalem Christians. *Genuine* and *proof* are words expecting the Corinthians to act.

---

[5] 9:2, 3.
[6] NIV.
[7] NIV.
[8] *Our love for you* is the harder reading, but the next verse mentions their love for Paul, giving plausibility to that meaning.

Paul had written before about the *collection (logeia).*[9] Here he wants it to be a *willing gift (eu-logeia,* 9:5), a *blessing* coming in genuine love, and with concern and prayer.

Summarizing his appeal, Paul twice calls the collection a *service* (9:12, 13), which raises the theological stakes. Literally, the collection is 'a ministry of priestly service', using the word *leitourgein,* from which we derive the English word 'liturgy'. He means that giving money to the poor Christians in Jerusalem is an act of worship, and essential to their Christian walk.[10]

Paul admires the Macedonian churches for *begging us earnestly for the favour of taking part in the relief of the saints* (8:4), and he anticipates that people *will glorify God because of . . . the generosity of your contribution for them and for all others* (9:13). Behind *contribution* lies *koinōnia,* a word often translated *fellowship,*[11] but here with a new and inescapably financial flavour.[12] From this point on, it will be impossible to think properly about the idea of *fellowship* or *sharing* without considering that finances will be involved.

Two conclusions follow. Fellowship is shrivelled when we define it as something over coffee after church, or at our Bible study, or a great conference. We need to broaden our thinking to a more biblical span: unless our regular giving includes a conscious element, then our understanding of *love, fellowship* and *blessing* are defective. We should work at *generosity in sharing* (9:13).[13] And secondly, Paul deliberately uses 'worship' language in this context, so we need to stretch our language to match. Worship here is expressed with our cheque books.

For a rounded picture of giving, there are two other groups needing support.

b. The pioneers

In 2 Corinthians 11:1–12 (especially vv. 7–9) Paul describes his financial situation. He is in an embarrassing position, answering two simultaneous accusations. Some think he 'robbed other churches' (11:8), so he needs to be financially scrupulous and transparent. But others are fans of teachers who charge extravagant fees, with the clear

---

[9] 1 Cor. 16:1–2.
[10] See Phil. 4:18; Rom. 15:27.
[11] Good (2 Cor. 13:14) or bad (2 Cor. 6:14).
[12] 'Paul creates a new meaning for the word . . . This is the first use of the word for monetary collections'; D. Garland, *2 Corinthians,* NAC (Nashville: Broadman & Holman 1999), p. 369.
[13] NIV.

implication that Paul's gospel cannot be worth much if he offers it 'free of charge' (11:7).

Paul's fundamental principle is to avoid being 'a burden' to non-Christians (11:7–9). The Corinthians saw how he worked as a 'tentmaker',[14] until 'Silas and Timothy came from Macedonia', and then he 'devoted himself exclusively to preaching'.[15] He explained in this letter, 'I did not burden anyone, for the brothers who came from Macedonia supplied my need'.[16] In other words, the generous Macedonian support meant that he need not earn his living. The Macedonians had seen the same pattern: 'For you remember, brothers, our labour and toil: we worked night and day, that we might not be a burden to any of you, while we proclaimed to you the gospel of God.'[17] Paul expected his converts to support him and his team when he moved to the next unreached place.[18] Evangelists and planters should expect similar support from us.

c. The pastors

Thirdly, Paul expects churches to pay their own pastors, where they can. He said this came from Jesus himself, 'in the same way, the Lord commanded that those who proclaim the gospel should get their living by the gospel'.[19] Leaving aside those circumstances where this might not be possible, it is a good and responsible duty to pay our pastors decent wages.

These groups, the poor, the pioneers and the pastors, help to answer the question: how do churches relate to Christian organizations which work alongside them? From the Greek for 'alongside' (*para*) we sometimes call them 'parachurch' organizations.

Keeping a worker housed and fed overseas, and ensuring they have adequate health cover requires expensive administrative support. So does monitoring money, food and personnel. Writing, publishing and distributing the books for a pastor's shelves, producing effective training courses, or running a discipleship programme for students, are all tasks for which Christians rightly have a concern. But, as with Paul's collection, it would complicate life if every church took on the full individual responsibility for them. So sharing the task, and centralizing the administrative burden, seems wise.

Parachurch organizations now often dwarf the churches, so there

---

[14] Acts 18:3; 1 Cor. 4:12.
[15] Acts 18:5, NIV.
[16] 2 Cor. 11:9.
[17] 1 Thess. 2:9. See too 2 Thess. 3:8.
[18] Phil. 4:10–19.
[19] 1 Cor. 9:14; Matt. 10:10; Luke 10:7. See ch. 12, and below on tithing (p. 126).

are occasional tensions between the two.[20] But parachurch organizations exist to support, simplify and serve the local church, and their attention should ultimately be the same as the centre of God's attention: the community of Christians gathered around him. To achieve that ultimate goal, they focus on tasks that are too difficult, expensive or distracting for a local church. Ralph D. Winter distinguishes a 'sodality' (a recognizable team, like Paul's, which exists to serve a task) from a 'modality' (a network of relationships which exists in its own right, like the local church).[21] A parachurch organization (the 'sodality'), perhaps Bible translators, or denominational officials, exists because it is beyond the resources of any church (the 'modality') to gather the specialist staff, and it would take them away from their biblical focus to do so. It would be foolish to argue that because it cannot be done by a local church then it should not be done. Conversely, it would be wrong for those organizations to think they were the centre of God's plan. They exist to serve the churches, including those yet to be planted. God can, has done, and will again achieve his saving purposes without publishers, conference centres and seminaries, but he has promised he will never do it without a church.[22]

So the poor, the pastors and the pioneers summarize those to whom churches should give. Paul focuses on the first, but much of what he teaches applies to all three.

2. Why do we give? (8:1–15)

To motivate the Corinthians to complete their giving, Paul gives two counter-examples, the Macedonian churches and the Lord Jesus, and then corrects two misunderstandings.

a. The Macedonians model grace leading to generosity (8:1–5)

Giving begins with God, in this instance giving these most unlikely Christians a desire to give; and they were unlikely because they faced *a severe test of affliction* and *extreme poverty* (2).[23] *Yet because of*

---

[20] See *Cooperating in World Evangelization: A Handbook on Church/Para-Church Relationships*, Lausanne Occasional Paper 24, http://www.lausanne.org/en/documents/lops/67-lop-24.html.

[21] R. D. Winter, 'The Two Structures of God's Redemptive Mission', reprinted in R. D. Winter and S. C. Hawthorne (eds.), *Perspectives on the World Christian Movement* (3rd ed., Pasadena: William Carey Library and Carlisle: Paternoster, 1999), pp. 221–230.

[22] See also ch. 9; as well as 'para-church', some are 'intra-church' ministries, facilitating relationships.

[23] Phil. 1:27–30; 1 Thess. 1:6; 2:14; 3:3–4, 7; 2 Thess. 1:4–10.

God's grace they did not despair but produced abundance of joy, and instead of self-centeredness they produced *a wealth of generosity* (2). Paul has experienced God's grace too ('In all our affliction, I am overflowing with joy')[24] and it is what he longs for the Corinthians.

We can see three aspects to the Macedonians' giving. First, they *gave according to their means*, and even *beyond their means* (3), neither of which would be true of the Corinthians. They were open hearted. Second, they saw it as *a favour* (*charis*, again) *of taking part* (*koinōnia*, again) *in the relief* (*diakonia*, service) (4). They were not even asked to contribute, because *of their own free will* they asked if they could give (3). The givers, not the fundraiser, did the asking! Third, they saw that they had to give themselves, and not just their money. Paul reminds the Corinthians, who did not take him with proper seriousness, that the Macedonians *gave themselves first to the Lord and then by the will of God to us* (5). They are models not only in their openheartedness towards *the saints* (4) but towards Paul as well.

b. The Corinthians should copy the Macedonian example (8:6–8)

Paul switches from *they/their* (2–5) to *you/your* (6–8ff.) as he contrasts the two churches. The Macedonians have experienced God's *grace* (1), and Paul wants the Corinthians to complete their *act of grace* (6) and *excel in this act of grace* (7). Overseeing it was delegated to Titus, recently returned from a warm visit to Corinth (7:13b, 15). Excelling is something the Corinthians were famously good at, or at least so they thought,[25] so Paul catches them on it. Since they excel in *faith*, *speech* and *knowledge*, and have a new 'earnestness' for Paul[26] he challenges them to excel in the area of giving too. He even uses the same word to say, just as the Macedonians experience of grace *overflowed* in being generous, now let the same experience of grace *excel* in you.[27]

One suffering church had experienced God's kindness, and another which claims to excel in experiencing him has become cold. Paul challenges the Corinthians to *prove* by comparison (8), see how far the Macedonians' experience of grace outstrips theirs, and live up to their own claims to knowing God. That comparison was to stimulate them, because Paul uses a blacksmith's word for proving and improving, testing for success.[28] And the proof lies with

[24] 2 Cor. 7:4.
[25] 1 Cor. 1:5, 7; 12:8.
[26] 2 Cor. 7:12.
[27] *Perisseuein.*
[28] *Dokimazōn.*

them, because Paul did not *command* (8), but left it to their own voluntary action.

c. The Lord Jesus models grace leading to generosity (8:9)

Having told the Corinthians he wanted them *to know . . . about the grace of God that has been given among the churches of Macedonia* (8:1), Paul now adds that they *know the grace of our Lord Jesus Christ.* Here is his second, contrasting model of *grace*, meaning the self-sacrifice which led the Lord Jesus to serve us. Here is the gospel laid out, showing how we benefit. The central idea is clear: *he became poor . . . so that you . . . might become rich*, but the financial language is startling. How were the Corinthians enriched by Christ's death for them? The explanation comes in two steps.

First, Jesus moved from being *rich* to being *poor*, meaning that he was 'in the form of God',[29] but stripped himself of all power and dignity, and died in poverty. For us. At his death our sinful condition was transferred to him: 'For our sake [God] made him to be sin who knew no sin.' But simultaneously, his righteous status was transferred to us: 'For our sake he made him to be sin who knew no sin, *so that* in him we might become the righteousness of God.'[30] That is the second step here, that *for your sake he became poor, so that you by his poverty might become rich.* By *riches*, Paul means the blessings that all Christians share, for 'the same Lord is Lord of all, bestowing his riches on all who call on him'.[31] His ministry therefore copies Jesus' pattern, 'poor, yet making many rich'.[32]

d. The Corinthians should copy the Lord Jesus' example (8:10–12)

Here is the sting in the tail. Paul's logic of double imputation (our sin laid on Christ, his righteousness laid on us) has been repeated, this time using financial language. Since the Corinthians have been enriched by Jesus' generosity, can they now find the same will to finish their promise to enrich others? Last year they were the first in the queue, and the first to indicate that if there were a queue they would be in it (*you, who a year ago started not only to do this work but also to desire to do it*). That *desire* is what Paul wants to re-activate,[33] so he is much more concerned about their hearts than the donation, *For if the readiness is* there, it (the gift) *is acceptable*

[29] Phil. 2:6.
[30] 2 Cor. 5:21.
[31] Rom. 10:12; 11:12.
[32] 2 Cor. 6:10.
[33] 8:11, 12, 19; 9:2.

(to the needy Christians in Jerusalem, presumably) *according to what a person has, not according to what he does not have.*

e. Equality (8:13–15)

The exchange of riches and poverty between Jesus and Christians is the model for their gift to Jerusalem. So should the Corinthians transfer all their money to Jerusalem, impoverishing themselves in the process? Paul anticipates some stingy members could exaggerate what he was saying. 'How absurd to impoverish ourselves by our generosity, so we have to ask for our own money back! It is obviously quite illogical to give in the way Paul suggests. Much better simply to pray for them.' Others might have taken a more fearful route to the same conclusion. 'It's all very well asking us to give, but God might have given us the money because he knows we will need it. Our rainy day might come too.' Paul addresses both misunderstandings.

His goal is not absurd, but an interrelationship, so that *your abundance at the present time should supply their need*, and in the future, *so that their abundance may supply your need* (14). At the least that implies partnership between the two churches, but quite possibly economic aid flowing back at some point. Paul's word for this interconnectedness is *equality*[34] or *fairness* (13, 14), which remains a sharp rebuke to many wealthy congregations. The *wealth of generosity* flowing out of the *extreme poverty* of the Macedonians as they *were begging* to take part in the *favour* of the collection contrasts with the lack of *readiness* trickling out of the Corinthians' *abundance*. Today, the disparity between rich and poor churches is even greater, yet the task of collecting and sending money is much simpler. And anyone who has travelled in poorer places has discovered Macedonian levels of generosity which shame those of us elsewhere. Most of us need to hear this rebuke.

But hear what Paul says about *equality* or *fairness* carefully. Every church has financial inequality within it, as the clothes we wear, the cars we drive and even the Bibles we carry testify. Does Paul intend to flatten out all differences of income? That would be demanding within one congregation, let alone between a church in the West and one in sub-Saharan Africa. We need to tread carefully here, but I think Paul means something other than financial equality. Verse 13 reads not *that there might be equality*,[35] but that their generosity flows 'out of equality' (*ex isotētos*). The equality is already there, as something that Paul can appeal to, despite the disparity of wealth

---

[34] NIV.
[35] NIV.

and a halted collection. Perhaps it is equal status. The Jerusalem church has no primacy over Corinth or Macedonia, nor have those congregations floated into independency. A mature interdependence between equals is the basis for giving; when that happens, *there will be equality*.[36] So without muting Paul's radical appeal for generosity, there is a new relationship between those who give and those who receive. The recipients have equal status with the donors, one of dignity and Christian love.

The story of Israel collecting manna in Exodus 16 seems rather odd here, because it has nothing to do with money, or sharing, or generosity, or willingness, or any of the obvious themes – except one. Moses said,

'This is what the LORD has commanded: "Everyone is to gather as much as they need. Take an omer for each person you have in your tent."' The Israelites did as they were told; some gathered much, some little. And when they measured it by the omer, the one who gathered much did not have too much, and the one who gathered little did not have too little. Everyone had gathered just as much as they needed.[37]

The point is trust. The Israelites learned that God would provide for what they *need*, and hoarding manna in case God did not, produced maggots, a stink and Moses' anger.[38] So too, in Corinth, a lack of trust in God must not kill generosity.

3. How do we give? (8:16–24)

Money and churches have a bad track record. Jesus warned that 'no-one can serve two masters. *Either* you will hate the one and love the other, *or* you will be devoted to the one and despise the other. You cannot serve *both* God *and* Money'.[39] He is quite clear: we think we can manage a *both/and* approach; he makes it an *either/or* choice. Not taking this warning seriously, many churches run into danger, because they do not see that money, especially the amount in a collection like the one Paul is organizing, is a serious temptation, even for Christians. Paul needs to ensure that everyone concerned with this large sum is seen to act appropriately. *We take this course so that no one should blame us about this generous gift that is being administered by us, for we aim at what is honourable not only in the*

[36] NIV.
[37] Exod. 16:16–18, NIV
[38] Exod. 16:20.
[39] Matt. 6:24, NIV.

Lord's sight but also in the sight of man (20–21). He is avoiding *blame
. . . in the sight of man*, an aspect of the Corinthian church with which
he was uncomfortably familiar.[40] As Calvin wrote, 'There is nothing
which is more apt to lay one open to sinister imputations than the
handling of public money.'[41] Three men have been chosen to
accompany the collection: *Titus* (16–17), and two unnamed Christian
brothers (18–19, 22).

a. Choose Christians

Titus was one known Christian leader, but the Corinthians also knew
of another *who is famous among all the churches for his preaching
of the gospel* (18) and that both were *the glory of Christ* (23). Choosing
Christians is not the end, but it is the right start.

b. Choose several of them

These people travel together. We must not be gullible, so making
sure the collection is always counted by two people, and that cheques
are counter-signed, are good practices. To the person who says
'Don't you trust me?' the answer is, 'No, and please don't trust a
sinner like me, either.'

c. Ensure the choice is public and accountable.

Titus was known to be trustworthy, and the first brother from Macedonia passes similar tests. He was *famous among the churches* (18),
so they knew him, and he was *appointed by the churches* (19), which
possibly indicates a show of hands.[42] Both are *messengers of the
churches* (23),[43] so if anything goes wrong, the Macedonians are
responsible.

d. Choose people who are competent with money

The specific reason for choosing the first brother (*he was chosen by
the churches to accompany us as we carry the offering*, 19)[44] may
imply he had financial abilities to keep track of the cash.

---

[40] 2:17; 4:2; 7:2–4; 11:7–12; 12:14–18.
[41] Quoted by Philip Hughes, *Second Epistle to the Corinthians*, NICNT (Grand
Rapids: Eerdmans, 1962), p. 317.
[42] *Cheirotonētheis.*
[43] *Apostoloi*; 'apostle' means a delegate, appointed by the church, not directly by
Jesus.
[44] NIV.

e. Make sure they share the vision

Titus's qualifications are transparent. *God* had given him *the same earnest care* as Paul's to rectify the Corinthians' sluggishness, so he not only *accepted* Paul's *appeal* but offered to travel *of his own accord.* Similarly, one of the others is commended for being *earnest* in his work with Paul, and having *great confidence* in the Corinthians (22).

All three have authorization from Paul (16, 18, 19, 22, 23), the churches (16, 18, 19, 23) and indirectly from the Lord Jesus himself (19, 23). Again, the relationships have transparency, accountability and authority: *As for Titus, he is my partner and fellow worker for your benefit. And as for our brothers, they are messengers of the churches, the glory of Christ. So give proof before the churches of your love and of our boasting about you to these men* (23–24). The Corinthians can be confident that *the offering, the generous gift* will be handled honestly. Paul is taking great care to do what is right.

4. When do we give? (9:1–5)

Therefore they must plan their giving. Whatever their past *readiness* (8:12; 9:2), if they delay now it will look like they are contributing grudgingly. So, Paul stresses they must *be ready* (3, 5) rather than *not ready* (4); the three men will *go on* ahead of Paul, and *arrange in advance* for the gift. And to force it home, in verse 5 Paul uses three words with begin with *pro-*, meaning 'forwards': *proelthōsin* (to arrive in advance); *prokatartisōsin* (to organize in advance); and *proepēngelmenēn* (to promise in advance). Even a *willing gift* can be planned.[45]

5. How much do we give? (9:6–11)

Paul's next concern is how God relates to generous and to mean churches: *Whoever sows sparingly will also reap sparingly, and whoever sows generously will also reap generously.*[46] Paul tailors this biblical idea to his argument:[47] *sparingly*, is unique in the New Testament, but, *generously* came twice in the preceding verse: *the generous gift . . . a generous gift.* A rhythm breaks out, as Paul alternates between sowing generously (7a, 8b, 11b) and reaping generously (7b–8a and 9–11a).

[45] 1 Cor. 16:1–3.
[46] NIV.
[47] Prov. 11:24–25; Gal. 6:7–9.

a. Sowing generously – how much do we give? (7a)

Paul never mentions a specific amount.[48] Giving is connected to payday ('on the first day of every week') and salary ('as he may prosper'),[49] but that is as far as Paul is willing to be prescriptive. Family circumstances, age or personal liabilities make any rule harsh, so Paul is resolute in allowing freedom of choice: *each one must give as he has made up his mind.*[50]

b. Reaping generously – what do we get? (7b–8a)

The first response from God is his love, *for God loves a cheerful giver*. It summarizes the biblical thought, 'You shall give to [a needy person] freely, and your heart shall not be grudging when you give to him, because for this the LORD your God will bless you in all your work and in all that you undertake'.[51] God observes our attitudes, and loves us when we reflect him. Being a *cheerful* giver is the same as giving *generously*, or any of the other terms Paul has used.[52] The Macedonians, were *begging us earnestly* to be involved (8:3–4), and Titus was acting *of his own accord* (8:17), so Paul expects the Corinthians to be pleased to echo God's generosity. God *loves* that.

Then God will shower his *grace* on them, the same *grace* that he had *given among the churches of Macedonia* (8:1). God's generosity is described in a series of all-encompassing phrases: *all grace*, having *all contentment*, in *all things*, *at all times*. However generous Christians are, we cannot be more generous than God. Is that a promise that the Corinthians' bank-balance will swell? No, because the Macedonians' experience of *grace* had been that it made them generous despite their *extreme poverty* (8:2). This is no blank cheque from God, then, that all you have to do to become financially rich is to give money away, but a promise that someone who seeks honestly to be generous to a generous God will find that God loves that trust.

c. Sowing generously – what do we give? (8b)

However, there is one specific way in which we grow rich. The final action God's grace unlocks is that we *may abound in every good*

---

[48] Rom. 15:25–32; 1 Cor. 16:1–4.

[49] 1 Cor. 16:2. The singular ('each one of you') suggests this was payday; a plural ('all of you') might suggest it was the day of a church collection.

[50] The absence of tithing, and the mention of choice, suggests no amount was prescribed. See Additional note: Tithing, p. 126.

[51] Deut. 15:10.

[52] *Hilaron* gives us the more intense 'exhilaration'.

work. The sequence is emphatic: *all (pasan) grace, in all things (panti), at all times (pantote), all (pasan) contentment, abound in [all] (pan) good work*. By *good work*, Paul presumably has the collection in mind, first – he has already appealed to them to *finish the work* (8:11).[53] So in wonder at God's generosity, we receive the gift of being generous, and we ourselves give back. We *abound*, we overflow in good work.

d. Reaping generously – what do we get? (9–11a)

What do they get, those who are generous to God? Paul quotes three Old Testament texts describing Israel as land, producing crops for God's obedient people.

As it is written:

> '*He has distributed freely; he has given to the poor;*
> *his righteousness endures forever;*' [Ps. 112:9]

Now '*he who supplies seed to the sower and bread for food*' [Isa. 55:10] *will supply and multiply your seed for sowing and will increase* '*the harvest of your righteousness*' [Hos. 10:12].

In Paul's context, *sowing* and *seed* means money for the collection, and in line with those other promises to generous people, Paul says God *will supply and multiply your seed for sowing* – that is, God will reward you by making you even more generous. That store of seed is not there for a rainy day, for a Corinthian second home or comfortable retirement. Those who are generous find that God gives them ways of being even more generous. That is the reassurance to the cautious Corinthians.

But to those who complain that all God promises to generous people is that they will be more generous, Paul twice says that they will indeed receive a harvest, for themselves, that they will not have to give away. In the psalm, God has *given . . . righteousness*, and in Hosea, he *will increase the harvest of your righteousness*. They receive *righteousness*, God's own character. As the great exchange verse earlier in 2 Corinthians puts it, 'For our sake he made him to be sin who knew no sin, so that in him we might become the righteousness of God'.[54] Once again there is no backing for a crude model in which we give money away so that God gives us more. No, God gives us much, much more than mere money.

[53] NIV.
[54] 5:21.

e. Sowing generously – when do we give? (11b)

So the sequence ends. *You will be enriched in every way for all your generosity, which through us will produce thanksgiving to God.* The 'all' words continue: *in every way (panti), all your generosity (pasan),* but what is the *every way* kind of wealth Paul promises? The easy suggestion is it is the same grace God lavishes on us that we want to be radically generous, but there is an obvious but tough question we have been avoiding. Does Paul in any way at all mean that if we are generous financially, God will be financially generous to us? I think we have to say that he does, but we must be very careful in understanding him.

Given that the context of sowing here is the collection, the promise that God will *increase your store of seed* (9:10, NIV) must be a financial one. So too, God *will supply and multiply your seed for sowing* does not mean 'in every way except financial'. Both these promises necessarily mean that those who are financially generous will find, amidst all the other blessings God showers on them, financial blessing.

But, why does God *supply and multiply your seed? For sowing.* Why will the Corinthians *be enriched in every way? For all your generosity.* This is not a 'prosperity gospel'. It is a 'generosity gospel'. This is a particular pastoral argument to get a reluctant church to move out of meanness into generosity. It would twist Paul's words to promise that if the Corinthians unlock their wallets and purses they will find them increasingly full. That was certainly not the experience of either the Jerusalem or the Macedonian churches. They were destitute. Nor was it the experience of Paul, who repeatedly has emphasized in 2 Corinthians just how dire his own circumstances were.[55] No decent hotels and expense accounts for him. Like his Master, Paul wore chains, not a Rolex (11:23). He even promises that the Corinthians might find themselves needing Jerusalem's generosity if they fall on hard times *and their abundance may supply your need* (8:14). No, this is no crude promise of prosperity. It is hard for wealthy churches to give away what they think they rely on and actually to trust God the generous giver. But says Paul, trust him – and you will find he will supply what you need. What, then, do we say to the church that has not experienced this generosity from God? I suspect that for many of us, we need to say something like this: 'Sisters and brothers, our plenty has been given to supply your need. We are sorry that our lack of generosity has stopped you from receiving God's generosity. The seed has been sitting idle in the store house. The gift to you came from God, but we held it up on the way.'

---

[55] 1:5–6; 2:14; 4:8–10, 17–18; 6:10; 8:9, 14.

6. Giving to God (9:11b–15)

When we are given a generous or thoughtful gift, we write a note. Perhaps the Corinthians were already planning what they could do with the letter of thanks from Peter, James and the Jerusalem Christians. Frame it, perhaps, and hang it on the wall? Make sure the ten largest donors had copies? Perhaps they were wondering if it would be better than the Macedonians'. Paul is sure that there will be thanks because of their actions, but of another kind: *You will be enriched in every way for all your generosity, which through us will produce thanksgiving to God* (11). The final resting point in the sequence is that God is honoured. There will be multiple *thanksgivings to God* (12), and people *will glorify God* – not people. Paul even begins to anticipate the Corinthians' generosity and the resulting praise as he concludes this section: *thanks be to God for his inexpressible gift!* He again describes the collection as worship, as he calls it, twice: *service* (12, 13) – ministry.

Three other observations conclude his teaching on generous churches. First, generosity is part of what it means to be a church. Paul has used major themes to support this simple idea of collecting money, and now adds that people *will glorify God because of your submission flowing from your confession of the gospel of Christ.* Their contribution is not even an inevitable outworking of their corporate Christian confession, but an act of *submission*. Not to give would be an act of disobedience. So the Corinthians are to *prove* that their love is *genuine* (8:8).

Second, they can be generous because God has made them like the Macedonian churches, giving them his grace.[56] Paul began by reminding them of *the grace God has given the churches of Macedonia* (8:2) and he ends with *the surpassing grace of God upon you* (plural). These arguments, to produce Christ-likeness among the Corinthians, remain true, so we need never descend into manipulation or deceit. Such means, superficially effective in the short-term, produce neither Christ-likeness, nor praise to God.

Third, there is one tangible benefit for the Corinthians, which is that in Jerusalem, *they long for you and pray for you* (9:14). They will be prayed for, with affection. It is often noticed that it is those with least material resources who display most spiritual strength, and those which are the wealthiest who are the weakest. Here is the clear benefit for the Corinthians, one they sorely needed.

So Paul concludes his appeal as he began in 8:1, with God's generosity in Christ and all that he has won and done. Paul runs out of

[56] 8:4, 6, 7, 9, 16, 19; 9:8.

125

words to describe Christ, because the word translated *inexpressible* (*anekdiēgētos*) is one which had never appeared before he wrote this sentence. Maybe he coined it especially for this moment, to join the everyday subject of money with the Christ who is beyond words. Our only proper response is to give God *thanks* (*charis*, *grace*).

Additional note: tithing

These chapters have put tithing into the spotlight. Paul has not mentioned it, but many Christians assume it, and more broadly it shows different understandings of the Old Testament's guidance about 'church', which we began to see with baptism. There are three different approaches, all of which we need.[57]

a. Three approaches

(i) Completion
The differences between an Old Testament believer and a Christian have Jesus' death at their centre. The Old Testament contains practices that have no place in a Christian church, like one meeting place for a whole nation, the priesthood, and sacrifices. Jesus' death means some biblically sanctioned practices have ceased to be binding, and explains why.

(ii) Continuity
Other practices are common for believers across the Scriptures, so prayer, preaching and praise are Old Testament elements still found in all churches. 'Continuity' helps us appropriate the Old Testament, while 'completion' ensures we do not become legalists.

(iii) Change
Yet other practices have been changed, but still exist in some way for the church, and this approach gives us our undergirding theology of a God who encourages us to disobey Old Testament laws without fear, but puts them in fresh ways which require new obedience.

(iv) The parting of the ways?
Jesus taught all three approaches,[58] but Christians differ over which is right on some issues, and tithing is a clear example. As a Christian leader who needs to raise funds, I would really like it to be the way of continuity, but how would I know? Are all Old Testament

---

[57] These three ways are a simplification, so see Sidney Greidanus, *Preaching Christ from the Old Testament* (Grand Rapids: Eerdmans, 1999), pp. 227–277.
[58] Mark 7:1–23 contains all three.

practices binding unless the New Testament explicitly lifts them, or automatically lifted unless the New Testament imposes them? These questions still split churches.[59]

b. The temple and tithing

The house for God's glory began with his plans for the tabernacle,[60] and then David's designs for the Jerusalem temple, built by Solomon.[61] God dwelt there[62] but subsequently abandoned it,[63] and although it was rebuilt and continually enhanced, most spectacularly under Herod in Jesus' day, God did not arrive.

Instead, Jesus was the true place where God's glory came to earth again. John says, 'the Word became flesh and dwelt [tabernacled] among us, and we have seen his glory'.[64] *He was the true temple who, like the prototype, would be destroyed and rebuilt:* '"Destroy this temple, and in three days I will raise it up." The Jews then said, "It has taken forty six years to build this temple, and will you raise it up in three days?" But he was speaking about the temple of his body.'[65]

There is now a physical place where we encounter God's glory today, but it is not a building. 'Do you not know that you are God's temple, and that God's Spirit dwells in you? If anyone destroys God's temple, God will destroy him. For God's temple is holy, and you are that temple.'[66] Both those words translated 'you' are plural, because God's dwelling is now church-based: we are his temple.[67]

Because the temple has been replaced, we must query the practices which were designed to support it, like the tithes and offerings, or which flow directly from it, like the festivals and fasts, or even the

[59] The Regulative Principle asserts that the Bible contains all, and only, what we may do as church. Its most frequents adherents are Presbyterian, with tension between those who find freedom for contemporary songs, announcements or even dance (J. Frame, *Worship in Spirit and Truth* [Phillipsburg: Presbyterian and Reformed, 1996]) and those who deny that (R. Reymond, *A New Systematic Theology of the Christian Faith* [Nashville: Thomas Nelson, 1998] pp. 869–877). The alternative, the Normative Principle, identifies both required and forbidden practices, but argues for freedom between them. It is the position I argue from here.

[60] Exod. 25:1 – 31:11.

[61] 1 Chr. 28.

[62] 2 Chr. 7:1–3.

[63] Ezek. 10.

[64] John 1:14.

[65] John 2:18–21.

[66] 1 Cor. 3:16.

[67] Later in 1 Corinthians, the individual Christian is also God's temple, which is a reason for personal holiness (1 Cor. 6:19).

attitudes to our buildings. Before we consider what changes, however, we need to consider what continues. The most obvious point of continuity between the Old Testament giving and ours is, as we have seen, God's generosity to us, and our echoing generosity to others.

c. The way of change: the tithe

So we come at last to the question of tithing, which is a topic on which there are a variety of Christian views, from scrupulous observation as a matter of covenantal duty, through to complete Christian freedom.[68]

Precision is difficult, but it seems there were two or three tithes (payments of ten per cent of a particular sum) that were expected in Israel. One was paid from the harvest, annually, to support the Levites, who themselves tithed to support the priests.[69] Neither priests nor Levites were given land as their inheritance, but the land was fruitful enough to support them. A second tithe was paid to provide for the yearly festivals.[70] A third, paid every three years, provided food for the Levites, the poor and the foreigners, probably for them to enjoy the festivals rather than as food aid.[71] With some overlap between these tithes,[72] there was probably an annual average of over twenty per cent being expected.

When Christians today discuss tithing, and whether it is gross or net, they are usually describing something quite different. No Israelite would have given a flat ten per cent of income, before or after tax. The level of tithing was much higher. But who paid it? What was the expectation of, say, a fisherman, cobbler, carpenter or builder? Was the produce of the land an example to a fisherman, to give one-tenth of his catch? Or was it only the agricultural blessing of the farms which was tithed?

Secondly, we must consider how the cross fits into the discussion. Remember that all those tithes were part of the sacrificial system that is no longer needed because of the cross. It would not do to say that their priests and/or buildings were supported by tithing, and so must ours be. The local church is a temple and a priesthood; but unlike the Jerusalem temple, our buildings are merely functional, and any staff are no more priests than any other Christian.

---

[68] D. A. Crouteau, *Perspectives on Tithing: 4 Views* (Nashville: B&H Publishing Group, 2011). There are two references to tithing before the Law, but their rationale is not explained: Gen. 14:18–20 (cf. Heb. 7:1–10) and 28:18–22.
[69] Lev. 27:30–34; Num. 18:25–29.
[70] Deut. 26:1–11.
[71] Deut. 14:28–29; 26:12–15.
[72] Cf. Deut. 14:22–27.

Continuity would make the tithe binding for Christians. Jesus did commend the Pharisees on this,[73] but their tithes were not an act of generosity; it was obedience to the covenant before the cross. No New Testament passage about money, written for believers after the cross, talks in those terms of the tithe,[74] because those covenantal provisions are over. Paul nearly aligns Christian ministers with temple priests in 1 Corinthians 9:

> Do you not know that those who are employed in the temple service get their food from the temple, and those who serve at the altar share in the sacrificial offerings? In the same way, the Lord commanded that those who proclaim the gospel should get their living by the gospel. But I have made no use of any of these rights, nor am I writing these things to secure any such provision.[75]

There is an equivalence ('in the same way'), but it is not over the amount (which Paul does not mention) but over the *rights* which Paul refuses to claim. The principle is voluntary generosity. We have to bring in some element of change, otherwise we risk living under the wrong covenant.

If we do introduce change, we must be honest. Malachi 3:10 is a good example: 'Bring the full tithes into the storehouse, that there may be food in my house', with blessings and curses promised and warned. We cannot take that language about God's house, and apply it to any building today. It must not be used to raise funds for a capital campaign. The 'food' was needed for the priests and Levites involved in the sacrificial system; no pastor, elder or minister fulfils that role today. That would be grotesque, implying that Jesus' priesthood needs supplementing in some way. All these muddles come from not grasping the simple fact that tithing is not appropriate for Christians, because the reason for tithing has passed. It is hard not to suspect that many church leaders know this, but the habit of asking for or requiring a tithe is hard to break because it is a simple and apparently biblical way of getting Christians to give. But it is not gospel-based fund-raising.

So what can we say? At most, that we may use the tithe as a template. Fundamentally, the idea that Christians do not need to tithe is fabulous news because we no longer need temple or sacrifice. That time is over. And so is the tithe.

---

[73] Matt. 23:23.
[74] Heb. 7 anticipates 12:28 – 13:21, that appropriate worship in the New Covenant is the entire lifestyle.
[75] 1 Cor. 9:13–15.

1 Corinthians 11:17–34
8. The church's meal

Jesus left two actions, using everyday items. What could be simpler than having a wash or sharing a meal? But what they mean is far from simple. When Jesus told his disciples 'the cup that I drink you will drink, and the baptism with which I am baptised, you will be baptised', he meant that they would die with him.[1]

The Lord's Supper appears in Matthew, Mark, Luke and 1 Corinthians,[2] and because it is so emphasized, churches have taken it seriously. Yet the World Council of Churches 1982 report *Baptism, Eucharist and Ministry* reported irreconcilable disagreements over what the Lord's supper is, how the Lord Jesus is related to it, how the Holy Spirit is at work during it, the relationship between communion and baptism, and whether the bread and wine change.[3]

1 Corinthians is the account that was written to a church, but we must be careful. This church, shockingly, was not in fact holding a Lord's Supper. Paul says explicitly: *When you come together it is not the Lord's supper that you eat* (20). We can imagine their indignant reply. 'What do you mean? Do we have the wrong bread, or wine? Should we start using grape juice? Should we *stop* using grape juice? Are we using the wrong words, or the wrong theology, or is the wrong person leading? What are we doing wrong?'

None of those is close to why their meal was *not the Lord's supper*. Neither the bread and wine on the table, nor the person at the head

---

[1] Mark 10:39.
[2] Matt. 26:17–29; Mark 14:12–26; Luke 22:7–20; 1 Cor. 11:17–34. On the differences, I. H. Marshall, *Last Supper and Lord's Supper* (Exeter: Paternoster Press, 1980). On John 6, A. J. Köstenberger, *John*, ECNT (Grand Rapids: Baker, 2004), pp. 196–223.
[3] Responding to *BEM*, G. T. Smith, *The Lord's Supper: Five Views* (Downers Grove: IVP Academic, 2008) contains Roman Catholic, Missouri Synod Lutheran, Reformed, Baptist and Pentecostal views.

of the table invalidated their meal: it was the torn relationships around the table. This letter is a correction.

1. The Corinthian's meal (11:17–22)

Previously Paul wrote, 'Now I *commend* you, because you remember me in everything and maintain the traditions even as I delivered them to you',[4] but here he begins, *I do not commend you*, and ends, *shall I commend you in this? No, I will not commend you* (17, 22, emphasis added). An encouraging reminder of Jesus' death had turned into something so hurtful that *when you come together it is not for the better but for the worse* (17). Their questions no longer shape this letter, 'a certain report' has come Paul's way, and provoked this rebuke.[5]

At its heart is how they *come together*, underlined five times (17, 18, 20, 33, 34). Although some Christians talk about 'making my communion', our relationships are critical to a true expression of the meal, precisely because we are coming together *as church* (18).

a. Divisions

They were playing status games, subverting the meal's meaning. Paul describes it rather strangely: *for there must be factions among you in order that those who are genuine among you may be recognised* (19). He could be writing straightforwardly, although it is difficult to see *factions*, which he calls 'a work of the flesh' elsewhere, ever being a good thing.[6] Alternatively, this could be quite sharp, saying something like 'because the élite really ought to stand out, oughtn't they?' That seems plausible, because Corinthians loved prestige (1:11–31), and later succumbed to the glib prosperity of 'super-apostles'.[7] Paul's repeated 'coming together' rubs against their carelessness over divisions.

b. Dinners

A first-century house large enough to host a modest meeting was excavated in Corinth in the 1970s. Its dining room could hold maybe nine guests, lying on couches. The courtyard could seat thirty on benches, with more squashed on the rim of the central

[4] 11:2.
[5] See B. Winter, *After Paul Left Corinth* (Grand Rapids: Eerdmans, 2001), pp. 159–163.
[6] *Haereseis*, Gal. 5:19–20. The word does not imply 'heresy'.
[7] 2 Cor. 11:5.

pool.[8] And perhaps that was how they divided: first-class and second-class. And the word 'supper' is potentially misleading, if it implies a snack. This was the main meal of the day, and could even mean a banquet.[9]

Paul seems to be describing two meals: one which satisfied physical hunger after a day's work, where people could *eat and drink*, and even *get drunk* (21–22), and *the Lord's supper*, which seems to have involved Jesus' words, and shared resources (*the bread* and *the cup*, 26).[10]

The broad shape is clear, even if the details are not. Perhaps some people arrived early because they had the time for a leisurely meal, and slaves and other workers arrived later, hot, dirty and hungry – and there was nothing decent left from the bring-and-share meal. Possibly, though, the issue was that everyone brought their own meal, of wildly different quality; the wealthy assumed their cultural status and ate privately, becoming *drunk* in their dining room within metres of fellow Christians who were still *hungry* in the courtyard. Whichever Paul meant, the phrase *each one **goes ahead** with his own meal* (21) contrasts the Corinthian who selfishly *goes ahead* (*paralambanein*), with Jesus who *took* bread (*lambanein*, 23).

Paul's criticism is aimed at the dining room. *What! Do you not have houses to eat and drink in?* (22) The poorer people out in the courtyard did not; their huddled apartments had neither kitchen nor dining rooms, and they relied on filthy fast-food stalls. So the well-off could *humiliate* their sisters and brothers, the ones who *have houses* showing they *despise* the ones who *have nothing*.[11]

By blindly going ahead with their own meal without noticing their fellow believers – or, at least, only noticing the pleasant believers of their own caste – the 'élite' of this self-absorbed church were missing the point. It really had become their own supper, not the Lord's. The householder was a generous host, but only to his friends; by contrast, Paul wants them to pay attention to the meal where the Lord Jesus is the host.

2. The Lord's meal (11:23–26)

Different churches use different words for this meal. 'The Mass' is the Roman Catholic term, from the closing words of the Latin

---

[8] For the details, see Anthony Thiselton, *The First Epistle to the Corinthians*, NIGTC (Grand Rapids: Eerdmans and Carlisle: Paternoster, 2000), p. 860f.

[9] Meal: John 12:2; banquet: Mark 6:21.

[10] Emphasis added.

[11] The word *oikia* emphases the physical 'house' (v. 22), rather than 'home' (v. 34).

service, 'Ite, missa est'. The phrase is ancient, but there is no consensus on its meaning; it probably relates to 'dismissal'. 'Eucharist' is even older, going back to the *Didachē*, from the late first or early second century. It means 'the Thanksgiving', reflecting *when he had given thanks (eucharistēsas)* in 11:24.[12] It is widely used today, but perhaps we would do better to translate it and link to Jesus' words.[13] 'Communion', or 'Holy Communion', probably arises from the word 'fellowship', *koinōnia*.[14] 'The Lord's Table' or the 'Breaking of Bread' are other biblical terms.[15]

Whichever name we use, we go back to the night before Jesus died. The links in Paul's chain are careful: *I received from the Lord what I also delivered to you* (23),[16] forcing these individualist Corinthians to remember the meal Jesus shared, and think through its implications.[17]

a. The bread (23–24)

The Lord Jesus on the night when he was betrayed took bread, and when he had given thanks, he broke it, and said, 'This is my body which is for you. Do this in remembrance of me.'

Every detail comes for a reason. When did it occur? *On the night when [Jesus] was betrayed*, or 'handed over'. That word later describes Judas' treachery, then how Jesus was 'handed over' by the chief priests to Pilate, and then 'handed over' to the executioners. Paul used it in the previous sentence: *what I also delivered* – 'handed over' – *to you*. The Corinthians are part of this story.

All the accounts watch Jesus' hands, as after he had *given thanks he broke* [bread], *and said, 'This is my body which is for you . . .* '[18] They are not so much looking at the bread, but at what Jesus does

---

[12] *Didachē* 9:1; see chs. 10–11.

[13] Thiselton, *Corinthians*, p. 864.

[14] 'The cup of blessing which we bless, is it not the communion of the blood of Christ? The bread which we break, is it not the communion of the body of Christ?' 1 Cor. 10:16, KJV.

[15] The Lord's Table: 1 Cor. 10:21; Breaking of Bread: Luke 24:35; Acts 2:42, 46, 20:7; 1 Cor. 10:16. The Lord's Supper and baptism are sometimes together called 'ordinances' (Exod. 12:14 and Heb. 9:1 in KJV).

[16] *Received* and *delivered* are 'technical terms from Paul's Jewish heritage for the transmission of religious instruction' (Gordon Fee, *First Epistle to the Corinthians*, NICNT [Grand Rapids: William B Eerdmans Publishing Co, 1987], p. 548).

[17] Thiselton says Marshall, *Last Supper*, is 'utterly convincing' that the Gospels recount the Last Supper as a Passover (Thiselton, *Corinthians*, p. 874).

[18] Inserting 'broken' is understandable but, despite the KJV, should not be there. See NKJV footnote. C. L. Blomberg, *1 Corinthians*, NIVAC (Grand Rapids: Zondervan, 1994), p. 229, fn. 4.

with it: he rips it up. Imagine the scene: Jesus, holding the bread, says, 'this is my body' while he rips it to pieces. Slow down again: 'Watch – *this*, is my body.' Technically, the word translated *this* cannot refer to the word translated *bread*; Bruce Winter says it refers to an action, and although he suggests that the action referred to is Jesus' death, I suspect that even more closely, it is his tearing the bread.[19] Jesus was acting out with the bread what was about to happen to his body on the cross.

Keep the movie running – Jesus gave them each a piece of ripped bread, saying: *which is for you.* 'My death,' he says, 'will benefit you.' How? 'For' translates the little Greek word, *hyper,* which Paul used frequently with one emphasis: 'I delivered to you as of first importance what I also received: that Christ died for (*hyper*) our sins in accordance with the Scriptures.'[20] It describes the glorious transfer of our sins onto Christ. It means 'as a substitute for', and its range in translation shares one tremendous truth: 'In my place, condemned he stood.'[21] That is how his death benefits us.

And then, Jesus said *Do this in remembrance of me.* That is, 'By having this meal, keep central to your understanding that why I came, all I have said and done, and am about to do, is made sense of by my death.' Biblically, 'remembering' God means we consciously organize our lives around his priorities and glory; 'forgetting' him means we move him out of our sight.[22] So 'remembering' Jesus means we take ourselves back to the events themselves, examine our hearts to find the cause of those events in our own sin, and marvel at the forgiveness that flows.

b. The wine (25)

In the same way also he took the cup, after supper, saying, 'This cup is the new covenant in my blood. Do this, as often as you drink it, in remembrance of me.'

Jesus stripped the Passover liturgy to its barest essentials: *the cup, after supper.* Wine is a biblical picture of delight and celebration in God's blessing – that is 'the cup of salvation'.[23] But it also portrays God's judgment: 'For in the hand of the LORD there is a cup with

---

[19] The relevant word is a neuter demonstrative pronoun, but bread (*artos*) is masculine. Winter claims that sixteen of the seventy-four occurrences in Paul refer to an action (Winter, *After Paul*, p. 153).

[20] 1 Cor. 15:3. See Rom. 5:6–8; Gal. 3:13; 2 Cor. 5:21.

[21] 'Man of sorrows! What a name', by Philip P. Bliss.

[22] Deut. 8:18; Judg. 8:34; Ps. 22:27. Thiselton, *Corinthians*, p. 879.

[23] Ps. 116:13.

foaming wine, well mixed, and he pours out from it, and all the wicked of the earth shall drain it down to the dregs.'[24]

Jesus drained the cup of God's wrath. In Gethsemane he prayed, saying, 'Father, if you are willing, remove this cup from me. Nevertheless, not my will, but yours, be done.'[25] There is no doubt about which cup he drank. Which means that the cup he leaves for us is the other one, the cup of thanksgiving and salvation.

Here is Jesus' explanation about the *cup of salvation*: '*This cup is the new covenant in my blood.*' We have seen that covenants were sealed with blood. 'And Moses took the blood and threw it on the people and said, "Behold the blood of the covenant that the LORD has made with you in accordance with all these words".'[26] A covenant with God but without blood was impossible, because the death of the animal stood in for the inevitable death of the sinful human. Before God, I deserve to die. In order for me as a sinful human being to be in a loving relationship with him, he allows a death in my place.

Jesus' words make sense in that context: '*This cup is the new covenant in my blood.*' His death, bearing our sin once and for all, makes this new covenant exist forever. It is to remind ourselves of that, repeatedly, that we *drink* that cup of wine repeatedly.

c. Passover

Since Passover lies behind the Last Supper, it is worth noticing the similarities and differences.[27] There are two biblically mandated elements in that family meal to remember God's deliverance of his people from Egypt and 'passing over' their sin. One was a lamb, killed, roasted and eaten in haste while its blood was daubed on the doorposts.[28] The blood marked that the lamb had died in place of the first-born child of the house, and God's wrath was averted. The second element in the Passover was unleavened bread, bread which had to be baked quickly, and so used a recipe that did not require waiting for yeast to rise.

Both meals use bread, but where one uses lamb every year, the other remembers the one great sacrifice of the Passover Lamb of God, and uses the wine to symbolize his blood.[29] Both are for God's saved people, but where one is for close family, the other is for

---

[24] Ps. 75:8. See too Isa. 51:17 and Jer. 25:15.
[25] Luke 22:41–42.
[26] Exod. 24:8
[27] On the influence of Passover liturgies on the New Testament, see Marshall, *Last Supper*.
[28] Exod. 12:12–13.
[29] 1 Cor. 5:7

God's diverse, international new people. One is a dedicated, annual event, a meal in itself, the other is a frequent, probably weekly, event around a normal meal. Both meals look backwards, but one looks forward as well, *until he comes.*

d. Death (26)

Over time Christians developed rich ceremonies for this meal, and as they added creeds, readings and prayers to match different occasions, so different emphases emerged. My own denomination has moved from having one authorized form of prayer to eight, including traditional and modern variants, each with seasonal variations and permissible changes. In common with many Christians, the resources have broadened out what we can do.

But we risk losing clarity. Paul insists that the Lord's Supper is about one thing: *For as often as you eat this bread and drink the cup, you proclaim the Lord's death until he comes.* Did Paul not believe in the incarnation? Of course he did.[30] If Jesus had not been born he could not have suffered *death.* Was Paul confident about the resurrection? Certainly.[31] If Jesus had not been raised he would not be *the Lord.* Did Paul believe in the gift of the Holy Spirit? Surely.[32] Without the Holy Spirit we could not *proclaim.* Did Paul have a firm grasp of Christ's return? Of course.[33] We have this meal *until he comes.* Such doctrines are to be taught, believed and lived out, but they are not what the Lord's Supper is about. It recalls *the Lord's death.* And Paul insists that we **proclaim** the Lord's death in this meal, which 'transforms the participants into preachers'.[34] All of us who take part remind each other, and the world, that the absolute centre of what we believe is Jesus' death for us.

The Corinthians found this hard. They were wary of the cross, not because it was gruesome but because it was unimpressive, and that infected their meal. As David Garland says, 'The Corinthians "take" on their own behalf; Jesus "takes" on behalf of others. The Corinthians act selfishly; Jesus acts unselfishly in giving his life for others.'[35] If I think that God's acceptance and adoption of me is based on anything other than Christ's shed blood, I have ceased to believe the gospel. If I think I am part of a spiritual 'élite' that stands

---

[30] Phil. 2:6–7.
[31] 1 Cor. 15:14–15.
[32] Gal. 3:1–6.
[33] 1 Cor. 15:22–24.
[34] Marshall, *Last Supper*, p. 113.
[35] David E. Garland, *1 Corinthians*, BECNT (Grand Rapids: Baker Academic, 2003), p. 542.

in a superior relationship to God, I have ceased to trust in the *Lord's death*. Paul would not let the Corinthians shirk this responsibility: *you proclaim the Lord's death until he comes.*

Jesus joined the biblical voices describing God's future kingdom as a feast:[36]

'I have earnestly desired to eat this Passover with you before I suffer. For I tell you I will not eat it until it is fulfilled in the kingdom of God.' And he took a cup, and when he had given thanks he said, 'Take this, and divide it among yourselves. For I tell you that from now on I will not drink of the fruit of the vine until the kingdom of God comes.'[37]

So, as well as looking back, we look forward to his return. This is where we live, and we proclaim the Lord's death until he comes.[38]

3. The meaning of the Lord's meal (11:27–32)

All this matters because Paul has an astonishingly high view of the meal. Here and now, in the present, the Lord himself hosts his supper.

a. Eating 'unworthily' (27)

Paul's overarching concern is clear: *Therefore whoever eats the bread or drinks the cup of the Lord in an unworthy manner, shall be guilty of the body and the blood of the Lord (27)*.[39] These two questions strike any sensitive Christian: what does it mean to eat or drink in an unworthy manner; and what does it mean to be guilty of the body and blood of the Lord?[40]

The word *unworthy*[41] means something like 'inappropriately', referring to the Corinthians' status games that characterized their meetings. So our first concern should be the relationships between Christians in church. Understandably, the KJV's translation 'unworthily' made people turn inwards, looking at our own attitudes towards the bread and wine, and whether we are 'worthy' of eating and drinking. Anxious souls search their hearts for unconfessed

---

[36] Isa. 25:6–9; 65:13–14; Matt. 22:1–14; Rev. 19:6–10.

[37] Luke 22:15–18.

[38] 1 Cor. 15. Everything in Corinth is to be resolved by living between the cross (1 Cor. 1 – 2) and the resurrection (1 Cor. 15).

[39] NASB. See next footnote.

[40] The ESV expands this to 'guilty of profaning', HCSB to 'guilty of sin against', and the NIV to 'guilty of sinning against'.

[41] *Anaxiōs.*

sin. The place for self-examination will come, but the issue here is different. Does our pride towards other members of the congregation effectively rub out the message of the cross?

In fact, it does more than rub it out: we partner with the people who howled for Jesus' death. The word translated *guilty* (*enochos*) is found on the lips of the crowd: 'And they all condemned Jesus as deserving (*enochos*) death.' Paul is being shockingly consistent when he concludes that the loveless actions of the Corinthians are equivalent to spitting on Jesus.[42] They are *guilty of the body and blood of the Lord.*

b. Self-examination (28)

First, we *examine* ourselves, individually, to see if our own relationships run against the cross. The issue is not a generalized warning against sin, because if it were no-one would ever *eat of the bread and drink of the cup* (28). No, he assumes that people can *eat* and *drink* rightly, and even begins this instruction with an encouraging little word of invitation, which we might add as 'so', or 'but';[43] it tells the cautious Christian, 'yes, you may', not 'no, you are not worthy'. But we must examine our attitudes to each other. That is his concern.

c. Discerning the body (29–32)

The word *guilty* in the previous verse introduced a running theme. Paul uses a range of words which share a family resemblance:

* *discern* (*diakrinōn*), 29
* *judgment* (*krima*), 29 (and in 34, as a summary)
* *judged* (*diekrinomen*), 31
* *judged* (*ekrinometha*), 31
* *judged* (*krinomenoi*), 32
* *condemned* (*katakrithōmen*), 32

The important one is the first, because the rest explore what happens to *anyone who eats and drinks without discerning the body* (29).

The most immediate thought is that Paul is repeating verse 27, and *discerning the body* means the same as *whoever, therefore, eats the bread or drinks the cup of the Lord in an unworthy manner.*[44] The

---

[42] Mark 14:64–65.

[43] The word is *de*. Its nature as an invitation makes it worth translating.

[44] The text behind KJV has compounded this error by bringing in words from v. 27: *For he that eateth and drinketh **unworthily**, eateth and drinketh damnation to himself, not discerning **the Lord's** body* (emphasis added).

long history of Christian disputes about how exactly Christ is present at his supper have focused attention on what it means to discern, or judge rightly, the bread on the table, and therefore whether an individual's understanding is adequate.

But Paul does not talk about 'the bread *and* the cup' here as he does in verses 26, 27 and 28, nor about 'the body *and* blood' as he does in verses 24–25 and 27. He talks here only about *discerning the body*. It could be a slip, or a summary,[45] but more likely Paul is using the phrase *the body* with his usual meaning, 'the church'. Earlier, introducing the theme of unity at the Lord's Supper, he had written,

> The cup of blessing that we bless, is it not a participation in the blood of Christ? The bread that we break, is it not a participation in the body of Christ? Because there is one bread, we who are many are one body, for we all partake of the one bread.[46]

He looks backwards ('a participation in the blood of Christ') but also around ('we who are many are one body'). Following this section on the Lord's Supper comes the exploration of gifts, which depends on the metaphor of the church as 'one body'.[47] So here too, the issue is 'not just the piece of bread *on* the table, but the body *at* the table'.[48]

How, then, were the Corinthians failing to *discern* the body? Why, by the very divisions Paul has just described. Their selfishness meant some were refusing to acknowledge the equal standing of other members of the church, and whether it was preferring wealth, or particular gifts,[49] or other ways of being 'arrogant',[50] the Corinthian church was riddled with lack of *love*.[51] The consequences are serious, for anyone who acts in such a loveless way *eats and drinks judgment on himself* (29).

d. Judgment and discipline (29–32)

Recall that list of related words: *Discern* (*diakrinōn*), *judgment* (*krima*), *judged* (*diekrinomen, ekrinometha* and *krinomenoi*), and

[45] So Thiselton, *Corinthians*, p. 893.
[46] 1 Cor. 10:16–17.
[47] 1 Cor. 12:12.
[48] This is Garland's phrase, although he prefers a different understanding of what was happening, *Corinthians*, p. 552, emphasis original.
[49] 1 Cor. 12:21.
[50] 1 Cor. 5:2.
[51] 1 Cor. 13 occurs here for this reason.

condemned (katakrithōmen). They describe God's attitude towards the Corinthians, because of their attitudes towards each other.

Paul is clear about the reality of judgment, which is what he means by being *condemned*, and he is also clear about the reality of salvation, which is why he says Christians will *not be condemned along with the world* (32). But in addition, we must account for God's present *discipline* of his people. All those related 'judgment' words refer to present actions, both God's and ours, apart from that final condemnation.

Present judgment	*For anyone who eats and drinks without discerning the body eats and drinks judgement on himself. That is why many of you are weak and ill, and some have died. But if we judged ourselves truly, we would not be judged. But when we are judged by the Lord, we are disciplined . . .*
Future judgment	*. . . so that we may not be condemned along with the world.*

It is quite unusual today to think that God disciplines us in the present *so that* (the idea of purpose is clear in the Greek) *we may not be condemned*. The idea is repeated in verse 34: *so that when you come together it will not be for judgement.* We should remember that the Corinthians' behaviour aligned them with those who crucified Jesus. Those with tender consciences always examine themselves most closely, but Paul addresses the arrogant, insisting that God loves them too much to abandon them to their own devices, but disciplines them so that they would not be condemned.

In Corinth that discipline takes a particular form: *that is why many of you are weak and ill, and some have died* (30). Gordon Fee suggests that 'Paul is here stepping into the prophetic role',[52] and that might be correct. After all, key members of Paul's team were seriously ill, and one nearly died, and there is no hint there of any necessary connection between sickness and discipline.[53] When Jesus was asked about a blind man, 'Rabbi, who sinned, this man or his parents, that he was born blind?', his response was that neither was the cause.[54] Lazarus was sick, died, and raised to life again without any hint of discipline.[55] So, although all sickness and death

[52] Fee, *Corinthians*, p. 565.
[53] Trophimus was so ill he could not travel (2 Tim. 4:20); Epaphroditus nearly died (Phil. 2:27).
[54] John 9:2–3.
[55] John 11.

is caused ultimately because we live in a fallen world under God's judgment, we are not encouraged to find a particular connection between any individual illness and God's discipline. People who think like that either become obsessed over trivial problems in case it is God's judgment, or more cruelly, insist that the reason Christians are not healed from a serious sickness is some unrecognized and unrepented sin.

But of course, no-one at Corinth was agonizingly soul-searching about an unrecognized sin. They were engaging in blatant rebellion against God, and Paul had already warned them that their tolerance of idolatry was testing God to the limit. 'You cannot partake of the table of the Lord and the table of demons. Shall we provoke the Lord to jealousy? Are we stronger than he?'[56] So, for all that we would want to be very cautious about attributing a connection between sin and sickness in our churches, and for all that we might wonder why God is so patient with us that he does not behave in this striking way today, at least as far as we can see, we should take this matter very seriously. Paul had already warned about learning from Israel's history as we read it:

> Now these things took place as examples for us, that we might not desire evil, as they did . . . We must not put Christ to the test, as some of them did . . . Now these things happened to them as an example, but they were written down for our instruction . . . therefore let anyone who thinks he stands take heed lest he fall.[57]

e. Real presence

Roman Catholic theology, and circles influenced by it, talks of the 'real presence' of Christ in the bread and the wine, and therefore its automatic benefits.[58] Martin Luther, even while he refused to agree that the bread and wine had unalterably changed ('*tran*substantiation'), still described Christ being present in, with or under the bread and wine in some way (sometimes summarized, although not by Luther, as '*con*substantiation'). Reformed thinkers occupy a spectrum, but they concentrate on Christ's finished work on the cross, and therefore the permanence of his ascended physical presence

---

[56] 1 Cor. 10:21–22.
[57] 1 Cor. 10:6, 9, 11, 12.
[58] This theology was expressed in Lateran IV (1215), the Council of Trent (1545–63), Vatican II (1962–5) and the 1992 catechism. The phrase *ex opera operato* is often used, meaning that the bread and wine have effect by the very fact of their being consecrated.

in heaven.[59] The bread and wine remain bread and wine, although their significance changes for the duration of the meal,[60] and can be summarized as saying that the bread and wine are a sign, a promise and a means of God's grace.[61]

Nothing, to my mind, justifies anything for a biblically minded Christian other than a position on the Reformed spectrum. Nothing in 1 Corinthians or the Gospels gives any hint of a change in the bread and wine, and Jesus' full, physical presence while he said *this is my body . . . this is my blood* means that he must have intended a representative or symbolic meaning. 'This stands for my body, my blood.' Those words mean the same whether he was physically present, as then, or physically absent, as now. Just like a retired colonel grabs the cutlery after dinner and re-enacts a famous battle, 'This vinegar is Napoleon, d'you see, and that serving spoon is Blücher', so at the very least, the bread and wine stand in for, re-present to us, and show our attitudes towards, Jesus' death. That is what is meant by saying the bread and wine are a sign or symbol.

But that is not a trivial idea. A symbol does not have to be a 'mere' symbol like a sauce bottle or a spoon: an engagement ring is no 'mere' piece of jewellery, as anyone who has searched a muddy field to find a lost diamond knows well. The physical nature of bread and wine, their taste and texture, remind us of what it means to feed on Christ, to trust him for our spiritual survival just as we rely on food and drink for our physical survival, to taste his promise that because he died for me I will not be *condemned* (32). The bread and wine are, as one Reformer, John Jewel, called them, 'visible words'.[62] That is what is meant by saying the bread and wine are a 'promise'.

---

[59] A spectrum from Zwingli (the Lord's supper is a memorial act, although he would not have said a 'mere' memorial), through Luther (it was his biggest disagreement with Calvin) and Bullinger to Calvin, whose mature thought that the bread and wine (and, indeed, baptism) are a sign, a means of grace and a promise, is expressed in Book IV of the *Institutes*. See R. Reymond, *A New Systematic Theology of the Christian Faith* (Nashville: Thomas Nelson, 1998), pp. 996–967. Anglican Reformers aligned with Calvin's theology rather than Luther's: see P. E. Hughes, *Theology of the English Reformers* (London: Hodder and Stoughton, 1965), ch. 6.

[60] See Smith, *Lord's Supper*, for a contemporary expression of the spectrum, although John R. Stephenson is not properly representative of the Lutheran position. See too D. Bridge and D. Phypers, *The Meal That Unites* (London: Hodder and Stoughton, 1981).

[61] I am avoiding using the word 'sacrament' (from the Latin, 'sacramentum', a sacred thing), partly because it is not a biblical way of speaking, partly because Catholic listing of sacraments is longer than Reformed thinking (seven, rather than the two of meal and baptism), and partly because 'sacramental' sits uneasily with my preferred simplicity of practice.

[62] Quoted in Hughes, *English Reformers*, p. 192. On transubstantiation, Baptist theologian Roger Olsen writes, 'Protestants will probably always find this mystery too mysterious. And they will find such a mystery unnecessary' (Smith, *Lord's Supper*, p. 37).

We can go further. My wedding ring does not just represent my promise to be faithful to my wife, it reminds me of it, and in some circumstances would prevent me from breaking it. Symbols do things, and in Corinth they exposed the sinful heart of the participants. Paul longed that instead they would show up the Corinthians' restored relationships. They should produce, between Christians, the very blessings of forgiveness and love that they promise. In that way, as Roger Olsen says, 'the grace of Christ can be experienced and Christ himself personally encountered without any change in the elements'.[63] In the famous summary of the twelfth-century theologian, Peter Lombard, they are 'a visible form of an invisible grace'.[64] That is what is meant by saying the bread and wine are a 'means of grace'.[65]

Moreover, although the bread and wine are symbols, the Lord's Supper is not a symbol: it is precisely what it says it is, the *Lord's* Supper. While Jesus is not physically present in the bread and wine (he is, after all, physically in heaven), he is not absent; by his Spirit he is personally present among us. Christ calls the assembly together, speaks through his word, and – as we have seen – may discipline his people for their good.

4. Making our meal meaningful (11:33–34)

So then, my brothers, when you come together to eat, wait for one another – if anyone is hungry, let him eat at home – so that when you come together it will not be for judgement. About the other things I will give directions when I come.

Paul's conclusion is positive because the Corinthians' misbehaviour is not beyond repair. The solution is to *wait for one another*, rather than 'each one going ahead with his own meal' (21). We have the reverse problem here to verse 21: there Paul could mean either 'go ahead' or 'devour'; here he could mean 'wait for' or 'welcome, serve, receive hospitably'. But whether some people started earlier than others, or were selfish,[66] the underlying issues remain lovelessness.

[63] Smith, *Lord's Supper*, p. 37.

[64] *Invisibilis gratiae visibilis forma.* Sentences IV.I.4.

[65] Since the Reformation this phrase has described baptism, the Lord's Supper, praying and preaching as the effective mechanisms God uses to sustain his people. I would want to insert 'fellowship' as well. This was identified in the Westminster Assembly (Larger Catechism, Qn.195), the Belgic Confession, the Helvetic Confession, and the Anglican Article 19.

[66] The commentators are split: Fee supports 'devour/welcome' (Fee, *Corinthians*, p. 567), where Thiselton writes, 'the common translation . . . wait for (one another) . . . is entirely correct' (Thiselton, *Corinthians*, p. 899).

Whether the translation is *wait for* or 'welcome', the emphasis lies on *one another*. And whether they are ravenous or gluttonous, *if anyone is hungry, let him eat at home*. The repeated phrase *come together . . . come together* echoes the opening repetition of verses 17 and 18, and emphasizes that the horizontal relationships in Corinth were at the forefront of Paul's mind, because of the seriousness with which God views them.

When Paul writes *about the other things I will give directions when I come*, that leaves us unsatisfied, but it is worth noticing three issues where we might be surprised he says nothing.

a. When were they supposed to be meeting?

There was no weekly day off in the Roman Empire, so presumably they met on an agreed day, after work.[67] Jewish Christians might assume the Sabbath, but quite early, the habit seems to have begun of meeting on the first day of the week, perhaps because that was the day the risen Jesus appeared.[68] Paul directed, 'On the first day of every week, each of you is to put something aside and store it up, as he may prosper, so that there will be no collecting when I come',[69] but that does not necessarily imply that there was a church meeting with a collection on that first day, merely that everybody should be regular in planning their saving for the Jerusalem collection.[70] Luke mentions Christians meeting on the first day of the week once, but does not make anything of it.[71] John talks of 'being in the Spirit on the Lord's day',[72] but that is not a transparent reference to Sunday, and the alternatives (Easter Sunday or the Sabbath) are as likely.[73] Clear evidence that the Christians met regularly on what we call Sunday does not emerge until the second century.[74] At the best we can make a likely guess that the Corinthians met on a Sunday evening.

We might conclude that weekly sharing the Lord's Supper might be good too, and since it is *probably* what they were doing it is

[67] Blomberg, *Corinthians*, p. 228.
[68] Matt. 28:1, etc.
[69] 1 Cor. 16.2.
[70] See ch. 7.
[71] Acts 20:7.
[72] Rev. 1:10.
[73] See G. K. Beale, *The Book of Revelation*, NIGTC (Grand Rapids: Eerdmans and Carlisle: Paternoster, 1999), p. 203, although he is anachronistic in his use of 'Sunday'.
[74] Contrast D. A. Carson (ed.), *From Sabbath to Lord's Day: A Biblical, Historical and Theological Investigation* (Grand Rapids: Zondervan, 1982), concluding that the Lord's Day is not to be understood as a Sabbath, with R. T. Beckwith and W. Stott *This is the Day* (London: Marshall, Morgan and Scott, 1978) concluding that it should. See too R. B. Gaffin, *Calvin and the Sabbath: the Controversy of Applying the Fourth Commandment* (Ross-shire: Christian Focus, 2009).

probably what we should be doing. But remember, this was one element of a much wider kind of meeting; the Corinthians were not gathering to hold a liturgically complex and formal 'Holy Communion'. Provided we make time for proper fellowship, prayer, teaching and so forth, then this is *probably* a good habit.

b. Who might have led the meeting?

At no point does Paul instruct any single person in leadership to sort out the problems. That is not to say that he wanted a free-for-all, because chapters 12 – 14 argue the opposite, but on the manner of holding the Lord's Supper, who speaks Jesus' words is not Paul's concern. That is counterintuitive to many of us whose experience is that someone authorized must 'lead'. Some see that reading the words of Jesus and praying for the people is something only an elder or pastor should do, because it is akin to preaching, or on the Passover model, then the elders function as the 'head of the table' figures in the family. Yet others see the role of the person leading as 'priestly'.[75] But neither here nor anywhere else does the New Testament draw those conclusions. It is not just that there does not seem to be guidance of who may lead the meeting; there is not necessarily an assumption that the meeting will be 'led'. Those implications were drawn early in church history, but that was to buttress a sacrificial understanding of the meal and a priestly understanding of the role, which is not the biblical way.

Reading out Jesus' words of institution could be done by anyone with a clear voice. If it is analogous to preaching, then we could allow anyone whom we allow to preach to do it. Early Christians called this role 'presiding', and described 'the President', but that is deeply misleading.[76] We have repeatedly seen in 1 Corinthians, that it is the Lord Jesus who presides; it is the *Lord's* Supper. If I presided it would be Chris Green's supper, but it is the Lord Jesus who is the host, not me.[77] Many denominations which specifically require the leadership of ordained ministers, find there are congregations which cannot hold a Lord's Supper because of the lack of clergy, and a little thoughtfulness could make the case that severing the connection

---

[75] Again, my objection to such language is that it is the Lord Jesus who is the active priest, not any ordained minister.

[76] Justin Martyr, *First Apology*, ch. 66–67 (approximately AD 150).

[77] It would be helpful to drop the term 'lay presidency' for this position: the clergy no more preside than the laity. J. R. W. Stott (ed.), *The Anglican Communion and Scripture: Papers from the First International Consultation of the Evangelical Fellowship of the Anglican Communion, Canterbury, UK, June 1993* (Oxford: Regnum, 1996).

between being ordained and this role would be thoroughly beneficial, both in terms of thinking more biblically about the Lord's Supper, and about ministry.

c. Who was eating?

Traditionally, churches have monitored the age of taking part in the Lord's Supper. Churches who practice infant baptism have had some kind of teaching class and service to mark transition to adult membership; churches who practice adult baptism have the transition there.[78] But two recent developments have challenged that: one, across all churches, has been seeing the Lord's Supper as a family meal, based on the Passover, and the second, for some churches, has been seeing infant baptism as a complete entry point to full church membership.[79]

I think 1 Corinthians questions both developments. First, the Lord's Supper was not the meal; Paul's phrase *after supper* (25) means that they probably framed the meal with bread and wine. For children to take a full part in the meal does not necessarily mean that they took part in the Lord's Supper. Secondly, the closer we think the Lord's Supper was to the Passover meal, the more likely it is we might think children naturally participated. But we have seen that Jesus drew away from that. Our new meal is precisely not a Passover family meal with the father carving the lamb for the children and conducting a full liturgy, and the parallel should not be pressed.[80]

But what is decisive, in my view, is the note of judgment running through this section, and the seriousness of *discerning the body*. Our children are part of *the body*, but we should shield them from a responsibility towards other Christians which they are too young to take on.

4. Our meal

Historically, Christians have discussed mostly the ways in which Jesus might or might not be present. Paul has taught here that the Lord Jesus most decisively is present, as the host, but not in the bread or wine. Christians have also discussed the personal aspect, and how the Lord Jesus feeds us individually, as we chew over his promises, but we have rarely discussed the horizontal elements which are so central here.

[78] See J. I. Packer and G. A. Parrett, *Grounded in the Gospel* (Grand Rapids: Baker, 2009) for a contemporary catechism.

[79] See ch. 2.

[80] There were no children at the Last Supper; nor Gentiles, or women.

First, we must downplay, or at least correctly position, the emphasis on 'my personal communion'. There is a treasured history of Christian devotional writing on this, but it is not central for Paul, and we must not make it so. The critical issue is the nature of our relationships with each other, and if our meetings do not attend to them, we need to change our ways.

Second, there is an emphasis on the Lord's death. There is an understandable tendency to want to celebrate and safeguard every element of Christian thought and experience, but the Lord's Supper has a single focus, which is to *proclaim the Lord's death, until he comes* (26). We must insist that remains so, to challenge our pride and self-centredness. As David Garland says, ' . . . if they are proclaiming the Lord's death in what they do at the Lord's Supper, they will not overindulge themselves, despise others, shame them, or allow them to go hungry'.[81]

Third, two thousand years of Christian thought have not only delivered precious devotional thinking, but also unhelpful theology and liturgical clutter. So it is worth underlining that a very high view of the Lord's Supper is utterly consistent with seeing the bread and wine as remaining bread and wine, and a richly symbolic view of the bread and wine is utterly consistent with an understanding of *discerning the body* that focuses on people. A right view of Christ's ascended body is utterly inconsistent with seeing him physically present in any way; a right view of his once-for-sacrificial death is utterly inconsistent with seeing our meal as any kind of sacrifice; and a right view of his eternal high priesthood is utterly inconsistent with referring to any particular human role as essential.

There will always be pressure for churches to have a Lord's Supper as a weekly and central event, and that can happen if we find ways to eat it simply, and with a clear focus on what it means.

---

[81] Garland, *Corinthians*, p. 549.

Colossians 3:15–17
9. The church's praise

When people are frustrated with their churches they often express a desire to go back to the New Testament church. It is understandable but quite hard to do, because although we can access what Christians believed and how they lived, their meetings are rarely described. In fact, this is one of only two passages where Paul gives a brief insight into the normal meeting of Christians.[1] Here he describes what the church should be and do, with a hint of correction because of the errors within the congregation in Colossae.

1. Being church (3:15)

The church, or *body*, in Colossae was drifting into doctrinal dangers which could not be ignored. Paul's warnings were sharp, because the patronising false teachers were excluding ordinary church member from their charmed circles, and luring others away from Christ:

> See to it that *no one takes you captive* by philosophy and empty deceit, according to human tradition, according to the elemental spirits of the world, and not according to Christ.

> Therefore let no one *pass judgement on you* in questions of food and drink, or with regard to a festival or a new moon or a Sabbath.

> Let no one *disqualify you*, insisting on asceticism and worship of angels, going on in detail about visions, puffed up without reason by his sensuous mind.[2]

[1] The other being the similar Eph. 5:19–20. 1 Cor. 11 – 14 is longer, but it is also a sustained correction of the church where Paul introduces a better pattern, for instance over the Lord's Supper.
[2] Col. 2:8, 16, 18.

The false ideas, which looked hugely impressive, were actually pointless. The false teachers' practices, he says, 'have indeed an appearance of wisdom in promoting self-made religion and asceticism and severity to the body, but they are of no value in stopping the indulgence of the flesh'.[3] In fact they are simply 'puffed up', and have 'lost connection with the Head', Christ.[4] By contrast, the Colossian Christians were to remain close to Christ and the truth of his gospel, and their relationships should be markedly free of status. In this verse Paul gives them three resolves about repairing their life together.[5]

a. Resolve to be at peace

Jesus Christ 'both embodies and brings' peace,[6] and such a torn church needs to hear that 'in him all the fullness of God was pleased to dwell, and through him to reconcile to himself all things, whether on earth or in heaven, making peace by the blood of his cross'.[7] We were once 'alienated and hostile', but now we have been 'reconciled',[8] both to God and to one another. Indeed, in the verses introducing our section Paul has been at pains to describe the interpersonal nature of discipleship:

> Put on then, as God's chosen ones, holy and beloved, compassionate hearts, kindness, humility, meekness, and patience, bearing with one another and, if one has a complaint against another, forgiving each other; as the Lord has forgiven you, so you also must forgive. And above all these put on love, which binds everything together in perfect harmony.[9]

C. F. D. Moule says that these practices are 'precisely those which reduce or eliminate friction: ready sympathy, a generous spirit, a humble disposition, willingness to make concessions, patience, forbearance',[10] and they certainly stand in marked contrast to 'anger, wrath, malice, slander, and obscene talk'.[11]

---

[3] Col. 2:23.

[4] Col. 2.19, NIV.

[5] The resolutions are separated by three occurrences of the connective *kai*, which is usually translated 'and', but which it is impossible to translate identically here. If they all need translating, ESV's *and . . . also . . . and . . .* is close.

[6] P. T. O'Brien, *Colossians, Philemon*, WBC (Waco: Word Books, 1982), p. 204.

[7] Col. 1:19–20.

[8] Col. 1:21–22.

[9] Col. 3:12–14.

[10] C. F. D. Moule, *The Epistles to the Colossians and to Philemon*, CGTC (Cambridge: Cambridge University Press, 1980), p. 123.

[11] Col. 3:8.

This relational aspect means that it is unlikely Paul has in mind a personal, privatized *peace of Christ* (15) in which my evaluation of a good church meeting is whether I leave feeling soothed. Rather, the peace that Jesus brings is to be expressed in the way we speak and deal with one another. The arrogant false teachers have tried to 'disqualify' (*katabrabeuetō*) them,[12] but the peace of Christ will arbitrate between or *rule* (*brabeuetō*) them. Put simply, relationships between Christians are so important, that they put a potential question mark against anything which divides them. That is not to ignore doctrinal questions of course, as Paul has shown in his attitude to the false teachers who have tried to *delude* the Colossians with their 'plausible arguments'.[13] But it is quite common in churches to have people who hardly talk to each other, not because they disagree over the doctrines of grace, but because of a disagreement over rubbish bins, comments about someone's cooking, or the purchase of toys for the crèche.[14] Such foolishness should be named for what it is and put behind us, ruled out-of court by the importance of *the peace of Christ*.

b. Resolve to be a body

Relationships matter because we are not individuals who occasionally collide, but a *body*. Three times previously in this letter Paul has identified the church as Christ's *body* (1:18, 24; 2:19), but on each occasion the church in question has been the one, cosmic assembly rather than its local expression. And although Paul does elsewhere refer to the local congregation as a *body*, and does so extensively in 1 Corinthians 12, that is probably not his direct focus here. The NIV is potentially misleading, because it has added the words *members of*, which seems to draw a clear parallel with that idea,[15] but Paul's point is probably more prosaic: we are part of one organism, the heavenly congregation, and that means we are fundamentally *one*.

The peace of Christ, then, is not something which just 'happens' when we turn up with other Christians. It is a definite target, something we should have a high commitment to work at, because it is the essence of being a *body* that we have been *called* to peace. So we must not think we can devolve this goal to denominational committees working on 'Christian unity'. Whatever their value,

---

[12] Col. 2:18.

[13] Col. 2:4.

[14] I did not invent those, sadly.

[15] Compare ESV: *let the peace of Christ rule in your hearts, to which indeed you were called in one body.*

Paul here wants us to address our day-by-day relationships with each other, and confront those niggling issues which threaten our *peace*.

c. Resolve to be thankful

Gratitude is a theme here: not only must we *be thankful* (15) but we must *sing . . . with thankfulness* (16), and everything must be done *giving thanks to God the Father* (17). All three verses mention it.

That is a wider issue in Colossians (1:3, 12; 2:7; 4:2), and led Lightfoot to comment that 'in this epistle especially the duty of thanksgiving assumes a particular prominence by being made a refrain'.[16] The false teachers were obviously tempting the Colossians to be dissatisfied with Christ, and to look elsewhere for an experience of 'angels' and an understanding of 'wisdom' (2:18, 23). But Paul has reinforced that in Christ 'the whole fullness of deity dwells bodily, and you have been filled in him, who is the head of all rule and authority'[17] – including the very angels who fascinate the gullible Colossians – and that in him are 'hidden all the treasures of wisdom and knowledge'.[18] The false ideas 'are of no value in stopping the indulgence of the flesh', but the true gospel has the power to enable us to 'put to death . . . what is earthly in you'.[19] The gospel locates us 'in Christ'[20] and 'with Christ';[21] 'with Christ' they have 'died',[22] and were 'made alive together with him';[23] they have been 'raised with Christ',[24] and their life is 'hidden with Christ' where he is 'seated at the right hand of God'.[25] One day they will 'appear with him',[26] and they will be 'mature in Christ'.[27] In their own experience they can remember when they 'received Christ',[28] and Paul can appeal to the fact that they have 'faith in Christ',[29] and that in all their activities they 'are serving the Lord Christ'.[30] Paul's message

[16] J. B. Lightfoot, *The Epistles of St. Paul: Colossians and Philemon* (Grand Rapids: Zondervan, 1959, from the revised 1879 edn), p. 243.
[17] Col. 2:9–10.
[18] Col. 2:2–3.
[19] Col. 2:23; 3:5.
[20] Col. 1:2, 4, 17, 28; 2:5–7, 9–11, 17.
[21] Col. 2:12–13, 20; 3:1, 3–4.
[22] Col. 2:20; 3:3.
[23] Col. 2:13.
[24] Col. 2:12; 3:1.
[25] Col. 3:1–3.
[26] Col. 3:4.
[27] Col. 1:28.
[28] Col. 2:6.
[29] Col. 1:4; 2:5.
[30] Col. 3:24.

is not just 'God's mystery, which is Christ'[31] as objective truth, wonderful though that is, but 'the riches of the glory of this mystery, which is Christ in you, the hope of glory'.[32] The existence of the Colossian church is a positive demonstration of Christ's victory and rule.

So Paul's message identifies gratitude with the Colossians' satisfaction with Christ. In what could be the two central verses of the letter, he writes: 'Therefore, as you received Christ Jesus the Lord, so walk in him, rooted and built up in him and established in the faith, just as you were taught, abounding in thanksgiving.'[33] It is a call not to be distracted by other messages, but to be delighted in Christ. What distracted Christian could not be satisfied with 'the full assurance of understanding'[34] all those blessings? We should indeed be thankful.

Peter O'Brien emphasizes the corporate nature of this gratitude, which leads into the next section: 'Within the Pauline letters the *eucharisteō* word group regularly denotes gratitude that finds *outward* expression in thanksgiving; there is an emphasis on the *public* aspect of thanksgiving.'[35] So we turn to the words we use to address to one another.

2. Doing church (3:16)

Having told the Colossians what they are to *let the peace of Christ* do when they meet, Paul now tells them what they are to *let the word of Christ* do on those occasions. It is an artificial distinction, of course, and David Garland is right to observe that 'the peace of Christ rules where the word of God dwells'.[36] People who commit to the hard work of loving each other as Christians, do so as an act of obedience to Christ's word, and Christians who teach and sing the word to each other, do so as an expression of being at peace with each other. So although Paul could mean that the *word of Christ* dwells either 'in you' or 'among you', the corporate ideas are uppermost. Peter O'Brien describes the congregation governed by God's word here, when he sees that 'this rich indwelling would occur when they came together, listened to the Word of Christ as it was preached and expounded to them . . . and bound to its authority'.[37]

---

[31] Col. 2:2; 4:3.
[32] Col. 1:27.
[33] Col. 2:6–7.
[34] Col. 2:2.
[35] O'Brien, *Colossians, Philemon*, p. 205, emphasis added.
[36] D. E. Garland, *Colossians, Philemon*, NIVAC (Grand Rapids: Zondervan, 1997), p. 212.
[37] O'Brien, *Colossians, Philemon*, p. 207.

Paul's theme is the way in which the *word of Christ* (or 'the word of the truth', or 'the word of God')[38] is to *dwell* in us *richly* as we engage in various activities together. By *the word of God* he cannot yet mean the Bible, but the message of the gospel, and the collections of truths and teachings which guided the churches as they emerged. In time, they became the Bible, which is how we should apply the phrase. The reason for the emphasis was because there were other gospels, giving other truths to express, other ways to behave, and other songs to sing. There were other emphases, with impressive intellectual arguments to support them (2:8), powerful personal testimonies to authenticate them (2:18), and disciplined rules of life to experience them (2:20–22). It is almost impossible to see how those would not form an attractive teaching, 'and if so (and how else did they get their authentic messages?), this must have greatly influenced the teaching they gave, and the type of songs they used for praise'.[39] That is right, and Paul stresses that it is *the word of Christ* which must validate our teachings and our songs. In this sentence, *the word of Christ* governs four participles, literally: 'teaching', 'admonishing', 'singing' and 'thanking',[40] but we can take the first two as closely tied together.

a. Let the word of Christ dwell in your teaching

It might be obvious that we should *let the word of Christ dwell in [us] richly, teaching and admonishing one another*, but how hard it is to keep to the central focus. It was Paul's constant objective, because in describing the work that he and Epaphroditus did, he wrote, 'we proclaim [Christ], warning everyone and teaching everyone with all wisdom, that we may present everyone mature in Christ. For this I toil, struggling with all his energy that he powerfully works within me'.[41] His double effort, of 'toil' and 'struggling', was produced by Christ's 'energy' and 'mighty power',[42] and produced the same double result as here: *admonishing* and *teaching*. The difference between the two words is that where *teaching* has the idea of imparting information,[43] *admonishing* has the idea of pressing it home so that people see the implications and act on them, sometimes with the note of warning[44] and sometimes with encouragement.[45]

---

[38] Col. 1:5, 25.
[39] R. C. Lucas, *The Message of Colossians and Philemon: Fullness and Freedom* (Leicester: IVP, 1980), p. 154.
[40] *Didaskontes, nouthetountes, adontes* and *eucharistountes*.
[41] Col. 1:28–29.
[42] So NLT.
[43] E.g. 1 Tim. 2:7, 'a teacher of the true faith to the Gentiles' (1984 NIV).
[44] 1 Cor. 10:11; Titus 3:10.
[45] Rom. 15:4.

The word of Christ was becoming rarer in Colossae, and we too need to take care on precisely the same issues. The false message had 'an appearance of wisdom',[46] but we are to instruct one another *in all wisdom*, which does not mean we are to be clever, or intelligent, but that our instruction is in accordance with the wisdom of the gospel.[47] Our teaching must find its satisfaction in Christ.

We are expected to be *teaching and admonishing one another*. That is a demanding expectation, because most Christians would probably admit that their grasp of doctrine is hazy, and their understanding of how to derive life-changing principles from God's word is vague. Yet this mutual teaching and admonition is precisely how Paul expects the Colossian church to inoculate itself against the error in its midst. He had high standards of how much the regular Christian would know and understand, and would therefore be able to teach and admonish.

Pastors, on the other hand, have often been to seminary, and they are perhaps more aware of the dangers of false teaching. Good ones study hard to be faithful in what they say, so their dangers are perhaps less that they will stray into ignorant or wilful doctrinal error, than in the *admonishing*. Haddon Robinson, who has taught and written extensively on preaching, has noticed that 'It's when we're applying scripture that error most likely creeps in',[48] and every preacher has some experience of that. It is right that we long for our preaching to make a difference, but we should take care that we do not reproduce the false teachers' sterile applications (2:1–23); it is right that we teach our churches to avoid the heresy in the trends evident in the Colossian church, but we should take care that we do not retreat into the unapplied doctrine which would ignore Colossians 3 and 4. Ours is a twin task, to instruct and to exhort.

b. Let the word of Christ dwell in your singing

Three kinds of songs are mentioned here: *psalms and hymns and spiritual songs*, and it is hard to distinguish them. All three terms are sprinkled through the Greek Old Testament, and Garland is typical of most modern commentators when he says that 'any distinction between these three words . . . is merely guesswork, since we have no direct evidence'.[49] Lohse seems persuasive in

[46] Col. 2:23.
[47] Col. 1:9, 28; 2:3.
[48] Most recently republished in H. Robinson and C. B. Larson, *The Art and Craft of Biblical Preaching* (Grand Rapids: Zondervan, 2005), p. 306.
[49] Garland, *Colossians, Philemon*, p. 212.

saying that that 'taken together they describe the full range of singing'.[50]

What would that full range look like? At the very least, of course, they would have sung psalms of the Old Testament,[51] and in that they followed the explicit example of psalm-singing by Jesus,[52] but there are many accounts of people singing other songs in the Old Testament and the New.[53] We know that the early church adapted Old Testament material for their own songs,[54] that they followed Jesus' own example in seeing him in the Psalms[55] and also that they wrote new material.[56] Paul seems actively to encourage church members to write new songs.[57] So the range includes formal, informal, new, traditional, Old Testament both adapted and unadapted, and probably many others.[58] That would allow them to sing *to God* but also to *one another*. Even within the Psalms, there is great variety in what we may sing. There are psalms of petition, or lament, asking God to act, psalms of thanksgiving for what God has done, and psalms of praise for who God is.[59] All three have horizontal as well as vertical elements, where we involve other people as well as God, and their place in the book of Psalms means that even the individual prayers find a corporate voice. In our singing, as we use the same words at the same time to God, we are praying with *one another*, lamenting with *one another*, thanking with *one another*, and praising with *one another*. Singing together forces me out of my individual concerns on to the great themes all Christians have in common, and makes me see my life in the light of his great plan.

This suggests three implications for today. First, singing biblical material gives far greater range to our expressions than modern Christians often allow themselves. If we start with the psalms we shall sing praises, but also laments, deep gratitude but also deep sorrow. Christians who are going through hard times often notice that the songs at church are relentlessly upbeat, and while they do

[50] E. Lohse, *Colossians and Philemon*, Hermeneia (Philadelphia: Fortress, 1971), p. 151.

[51] Luke 20:42; 24:44; Acts 1:20; 13:33.

[52] Matt. 26:30/Mark 14:26. In all likelihood, the meal being a Passover, the 'hymn' would have been one of the psalms appointed for the Passover celebrations, Pss 113 – 118.

[53] Exod. 15:1–18, 21; Judg. 5; 2 Sam. 22; Luke 1:46–55; 67–79; 2:29–32; Acts 16:25.

[54] Rev. 5:9–10; 15:3–4.

[55] Luke 24:44–49.

[56] John 1:9–11, 15; Rom. 10:9–13; 1 Cor. 12:3; Eph. 5:14; Phil. 2:6–11; Col. 1:15–20; 1 Tim. 2:5–6; 3:16; 2 Tim 2:11–13; Heb. 1:3; 1 Pet. 3:18c–19, 22.

[57] 1 Cor. 14:26.

[58] It covers biblical, historic Christian and contemporary song, but to identify that sequence as *psalms, hymns and spiritual songs* would be a mistake.

[59] NIDOTTE 4.1103ff.

not wish to deny faith in the living God, they still ask, 'What do sad Christians sing?'. The answer is we can sing the psalms, and church should encourage us to do so.

Second, the range of the New Testament practise shows that we are not bound only to sing explicitly biblical material. We are encouraged to write new songs, and to adapt the biblical material. So we are not restricted into a particular musical genre which is designed to sing only the text as it was written. Traditional churches often chant the psalms as a way of singing the text together: the gain can be increased biblical literacy, but the loss can be the cultural distance between that musical style and the culture of most people present. In my experience, it is also hard to imagine anything less like how we might imagine the wild exuberance of Psalm 150 than traditional church chanting. It is surely no mistake that God has ensured that although we know that David's words were sung to instruments, to tunes with lovely names like 'The Doe of the Morning' and 'Lilies', we have no idea what they sound like. Probably, to our ears, they would have sounded alien, and possibly ugly. But in his goodness God made sure the book of Psalms was a libretto not a score, and that means we can sing in a wonderful range of music, whether we like driving rock rhythms or the quarter-tones of an Indian raga.

Third, and most important of all, Paul is not concerned here with musical styles, or the precise limitation of his three words. He has chosen deliberately all-inclusive terms, because his prime concern was that, whatever form their songs took, he does not want the Colossians to sing nonsense. *Let the word of Christ dwell in you richly . . . as you sing.* It is probably too tight to say their singing and their teaching one another were identical, but Paul definitely wanted the false teaching removed from the songs as much as the sermons, because as Gordon Fee puts it, 'Show me a church's songs and I'll show you their theology'.[60] Songs teach us. That is, as we *Let the word of Christ dwell in [us] richly, teaching and admonishing one another in all wisdom*, our minds are engaged to understand more. A good song might explore a great biblical doctrine, or tell a story, as 'My Song is Love Unknown' takes us through Easter week; perhaps, like 'Guide me, O thou great Redeemer' it teaches us how to read the Old Testament as a Christian; perhaps it just takes up a scripture and celebrates it.

Even within the Bible we can see writers doing that, as the book of the prophet Habakkuk ends with the instruction 'to the choirmaster' that it is to be sung 'with stringed instruments'.[61] More than

---

[60] Quoted in B. Kauflin, *Worship Matters* (Wheaton: Crossway, 2008), p. 101.
[61] Hab. 3:19.

that, though, a good song-writer will have thought about how to put the words so that they can be easily remembered. We can see that in the Psalms, where almost every one has a clear logical path through, a movement of thought which connects up. Some, like Psalm 119, were written in a way that was obviously designed to be memorable, working its way through the Hebrew alphabet so that anyone trying to remember it knows how the next verse should start. Unlike most sermons, songs are crafted to be memorable, with a shape, a rhythm and a logic which is supposed to stick in our heads, set to a tune to help that process.

That makes songs wonderful blessings, but also potentially lethal carriers of false doctrine. And of course, the very attractiveness of the music, and the emotional impact it has on us, may blind us to that danger, by elevating silly words with gorgeous settings. God hates it when that happens, and his judgment is severe: 'Take away from me the noise of your songs; to the melody of your harps I will not listen.'[62] We live in an age which places an extraordinarily high value on music, and which looks to be moved by it. Of course, other cultures have looked to be moved too, and singing dangerous nonsense to great music is not unique to our day.[63] Augustine was so concerned that his emotions would override his mind that he reflected,

> I am inclined – though I pronounce no irrevocable opinion on the subject – to approve the use of singing in the church, so that by the delights of the ear the weaker minds may be stimulated to a devotional mood. Yet when it happens that I am more moved by the singing than by what I sung, I confess myself to have sinned wickedly, and that I would rather not have heard the singing.[64]

But the impact of today's technology on the availability, quality and effect of music is quite new. If we bring those cultural assumptions to church we will find that we evaluate songs less by their words than their effect, but that can be a dangerous lie, as the Colossians had discovered to their cost: Paul insists that *the peace of Christ* is a product of *the word of Christ*. Good songwriters know both these things, and will be alert to the dangers of making truth bland, or error memorable. So John Stott is right, that 'All true worship is a response to the self-revelation of God in Christ and Scripture, and arises from our reflection on who He is and what He has done . . .

---

[62] Amos 5:23.

[63] As I typed these words, Verdi's *Requiem* was on the radio. We should not pray for the dead, no matter who wrote the music.

[64] *Confessions*, 10.33.50.

The worship of God is evoked, informed, and inspired by the vision of God ... The true knowledge of God will always lead us to worship.'[65] And Bob Kauflin is right to warn that 'the better (i.e. the more accurately) we know God through his Word, the more genuine our worship will be. In fact, the moment we veer from what is true about God, we're engaging in idolatry. Regardless of what we think or feel, there is no authentic worship of God without a right knowledge of God'.[66] Paul reminds us of the dangers of mindless praise when he wrote, 'I will pray with my spirit, but I will pray with my mind also; I will sing praise with my spirit, but I will sing with my mind also'.[67] A concern for truth in our songs is not the enemy of a living encounter with God.

A songwriter knows that varying rhythm, volume, pace and style changes peoples' moods. A service in a vast cathedral begins with a thunderous organ, massive choirs, and echoes to send shivers down the spine; a meeting in the evening on a student campus serves coffee with some laid-back jazz in the background; elsewhere on campus a different group of Christians are powering rock through enormous speakers, while a local church is offering Christianity 'unplugged', with acoustic guitars and simplicity. None is right, none is wrong – and none is 'Christian'. There is no Christian musical 'style', merely Christian lyrics set to music. There are questions to be asked about singable tunes and audible lyrics, but they apply as much to the choir singing a Latin canticle as to the band with its amplifiers.

What do the notes on the page do, then? We are repeatedly commanded to 'Sing praises to God, sing praises! Sing praises to our King, sing praises!'[68] – but why? There are various biblical responses which might make up the answer:[69]

- *Singing makes us more like God.* Zephaniah promised that when God saves his people, 'he will rejoice over you with gladness; he will quiet you by his love; he will exult over you with loud singing'.[70] Almost the last act of Jesus with his disciples before his death was that he sang with them.[71] And Hebrews reminds us that Jesus sang the psalms about himself on earth, and still sings them today in heaven.[72] So one aspect of the work of the

---

[65] J. R. W. Stott, *Authentic Christianity* (Downers Grove: IVP, 1996), p. 250.
[66] Kauflin, *Worship*, p. 28.
[67] 1 Cor. 14:15.
[68] Ps. 47:6. There are over fifty commands to 'sing'.
[69] See too, Kauflin, *Worship*, pp. 98–99.
[70] Zeph. 3:17.
[71] Matt. 26:30.
[72] Heb. 2:12.

Holy Spirit as he makes us more like Christ, is to stir up that same song-singing in us.[73]

- *Singing helps us to understand and remember God's plan.* Good songs help us to engage with the truth. Maybe they tell a story, or walk around a truth to delight in it, or adore some aspect of God's character, but however they do it, they make the gospel memorable when we need it, whether we are washing the dishes or weeping over a coffin.

- *Singing helps us to engage with the truth emotionally as well as rationally.* One common factor across all cultures is that music moves us. Music is influential. What makes it manipulative is when it seeks to affect us in ways that are inappropriate. A love song between a husband and wife can lead to a physical expression which would be quite wrong if they were not married. The music has moved them, which is what it does, but other factors need to say whether that movement is good or not. Excellent Christian music aligns our minds and emotions, so that we are encouraged to feel what the gospel would say is the right way to feel. The music serves the words. On some occasions, what the music will do therefore is to express our emotions; since joy is an appropriate emotional reaction to the gospel, the right music will help us express our joy. So the music is the servant of the lyrics, in the same way that the lyrics are the servant of the Scriptures. It ensures that God's word is heard and appropriated. So we cannot choose to sing a song just because the tune is uplifting or upbeat. Aesthetics do matter, because a dull tune, unimaginative arrangement or tone-deaf performance detracts from the words that are being sung, but aesthetic considerations on their own do not validate a piece of music.

- But singing can do even more. *Singing can encourage me out of my gloom into joy.* The reason music is so powerful is that it can change our moods, and responsible songwriters know that what they are doing is stirring up the right kind of change. As Jonathan Edwards wrote, 'The duty of singing praises to God seems to be given wholly to excite and express religious affection. There is no other reason why we should express ourselves to God in verse rather than in prose and with music, except that these things have a tendency to move our affections.'[74] So some of the psalms identify the musical instruments suitable for the songs: sometimes 'flutes',[75] sometimes 'strings'[76]

---

[73] Eph. 5:18–19.
[74] Cited by Kauflin, *Worship*, p. 98.
[75] Ps. 5:1.
[76] Pss 4:1; 6:1; 54:1; 55:1; 61:1; 67:1; 76:1; probably the harp, Ps. 33:3.

and in the case of Psalm 150, an entire orchestra and choir entering section by section. Each must have been chosen because of the mood it evoked. The scores have been lost, but not the idea that the songs were set appropriately. No-one today knows what a *shiggaion* was, but it evoked David's intention for Psalm 7, just as a *miktam*[77] or a *maskil*[78] did for others. Someone had to choose a setting that was right for 'The Memorial Offering'[79] or 'Do Not Destroy'.[80] There are fifty-five psalms which have instructions for the music director, telling him to choose an appropriate tune, to fit the intention of the writer.

- *Singing together helps us to teach and admonish one another in large numbers.* Even in a church of a hundred people I cannot have a hundred conversations to encourage every individual. But I can sing to a hundred or a thousand – and have a thousand people teach and admonish me!
- Finally, the way we sing, men and women, someone adding a descant, a group following the bass line, seems to be a small demonstration of the ideas of variety and unity which are biblically so strong. There is no biblical verse which supports this that I have found, but it appears to be such a natural concomitant of singing together that it is worth bearing in mind, at least. Martin Luther put it like this:

> When man's ability is whetted and polished to the extent that it becomes an art, then do we note with great surprise the great and perfect wisdom of God in music, which is, after all, His product and his gift; we marvel when we hear music in which one voice sings a simple melody, while three, four, or five voices play and trip lustily around the voice that sings its simple melody wonderfully and adorn this simple melody with artistic musical effects thus reminding us of a heavenly dance where all meet in a spirit of friendliness, caress and embrace ... A person who gives this some thought and yet does not regard it [music] as a marvellous creation of God must be a clodhopper indeed and does not deserve to be called a human being; he should be permitted to hear nothing but the braying of asses and the grunting of hogs.[81]

[77] Pss 16:1; 56:1; 57:1; 58:1; 59:1; 60:1.
[78] Pss 32:1; 42:1; 44:1; 45:1; 52:1; 53:1; 54:1; 55:1; 74:1; 78:1; 88:1; 89:1; 142:1.
[79] Ps. 70:1.
[80] Ps. 57:1.
[81] Cited by B. Kauflin, 'Words of Wonder: What happens when we sing?', in J. Piper and J. Taylor (eds.), *The Power of Words and the Wonder of God* (Wheaton: Crossway, 2009), pp. 121–122.

So the Colossians should sing *with thankfulness in [their] hearts to God*. The American humorist H. L. Mencken once observed that 'the chief contribution of Protestantism to human thought is its massive proof that God is a bore',[82] and Garland who quotes him, observes how ironic it is that Mencken wrote that observation in a book called *Minority Report*, when it is probably a majority view, even among Christians. So we need to change that. Exuberant, delighted praise of God is a good thing.

But even that is not quite what Paul has in mind, because the word *thankfulness* (or *gratitude*)[83] cannot be separated from its root idea of *grace*,[84] any more that the adjective *spiritual* can be severed from the person and work of the Holy Spirit.[85] *Grace* is another motif in Colossians, occurring in both the opening (1:2) and closing (4:6) verses of the central section, and is a different way of talking about the same gospel of Christ. Just as the theme of thankfulness was tied to the idea of finding our satisfaction in Christ, so the idea of gratitude is linked to the idea of standing in God's grace through Christ.

Of course that does not mean we do not thank God for his vast goodness towards us in so many ways, but that the centre of our singing must be *gratitude* for *grace*, and if we begin to see that the songs at church are veering off that centre, or we are becoming tired of the gospel, that is a warning light. But if we keep grace central, it is a delight to sing. Again, as Luther put it, 'Music is a beautiful and glorious gift of God and close to theology. I would not give up what little I know about music for something else which I might have in greater abundance.'[86]

3. When we are not at church (3:17)

Paul's closing concern is that their thankfulness should operate in all of life, *in word or deed*. Just as the terms for teaching and praise were designed to cover the entirety of what they do together, this phrase is designed to cover the entirety of what they do when they are apart. It is how they are to 'continue to live in [Christ]',[87] and

---

[82] Quoted in Garland, *Colossians, Philemon*, p. 238.

[83] NIV.

[84] Reinforced by an untranslatable definite article: *en tē chariti*.

[85] It seems safest to take *spiritual* in this way, meaning 'an authentic expression of the gospel which gives the Spirit', and so O'Brien argues that the adjective covers all three types of songs, not just *songs* (*Colossians, Philemon*, p. 210). It would be perverse (*pace* J. D. G. Dunn, *The Epistles to the Colossians and to Philemon*, NIGCT [Carlisle: Paternoster, 1996] p. 239) for it to mean singing in tongues, because Paul's focus here is on the understood content (cf. 1 Cor. 14:19).

[86] Cited in Kauflin, 'Words', p. 165.

[87] Col. 2:6, NIV.

is an overarching introduction to the all-encompassing instructions of the rest of the letter. The gratitude which flows from grace flows into the whole of everyday life.

Ephesians 4:1–6
10. The church's unity

How should all the Christians across the world relate to each other? Is that even a necessary goal? Given that neither Catholics nor Southern Baptists are part of the 'the World Council of Churches', is it truly a *World* Council?[1] Given what we have seen about the core idea of 'church' being 'a gathering', is it correct even to call this a Council of Churches? Is it not properly, a council of 349 denominations? Who is to arbitrate on the major fault lines that caused some of these denominations to come into existence? Who is to arbitrate when a minority disagree with documents that command widespread assent?[2]

Yet something in this instinctive pull towards one another is surely right. Christ has one bride, not 349: one body, one temple, one house. Jesus' final prayer was for unity:

> that they may be one, even as we are one . . . that they may all be one, just as you, Father, are in me, and I in you, that they also may be in us, that the world may believe that you have sent me . . . that they may be one even as we are one, I in them and you in me, that they may become perfectly one.[3]

Whatever one thinks of the World Council of Churches, the question remains: what counts as an answer to Jesus' prayer? Is it that experience of meeting new people, and discovering an instant bond of love, fellowship and family?

---

[1] Nor the Orthodox, among others.

[2] The report *Baptism, Eucharist and Ministry*, has been scathingly reviewed by the World Evangelical Fellowship, both in P. Schrotenboer (ed.), *Baptism, Eucharist and Ministry with an Evangelical Response* (Carlisle: Paternoster, 1992) and independently by D. J. Tidball, *Ministry by the Book: New Testament Patterns for Pastoral Leadership* (Nottingham: Apollos, 2008). I think their judgments are correct.

[3] John 17:11, 21–23.

To answer, we need to turn to the hinge of Ephesians. Chapters 1 – 3 describe God's magnificent grace in salvation, which Paul calls here, *the calling to which you have been called*, and chapters 4 – 6 will explore the implications for every aspect of a Christian's life as he calls us to *walk in manner worthy of the calling to which you have been called* (1). The word *therefore* indicates that division.[4] Our passage, 4:1–6 is a highly compact sentence in Greek, typical for this letter,[5] and it is the theme for what follows as Paul's central ideas of grace, truth, faith, love and hope are all developed.

Chapter 3 climaxed with Paul praising God, and seeing 'glory in the church and in Christ Jesus throughout all generations, forever and ever'.[6] But before we are carried away with that idea, he wants us to know what it will look like. It will not mean a life of unopposed church growth and triumph, because he, Paul, is a *prisoner in the Lord.*[7] That is a wonderful double-facing phrase, because even in his chains he knows he is also *in the* Lord, another theme in Ephesians.[8] He lives in one place, by the light of another reality. The word *Lord* is significant too, because Klyne Snodgrass notices 'Paul's tendency to use "Christ" in texts about salvation and "Lord" in texts about ethics'.[9]

The *calling to which we have been called* can mean only one thing in Ephesians. It is a reference to the gospel 'hope to which he has called you',[10] and it covers the future glory which God has planned for his people. It begins with being selected by the Father, saved by the Son, and sealed by the Spirit (1:1–13), but Paul's readers will have already discovered what spills out from that. Each of the four great sections which follow (1:15–23; 2:1–10; 2:11–13; 3:14–21) explain the logical consequence of that gospel and each applies it to relationships in the local church. That continues in the last three chapters too. *Walking* is the repeated metaphor (4:17; 5:2, 8, 15), and how we behave differently together is the centre of Paul's attention.

So we should remember that Paul began this section talking about 'glory in the church'. When we are called to be Christians, we are called into membership of God's church, and our walk must be worthy of our common life. He will discuss high truths, but basic

---

[4] H. Hoehner, *Ephesians* (Grand Rapids: Baker, 2002), p. 502, for what Paul referred back to.

[5] E.g. 1:3–14, 15–23; 2:1–7; 3:2–13, 14–19; 4:1–6, 11–16; 6:14–20.

[6] 3:21.

[7] ASV.

[8] Used twenty-six times in the letter, twenty of them in chs. 4 – 6.

[9] K. Snodgrass, *Ephesians*, NIVAC (Grand Rapids: Zondervan, 1996), p. 196.

[10] 1:18. See too Rom. 8:29–30; 11:29; 1 Cor. 1:26; 2 Thess. 1:11; 2 Tim. 1:9; Heb. 3:1; 2 Pet. 1:10.

and day-to-day ones too. Christian unity is something that involves each of us.

1. Christian unity is visible and real (4:1–3)

Paul gives flesh to what he means by *walk in a manner worthy* (1), with five challenging tests for our relationships in any local church, to push us beyond superficial niceness into a serious, but right, ordering of relationships.[11]

a. Walk with all humility (1)

Humility is not much admired in contemporary culture. Our sports-people, politicians and entrepreneurs are all expected to be thrusting and aggressive to achieve what should be done. Nor was it admired in Paul's day. One contemporary philosopher, Epictetus, said it should be first on the list of characteristics to be avoided.[12] So why is Paul so countercultural that he puts it first on the list to be adopted?[13]

Probably because pride is one of the most obvious ways to develop a fault line in a church. Pride will inevitably lead to disunity, because people build empires which they can lead to their own satisfaction, and they can find a place to stand uncorrected and unchallengeable. Pride is ugly, and as unlike the Lord Jesus on the cross as it is possible to imagine.

Humility starts with our view of ourselves. It is a challenge to the pastor who sees contemporaries from college asked to speak at big conferences, lead significant churches or write best-selling books. It is a challenge to the person who has been running the children's work for twenty years, when they are asked to stand down. But both those examples show that humility inevitably involves how we treat others. Do we avoid people, or cut them dead? Or are we genuinely glad that other people have an opportunity to serve?

b. Walk with all gentleness (2)

The second side of humility is how we relate to people who are perhaps less able or gifted than we are. The shy person who finds it hard to contribute in a Bible study. The older person who is slower in the coffee queue. *Gentleness* will mean taking time with them

[11] This list is constructed in four clauses. See, especially, A. T. Lincoln, *Ephesians*, WBC (Dallas: Word, 1990), p. 237.
[12] Hoehner, *Ephesians*, p. 506.
[13] See too Acts 20:19; Phil. 2:3; Col. 2:18, 23; 3:12; 1 Pet. 5:5.

165

and for them, listening before we speak. New Testament writers frequently draw *gentleness* to our attention, presumably because while it is a characteristic that should mark our lives, all too often it does not.[14]

c. Walk with patience (2)

Patience is just *gentleness* repeated, on every Sunday, at every Bible study. Pastors can easily start to hurry churches into new, different, or better programmes or events. How many times, they wonder, do they have to explain why we are doing such-and-such a thing? For how long do we have to carry that hurting person? And the answer is, every time, for as long as it takes. The early preacher, Chrysostom, said that this word meant 'to have a wide and big soul', which is a fine description.[15]

If this sounds demanding, remember that Paul is not describing the natural characteristics of some Christians, but the expected character of us all. It should be demanding, because it is not natural to sinful people. It takes work.

d. Bearing with one another in love (2)

Paul knows that because churches involve redeemed sinners, there will be bad days, snapped tempers and gossipy comments. Even long-standing Christians can be pushed too far and say something which is immediately regretted.

We need to remember that, and not expect each other to be perfect. It is difficult to remember in the middle of a tense discussion in a church committee at 11 pm after a hard day's work, but we need to encourage each other to keep on trying to live up to it. *Love* is much on Paul's mind, because this section will conclude with a second reference to it.

e. Eager to maintain the unity of the Spirit in the bond of peace (3)

Peace is also on his mind, appearing eight times in this letter (1:2; 2:14, 15, 17 (twice); 4:3; 6:15, 23). The tensions between the believers in the early church were, as we have seen, highly visible and ran the risk of dividing churches into different camps. Two words should make us pause before we tolerate similar splits.

---

[14] 1 Cor. 4:21; 2 Cor. 10:1; Gal. 5:23; 6:1; Col. 3:12; 1 Tim. 6:11; 2 Tim. 2:25; Titus 3:2; Jas 1:21; 3:13; 1 Pet. 3:16.
[15] Quoted by Snodgrass, *Ephesians*, p. 197.

(i) Eagerness

Paul wants us to be passionate about the relationships in our church. His language here is terse, as he encourages and warns us not to give in to the easy practice of forming hard little cliques. It is, of course, much easier to remain in a self-reinforcing world, to stay with the people whom you know and like, and not make time for others, but the fact that it is easy only redoubles Paul's energy. 'Go on,' he says, 'be the first to apologize. Be the first to speak. Be the first to offer to serve.'

(ii) Maintaining

The basis for taking that initiative to be first is not, as we might expect, because Christian unity is so desirable, or because otherwise non-Christians will think we are hypocrites. Instead, Christian unity is a gift *of the Spirit*, already in place, but needing to be maintained.

The fundamental disunity is between us and God. We were 'by nature children of wrath'.[16] But by the cross he overcame that, and our subsequent disunity as well:

> But God, being rich in mercy, because of the great love with which he loved *us*, even when *we* were dead in *our* trespasses, made *us* alive together with Christ – by grace you have been saved – and raised *us* up with him and seated *us* with him in the heavenly places in Christ Jesus.[17]

For Gentiles, it is even more wonderful. Here is our five-fold plight: '. . . at one time you Gentiles . . . were at that time (1) *separated* from Christ, (2) *alienated* from the commonwealth of Israel and (3) *strangers* to the covenants of promise, (4) having *no* hope and (5) *without* God in the world.'[18] Contrast that with what follows: 'But now in Christ Jesus you who once were far off have been brought near by the blood of Christ. For he himself is our peace, who has made us both one and has broken down in his flesh the dividing wall of hostility.'[19]

Once again, the magnificence of what God has done for us minimizes our petty squabbles, and because he has done that first, and overcome the primary obstacles, we cannot rest content with any secondary barriers in our churches.[20] We shall return to the issue

[16] Eph. 2:3.
[17] Eph. 2:3–6.
[18] Eph. 2:11–12.
[19] Eph. 2:13–14.
[20] See below for what this might mean about relationships and barriers between churches.

of relationships, but where Paul turns next is to look at the full magnificence of what God has achieved, which is not visible, but no less real.

2. Christian unity is invisible and real (4:4–6)

The other side of our visible unity that we must work to accomplish, is the invisible unity which God has already accomplished. Paul has a grand list of seven consequences, held together by two features. Most obviously, each of the seven is introduced by the word *one*. They are shared in common, by all Christians, everywhere.[21] More subtly, it looks as though he has given the list a Trinitarian shape, as he begins with the *body* being given life by the *Spirit*, then *faith* in the *Lord*, and concluding with the *Father*. And it is fundamentally the *Father* who is the basis for this, because he reigns supreme *over all* of us, works *through all* of us, and lives *in all* of us. Whatever God has done, this is his supreme masterpiece.

a. There is one body (4)

Elsewhere we have seen the local church described as the body of Christ,[22] but here Paul is looking at the church from the heavenly viewpoint. He describes all Christians, together, as *one body*. How can this be, since we are all individuals, and our congregations are so separate?

The answer lies in that repeated phrase: 'in Christ'. Since we are all 'in Christ', then that is where we are gathered together, or assembled. 'In Christ' is another way of describing the great heavenly assembly of which we are all members, those who are alive and those who are dead; the dead, after all, are 'in Christ' just as much as those who are alive.[23] All believers are in one heavenly assembly, gathered around and in Christ.

This is a challenge to some of our ways of thinking. For example, sometimes Christians distinguish between the visible church and the invisible one, as if the invisible (heavenly) one is for dead Christians, and the visible one for living ones. But if it is a fundamental meaning of 'church' that it assembles, where does this visible, earthly one meet? Or again, Christians occasionally talk about the heavenly church as if it were not seriously important, or real. Ethereal, perhaps, and a bit misty.

---

[21] Behind the translation *one* Paul uses three Greek words, but they function as synonyms.
[22] 1 Cor. 12:27.
[23] 1 Cor. 15:18.

How different to Paul! If being 'in Christ' describes being a Christian, and we are all 'in Christ' together, as *one body*, then nothing could be more central than that great heavenly assembly. And we need no earthly, visible counterpart to make up for the fact that we are not yet in the heavenly, invisible one, because we already are, permanently. Nor do we need to defer it as if we will only be part of one church when we come to the new heavens and the new earth. Every Christian on the planet is at this moment already taking part in the heavenly assembly.

That means we should perhaps stop using terms like 'universal church' or 'visible church', at least if by that we mean 'all Christians now living'. There is not a New Testament term which covers all living believers to the exclusion of the dead ones. There certainly is not one to describe a denomination. The principle stands: if it does not meet, it is not a church, however good it is. But that is not a demeaning idea because, as we have just seen, we are all in church all the time, anyway. It does mean, though, that even if all Christians everywhere settled all their theological differences, and resolved all their denominational differences, and formed a completely united movement, with a completely uniform pattern of services, with a completely harmonious leadership, that would still not be what Paul calls here *one body*. Because that one body is not something we have to work to achieve by denominational merger, but something that already exists, and will exist for ever.

b. There is one Spirit (4)

The Holy Spirit is the one who gathers us together, individually, into that heavenly assembly. The Holy Spirit has already been mentioned twice in Ephesians, each in a church context.

Paul had explained that 'we both' (by which he means, both Jews and Gentiles) 'have access in one Spirit to the Father' (2:18), which gives a further window into his *one*. Each of these elements will confront the lines along which Christians will be tempted to divide, modelled in the Jew/Gentile division. We have already seen from Galatians that some teachers were saying that the way for the Gentiles to be filled with the Spirit was to keep the Jewish Law, and others insisted that the appropriate pathway was to keep Jews and Gentiles separate. No, says Paul, let me ask you some questions.

Did you receive the Spirit by works of the Law, or by hearing with faith? . . . Does he who supplies the Spirit and does miracles among you do so by works of the law, or by hearing with faith

169

– just as Abraham believed God, and it was counted to him as righteousness?[24]

Faith, for both Jews and Gentiles, is the way we are put right with God, and receive the Spirit.

Second, Paul had explained that we are being 'built together into a dwelling place for God by the Spirit'.[25] Here is the necessary counterpart to the idea of the fully present, fully real heavenly assembly. There is a considerable amount of work for the Spirit to do, still. There will be a day when the heavenly assembly becomes the visible one, but until that day the Spirit is changing each of us to make us more like Christ – and here that means he is at work on our relationships, so that our earthly, visible ones better reflect the heavenly, invisible ones.

c. There is one hope (4)

We have already described *calling* in verse 1, but it is worth expanding on the one great *hope* that directs it. God will 'unite all things in [Christ], things in heaven and things on earth',[26] to display his victory in the heavenly realms (2:6–7) by the fact that we are united and reconciled in him (2:11–13). There is no greater, grander plan.[27]

Remember, too, that in our lost state we were without 'hope',[28] meaning not that we were all gloomy pessimists, but that we were ignorant of and outside that one great plan. But now there is a certainty for us that rises beyond mere optimism; as Harold Hoehner says, 'Hope for believers is not the world's "hope so" but the absolute certainty that God will deliver what he has promised'.[29]

d. There is one Lord (5)

The Lord Jesus Christ is yet another theme of Ephesians: every spiritual blessing is found in him (1:3), our faith is rightly placed in him (1:15) and we are becoming a new temple in him (2:21). He fills the cosmos and is the head of the church (1:22).

[24] Gal. 3:2, 5–6.
[25] Eph. 2:22.
[26] Eph. 1:10.
[27] This means that, in the context of Paul's logic here, God does not have one hope for Gentile Christians and another one for Jewish ones, or one hope for Israel and another for the church. There is only *one hope*.
[28] Eph. 2:12.
[29] Hoehner, *Ephesians*, p. 515.

He is, then, not just Lord of Israel, nor Lord of a Gentile church, but Lord of Jew and Gentile, for 'Gentiles are fellow heirs, members of the same body and partakers of the promise in Christ Jesus through the gospel'.[30]

Paul uses the language of lordship when issues particularly press on us in terms of obedience: 'Lord' has its mirror image in the words 'slave' or 'servant'. Many of the issues which currently cause rifts between Christians have their roots in issues of ethics, morality or behaviour. And it might be tempting to think that if we all profess to believe the same things, then perhaps we should not divide over behaving in different ways. But the word *Lord* encompasses both, for we cannot profess him in what we believe, and then disobey him in how we behave. To confess him as *Lord* means to obey him as *Lord*.

e. There is one faith (5)

There is a question to be resolved here, and it is not obvious which of two options we should take. The question is simple: by *faith*, does Paul mean something objective (as when we talk of 'the faith') or subjective (as when we talk of 'my faith')?

Both could fit neatly with Paul's argument, and both have senior scholars supporting them. Harold Hoehner argues for the 'subjective' translation. He notices that in 1:13 and 1:15 Paul has clearly identified their own faith as something he commends. So here, he suggests, we should understand Paul to mean something like 'their one faith in the one Lord'.[31] By contrast, both Ernest Best and Peter O'Brien prefer the 'objective' translation. They notice that Paul mentions *the faith* in 4:13, and that seems to fit with the way a number of other New Testament authors wrote.[32]

It is difficult to decide, precisely because each is true and could fit the question of unity, even with the focus on Jew/Gentile: they both have faith, and they both believe the same unifying gospel. I suspect there is most plausibility in the objective interpretation, because Paul is focusing more on the heavenly, objective realities than the personal subjective ones.

Whichever is correct, they both explain the reality that nearly all Christians have in common, which is discovering instant fellowship

---

[30] 3:6. See too 2:13–18.

[31] Hoehner, *Ephesians*, p. 517.

[32] Acts 6:7; Jude 3, 20; cf. 1 Tim. 3:9; 4:1, 6. See P. O'Brien *The Letter to the Ephesians*, PNTC (Grand Rapids: Eerdmans and Leicester: Apollos, 1999), p. 283; E. Best, *Ephesians*, ICC (London/New York: T&T Clark International, Continuum, 1998), pp. 368–369.

with believers they have never met before. Visiting a strange church, perhaps in a foreign country, even with a language barrier, we discover the common element of believing in a common Lord. And this is no intellectual exercise, but a heart-to-heart immediacy of relationships that is hard to put into words, but is every Christian's birthright.

f. There is one baptism (5)

This is the only reference to baptism in Ephesians, and it makes most sense to take it straightforwardly.[33] Frustratingly, though, Paul does not give us details of his practice of baptism, other than the obvious implication that he assumed that a church in one place would automatically accept as valid the baptism of someone who was baptized in another.

There are good resources exploring the two main positions which claim to be biblically serious, and we shall not be able to resolve it here.[34] Instead, I think the challenge from Paul is that while there may be differences over how much weight we give to arguments from Christian tradition, there is a place to respect a different view if it is making a serious claim to be biblical. Any discussion which divides senior evangelical leaders must be one we approach with seriousness and scholarship, and we must take care to evaluate it properly, allowing for someone else's viewpoint. This is a matter, we should recall, which demarcated Calvin from Spurgeon, and John Stott from Billy Graham. It is not one we should treat lightly, but as Klyne Snodgrass, himself a Baptist commentator puts it, 'we do not have to agree on the theology of baptism to accept each other'.[35]

g. There is one God and Father of all (6)

The great Jewish prayer, the *Shema*, derives its name from its first word in Deuteronomy 6:4: 'Hear, O Israel: The LORD our God, the LORD is one'; that prayer both demarcates Israel and makes her the particular object of God's blessing. How even more wonderful

---

[33] Hoehner argues for baptism into Christ's death, which avoids the difficulty of accepting one another's different modes of baptism (*Ephesians*, p. 518). Some scholars suggest 4:22–24 or 5:26 might allude to baptism.

[34] See D. Bridge and D. Phypers, *The Water that Divides* (rev. ed., Ross-shire: Christian Focus, 2008) or, with a wider range of views, P. E. Engle and J. H. Armstrong (eds.), *Understanding Four Views on Baptism* (Grand Rapids: Zondervan, 2007).

[35] Snodgrass, *Ephesians*, p. 211.

is the transformation here, for this *one God* is revealed to be also *the Father of all*, both Jews and Gentiles who believe.[36]

This *one God*, then, exercises sovereign rule (he is *over all*), using his people (he works *through all*) and knowing them individually (he is *in all*). If there were any doubt that God has decisively broken down the Jew/Gentile barrier, this verse removes it. There is no exception to God's work among his people: *all . . . all . . . all . . .*

3. Real Christian unity

The twentieth century saw three major changes in the Christian landscape. The first was a growing awareness of the truly global nature of Christianity, numerous and growing, with a vibrant leadership emerging from what we now call the global south. The centre of energy shifted from Europe and North America, to Africa, South America, India and Asia. That was already foreseen clearly in the great World Missionary Conference held in Edinburgh in 1910. It was the climax of a series of international missionary meetings, but here soundings were taken of the condition across the world, and concrete plans made for, in the words of one leader, John R. Mott, 'the evangelization of the world in this generation'.[37] The presence of indigenous leadership from churches around the world meant that the global south had to be taken seriously for the future of the work of mission. This was enormously significant, even though the attendees could not foresee two world wars, the end of empires or the political upheavals in Russia or China.

The Edinburgh conference also saw the need for cooperation in the work of mission, and it began a series of conferences which eventually produced the World Council of Churches. This is evidence of the second great change in the landscape: the twentieth century was one of ecumenical dialogue. Even the monolithic Roman Catholic Church shifted in its views, and the Second Vatican Council which met between 1962 and 1965 produced an understanding of other denominations which would have been unthinkable fifty years before. This has been reflected at a local level too, with congregations meeting across denominational boundaries in times of prayer

---

[36] Although the translation *all things* is equally possible, reading the word as masculine rather than neuter seems to fit with the context slightly better. For the title, *God and Father*, see Rom. 15:6; 1 Cor. 15:24; 2 Cor. 1:3; 11:31; Gal. 1:4; Eph. 1:3; 5:20; Phil. 4:20; 1 Thess. 1:3; 3:11, 13; Jas 1:27; 1 Pet. 1:3; Rev. 1:6.

[37] A key phrase throughout his ministry, and the title of his *The Evangelization of the World in This Generation* (New York: Student Volunteer Movement for Foreign Missions, 1901).

or Bible study, using shared discussion documents and common liturgies.[38]

The third major change runs in an apparently different direction to the second, but it is actually connected. That is that the average church member identifies more lightly with denominational allegiances than was the case a century ago. The rise of large and influential congregations which either have no denominational identity, or sit so loosely to them that they are not recognized as such, means that many churches and pastors look more to conferences and speakers for leadership and resources than they do to the denominations, and they find more fellowship between like-minded believers across denominational lines, than they do with people in the same denomination but with different beliefs.

These three interplay in different ways, but together they mean that we are living in an unprecedented era of both formal and informal Christian thinking about Christian unity. This should not surprise us given what we have seen in Ephesians, because what we fundamentally hold in common is the greatness of our salvation, and our experience of the transforming grace of the gospel. Travel and technology have combined for many of us to produce the experience of meeting new Christians from other cultures and discovering that our differences over food and clothing are nothing compared to our unity in Christ. That is always very exciting.

We shall need to consider the necessary boundaries to this.[39] For instance, how do we relate to someone who claims an identical experience of grace, but yet belongs to a denomination or congregation which endorses error? Does their experience outweigh the theology, or does the theology call into question the apparent experience? Denominations are increasingly aware of tensions caused by having someone who claims to be a leader in authority, but whose doctrine or lifestyle is in error. Does their theology outweigh their position, or does their position still mean faithful believers are accountable to them? How do we approach an issue from the past, like the Reformation, which split the Lutheran and Reformed families from Catholicism? Are we required to hold to sixteenth-century positions, because they are biblically mandated, or are we required to find different formulations on which we can all agree, in the face of rising secularism? Or, to take a different example, one set of differences between the Orthodox and Western groups rests on the position of just one word in the creed: the Latin word *filioque*, meaning 'and from the Son'. Western creeds affirm that the Holy

---

[38] On developments following Edinburgh 1910, see the relevant articles in S. Moreau, *Evangelical Dictionary of World Missions* (Grand Rapids: Baker, 2000).

[39] See ch. 14.

Spirit 'proceeds from the Father and the Son', the Orthodox, that he 'proceeds from the Father', leading to a final separation between the two in 1054 when Cardinal Humbert, the papal legate, laid the document of excommunication against Patriarch Cerularius on the altar of the cathedral in Istanbul. It was 900 years before Pope John XXIII and Patriarch Athenagoras asked each other's forgiveness at Vatican II. Does it matter that we still have two different creeds? Who should arbitrate between them?

Unity, then, is a never-ending challenge. On occasions, like a great Christian celebration, we know it, we are sure we have experienced it, and we have little time for theological niceties. On other occasions, like an ecumenical Bible study, we fall apart at the first discussion, over the roles of bishops or elders. Or the pope. Which is the better route?

Putting it all together: Part one
How churches relate to each other

So far in successive chapters we have seen many different truths about how churches relate to each other, and at this point it is useful to pause and simplify. There are basically four aspects to our relationships, which we can diagram like this:

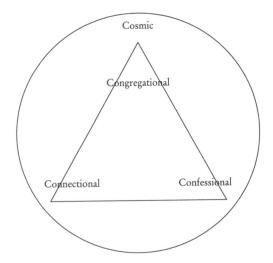

The *cosmic* aspect refers to the great heavenly assembly in Christ of which all believers are permanently members, and which one day will be as visibly real as it is now spiritually real. For the reasons we have seen in this chapter, I have tried to resist calling this the 'invisible' or 'heavenly' church, because can both of those sound unreal and lightweight, which as we saw in chapter 1 is the direct opposite of Christ's reign. It is sometimes commented that 'the Church is one, holy, catholic and apostolic – and is nowhere to be found', but that is to trivialize the profound foundational magnificence of this cosmic church where all those marks are fully true. One of the tasks of the subsequent expositions will be to consider such issues, so that even if we do not produce agreement, we are at least aware of the problems. The next six chapters will consider four overlapping truths that are affirmed in the Nicene Creed: that the church is one (both in our heavenly unity and in its local expression), holy (both declared righteous by God and living that out with members who sin, in a sinful world), catholic (both diverse and with boundaries) and apostolic (both built on the apostles' work and copying their pattern of ministry). All these are based on Paul's insight that Christian unity is fundamentally something we have already been given. Every Christian is already united to every other Christian, 'in Christ'.

The *congregational* aspect shows that Christ's cosmic victory erupts in visible expression in the local meetings of Christians. Where 'heavenly' is the opposite of 'earthly', and 'invisible' is the opposite of 'visible', something is in either one or the other. But Christians have dual citizenship, as Paul described it to the Philippians: 'To all the saints *in* Christ Jesus who are *in* Philippi.'[1] This is where we enjoy and obey the fifty-five or so 'one-another' commands of the New Testament.

The *connectional* aspect is where we pay attention to the relationships between congregations, and to organizations that work alongside us (publishers, missionary organizations, seminaries) to resource us. The latter we call 'para-church'; the former we might call 'intra-church', because structures like denominations and accountability are not separate from the congregations, but should be like a living web of service and love.

The *confessional* aspect addresses the issues of our foundational beliefs, guards the gospel and protects us from false teachers. The three great Creeds (Apostolic, Nicene and Athanasian) are shared by all Christians, as are the councils which produced them. The Reformers wisely added both confessions and catechisms to teach truth and refute error. These are public, shared truths.

Simply put like that, it is obvious that every healthy church will pay attention to all four aspects. But it is also obvious that a church can pay disproportionate emphasis to one particular aspect.

An over-emphasis on the cosmic aspect can produce great beauty and organizational unity as we seek to echo the heavenly assembly, but it frequently produces a lack of contemporary place and time. Churches that place great emphasis on what has been said and done

---

[1] Phil. 1:1, HCSB. Neither ESV nor NIV catches the repeated *in* (*en*) in translation.

everywhere, always, by everyone[2] tend to lose sight of what must be done here, now, and by us, and many of the great historically rooted denominations (Roman Catholic, and both the Orthodox and Anglican families) are sluggish when it comes to obedient reform.

An over-emphasis of the congregational aspect produces an unhealthy self-obsession. Our focus on loving each other leads us to be blind to the needs of those outside the church circle, or even to other believers elsewhere. Our study in 2 Corinthians should correct that, but as Paul reminded the Galatians, 'let us do good to everyone, and especially' (note – not 'only') 'to those who are of the household of faith'.[3] At various points I have been critical of some elements in self-styled 'post-Christendom', 'emerging' or 'missional' church practice, but they rightly force us to address our sinful narcissism, and to embrace those who are sometimes called 'the least, the last and the lost'.

The confessional aspect is critical, because the creeds and confessions fought necessary battles, most if not all of which are still with us today, and continue to need to be resisted.[4] But it contains a double danger. One the one hand, we can become so fascinated with our own logical processes, and so unable to correct our theological systems from Scripture, that we continually separate from true Christians. Our sermons and conversations become marked by divisiveness, and that is called schism.[5] But on the other, we can become antiquarians, fighting the battles of yesterday with increasing clarity, yet dangerously naïve before contemporary error. Neither the creeds nor the confessions address, for instance, the definition of marriage, which is why some call us 'schismatic' if we insist on the traditional view. If the creeds do not mention the issue, they say, it must be a secondary matter over which it is sinful to divide – and that is an argument I have heard both from campaigning liberals (who want to force the issue through) and troubled orthodox (who see the issue's importance, but fear to break creedal unity). But the Reformers faced exactly this issue, because both sides agreed on the creeds but disagreed over justification, and as one reformer argued, 'That which they call Schism, we know to be our reasonable service unto God.'[6]

[2] The phrase is attributed to a fifth century theologian, Vincent of Lerins.

[3] Gal. 6:10.

[4] In general, see C. FitzSimmons Allison, *The Cruelty of Heresy* (London: SPCK, 1994); on recent theology of the Trinity, see Stephen Holmes, *The Holy Trinity* (Milton Keynes: Paternoster, 2011).

[5] See for instance the alarming diagrams of the history of Presbyterianism in Scotland and in the United States, in John H. Leith, *Introduction to the Reformed Tradition* (Atlanta: John Knox Press, 1977 and Edinburgh: The Saint Andrew Press: 1978).

[6] Richard Hooker, 'Two Sermons Upon a Part of St. Jude', in *The Works of Richard Hooker*, vol. 3 (Oxford: Clarendon, 1793), p. 559.

Finally, an over-emphasis on the connectional aspect means that we give automatic deference to structures, even when they hinder health and promote error. It is often said that Evangelicals have no ecclesiology, and I have discovered that often what is meant by that is that we have no theology of our unique denominational structures. But that is not necessarily a lack of an 'ecclesiology'. If I am asked for a theology of my being an Anglican which differentiates me from my colleagues who are Baptist, Presbyterian or belong to other free churches, then I can reply – if am being asked how my understanding of biblical oversight differs from theirs. But if I am being asked to relate to them more distantly than to an episcopalian who is teaching error then I must decline. I cannot have an ecclesiology which privileges an Anglican heretic over a Presbyterian evangelical; that would not be ecclesiology but 'denomination-ology' – and arguably 'denomination-olatry'.

How do we relate these four aspects to each other? I would suggest that any attempt to achieve balance between them is probably futile, and also unwise. Achieving balance implies being static; it does not ask us to address the relationships between them, nor the priorities. Instead, I think we to say that to *define* 'church' we must start with the first two, the cosmic and the congregational, related as cause and effect, permanent and temporary expressions of the victory of Christ. Between them they exhaust the New Testament uses of the word 'church'.[7] But to *explain and experience* 'church' we need the other two elements as well, to inform and guide us. Every church probably heads to one corner of the triangle, and needs to pay close attention to the necessary content of the other two. Where would you put your church on the diagram?

[7] On the one possible exception, Acts 9:31, see ch. 16, where I suggest it refers to the now-scattered Jerusalem assembly rather than being a term for all the Christians on the planet.

Ephesians 4:7–16
11. The church's maturity

The church of Agia Sophia, 'Holy Wisdom', dominates Istanbul. Today a museum, and for five hundred years a mosque, it was built by the Emperor Justinian in the 530s. For a millennium it was the largest cathedral in the world. Even today it is breathtaking, despite being ransacked and defaced over many centuries, but in its time it was unequalled. Extravagant chambers surrounded the great central nave, and soaring high above in the great dome was a mosaic of *Christ Pantokrator*, Christ the Ruler of all; a rich, deep, wise face, constructed from hundreds of thousands of pieces of precious stones and metals.

I love the image of a mosaic for a church. Beautiful, but made from broken pieces, each one contributing to something grand and coherent – the image of Christ.

Agia Sophia had a smaller, but still magnificent predecessor. There, week after week, John Chrysostom opened and explained the Bible before vast crowds, a brave preacher who was twice exiled for his message. He was nicknamed Chrysostom, 'Golden-Mouth', because of that preaching. And the people of Constantinople, from street-sellers to courtiers, drawn from across the empire, jammed that building to hear God's word. Under the stone mosaic of *Christ Pantokrator* there assembled a living mosaic of God's people, just as in Ephesians.

So far, Paul has stressed unity. All Christians share the same calling, and the same responsibility, to 'walk in a manner worthy of the calling'.[1] Now he shows the foundational gifts Christ gives every church, and how they produce both unity and maturity (13).[2]

---

[1] Eph. 4:1.

[2] My interpretation challenges, in particular, M. Frost and A. Hirsch, *The Shaping of Things to Come: Innovation and Mission for the 21st-Century Church* (Peabody: Henderson/Erina/Strand, 2003). Rather than dialogue throughout, I will first explore the passage and then summarize the contrasts. Readers not interested in the debate can pass over 'Additional Note: APEPT', although the diagram might be helpful.

1. The victorious Christ gives gifts to the church (4:7–10)

The risen, *ascended*, and victorious Christ, showers his church with *gifts*. The picture comes from Psalm 68, from the victorious procession of the king of Israel, and here it is brought right up to date for Christians, as the one Lord gives *each one of us* the *gift* of *grace*.[3]

By *grace* Paul could mean the gospel, but several reasons suggest he means something else. First, he has moved from talking about 'all' to *each one*, a contrast he indicates by the word *but*. Secondly, he describes his apostolic role using this same *grace/gift* language:

> Of this gospel I was made a minister according to the *gift* of God's *grace*, which was *given* me by the working of his power. To me, though I am the very least of all the saints, this *grace* was *given*, to preach to the Gentiles the unsearchable riches of Christ.[4]

More carefully, when *grace* means 'the gospel', Paul gives it a definite article; without it he means a particular 'gifting' or enablement.[5] So here, *grace* and *gift* is used of each individual's ministry rather than every Christian's common experience.

Eternal life, the Holy Spirit, singleness and marriage, people, ministries and activities are all described in various passages as Christ's kind *gifts* to his people.[6] They are certainly not at all unusual – in fact some of them are quite mundane, and for at least two of them (singleness and marriage) everybody experiences at least one, and most, both.[7] So initially here, Paul talks about his apostolic ministry, but then he broadens it.

2. Some gifts release the other gifts (4:11–13)

a. Apostles (11)

The first of four ministries Christ has *given* are the *apostles*. The word meant, 'someone who is sent', so couriers between churches were 'apostles', although to prevent misunderstanding most modern

---

[3] Paul's citation is difficult, because Ps. 68:18 says the king *received* gifts, not *gave* them. H. Hoehner, *Ephesians* (Grand Rapids: Baker, 2002), p. 528, suggests Paul summarizes Ps. 68, where God is repeatedly described as generous.

[4] Eph. 3:7–8.

[5] See Hoehner, *Ephesians*, p. 522. *Grace* and *gift* overlap with *charisma* (1 Cor. 12:4, 9, 28, 30–31). Compare 1 Cor. 1:4, 7 and Rom. 12:6.

[6] Rom. 6:23; 1 Cor. 7:7; 12:28; Eph. 3:7–8; 4:8, 11. See K. Snodgrass, *Ephesians*, NIVAC (Grand Rapids: Zondervan, 1996), pp. 212–213.

[7] The gift passages are illustrative, not checklists (Rom. 12:6–8; 1 Cor. 12:8–10, 28–30; Eph. 4:11–12, 1 Pet. 4:10–11. See ch. 13.

translations use a blander title, like *messengers*.[8] That was because a second group, commissioned by the Lord Jesus as his couriers, have a unique status for the church.[9] This group, including Paul, not only met the risen Jesus and heard him (over five hundred people did that), and were taught by him (a number of men and women came in that category), but were commissioned by him, as his authorized teachers and church pioneers. One man, Joseph Justus, held every single qualification for being in this second group, save the critical one: Jesus did not choose him.[10] Distinguishing these groups is helpful, because we can see why Androcinus and Junia could be *outstanding among the apostles* without claiming they were two of the twelve.[11] The twelve were Jesus' irreplaceable representatives and ambassadors.[12]

b. Prophets (11)

Partnering the *apostles* are the *prophets*. Possibly, Paul means Old Testament prophets, which would give a neat balance between the Old Testament and the New, but more likely he means people with the authority to speak for God. The early church had a number of such prophets[13] who explained the present and foretold the future.[14]

This is an issue of tension today. Some argue that just as the *apostles* were a once-for-all gift to the church, so were the *prophets* – we should not expect any continuance. Others argue precisely the reverse, that since we have people who have the gift of prophecy today, so we should respect contemporary leaders as apostles.

Paul had already said in 2:20, the church is 'built on the foundation of the apostles and the prophets, Christ Jesus himself being the cornerstone', which would imply that they are irreplaceable. A building only needs its foundation laid once.[15] Perhaps it helps to remember that Paul has described the people, not their abilities, as gifts: *he gave the apostles, the prophets*, etc. If we separate those two

---

[8] 2 Cor. 8:23: *apostoloi ekklēsiōn* ('apostle of the churches'); Phil 2:25: Epaphroditus is *hymōn . . . apostolon* ('your apostle').

[9] Acts 1:21–22; Gal. 1:17 – 2:10; 1 Cor. 9:1.

[10] Acts 1:21–26.

[11] Rom. 16:7. Translating this verse is notoriously difficult, as the Greek construction seems to have only one known contemporary parallel (Psalms of Solomon 2:6), which by itself tentatively confirms ESV's 'well known to the apostles'. The consensus is that Paul means 'among', which still leaves open the question of whether Junia was an apostle, or just well-known among them. It is almost certain that the name Junia is feminine.

[12] On apostolic succession, see ch. 12.

[13] Acts 13:1; 15:32; 21:9; 1 Cor. 14:23.

[14] Present: 1 Cor. 14:24; future: Acts 11:27–28.

[15] Cf. 1 Cor. 12:28.

ideas we could say that, although we might have people who have similar supernatural abilities to those two groups, and we might say they are 'apostolic' or 'prophetic', it would be confusing to call them 'apostles' or 'prophets'. One early but sensible idea is that *evangelists* and *pastors and teachers* are the contemporary expression of the irreplaceable foundation gifts of the *apostles* and the *prophets*.[16]

c. Evangelists (11)

Evangelists are hard to pin down. Philip was called 'the evangelist', and Timothy was told to 'do the work of an evangelist', but that is the limit of references.[17] It is not unique in that limited range, because 'overseer' and 'elder' are mentioned only three times, 'deacon' twice and 'pastor' once (in this passage) – even 'Christian' only occurs twice. But those are usually explained by their context.

The writings of the early church give fascinating insights into these people's work, which is clearly recognizable today. Origen, in the third century, wrote, 'Christians do all in their power to spread the faith all over the world. Some of them accordingly make it the business of their life to wander not only from city to city but town to town and village to village in order to win fresh converts for the Lord.' And the historian Eusebius wrote of the second century, 'There were still many evangelists of the word eager to use their inspired zeal after the example of the apostles for the increase and building up of the divine word.'[18]

Yet little of that is in the biblical data. Philip owned a house, and Timothy was settled in Ephesus, so neither was itinerant.[19] Paul uses 'evangelism' for his enthusiasm to preach to Christians, as well as non-Christians.[20] And here, Paul says that the role of the *evangelists* is *to equip the saints*.

Perhaps we have adopted too narrow a definition. Peter O'Brien thinks they had 'a range of activities from primary evangelism and the planting of churches to the ongoing building up of Christians and the establishment of settled congregations', covering 'both intensive and extensive growth'. Harold Hoehner agrees that they 'worked inside and outside the church'.[21]

---

[16] See Eusebius, *Ecclesiastical History* 3.37.1–4; 5.10.2–4.
[17] Acts 21:8; 2 Tim. 4:5.
[18] Origen, *Contra Celsus* 3.9. Eusebius, *Ecclesiastical History* 5.10.2. See M. Green, *Evangelism in the Early Church* (rev. ed., Eastbourne: Kingsway, 2003), p. 237.
[19] Acts 21:8; 1 Tim. 1:3.
[20] Rom. 1:14–15 uses the verb *euangelizō*.
[21] P. T. O'Brien, *The Letter to the Ephesians*, PNTC (Grand Rapids: Eerdmans/ Leicester: Apollos, 1999), p. 299; Hoehner, *Ephesians*, p. 542.

Mark Mittelberg has suggested that we should adopt a range of different 'styles' of evangelist, both for training and encouraging (the inward focus), and explaining to outsiders.[22]

- *Bold.* I know someone who regularly stands in Speakers' Corner in Hyde Park in London, and engages Muslims, not only answering questions but challenging their assumptions, and provoking a strong response. It is not for everyone, but we should honour our bold friends.
- *Invitational.* Like most pastors, I regularly arranged events for people to invite their friends to, and gradually noticed that some people were especially effective in bringing guests. In fact, I thought I should have given almost all the tickets to just one person! But that person would be hopeless in Hyde Park.
- *Intellectual.* These people love interrogating the latest secular best-seller. Throw them into any book or film club and the conversations always turn to Jesus.
- *Befriender.* I know someone with an astonishing ability with non-Christians during sad times, who over many years gently turns those friendships into gospel opportunities. This is slow evangelism.
- *Testimonial.* Christians with a clear account of how God has worked in their lives, either at their conversion or subsequently, are 'shop windows' for the gospel. We need to be cautious, though. One speaker stopped giving his testimony because he found that people were more interested in him and his drug-gang past, than in Christ. And many Christians testify to God's faithfulness with no drama and in the midst of tragedy; those are testimonies too.
- *Personal.* Some Christians are at their best talking one-to-one over a cup of coffee or a golf ball. Help them to see that although they could never get their neighbours to a big meeting, they have conversational opportunities that big-name speakers would never have.
- *Explainer.* These people explain the gospel so clearly that non-Christians frequently become believers. We most naturally call these 'evangelists', although that narrows the idea too much. God uses these people significantly, and I have been humbled to listen to one such speaker, thought 'Well, that wasn't very special; I could have done that', and was then awed as non-Christians laid their lives before Christ.

[22] M. Mittelberg, *Building a Contagious Church: Revolutionizing the Way We View and Do Evangelism* (Grand Rapids: Zondervan, 2000).

We can extend Mittelberg's list (he does not pretend it is exhaustive):

- *Trainer.* Paul said that evangelists *equip the saints*; we can identify people with the gifts and passion to encourage others to do the work of evangelism. They are evangelists for evangelism!
- *Planter.* Since a clear element in Paul's understanding of his apostleship was that he planted and established churches,[23] we need to identify those who will start churches, either by themselves or with a team, to reach new communities and cultures with the gospel.

Because the biblical data is so scarce, it is pointless to ask whether this is what Paul had in mind, because we cannot know. Certainly, this is a creative range of ways of seeing the role, applicable to many more people than just those who are comfortable in front of a crowd.

d. Pastors and teachers (11)

In English this looks like two groups, and common sense seems to agree. An austere but clever person is said to be 'a good teacher, but not a great pastor', or people say they put up with thin and opaque sermons, because 'he is such a lovely pastor in a crisis'.

Neither of those comments match what Paul means. The way he has structured the list means that these are two words describing one group of people: the 'pastor-teachers'.[24]

This is the only place where Christian leaders are called *pastors*, or 'shepherds' as the word is more literally, although there are occasions where a church is described as a 'flock', and the task is 'to shepherd' them.[25] It has of a rich biblical background, because Israel was described as a 'flock' and God as their 'shepherd'.[26] By extension, their kings and leaders were called 'shepherds', from the tough men who could kill bears and lions with one stone shot from a sling. They needed to be tough, because their flocks needed protection as well as leadership, and good local knowledge of where water and grass were to be found. It should be no surprise that the young David was able

---

[23] See ch. 16.

[24] The Greek runs: *men* [apostles] *de* [prophets] *de* [evangelists] *de* [pastors-and-teachers, linked by *kai*]. Most modern commentators think they are a subset: 'all pastors are to be teachers, but not all teachers are to be pastors' (D. B. Wallace, *Greek Grammar beyond the Basics* (Grand Rapids: Zondervan, 1996), p. 284. But we know nothing else about the function of a 'shepherd', and plenty about a 'teacher'. What would a shepherd who is not a teacher do? I think it is a hyphenated description.

[25] John 21:16; Acts 20:28–29; 1 Pet. 5:2–3.

[26] Gen. 49:24; Pss 23:1; 28:9; 80:1.

to kill Goliath – the masked youths in the Middle East who fire stones at tanks from their slings can do the same. It was entirely natural that the military and political leaders were called 'shepherds'.[27]

When Jesus was described as a *shepherd*, we should see it as another way of describing his lordship, or divine monarchy. Israel's leader-shepherds had been a self-serving failure, so God had promised he would replace them himself.[28] So when Jesus described himself as *the good shepherd* he was claiming to be God, replacing the evil shepherds who preceded him.[29]

Christian leaders can never have that authority, for Jesus will never lay it down. He remains today, 'the great Shepherd' and 'the chief Shepherd'.[30]

Two consequences flow from that for those of us who call ourselves 'shepherds'. First, ours is not an ultimate authority. We are under the authority of 'the great Shepherd', and it is his flock, not ours, that we look after temporarily. Second, being a *pastor* is not a light duty, ideally suited for the religious introvert who cannot cut it in a tough, secular workplace. The flock will be threatened, externally and internally, by 'fierce wolves, not sparing the flock', and it is our job to protect it at whatever price.[31]

How are we to lead, feed, guard and protect this flock? By the other word that accompanies 'shepherd' – by being proper *teachers*. Once again, we must allow the Bible to determine the meaning of its words.

Teaching is not the mere sharing of information. *Teaching* means opening up and applying Scripture to the hearts and lives of the individuals and church under our care.[32] This is such an important issue, and so often repeated as a necessary part of the role of the Christian leader, that we shall revisit it when we consider the qualities needed in such a person.[33] But Jesus warns those of us who have this task not to flinch from carrying it out. That person who 'is a hired hand and not a shepherd, who does not own the sheep, sees the wolf coming and leaves the sheep and flees, and the wolf snatches them and scatters them. He flees because he is a hired hand and cares nothing for the sheep'.[34]

Perhaps we can now see the real danger of letting these two words float independently of each other. There is a rich biblical language

---

[27] 2 Sam. 5:2; Ps. 78:71; Jer. 23:2; Ezek. 34:2.
[28] Ezek. 34.
[29] John 10:11–18; cf. Matt. 18:12–14; Luke 15:3–7.
[30] Heb. 13:20; 1 Pet. 5:4; cf. 1 Pet. 2:25.
[31] Acts 20:29.
[32] Acts 15:35; 18:11, 25; Rom. 2:20–21; Col. 3:16; Heb. 5:12.
[33] Ch. 11.
[34] John 10:12–13.

for the need for leaders to be kindly, generous and peacemakers, but the word 'shepherd' is not part of it. There is probably a good place for being efficient administrators, but, again, that is not being a 'shepherd'. Jesus was not claiming to be 'the good administrator'. How foolish to think that we are only being pastored when someone is being nice or organized. No, it is the real pastors who discern danger, confront it and deal with it. And how foolish of those of us who are teachers to act as if all that mattered were decent handouts, flashy graphics or numbers of commentaries consulted. Every time we preach we engage in spiritual battle for the flock, and we follow 'the good shepherd' who 'lays down his life for the sheep'.[35]

There is one more feature about these four roles – apostle, prophet, evangelist, and shepherd-teacher – to notice. They all speak. These are 'word gifts' and that underlines the high responsibility that the New Testament gave to these positions. If the church is built on the foundation of the *apostles and the prophets*, and if the *evangelists and shepherds and teachers* are supposed to build on, not outside, that foundation, then it is critically important that they do their word-work sensibly, responsibly and knowledgeably. Many churches place other duties on their pastor's shoulders instead, and many pastors put different tasks in their diaries. The work of being the church's 'shepherd-teachers' is too serious to allow that to happen.

e. The saints (12)

Saints is another term for all God's people, meaning holy, belonging uniquely to him. It certainly does not imply a special few. So Paul now explains how those with speaking gifts release the *work* of all of us.[36]

(i) Equipping the saints

The fundamental *work* of 'evangelists and shepherd-teachers' is to *equip the saints*. The word translated *equip* only appears here in the New Testament, although the verb appears often and has a wide range of meanings: repairing, training, preparing or restoring. There

[35] John 10:11.
[36] This is a complex passage to translate. Lincoln, for instance, argues all these tasks are the work of the gifted people (A. T. Lincoln, *Ephesians*, WBC [Dallas: Word, 1990], p. 253). My understanding is that the first clause (12a, beginning *pros*) describes the work of the gifted ones, and the four that follow (12b, 12c, 13a and 13c, each beginning *eis*) describe parallel results among God's people. The context is God's people as whole.

is no obvious problem being sorted out among Paul's first readers, so although it can be used for restoring a fallen Christian[37] we should probably leave those ideas to one side. We are to help people whose lives are hurting, but that is not quite what Paul means here either.

Rather, Paul has four tasks for the members of the local church to perform, and they can only do them if they are taught properly from God's word.

(ii) Evangelists and shepherd-teachers equip the saints for ministry

The first task is *ministry*. Elsewhere the Bible can use this word for the unique role of the shepherd-teacher[38] but here the whole people of God is in view: we all, without exception, have a role to play in the church, as we serve, or minister to, each other. It was a word for waiting at table, or distributing money,[39] and more generally for a servant-hearted attitude that should characterize us all. As someone said to me recently, church is not like a restaurant where most of us consume and only a few serve; it is like a family meal, where everyone is expected to play their part.

To be precise, Paul writes in the singular here, *the work of ministry* (not, as in NIV, *works of service*), so this is one task that is required of all of us. It would be very neat if we could line up the teaching role of the pastor with this work of ministry and say that the shepherd-teacher's role is to encourage everybody in their own word-teaching ministry. That is a general truth, of course, because we are told to teach each other,[40] and presumably there should be a particular focus on equipping those with the gift of teaching.[41] But it is not obvious that this particular verse teaches that general truth. The verse that began this section, as Paul turned his argument, was that *grace was given to each one of us according to the measure of Christ's gift* (7). That not only moves the argument from talking about 'all' to *each*, but it seems to imply differences between Christians, and would make a similar argument to Romans 12 or 1 Corinthians 12 – 14 as they talk about the church as 'the body of Christ' and the need for each of us to play our different role. That is where Paul heads in this section too: the goal is *the whole body, joined and held together by every joint with which it is equipped, when each part is working properly* (16). There is such a wide range of Christian tasks and abilities in the New Testament, all of which have to be exercised with a servant spirit, that it makes most sense

[37] Gal. 6:1.
[38] 2 Tim. 4:5.
[39] Tables: Luke 10:40; Acts 6:1. Money: Romans 15:31; 2 Cor. 8:4.
[40] 1 Cor. 14:26; Col. 3:16.
[41] Acts 13:1; 1 Cor. 12:28; Gal. 6:6; 1 Tim 5:17.

here, to take *the work of ministry* in a broad way, to mean something like 'the work of serving each other'.

There is still, perhaps, no more difficult role for 'evangelists and shepherd-teachers' to adopt. Something about the function we take on, and the position we have as those who open God's word for others can give us the mantle of being the guru, the one with all the answers, which encourages us to think we are something special, and everybody else to think they are mere passive recipients.

Perhaps part of the answer is to notice that, while *the work of ministry* is in the singular, *evangelists* and *pastors-and-teachers* are plural. Since the New Testament norm is that local church leadership is plural, not singular, it becomes a central part of the *evangelists'* and *pastors-and-teachers'* task to multiply themselves, and raise up more for the future than there are in the present. A church with several hundred members but with only one regular preacher is not the New Testament norm.

Yet it is not quite true to say that the role of the 'shepherd-teacher' is to give their ministry away, or to work themselves out of a job. This passage teaches the precise opposite: the church will always need shepherd-teachers; they are critical for the health of each local congregation. But everybody needs to understand why. The church needs to have everybody exercising their ministry, and to do that the shepherd-teacher needs to have as a constant question. 'Am I equipping the saints, or just filling their notebooks? Is the goal of my sermon this week that people will be encouraged, resourced and trained for what they have to do, or will they just admire me for the skill with which I do what I have to do?' Christ has given the church shepherd-teachers as his *gift*. But they are a gift with a purpose behind them. Everybody else benefits.

(iii) Evangelists and shepherd-teachers build up the body

The second purpose of the shepherd-teachers is *building up the body of Christ*. Body language is familiar as a New Testament term, of course, and it gives us the familiar ideas of different parts playing different roles, interconnected and mutually cooperating. What stops this from being a mere sociological observation which is true of any well-meaning human organization, is that this is *the body of Christ*, owned by, and ruled over by him, *the head* (15).[42]

But how is this *body* to be *built up* by the *evangelists* and *pastors-and-teachers*? The answer lies in the second of those two words. Christ has given us teachers so that, as they teach, the body is built up. It would be silly for me, having been appointed as a teacher, to

[42] Col. 1:18.

189

scurry round a series of conferences on building up the body to find out if my job is clever marketing or good time-management skills. No, my role, as a teacher, is to build up the body by teaching.

But there is a trap here, and to spot it we need a small historical detour. When the Bible was put into Latin in the late fourth century, this phrase was translated, quite rightly as '*in aedificationem corporis Christi*', and when William Tyndale put it into English he carried over one of those Latin words: 'to the *edifyinge* of the body of christ'.[43] We still have some trace of why he used the word, because we retain the word 'edifice' for buildings. But whatever 'edifying' meant for Tyndale or architects, when it is used today it normally means something like 'mental or moral improvement'.[44] If someone, after a sermon, says 'that was deeply edifying', and assuming that it is not an ironic comment, it probably means 'I feel better informed', or 'that was very moving and satisfying'.

But it was not Paul's ultimate aim that individuals leave church better informed. When he uses the word he means it affects the way we treat it each other: 'let us pursue what makes for peace and for mutual upbuilding.'[45] It covers how we decide what to do when we meet together ('Let all things be done for building up');[46] it covers the purpose of his authority as an apostle ('which the Lord gave for building you up').[47] So this is a word that is mutual, and relational.

We may not fall into the trap of thinking that 'edifying' means 'being better informed'. But we may fall into the equally anachronistic trap of thinking that *building up the body* means getting larger, like a body builder. The trap is not that that the idea is wrong (it is a New Testament assumption that the local church should grow and multiply), but that this is not what this verse is saying. The language in this section is consistently to do with how we see each other, and Paul concludes this section saying that Christ *makes the body grow so that it builds itself up in love* (16).

So here is the second task for the *evangelists* and *pastors-and-teachers*. We must teach, and to that extent, people ought to leave church 'better informed'. Good teaching is good. But, that in itself is not building up the body. Building up the body requires attention to the relationship between the different members of the body. An exceptional preacher might be able to do that just with a sermon, but most of us will need to roll our sleeves up and sort out the hurts,

[43] Italics added. Retained by the KJV: 'for the edifying of the body of Christ'.
[44] SOED 1.630.
[45] Rom. 14:19.
[46] 1 Cor. 14:26.
[47] 2 Cor. 10:8.

insults, histories and misunderstandings that stop people serving each other, and then help them to flourish.

These two tasks have been the day-to-day tasks of the church, nourished by their shepherd-teachers. Neither is an alternative to teaching, both depend on it, but neither is done merely by giving a good talk. *Shepherds and teachers* make sure the teaching is put into practice. By contrast, the second pair of tasks have a longer term focus, indicated by the word *until* which begins verse 13.

(iv) Evangelists and shepherd-teachers equip the saints for unity
This is a bold plan for Christian unity, and it can be hard to take seriously when we see the proliferation of denominations and law suits between groups of believers. We might prefer to see this as the ultimate, future unity of all churches in the new heavens and the new earth. When we stand, together, around the Lord Jesus, then, and only then, will we see true unity.

The problem with deferring all the unity until that day, is that Paul's time markers in this passage do not work that way. It is true that the previous two tasks seem to build the highway to reach this goal, and the word translated *reach* is one that Luke uses in Acts of finishing journeys and arriving at destinations.[48] But looking at the parallel idea of *the knowledge of the Son of* God in verse 13, the destination in verse 14 with its emphasis on the absence of false teaching, and in verse 15 on *speaking the truth in love*, it appears more likely to be church as we experience it now, but much improved.

This makes it something that the *evangelists and pastors-and-teachers* should be consciously striving for now, as an achievable goal, and not something that we put on our 'wish list' for the Last Day. This unity is the direct consequence of teaching. One of the unhelpful sayings that Christians echo is that 'Doctrine Divides, Mission Unites'. It is true that nothing quite focuses the mind like addressing the needs of the lost and the least, and it has pulled Christians together for centuries. Mission unites. But the first half of that saying is wrong: true doctrine also unites, because its goal is agreement and unity. Paul is not going soft here: he knows the danger of false teaching and what he calls *craftiness in deceitful schemes.* He is not arguing for an end to doctrinal clarity. But such clarity should expect to attract, to compel agreement and to unite.

I recall visiting one church where the welcome leaflet began, 'We are not one of those churches who . . . ' In other words, they did not begin by defining themselves over against a lost world, and certainly not as people who have been rescued and long for others to be

[48] *Katanteō;* e.g. Acts 18:19; 20:15; 25:13; 27:12; 28:13.

rescued too; no, they began by defining themselves over against other churches. I do not think that it is healthy to make that the centre of your self-definition. *Shepherds and teachers* must point out the wolves and protect the flock; but it is dangerously easy to become more concerned with the wolf than with the lost sheep.

(v) Evangelists and shepherd-teachers equip the saints for maturity
With the goal of *maturity* the same question arises: is this a uniquely Last Day phenomenon, or something to be worked at now? The standard is certainly dauntingly high: the word was used of the unblemished animals used in the temple, and of being not merely blameless before our peers, but being blameless before God.[49] Throughout the New Testament it carries ideas of completion and perfection.[50] In the next phrase it is equal to *the measure of the stature of the fullness of Christ*.[51] Could such a glorious goal be achieved?

The reason it must, and can, be achieved is that this is the work of the *evangelists* and *pastors-and-teachers*. If this were a Last Day picture of our ultimate maturity, in which all our questions would have been answered and all our ignorance filled, then no *shepherd-teacher* on the planet could have achieved that. Such maturity is produced by the resurrection from the dead, when, as Paul puts it in 1 Corinthians, 'Now I know in part; then I shall know fully, even as I have been fully known'.[52] That will be a great day. But what Paul has in mind here is what happens in church as a result of ordinary sermons preached by ordinary *shepherd-teachers*.

3. Contrasts (4:14–16)

Perhaps the clearest way to see the nature of *unity* and *maturity* for our churches is to look at verses 14–16 as a series of contrasts. Paul sets it up that way, beginning with a series of negative properties headed *no longer*, and then a series of balancing properties, headed *rather*.[53]

- *No longer gullible infants but mature adults.* The contrast is between the naïve and dependent child, and the level-headed and responsible adult. The Christian who is constantly agitated by

[49] Animals: Exod. 12:5; before humans: Gen. 6:9; God: Deut. 18:13; 2 Sam. 22:26.
[50] Matt. 5:48; 19:21; Rom. 12:2; 1 Cor. 2:6; 13:10; 14:20; Eph. 4:13; Phil. 3:15; Col. 1:28, 4:12; Heb. 5:14; 9:11; Jas 1:4, 17, 25; 3:2; 1 John 4:18.
[51] Eph. 1:10, 23; 3:19.
[52] 1 Cor. 13:12.
[53] For these headings from a very similar list, see Snodgrass, *Ephesians*, p. 206.

the latest piece of theological fluff to have been published is an *infant*. The older, wiser Christian knows enough to take a deep breath, and reads and responds responsibly. Good shepherd-teachers will not only promote proper maturity, they will protect the gullible from the consequences of their immaturity.

- *No longer tossed about but joined and held together.* Error in the church derails Bible studies and hijacks conversations, its presence means that parents distrust what is being taught in the children's groups, and there is general instability. By contrast, a mature church is one where the teaching resources can be trusted, the groups are responsibly and accountably led, and there is a general sense of people pulling in the same direction.
- *No longer deception but truth.* The Bible is clear that false teaching has supernatural origins. Not that the demons are heretical – they know too much for that.[54] But behind *deceitful schemes* lies the evil one, and both the words *cunning* and *deceitful* are used of him elsewhere.[55] So error is designed to blow us off course, swirling in gusts, to get us marooned and up creeks – to extend Paul's sailing metaphor. By contrast, good teaching is straightforward. It does not manipulate, bully or use false guilt to achieve its ends, but is utterly transparent.
- *No longer cunning but loving.* This is an extension of that idea: people deliberately teaching error do so for their own ends, often to feed their egos or fill their wallets. By contrast, *speaking the truth in love* is the kind of teaching that wants the best for the hearers. This phrase is sometimes used to encourage honesty in our conversations, but the only other similar phrase in the New Testament is related to speaking gospel truth.[56] So, once again, the goal of teaching is found in the relationships between one another.[57]
- *No longer human lies but Christ's truth.* The nourishment, life and growth of the church come from Christ, our head. He wants the best for us, and it is therefore for our own blessing that he has given us these gifts of *shepherds and teachers.*
- *No longer crafty people serving themselves, but honest, loving people serving each other.* Paul has used the images of immature children and inexperienced sailors; his third, healthy, picture is of a healthy body working well. Paul does not press the image

---

[54] Jas 2:19.

[55] 2 Cor. 11:3; Eph. 6:11.

[56] More literally, 'truthing you in love' (*alētheuontes de en agapē*). Gal. 4:16: 'Have I then become your enemy by speaking the truth to (*alētheuōn*, 'truthing') you?' meaning, 'by speaking the true gospel to you'.

[57] *Love* is another theme in Ephesians: 1:4; 3:17; 4:2, 15, 16; 5:2.

here, and so we do not either; the image is the one we all enjoy when it happens, of the easy functioning of a fit runner taking 10k in her stride.

This final section summarizes much of Ephesians 4: it began with a call for humble gentle, patient love (2), and it has closed on that note (16); the great call for unity (4:3–6) is repeated (13, 16) in the light of divisive false teaching (14); the gifts of the word ministers (11, 13) are needed in the light of error and its opposite (14–15), and the use of all of our gifts (7–8, 11, 16) is the opposite of the self-serving nature of lies (14).

There will be a glorious day of ultimate maturity and unity. God has promised us that. But he does not allow us to park the idea until then. The church's *evangelists* and *shepherd teachers* are the people he has now given to us as the means to work at it in the present.

Additional note: APEPT

Michael Frost and Alan Hirsch have written a significant and highly praised book, which comes to very different conclusions to mine. Simply put, they argue that the five functions of apostle, prophet, evangelist, pastor and teacher (the names give the acronym APEPT) are God's ongoing gift for the continuing healthy maturity of the church. Moreover, in additional to the leadership of the church, they describe the characteristics of the whole local church:

> And here comes the revolutionary paradigm. What we have called the ministry matrix suggests that the fivefold ministry belongs to, and describes in some way, the whole church. If we take the phrase '*to each one of us*' together with the repeated distribution formula '*he ... gave some to be*' quite naturally, this implies that all Christians are included in some part of the fivefold APEPT structure.[58]

There is so much fizz and enthusiasm in this book that anyone calling it to account for careful exegesis is going to seem a boring academic killjoy. Nevertheless, because it presents itself as a careful exegetical correction for the health of the church, and since that is our task too, it seems a responsible thing to do. I have four observations and an alternative diagram.

First, as the acronym APEPT shows, they are confident that Paul describes five clearly separable functions, but he actually breaks the

---

[58] Frost and Hirsch, *Shaping*, p. 171.

rhythm for pastors and teachers, introducing the two nouns with one definite article. Commentators who think they are separate roles still argue they are held closely together, distinct even from *evangelists*, and some argue for a double-description function, as I have above.[59] This means that the list is nowhere near as simple as Hirsch and Frost make out: at worst for their case there are four, not five on the list, at best there are five, of which two can hardly be distinguished.

Second, therefore, the confidence with which they define and populate the list[60] must be largely guesswork. This is the only reference to a *pastor*, so it is unclear how they define it as 'one who cares' against the *teacher* as 'one who explains'. Remember that in Acts 20, Paul tells the 'elders' (who are also the 'overseers') to care for 'the flock', and they are to do so by watching for false teachers.[61] It is therefore extremely hazy once they extrapolate from continuing roles within the leadership to the equivalent characteristics in the church membership: 'Some will be called apostles, but the whole community is to be apostol*ic*. Some will be called to be evangelists, but the whole community is to be evangelist*ic*.'[62] That is great rhetoric, but not at all clear in content. They subsequently give that content over the next ten pages, drawn from history, current church practice and the social sciences, but it includes only one biblical cross-reference.[63]

Third, I think their model misreads the function of these five roles. Frost and Hirsch align the phrase *to each one of us* with the five roles, as God's continuing gift to each individual Christian. But that is too remote: the phrase comes from verse 7 but the functions come in verse 11. Verse 7 actually reads *but grace was given to each one of us according to the measure of Christ's gift.* There is an expectation here that we will each have a place for our individual service, but we have to wait until verse 11 for that to be explained, which is that the five exist *to equip the saints for the work of ministry.* Frost and Hirsch extrapolate out from the five to cover us all: they describe us all in some way. But Paul says that it is as we receive from them that we are equipped for our distinct ministries.

Fourth, I have suggested above that while Paul elsewhere uses the words 'apostle' and 'prophet' in ways that can find contemporary

---

[59] Hoehner, *Ephesians*, p. 544; Lincoln, *Ephesians*, p. 250; O'Brien, *Ephesians*, p. 300. Snodgrass, *Ephesians* (p. 204) follows M. Barth (*Ephesians 4-6* [New York: Doubleday, 1960]) in strongly identifying the two as 'teaching shepherds' (pp. 438–439). Ernest Best (*Ephesians*, ICC [London/New York: T&T Clark International, Continuum, 1998]) argues for fluidity between the three roles (p. 392).

[60] See the table in Frost and Hirsch, *Shaping*, p. 170.

[61] Acts 20:17, 28, 30.

[62] Frost and Hirsch, *Shaping*, p. 170, their italics.

[63] On p. 175, and I am being generous.

expression, it would misread this passage to see them in here; rather this passage assumes that we 'are fellow citizens with the saints and members of the household of God, *built on the foundation of the apostles and prophets*, Christ Jesus himself being the cornerstone'.[64]

Perhaps a diagram might make my understanding clearer. I think Paul means something like this, remembering that I have used a broad category for 'evangelist' to include church planters, apologists and so on.

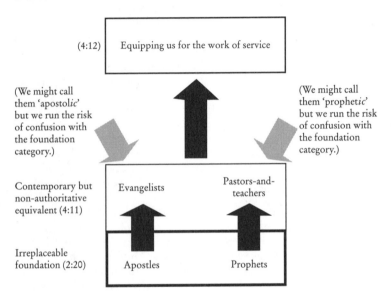

In summary, I am troubled that their missional passion (which I admire and envy) seems to have overridden their biblical carefulness.[65]

---

[64] Eph. 2:19–20.
[65] See the Introduction, and ch. 11.

1 Timothy 3:1–13; 5:1–25
12. The church's servants

Organizations seem to flourish when people take responsibility for their well-being, and so for centuries churches have had leaders.[1] But centuries of selfish, irresponsible, heretical, greedy, bullying, craven, chaotic church leadership show the dangers of power, especially if our models are culturally endorsed. Indeed, a new generation wants us rethink church leadership in a new and missional way: counter-cultural, communal, subversive and hidden, being 'an organism, not an organization'.[2] Michael Frost and Alan Hirsch are typical:

> [The] traditional church (Christendom) is hierarchical, deeply indebted to what we see as an overly religious, bureaucratic, top-down model of leadership, as opposed to one that is more structured around grassroots agendas. While some denominations are ideologically committed to a very-top-down hierarchical model that includes archbishops, bishops, priests and parish councils, others (who call themselves low church) are equally indebted to top-down approaches via regional superintendents, senior pastors, associate pastors, youth pastors, and deacons. From Pentecostals to the Orthodox church, from Baptists to Episcopalians and Presbyterians, the hierarchical model seems to be universal . . . Some younger leaders are discovering that in the emerging global

---

[1] Heb. 13:7.

[2] F. Viola, *Reimagining Church* (Colorado Springs: David C. Cook, 2008). See S. Murray, *Church After Christendom* (Milton Keynes: Paternoster Press, 2005) and *Post-Christendom: Church and Mission in a Strange New World* (Milton Keynes: Authentic Media, 2011); D. Kimball, *The Emerging Church: Vintage Christianity for New Generations* (Grand Rapids: Zondervan, 2003); L. Sweet (ed.), *The Church in an Emerging Culture: Five Perspectives* (Grand Rapids: Zondervan, 2003); and M. Frost and A. Hirsch, *The Shaping of Things to Come: Innovation and Mission for the 21st-Century Church* (Peabody: Henderson/Erina: Strand, 2003).

cultural context the hierarchical model has little to say to a generation that values egalitarianism and community.[3]

But experience shows that completely free-form relationships are just as open to abuse of power – possibly more so, since abuse is hidden.[4] The New Testament churches protected themselves from abusive leaders with shared expectations.[5] The principal teaching comes in 1 and 2 Timothy and Titus;[6] our focus is 1 Timothy, but first we should clear the ground.

1. Christian ministry

Jesus has the only essential ministry. 1 Timothy 3:8–11 describes *deacons* ('servants'), but their ministry is based on Jesus: 'For who is the greater, one who reclines at table or one who serves? Is it not the one who reclines at table? But I am among you as the one who serves.'[7] Jesus must serve us first, and if he is not our servant, then he is not our Lord. Because Christ served us, Christians serve one another,[8] and even high-profile Paul, Apollos, Timothy, Tichycus and Epaphras are only servants.[9] Having understood those two truths, some people were called *deacons*, 'servants' (3:8).[10] But calling them 'servants' does not mean everybody else stops serving.

This is true for 'oversight' or 'supervision' (*episcopē*) (3:1, 2) too. God 'oversees' everything,[11] and 'oversaw' his people in Jesus' birth.[12] Today, Jesus 'oversees' us as our shepherd.[13] Being a Christian means Jesus is our 'overseer'. Therefore, Christ-like Christians 'oversee' one another.[14] Everyone *in* the congregation is overseen *by* the congregation. So when a leader is caught in some sin, we must

[3] Frost and Hirsch, *Shaping*, p. 21. See too F. Viola and G. Barna, *Pagan Christianity* (Carol Stream: Tyndale House, 2012).
[4] See P. Ward, *Liquid Church: A Bold Vision of How to Be God's People in Worship and Mission: A Flexible, Fluid Way of Being Church* (Peabody: Hendrickson, 2002), and F. Viola and G. Barna, *Pagan Christianity? Exploring the Roots of Our Church Practices* (Carol Stream: Tyndale, 2002). For a critique, J. Belcher, *Deep Church: A Third Way Beyond Emerging and Traditional* (Downers Grove: IVP, 2009).
[5] Acts 14:23.
[6] Titus and 1 Tim. are similar; 2 Tim. addresses the individual leader.
[7] Luke 22:27.
[8] 1 Pet. 4:10.
[9] Paul: 1 Cor. 3:5; 2 Cor. 3:6; 6:4; Eph. 3:7; Col. 1:23, 25. Apollos: 1 Cor. 3:5. Timothy: 1 Tim. 4:6. Tichycus: Eph. 6:21; Col. 4:7. Epaphras: Col. 1:7.
[10] Rom. 16:1; Phil. 1:1.
[11] Luke 19:14; 1 Pet. 2:25.
[12] *Epeskepsato* Luke 1:48. LXX Ps. 8:4.
[13] 1 Pet. 2:25.
[14] Matt. 25:36, 43 (*visit* translates *episkeptomai*); Jas 1:27; Heb. 12:15–16.

ask, 'Who cared for, "oversaw", that person?' Hierarchy might suggest a denominational official, or the church board, but the right first answer should be, 'We, the other members of the congregation, should have overseen that person.' It is spiritually unhealthy to have denominational officials who are over but not in congregations. It is not good for those officials. Only when we have seen those two truths is it safe to see the third, which is that the Holy Spirit sets some apart as 'overseers'.[15]

That threefold pattern rolls out to almost every description. 'Pastors' (shepherds) are fellow sheep, under the Great Shepherd; 'teachers' must be taught by Christ, and by other Christians; even apostles were under the Great Apostle.[16] The living, active ministry of the Lord Jesus is uniquely and irreplaceably foundational.

This stops us being troubled by the historical gap between the churches today and Jesus. Some Christians stress an unbroken line of Christian clergy from then to now,[17] and others want strong characters as leaders. But those three aspects bridge the gap. Two thousand years do not make Christ increasingly remote from us; rather, his ascension means that he is active on our behalf, and present among us by his Spirit. He is always contemporary, as present today as he was for Spurgeon, Calvin, Augustine or any giant of the past. All human leaders recede over time, but not the Lord Jesus. In royal families the throne passes from generation to generation, and presidents exchange responsibilities as each one in turn lays it down. But not the Lord Jesus. He is still, constantly, overseeing his flock, and under him we are to oversee each other. He says we need overseers, but not because he is overstretched.

One title is never shared: 'head'. Christ is the 'head' of the church, both local and cosmic,[18] so we might expect human leadership of the congregation to share the word. But we need his ultimate authority, and his eternal generosity, forever. He will not delegate that. He does not need to. No-one else is the source of all our gifts and ministries. It is mistaken for any leader to claim headship, whether as a local pastor or an international pope. Every church depends on the Lord Jesus' active and ongoing headship over his body.[19]

We must underline this point: we are equal, nothing but each other's servants, and the idea of one group ('clergy') doing what most

[15] Acts 20:28.
[16] Christ the pastor: John 10:14, etc.; teacher: Matt. 8:19; Mark 4:38, etc.; apostle: Heb. 3:1.
[17] For 'apostolic succession', see below (p. 219).
[18] Col. 1:18.
[19] Paul derives the husband's 'headship' in marriage from Christ's as head of the church (Eph. 5:22–32).

('laity') cannot, is so wrong that it is almost denies the gospel. All a Christian teacher can do, however gifted, is remind us of what is already in the scriptures.

So we must rethink both 'clergy' and 'laity'. In the Old Testament Greek '*laos*' meant the entire people of God, distinct from the surrounding nations (*ta ethnē*). In the New Testament, it meant the new chosen people. James said that 'God has visited the Gentiles (*ta ethnē*), to take from them a people (*laos*) for his name'.[20] It is all-inclusive. The New Testament has language for leaders, but none for 'laity'. Not until the third century was there any distinction between 'clerics' and 'laity'.[21] We are all priests; and we are all laity.

2. Appointing elders/overseers (1 Tim. 3:1–7)

Paul first describes the qualities and gifts, but not duties, of overseers. A *trustworthy* saying is vital, and after deacons he concludes similarly.[22] He was fighting for the life of the church, and that depends on selecting the right people.

The first challenge is relating an *overseer* (*episkopos*), to the *elders* (5:17–25, *presbyteroi*). Both Episcopalians and Presbyterians obviously derive titles and roles from them, yet it appears the two were identical:

- Acts 20:17, 28: Paul summons the 'elders' and calls them 'overseers'. They are clearly the same group.
- Titus 1:5–7: Paul describes 'elders' and almost immediately calls them 'overseers'. Again, the same group.
- Philippians 1:1: Paul writes to the 'overseers and deacons'; if *elders* also existed they would be mentioned.

Evidence from the first centuries is unanimous that they remained identical. Jerome is typical: 'the bishop therefore is the same as the presbyter.'[23]

Wondering why there were two titles exposes how little evidence we have. 'Elders' was an Old Testament term for senior leaders,[24]

---

[20] Acts 15:14. See too 2 Cor 6:16; Heb 8:10–12.

[21] H. Küng, *The Church* (Tunbridge Wells: Search Press, 1968), p. 126, listing Origen, Jerome and others.

[22] A *trustworthy saying* was an important but threatened truth: 1 Tim. 1:15; 4:9; 2 Tim. 2:11; Titus 3:8. Here it makes most sense referring to the appointment of elders.

[23] Cited by M. Green, *Called to Serve* (London: Hodder and Stoughton, 1964), p. 42.

[24] See Gen 23:10, 18; Deut 21:1–4; 22:15; 25:7; Exod. 3:16; 24:1; Job 29:7–10; Prov. 24:7; 31:23.

later used in the synagogue.[25] The first Jewish Christians took their patterns into how they ran a church, so James can call a Christian meeting, a 'synagogue'.[26] Even if someone had not been a Christian for any longer than any other believers, a Jewish background gave better grasp of the Scriptures and therefore an ability to teach as an 'elder'.[27]

If 'elder' describes who they are, *overseer* describes what they do. The verb *episkeptomai* occurs frequently in both the Greek Old Testament and the New Testament, and means a visit for a reason.[28] Numbers uses it for the detailed census-taking; it describes a shepherd counting sheep,[29] or Paul and Barnabas' plan to *visit* churches.[30] It became used for someone overseeing a project.[31]

Churches with an 'episcopal' form of government, often encounter a 'bishop' as a distant figure. But although the single 'overseer' for a large area emerged in the second century, nothing in the New Testament anticipates that. Possibly Titus had a trace of such a ministry, but his visit to Crete was short. Overseers are congregationally based, and plural. That does not prevent the development of such a structure but it does prevent theological shortcuts, as if either second-century bishops or contemporary bishops are identical to New Testament *overseers*.[32] They are not. So one particular claim, that bishops are of 'the full essence' of the church (*plene esse*), is clearly wrong, since the New Testament church ran quite properly without them. Even more modest claims, that bishops are the 'good way of being' a church (*bene esse*) is wrong if it implies the best of all systems. No, working well, 'episcopacy' can support the local church healthily. As can many alternatives.[33]

---

[25] For example, Matt. 26:3, 47; Mark 7:1–5.

[26] Jas 2:2: 'synagogue' means 'gathering', so is identical to 'church'.

[27] Acts 14:23.

[28] 170 occurrences in LXX, eleven in NT. For a visit by people, e.g. Judg. 15:1; Matt. 25:36; by God, e.g. Gen. 21:1; Luke 1:68. The LXX background makes it unlikely that *episkopos* was used in Hellenized settings, and *presbyteros* in Jewish ones (so J. B. Lightfoot, *The Epistles of St. Paul: Colossians and Philemon* (Grand Rapids: Zondervan, 1959, from the rev. 1879 ed.), p. 194.

[29] E.g. 2 Chr. 24:6; Jer. 23:2; Zech. 11:16; Ezek. 34:11–12.

[30] Acts 15:36.

[31] E.g. Ezra 1:2, *charged me*; Acts 6:3, *pick out*.

[32] 'Bishop' comes from *episkopos* through coarse Latin ('[e]biscopus'), through Old English ('biscop') and Old High German ('biscof').

[33] On the development of episcopacy see Lightfoot's essay (*Epistles*, pp. 181–269); H. M. Gwatkin, *Episcopacy* (London: Fellowship of Evangelical Churchmen, (repr. 1962 [1914]); L. Morris, *Ministers of God* (London: IVP, 1964) and Green, *Called*.

a. Ambition (1)

It is sometimes suggested that anyone who wants to be a leader is automatically debarred. Churches need humble servants, not thrusting types. Paul would affirm part of that, but not the central idea. Humility is essential in an elder, but it must be found in someone who *aspires* and *desires* to do the work. Those who help people consider future ministry explore maturity and gifts, but Paul also weighs someone's passion for ministry, and keenness to serve.

b. A noble task (1)

Churches struggle to find volunteers, and many pastors feel they are always asking busy people for favours. What a contrast to Paul! Not only does he assume enthusiasm, he says that this is an excellent way for someone to spend their life.

Noble (*kalos*) opens the section on elders (*a noble* task) and closes the section on deacons (*a good standing*, 13). It appears in running a household *well* (4), and being *well thought of* by non-Christians (7). Deacons also must run their families *well*, with heavenly rewards for those who have served *well*. Being an elder demands and calls the best out of people.

But *noble* might attract those who like titles and ceremony. So it is tied to *task* – or, *work*.[34] It means hard duty, as when the Holy Spirit said, 'Set apart for me Barnabas and Saul for *the work* to which I have called them',[35] or in Paul's challenge: 'As for you, always be sober-minded, endure suffering, do *the work* of an evangelist, fulfil your ministry.[36]

Being an elder means putting effort into kingdom building. Someone who hopes to squeeze it in between other commitments is not the person. Nor is the talented business executive, travelling too frequently to make the meetings. Nor is the busybody who likes to be in the know. So who does qualify?

c. Exemplary Christians (2–7)

The most important quality is that elders *must be* (this is Paul's non-negotiable), model Christians, in private and in public. The headline is, *above reproach*. Not sinless, or no churches would ever have elders, but that there is nothing known against them. So churches should enquire about hidden problems. I have twice worked with

[34] HCSB.
[35] Acts 13:2.
[36] 2 Tim. 4:5.

Christian leaders who were engaging in serious sexual sin, and in neither case did I suspect. Perhaps I thought too highly of them, as if their high profile guaranteed they could not sin. But the impact that sin among the leaders has, both within the church and before the world, is too serious to leave it to chance. We consider each qualification in turn.

They should be *the husband of one wife*. First-century society was probably the most sexually explicit the world had seen, at least until today. Yet 'the sexually immoral', and 'men who practice homo-sexuality' have both been converted. Timothy also faced grim ascetics who 'forbid marriage'.[37] Critics sometimes say that Christians are obsessed by sex, but we should not be bashful: sexual behaviour heads Paul's list for good reason, and it is necessary that we do the same today.

The elder must be 'a one-woman man', which taken at its simplest, means 'faithful in heterosexual marriage'.[38] That is clear. But possibly, Paul could be banning polygamy (having more than one wife). If so, there are some helpful contemporary parallels. For instance, the Anglican Church in Kenya has converts in a culture where polygamy is widespread. Their position is that if the wife is converted, nothing more is required of her. She has only one husband. But if the polygamous husband is converted, he must remain faithful to his marriage promises, and be a spiritually responsible husband and father. That means he cannot abandon any of his wives and children into inevitable poverty, but he is forbidden from marrying any further wives, on pain of church discipline. They are also quite explicit that no-one involved in a polygamous marriage may hold office in the church. 'One-woman-man' means exactly that, even in a polygamous culture.

Our Kenyan sisters and brothers point out that Western Christians, tolerating sex before and outside serial marriages, also allow polygamy (and polyandry, one woman having several husbands), and they challenge us to be as distinctive in our culture as they are in theirs.[39]

Sober-minded means level-headed. Here is a grown-up, who does not panic when issues come thick and fast, or there is a tricky situation to resolve.

Being *self-controlled* is the twin of *sober-minded*. Here is someone whose diary, bank account, and prayer list show an awareness that each day is one for which an account must be given to God. Perhaps there are further implications. In the West there is an epidemic of

[37] 1 Tim. 1:10; 4:4.
[38] 5:9.
[39] D. M. Gitari, 'The Church and Polygamy', *Transformation* 1.1 (1984), pp. 3–10.

obesity. Although there may be multiple factors and causes, on the whole someone who is morbidly obese cannot preach convincingly on the issue of self-control. The same could be said of someone who finds it hard to break a habit, even a chemically induced one, like smoking.

The ideal elder is *respectable*. Simply by being in the room this person creates order, and people see why maturity is worth respecting.

Elders are also *hospitable*. Travelling teachers and evangelists needed safe, free accommodation, so elders must welcome guests cheerfully, and make them feel at home.[40] Elders (and remember, this is another way of describing 'pastors') are to be friendly, not the bookish sort for whom visitors are an irritating distraction from sermon preparation. The elders' homes were probably where the church met. Do they resent people coming to their house, every week, bringing mud and noise, and needing food and drink? Of course the church should not impose, and there should be sensible boundaries, but, nonetheless, hospitality is necessary for an elder.

We shall look at *able to teach* below.

Drunkenness is inconsistent with Christian living,[41] and yet Paul repeatedly insisted that an elder must *not be a drunkard*.[42] Perhaps we need to be more realistic about the temptations leaders face. Some of our elders need help to live up to this. Perhaps we need to expand this today, to include recreational drugs – they are absolutely forbidden, not only because they are illegal but because their mood-altering influence is the opposite of being *sober minded* and *self-controlled*.

They should *not be violent but gentle*. God is gentle[43] but Christian leadership is stressful, and many times an elder will feel pushed too far. The temptation to lash out can be strong, and – in the short term – punching someone on the nose might feel quite satisfying. But think what that does to that elder's reputation. Would anyone dare to disagree, ever again? Who would confront sin in that elder's life? Once again, this vice is the opposite of *self-control*. This connects with abuse of power. I have known of Christians in leadership who shouted and swore at colleagues, and others who have been as abusive without the obvious sin, but in both cases the imbalance in the relationship, and their strong personalities, meant no-one dared confront them. Bullies must be blocked.

[40] See ch. 14.
[41] Gal. 5:21.
[42] 1 Tim. 2:8; Tit. 1:7, 2:3.
[43] Ps. 18:35.

Following that comes *not quarrelsome*. Some people enjoy controversy, and get known for being edgy. They deliberately overstate
their case to get the other person coming back at them. Mounce calls
this 'active and serious bickering',[44] and Paul says this mindset
displays a love of trivia and foolish discussions.[45] The obvious forum
today is the web. It allows unaccountable self-expression, where
anyone can generate a bit of a storm with an exaggerated view. Jesus
could on occasion be scornful or sarcastic – but he was so sinlessly.
Perhaps bloggers need wise friends who can edit us, hold us to
account, and make us apologize when necessary. And perhaps an
on-line controversialist is unsuitable as an elder.

An elder should *not* be *a lover of money*. By and large, there is not
much money to be made in ministry – although false teachers are
often chasing people's cash.[46] But that is not quite the point. It is
not money, 'but the love of money' which is the problem.[47] One
can be poor, and still have a consuming love of it. Churches need to
watch this. Later Paul touches on salaries,[48] but as a general principle,
elders and cash should meet rarely. Many pastors arrange that they
cannot sign cheques, count the money or have a church credit card.
That is wise. My denomination pays all its pastors the same salary,
no matter the size of church or its physical location. Others always
publish what staff are paid. Some churches make it impossible for
leaders to know who are significant donors, in case it would stop
the elders from disciplining that person. One pastor asked a member
of the church to preach about giving, so that no-one would think he
(the pastor) was trying to feather his own nest.

Money, and the illusions of success, power and freedom it gives,
are inescapable. Once a church decides to collect and distribute
money, it risks having leaders who love it (in one case I know,
hoarding the church's money in plastic carrier bags). We must be
blunt about this in choosing them.

*He must manage his own household well, with all dignity keeping
his children submissive, for if someone does not know how to manage
his own household, how will he care for God's church?* (4–5). Households included family, business, slaves, finances and property – in
other words, a complex set of relationships – and the word
that occurs twice is *manage*. It is a bland word in English, from the
world of paperclips and offices. But it is strong concept, elsewhere

[44] W. D. Mounce, *Pastoral Epistles*, WBC (Nashville: Thomas Nelson, 2000),
p. 176.
[45] 2 Tim. 2:23; Titus 3:9.
[46] 2 Tim. 3:1–9.
[47] 1 Tim. 3:8; Titus 1:7; 1 Pet. 5:2; Heb. 13:5.
[48] 1 Tim. 5:17.

translated: *rule* or 'lead';[49] Paul used it to describe those who are *over you in the Lord.*[50]

This is an appearance of the gift of leadership, from Romans 12:8, which must be proved in the household before it can be used in church.[51] That becomes clear if we translate 1 Timothy using the Romans word: *He must **lead** his own household well, with all dignity keeping his children submissive, for if someone does not know how to **lead** his own household, how will he care for God's church? ... Let the elders who **lead** well be considered worthy of double honour.* The church is to identify people with the God-given ability to make the right thing happen; or, to put it negatively as Paul, if someone cannot control his own children, where there is natural authority in place, what would make us consider that such a person would be able to run a church?

He must not be a recent convert, or he may become puffed up with conceit and fall into the condemnation of the devil (6). Churches know they need mature leaders – until they want a new pastor, when they look for someone young and energetic. But Paul warns about hiring a neophyte (*neophytos*), and ignoring him has two consequences. First, young Christians given significant roles risk being 'puffed up with conceit', a trait of the false teachers.[52] I have seen a young man, given great responsibility with little accountability, lead a youth group into schism and factionalism. The elders should not have allowed that to happen. The terms *elder* and *recent convert* are so opposite in meaning that that should be warning enough. We should not appoint a younger as an elder.

Secondly, such a person will *fall into the condemnation of the devil* (6). Paul might mean 'fall into the condemnation which the devil also has fallen into' because of similar pride. But the parallel with *the devil's trap* in verse 7 (NIV) makes it more likely that he means Satan's active opposition, designed to make us fall into condemnation, and out of ministry.

Moreover, he must be well thought of by outsiders, so that he may not fall into disgrace, into a snare of the devil (7). When I was being examined to see if I should be ordained, the church took up a reference from my non-Christian employer as a way of fulfilling this criterion. What do non-Christians make of this potential elder? Did they know I was a Christian? Was I consistent in my lifestyle, or was there a façade that anyone could spot? Was I inappropriate in the way I expressed my faith?

[49] 5:17. See Rom. 12:8.
[50] 1 Thess. 5:12.
[51] See below, and ch. 12.
[52] 1 Tim. 6:4; cf. 2 Tim. 3:4.

Jesus was 'a friend of tax collectors and sinners',[53] meaning that he liked spending time with them, and they liked spending time with him. So we ask a potential elder, 'Who are your non-Christian friends? What do they think of you?' And we ask the non-Christians, 'What do you think of this person? Do you enjoy spending time together?' Some answers to those questions should alert us, especially if the potential elder does not know, or does not like, any non-Christians. Not liking Jesus' friends is a worrying sign.

Paul has now twice underlined Satan's plan to disrupt gospel ministry by undermining the character of the elder. We must learn this quickly and deeply. Secret sins are no secret: they are no secret to our Lord, nor to the evil one. His malign purpose is our public disgrace; that is his *snare*, and we must resist him on every occasion. We dare not let busyness drive out discipleship.[54]

d. Teachers (2)

This magnificent, daunting picture of Christian maturity contains one more qualification: *able to teach;* the only requirement based not on maturity, but on an ability or gift. Paul is even more explicit in Titus: 'He must hold firm to the trustworthy word as taught, so that he may be able to give instruction in sound doctrine and also to rebuke those who contradict it.'[55] That positive and negative task implies a deep knowledge of God's word, an ability to explain it with clarity and relevance, and fearlessness in confronting error. 2 Timothy embedded the same instruction: 'the Lord's servant must not be quarrelsome but kind to everyone, *able to teach*, patiently enduring evil',[56] and Timothy's training task is therefore 'what you have heard from me in the presence of many witnesses entrust to faithful men who will be *able to teach* others also'.[57]

This simple, single task of teaching has multiple aspects. Derek Tidball lists from Acts 20: teaching in public and in private; calling people to a decision about repentance and faith; testifying to God's grace in the elder's own life; proclaiming the whole will of God; watching over his own life as well as the flock; being a good shepherd; and preparing them to cope with the future.[58] Mark Driscoll's list goes further: praying and studying the Scriptures (Acts 6:4); ruling/

[53] Luke 7:34.
[54] 1 Tim. 1:20; 2 Tim. 2:26; 1 Pet. 5:8.
[55] Titus 1:9.
[56] 2 Tim. 2:24.
[57] 2 Tim. 2:4.
[58] Acts 20:20, 21, 24, 27, 28, 29–31. D. J. Tidball, *Ministry by the Book: New Testament Patterns for Pastoral Leadership* (Nottingham: Apollos, 2008), p. 104.

leading the church (1 Tim. 5:17); managing the church (1 Tim. 3:4–5); caring for the people in the church (1 Pet. 5:2–5); giving account to God for the church (Heb. 13:17); living exemplary lives (Heb. 13:4–7); rightly using the authority God has given them (Acts 20:28); teaching the Bible correctly (Eph. 4:11; 1 Tim 3:2); preaching (1 Tim. 5:17); praying for the sick (James 5:13–15); teaching sound doctrine and refuting false teaching (Titus 1:9); working hard (1 Thess. 5:12); rightly using money and power (1 Pet. 5:1–3); protecting the church from false teachers (Acts 20:17–31); disciplining unrepentant Christians (Matt. 18:15–17); obeying the secular laws as the legal ruling body of a corporation (Rom. 13:1–7); developing other leaders and teachers (Eph. 4:11–16; 2 Tim. 2:1–2).[59]

Occasionally people discover these lists and, expecting a list of the elders' duties, draw a blank. Did they distribute the Lord's Supper? Visit new members? Lead services? Baptize? Evangelize? For how long did they serve? Did they take funerals? Instead, Paul requires only an ability to teach.

Those who train future pastors know that there are many things to cover, and the pressures of a changing culture make increasingly complex demands on future ministry. But the fundamental task which we need to prepare people for is their duty to teach. That must come first, last and central to what we do.

There is a second possible gift in the list, in the word '*manage*' or '*lead*'. As far as it relates to households and children it is a necessary task and duty, but the appearance of the same word in the gift-list of Romans 12 is intriguing.[60]

I know gifted Bible teachers who preach superbly, write engagingly, and evangelize with passion. Conferences they speak at are overbooked. But those same teachers could not organize those conferences. Timetables would slip, room bookings would collide, and people would miss their car lifts home. They do not have the gift of leadership.

I also know leaders who cannot teach or preach. I watched with awe as one of them organized a conference for thousands, ran a charity, and supervised a building programme. He is a wonderfully gifted man. But under no circumstances would you want to listen to his sermons.

When the elder meets the double qualification, able to teach and having a proven ability to lead, I think we meet 'Christian leadership'. Someone who knows what we should do, and knows how we should do it; who can teach us and change us, not just individually

---

[59] M. Driscoll, *Vintage Church* (Wheaton: Crossway, 2008), p. 72.
[60] See ch. 13.

but as a church. Elders like these apply God's word to our habits and plans, our sins and our ambitions, our resources of time and talent and treasure, and they say 'this is what it means to obey God's word; let's do it'. A team of such people, all doubly gifted, is God's plan for our churches.

It has sometimes been fashionable to be rather condescending towards Paul's list. Where, critics say, is the fire and the passion, the revolution and the world being turned upside down? People who want to storm barricades and plot a new world order find Paul very bourgeois. Some theologians contrast the 'charismatic' passion of the first churches with the more settled, 'catholic' values here.[61]

But that is why we appoint 'elders' and not 'youngers'. Luke Timothy Johnson's observation would be echoed by every church planter making inroads into a pagan culture:

> Fidelity to one spouse, sobriety, and hospitality may seem trivial virtues to those who identify authentic faith with momentary conversion or a single spasm of heroism. But to those who have lived longer and who recognize how the administration of a community can erode even the strongest of characters and the best of intentions, finding a leader who truly is a lover of peace and not a lover of money can be downright exciting.[62]

That must be right. Every church needs a solidly dependable leadership team, and many churches need to develop one.

3. Appointing deacons (3:8–13)

Deacon (diakonos) means 'servant'; John used it for wine waiters at a wedding.[63] We saw at the outset that Christ serving us, and our serving each other, was a foundational concept, and even when there were identifiable deacons, the word still retained its more general use. Timothy is to be a good servant (diakonos) in his teaching role, and Paul says of himself that Christ appointed him to his service (diakonian).[64]

---

[61] Classically, E. Käsemann, 'Ministry and Community in the New Testament', in Essays on New Testament Themes, transl. W. J. Montague (London: SCM, 1964), pp. 63–94. Tidball observes 'The case largely rests on an underestimation of the order implicit in the concept of charisma and an over-estimation of the sense of structure and office in the pastorals', Ministry, p. 158. See too, R. Fung, 'Charismatic versus Organized Ministry? An Examination of an Alleged Antithesis', EQ 52 (1980), pp. 195–214.

[62] L. T. Johnson, Letters to Paul's Delegates (Valley Forge: Trinity Press, 1996), pp. 148–149.

[63] John 2:5, 9.

[64] 1 Tim. 4:6; 1:12.

Because *deacon* is another rare title with little content,[65] many churches assume a model from Acts 6:1–6, where seven men were appointed to distribute food, releasing the apostles for teaching. It looks promising, but we need to slow down. First, none of those seven is called 'deacon'. Second, when they reappear, none of them is serving food: Stephen turns out to be a wonder-worker, a preacher and a martyr;[66] Philip's title is 'the evangelist'.[67] Most seriously, Luke uses the same word for what the seven are to do with food, and what the apostles do with the word: 'it is not right that we should give up preaching the word of God to *serve* (*diakonein*) tables . . . But we will devote ourselves to prayer and to the *ministry* (*diakonia*) of the word.'[68] 'You serve up pizza, we'll serve up preaching.' 'Serving' is such an ordinary word it can be used equally for the Spirit-fuelled preaching of the apostles, and sorting out the food queue.

At some point, *deacons* were formalized. The looseness of the word can help, because from Acts 6, we can fill the role with any important work which would otherwise distract the teachers. Notice too that the apostles devote themselves 'to prayer and the ministry of the word'. Paul did not mention prayer in his list of qualifications, but it should feature in our expected duties.

a. Exemplary Christians (8–9)

Deacons, *likewise*, must be exemplary Christians. These lists overlap, so we shall pause only on what is unique to deacons, but because both contain general Christian characteristics, no-one is excused an aspect of discipleship just because it is on the other list.

Dignified is similar to *respectable* in 3:2.

Not *double-tongued* covers several temptations. One could be saying one thing to one person, but a different story to somebody else. Perhaps deacons were to be wary of church politics, and being eager to win support. Maybe it is a warning about gossip, and their tongues wagging so furiously it looks like the deacon has two of them. Our media desensitizes us to this, but gossip is false witness, and a serious sin.[69]

Not *addicted to much wine*, mirrors *not a drunkard* (3). That Paul said this twice, bluntly, should stop us idealizing the early churches. They were like us. So we should expect to identify, and be as repeatedly blunt about, the same issues.

[65] Also in Phil. 1:1; Rom. 16:1.
[66] Acts 6:8 – 7:60.
[67] Acts 21:8.
[68] Acts 6:2, 4.
[69] Rom. 1:29.

They should *not* be *greedy for dishonest gain*. The insistence applies to money too, so be prepared to ask hard questions about cash. People handling collections and distributing gifts must be above suspicion.

They must hold the mystery of the faith with a clear conscience. The most significant difference for deacons is that they do not need to teach. So a wider group qualifies, but they must be as doctrinally clear as the elders.[70] Then, as now, false teachers existed, and representatives of the church must defend and explain truth, and refute error. Churches must keep the gospel pure, in their serving as in their preaching. There is great risk when only the teachers are examined for their orthodoxy, and the serving arms of the church are left in the hands of those with a shallow theology.

b. Men and women as deacons? (11–12)

The next requirement can be translated three ways, and it touches a sensitive topic so clarity matters. *Women* might mean women generally, women deacons, or the wives of the deacons. The first is unlikely, because of the context. 'Deacons' wives' is plausible for several contemporary commentators,[71] although it seems odd to expect maturity of a deacon's wife, and not an overseer's, especially as the latter will be opening their homes to the church.

Long ago, John Chrysostom said, 'Some have thought that this is said of women generally; but it is not so, for why should be introduced anything about women to interfere with the subject? He is speaking of women who hold the office of deacon.'[72] And in 112 Pliny, a non-Christian Roman governor, asked his Emperor about interrogating Christians, among them 'deaconesses'.[73] This would be parallel to 'Phoebe, a servant ['deacon'] of the church',[74] identifying that being a deacon was open to both men and women.

Paul probably notes this because some requirements only apply to men (*the husband of one wife, managing their children and their own households well*), which might be misunderstood to mean that only men could be deacons. Paul clarifies that this role is open to any mature Christian. It highlights the absence of a similar clause for elders.

---

[70] Titus 1:9.

[71] E.g. Mounce, *Pastoral Epistles*, pp. 202–204; G. W. Knight, *Commentary on the Pastoral Epistles*, NIGTC (Grand Rapids: Eerdmans and Carlisle: Paternoster, 1992), pp. 170–172.

[72] Quoted by Morris, *Ministers*, p. 89.

[73] Pliny, Epistle 97.

[74] Rom. 16:1.

c. The benefit for the deacons (13)

The blessings we receive in ministry frequently outweigh those we give. Preparing a talk yields much more than it could contain, and visiting older Christians encourages us on hard days. Ministry is *work*, but has benefits, both visible and heavenly: *For those who serve well as deacons gain a good standing for themselves and also great confidence in the faith that is in Christ Jesus.*

d. The blessing of a properly ordered church

Elections for church boards become exciting once we grasp that we are 'the household of God', and the appointment of right leaders is how we 'ought to behave'.[75] The running of God's household must be done to his design, because the gospel itself is at stake.[76]

These prospective leaders faced a virulent error in Ephesus, argumentative ('contrary to sound doctrine') and ruinous ('made shipwreck of their faith').[77] So Paul is urgent: 'O Timothy, guard the deposit entrusted to you. Avoid the irreverent babble and contradictions of what is falsely called "knowledge", for by professing it some have swerved from the faith.'[78] Addressing that was Timothy's central task: 'remain at Ephesus that you may charge certain persons not to teach any different doctrine, nor to devote themselves to myths and endless genealogies, which promote speculations rather than the stewardship from God that is by faith.'[79] Hence the importance of appointing the right people, with the right beliefs, and excluding the wrong people with the wrong beliefs.

For this congregation was no mere club. Every church is 'the church of the living God', where false teaching is a blasphemy.[80] Every church is 'a pillar and buttress of truth'. Some congregations talk as if it is their leaders who are the pillars and buttress of the church, but Paul has put this the other way round – not because the gospel is weak, but because the church matters. If a church compromises on the gospel, then their message has no saving power; if they fail to defend it, it collapses. God constructed his gospel plan so that his people are actively involved in putting it on permanent, public display. Our task is to rally to, fight for and defend this gospel,

[75] 1 Tim. 3:15.
[76] This is 'the heart of the pastoral corpus', defining the church's true nature. Mounce, *Pastoral Epistles*, p. 214.
[77] 1 Tim. 1:10, 19.
[78] 1 Tim. 6:20–21.
[79] 1 Tim. 1:3–4.
[80] 1 Tim. 3:15. Deut. 5:26; Josh. 3:10a.

because it is the only message that will save a lost world. Chrysostom called this 'a work of protection', because the church must be kept pure, holding onto and holding out the only gospel that saves.[81] For that we need those who are *able to teach* (3:2).

4. Honouring elders/overseers (5:17–25)

A third passage returns to the *elders*, this time addressing their treatment, depending on whether they do the work *well* (17) or *persist in sin* (20, 22, 24).

a. Honouring elders (17–18)

The *elder* is to *rule*, another way to describe an accountable overseer. Some do a poor job, but those who perform *well* are worthy of *double honour*.

The two references in verse 18, quoting Deuteronomy 25:4 and Luke 10:7, show that this is about money. Elders should be recompensed, gladly.[82] But what does *double honour* mean? Do we pay those who do a good job twice as much as those who do a bad one? Or that we pay those who teach twice as much as those who do not? There is unexpected help from Isaiah, who prophesied that Israel would be punished until they received 'double for all their sins', where *double* means ' "the equivalent" or "that which exactly matches" '.[83] That works here too. The elders receive the equivalent money for what they otherwise might be doing. One who stops work to attend a meeting has that financial loss covered by the church. The one who works full-time is paid what might be expected for an equivalent role. The general rule is that churches should not take advantage of willing workers.

Calvin suggested Paul describes two kinds of elders: 'ruling' and 'teaching' elders, with the latter being full-time and therefore needing a salary. Many Presbyterians agree, but others have suggested that this might be pressing the translation too far.[84] The issue is how to understand *especially*: does it mean 'above all' (some elders are charged with *preaching and teaching*), or does it mean 'namely' (the two groups are the same). Either could be correct grammatically,

---

[81] Homily 10, NPNF 13:347.

[82] Gal. 6:6; Rom. 13:7. Paul had rights (1 Cor. 9:4–6), but had a different pattern (1 Cor. 4:12; 2 Cor. 11:7–9; 1 Thess. 2:9).

[83] Isa. 40:2. A. Motyer, *The Prophecy of Isaiah* (Leicester, IVP, 1993), p. 299.

[84] Calvin, *Institutes*, 4.4.1. See T. F. Torrance and D. F. Wright, in H. Wotherspoon (ed.), *A Manual of Church Doctrine According to the Church of Scotland* (London: Oxford University Press, 1960), and Marshall, *Pastoral Epistles*, p. 610.

but previously Paul expected all elders to be *able to teach* (3:2), and for me that is unambiguous; I find it unlikely that Paul conceived of a non-teaching elder.

How generous is your church towards those who *labour in preaching* (literally, *in the word*) *and teaching*? Do you recompense and resource them? Do you cover their expenses? Do you help them read, study and develop their preaching?

b. Evaluating elders (19)

Any public Christian attracts scrutiny. As someone once put it, 'Churches put their leaders on a pedestal – mostly to get a clearer view of the target!', and Paul wants us to plan what to do if someone makes an allegation against an elder.

This is legal language: *admit a charge ... evidence ... witnesses*, because serious matters need an appropriate process. *Two or three witnesses* enable checking of evidence, as both the Old Testament and Jesus taught.[85] A healthy system ensures that no-one stands outside appraisal, correction, and protection.

c. Disciplining elders (20–21)

Paul identifies those who *persist in sin*. Having been examined privately, and presumably rebuked, they carried on, so Timothy is to *rebuke them in the presence of all*. Perhaps there is a grading here, some sins rebuked before *all* the elders, others before *all* the church. But sin is to be rebuked appropriately, so everyone impacted knows it has been addressed.

Because the church is 'the household of God, the church of the living God',[86] being an elder is significant. They do a *noble task* (3:1), and those who take it on should know they are accountable to God for that church. Rebuking one should make the rest *stand in fear*. Jesus is no absent Lord, and he will punish those who abuse their spiritual positions.

Paul writes with his full authority: *I charge you*, because Timothy also works *in the presence of God and of Christ Jesus and of the elect angels*. Aware of the pressures of ministry, the need to act quickly without acting hastily, of contending without being contentious, of being fair without being weak, Paul says *keep these rules* (notice, they are *rules*, not 'hints') *without prejudging, doing nothing from partiality*.

[85] Deut. 17:6; Matt. 18:15–20.
[86] 1 Tim. 3:15.

What system does your church or denomination have for disciplining elders? People can occupy powerful positions for years, seemingly unmoveable, and pastors can be constantly frustrated because of the weakness of the rules that their church operates. Churches find they cannot remove their pastor or challenge their bishops for the same reason.

That is particularly important for paid staff. Our systems must be Christian, in line with this passage, and they must also be legal. Getting this wrong may mean we have to reinstate or compensate employees who have been illegally dismissed. Secular courts may misunderstand why we wish to remove a sinning staff member, and we must ensure we can address that.

d. Appointing elders (22)

No wonder Paul tells Timothy, *Do not be hasty* (22), most likely warning against *hasty* selection. Elders were 'appointed',[87] and Paul might have some election, or at least public agreement in mind. But *laying on of hands* has Old Testament roots, was how Jesus blessed people, and marked God giving the Spirit at conversion twice in Acts.[88] It also marked giving authority to people, and was part of Timothy's own story.[89]

So this is a double-edged practice. It is a powerful way of asking God to bless this person, right now, with the strength they will need for ministry. Timothy was to look back on it for comfort and courage from God in challenging times. But we are also reminding each other that this person has new duties, possibly having authority over us, and a new accountability to God.

5. Calling?

Paul's requirements cover three areas. *God's standards* require that elders are mature Christians, solid in doctrine and able to teach/refute, and that deacons are deeply considered in their faith.[90] They must possess a *personal conviction*.[91] *Corporate recognition* then follows, because these qualities are to be publicly known and tested, and the people then duly prayed for and authorized.[92]

---

[87] *Cheirotoneō*, Acts 14:23, relates to *cheir*, 'a hand'; 2 Cor. 8:19. Titus 1:5 uses *katistēmi*.
[88] Num. 27:22–23; Mark 10:16; Acts 8:17–19; 19:6.
[89] Acts 6:6; 13:3; 1 Tim. 4:14; 2 Tim. 1:6.
[90] 1 Tim. 3:6; Titus 1:9.
[91] 1 Tim. 3:1.
[92] 1 Tim. 5:22.

There is one remarkable omission. Paul does not require that a particular person is, or feels, 'called' into ministry. A phrase which is almost a definition for starting to think about ministry in contemporary Christian circles, is not here.

a. What calling was

The Old Testament uses 'calling' in two ways. One describes salvation. God said through Isaiah, 'But now thus says the LORD, he who created you, O Jacob, he who formed you, O Israel: "Fear not, for I have redeemed you; I have *called* you by name, you are mine"'.[93]

Within that understanding, significant individuals received a call from God to do a particular work. Moses, Aaron, Samuel, David, Isaiah, Jeremiah and Ezekiel all remembered that calling distinctly.[94] But they ministered under different covenant expectations, and together were the prophets, priests and king who formed the template for what Jesus would be and do.

This puts them in an unusual position. We have seen repeatedly that different approaches to the Old Testament produce different understandings of the church and its life, and this is another. On this occasion I understand the prophets, priests and kings to function primarily as working models, or 'types' of Christ. Once he came, the line of all three could cease, and no contemporary prophet could ever claim that typological role. They were in that sense unique. Therefore their 'calling' (which was unique to those roles even in the Old Testament) ceases as well.

b. What calling is

The New Testament uses 'calling' to mean 'salvation'. Paul identified 'the hope to which he has called you',[95] and Peter tells us to 'make our calling and election sure'.[96] We have all been called.[97]

c. What calling is not

There are only two exceptions to that. Jesus was 'called' to his ministry. He is our high priest: 'And no-one takes this honour to

[93] Isa. 43:1.
[94] Exod. 3:1 – 4:17; 28:1; 1 Sam. 3:1–4; 16:1–13; Isa. 6:1–13; Jer. 1:4–19; Ezek. 1:1 – 2:10.
[95] Eph. 1:18.
[96] 2 Pet. 1:10.
[97] Jude 1.

himself, but receives it when called (*kaloumenos*) by God.'[98] Jesus is unique, and although Hebrews later addresses Christian leaders, 'calling' is reserved for Jesus alone.

The apostles were also 'called'. Jesus '*called* the twelve disciples to him and gave them authority to drive out impure spirits and to heal every disease and illness. These are the names of the twelve apostles . . . ', and then Matthew lists them.[99] Paul understood his apostleship similarly ('*called* to be an apostle').[100] Jesus and Paul heard a voice no-one else could hear;[101] Paul and John saw visions no-one else could see;[102] Jesus and the apostles have vocations no-one else could share. The voices and the visions are connected to the vocations, the calling they uniquely occupy.

Other than that, the biblical language of calling is unrelated to ministry; the biblical language of ministry is unrelated to calling. All Christians are 'called', because we are Christians, and because 'his divine power has given us *everything* we need for life and godliness when he *called* us by his own glory and goodness',[103] there is no requirement for any subsequent 'calling'.

Yet many churches look for a 'calling' to ministry, or a 'vocation' (the Latin equivalent). Martyn Lloyd-Jones described it, and concluded, 'Nothing but this overwhelming sense of being called, and of compulsion, should ever lead anyone to preach.'[104] But I suggest we reach a different conclusion. The experience described is vital, and hard questions should be asked about fitness for ministry, gifts and personality, passion, experience and Christian maturity. 'Are you aspiring to be an overseer, which is a noble task (1 Tim. 3:1), or are you a selfishly ambitious person who loves to be first (2 John 9)?' 'Do you love to teach, or do people love to learn from you?' 'Will you feed God's flock, or attract followers for yourself (Acts 20:28–31)?' Those are proper questions. But even though some people have a strong sense of God propelling them into a particular role, 'calling' is not the right biblical category. So, 'Do you feel called to ministry' is a well-intentioned but misguided question, and possibly excludes people who should be in ministry. We should ask the hard biblical questions,

---

[98] Heb. 5:4, NASB. See 5:5, 10.

[99] Matt. 10:1–2, NIV.

[100] Rom. 1:1; 1 Cor. 1:1.

[101] John 12:29; Acts 22:9.

[102] 2 Cor. 12:1–4; Rev. 1.

[103] 2 Pet. 1:3.

[104] M. Lloyd-Jones, *Preaching and Preachers* (London: Hodder and Stoughton, 1971), p. 107.

and retain the high biblical standards, but lose the unbiblical language.[105]

6. Men and women as elders?

The discussion about men and women in ministry is probably the most controversial facing churches today. Significant pastors structure their churches in starkly different ways; theologians and commentators dispute detailed exegesis and the broad contours of Scripture. Splits are occurring, from small groups through to entire denominations.

We cannot resolve this here. Indeed, the heat of the controversy meant I decided not to cover the most contested passages, including the nearby 1 Timothy 2:11–15, because proper exposition would require too much detail.[106] But these two passages contribute to the debate. Some questions always arise, such as whether Paul was giving local or universal instructions; whether he argues from culture or creation; whether theology is based before or after the fall; whether subsequent societal or theological insights modify his thinking; which passages overrule others, or whether there is a deep biblical trajectory leading to one conclusion, even though particular passages may lead to another.[107]

Two reasons persuade me that here, Paul restricts eldership to men. First, Paul wrote with explicitly masculine referents. An overseer is to be *the husband of but one wife* (3:2)[108] (contrast the widow of 5:9, 'the wife of one husband'); those are both one-way references, and Paul uses masculine pronouns for the elder, *he*, throughout. That alone might be cultural, but when Paul fears he might be misunderstood to teach that only men can be deacons, he explicitly addresses the issue of qualified women (3:11–13).[109]

All the relevant passages require careful study, but these two seem to me to support women's involvement equally in a huge range of church ministries, but not in eldership.

[105] Lloyd-Jones' section on 'call' contains no biblical references (*Preaching*, pp. 103–107), although he opposes an 'unscriptural' model (*Preaching*, p. 101). I agree with him that not every Christian can or should preach.

[106] See also W. Grudem, *Evangelical Feminism and Biblical truth: An Analysis of 118 Disputed Questions* (Leicester: Apollos, 2005), contrasted with R. W. Pierce and R. M. Groothuis, *Discovering Biblical Equality: Complementarity Without Hierarchy* (Leicester: Apollos, 2005). For a range of views in one volume, see J. R. Beck and C. Blomberg (eds.), *Two Views on Women in Ministry* (Grand Rapids: Zondervan, 2005).

[107] Others ask whether Paul was wrong, inconsistent, or binding.

[108] See A. J. Köstenberger and T. L. Wilder, *Entrusted with the Gospel: Paul's Theology in the Pastoral Epistles* (Nashville: Broadman and Holman, 2011), pp. 22–23.

[109] See above, and Köstenberger and Wilder, *Entrusted*, pp. 24–25.

7. Apostolic succession

We saw above the historical gap between us and Jesus, and the Roman Catholic claim to a line of leaders, unbroken from Peter.[110] It is initially attractive. Peter was martyred in Rome,[111] and it is plausible that he passed on his authority. The nineteenth-century English historian, Macaulay was more romantic:

> No other institution is left standing which carries the mind back to the times when the smoke of sacrifice rose from the Pantheon, and when camelopards and tigers bounded in the Flavian amphitheatre. The proudest royal houses are but as yesterday, when compared with the line of the Supreme Pontiffs. That line we trace back in unbroken series, from the Pope who crowned Napoleon in the nineteenth century to the Pope who crowned Pepin in the eighth; and far beyond the time of Pepin the august dynasty extends, till it is lost in the twilight of fable.[112]

But Peter's death aside, those first few centuries are guesswork; the popes disappear during Macaulay's 'twilight of fable'.[113] The Catholic theologian Hans Küng writes, 'Our information about the Roman church and its bishops is very fragmentary up to the middle of the third century; the first precise chronological dating of a Roman pontificate is the resignation of Pontian on 28 September 235.'[114] Can it be proved to go back to Peter? No.[115]

The deeper problem with apostolic succession is that the New Testament contains no hint that the apostles thought successors were needed. After Judas' suicide, Peter said:

> 'So one of the men who have accompanied us during all the time that the Lord Jesus went in and out among us, beginning from the baptism of John until the day when he was taken up from us – one of these men must become with us a witness to his resurrection.' And they put forward two, Joseph called Barsabbas, who was also called Justus, and Matthias. And they prayed and said, 'You, Lord, who know the hearts of all, show which one of these two you have chosen to take the place in this ministry and apostleship from which Judas turned aside to go to his own place.' And they cast

[110] Versions are occasionally found in other denominations.
[111] Eusebius, *Church History* III.1.
[112] Cited in Küng, *Church*, p. 24.
[113] For the history, see Morris, *Ministers*, pp. 70–80, and Green, *Called*, pp. 69–75.
[114] Küng, *Church*, pp. 460–461.
[115] Green, *Called*, p. 69.

lots for them, and the lot fell on Matthias, and he was numbered with the eleven apostles.[116]

As we saw, apostles accompanied Jesus before his death, witnessed his resurrection, and then were selected by him for this ministry – that is why they cast lots. Hundreds of men and women fulfilled those first two criteria, but only one fulfilled all three. Not even the women who met Jesus in the garden and whom he sent were included. But after this, there were twelve again.

What happened after the next apostle died, and the number dropped down?[117] Nothing. Not even the appointment of Joseph Barsabbas, who had come second. They remained eleven, then presumably ten, until all died. Jesus commissioned Paul,[118] but as 'the apostle to the Gentiles', and 'the least of the apostles',[119] and although Paul laid hands on Timothy, and expected Timothy to copy that, the apostolic title died.[120] No-one lays a foundation twice, and the twelve are the foundation of the heavenly Jerusalem for eternity.[121] Instead, as we obey what Paul told Timothy to pass on, we travel back two thousand years, and Timothy lays his hands on us.

8. Names

Different churches use these passages in startlingly different ways. Gordon Fee writes,

the entire spectrum of church government, from the hierarchical episcopacy of Roman Catholicism, through the mediating expression of Presbyterianism, to the extreme congregationalism of the Plymouth Brethren, all find support for their polity in [the Pastoral Epistles]. If the Pastor intended these letters to set the church in order, he seems not altogether to have succeeded.[122]

There are basically only three ways for churches to be organized, and there are biblically-minded believers in each.

- *Episcopalian.* One person, the 'bishop', the *episkopos,* is the focal leader in a particular area. Within a few decades of the death of

[116] Acts 1:21–26.
[117] Acts 12:2.
[118] Rom. 1:1, etc.
[119] Rom. 11:13; 1 Cor. 15:9.
[120] 2 Tim. 1:6; 1 Tim. 5:22.
[121] Acts 6:2; 1 Cor. 15:5; Rev. 21:14.
[122] G. Fee, *1, 2 Timothy and Titus*, NIBC (Peabody: Hendrickson, 1988), p. 21.

the last apostle, this became the only model for around 1,500 years, and still functions in many denominations. Episcopalians value that tradition, but the biblically-minded also draw on Timothy, Titus, and 'overseers'.[123]

- *Presbyterian.* The elders, *presbyteroi*, within a congregation, relate to other congregations through their meetings at a local and national level. It is associated particularly with Calvin's legacy,[124] and there was mutual acceptance of episcopalian and presbyterian ordination at the Reformation.[125]
- *Congregational.* There may be, one, many or no pastors, with or without elders or deacons, but each congregation is accountable only to Christ, and relates to any other church only through him.[126] The ultimate authority is the congregation itself, even within denominations. It emerged at the Reformation, often in deliberate contrast to Calvin, and is associated particularly with a Baptist legacy.[127] The other two models generate officers in authority over congregations and oversee relations between them (they are 'Connectional'); congregational churches are independent. Some developed into the 'Radical Reformation', a position which has recently re-emerged as a basis for mission to challenge the historic ('Christendom' or 'Magisterial Reformation') legacy of the

---

[123] See C. Buchanan, *Is the Church of England Biblical?* (London: Darton, Longman and Todd, 1998), p. 255, and T. Bradshaw, *The Olive Branch: An Evangelical Anglican Doctrine of the Church* (Carlisle: Paternoster Press, 1992). Contrast P. Toon, 'Episcopalianism', in P. E. Engle and S. B. Cowan (eds.), *Who Runs the Church? 4 Views on Church Government* (Grand Rapids: Zondervan, 2004), pp. 19–41, or P. Zahl, 'The Bishop-Led Church', in C. O. Brand and S. E. Norman (eds.), *Perspectives on Church Government: Five Views of Church Polity* (Nashville: Broadman and Holman, 2004), pp. 209–254. Toon and Zahl both depend on the authority of tradition, and their fellow contributors accuse them of not being properly evangelical.

[124] See R. Reymond, 'The Presbytery-led Church', in Brand and Norman (eds.), *Perspectives*, pp. 87–156, and L. Taylor 'Presbyterianism', in Engle and Cowie (eds.), *Who Runs the Church?*, pp. 71–98.

[125] J. W. Hunkin, 'The Anglican Pattern of Episcopacy', *Churchman*, 62.2 (1948).

[126] For the range see P. Patterson 'Single-elder Congregationalism', in Engle and Cowie (eds.), *Who Runs the Church?*, pp. 131–152 and D. Akin, 'The Single-Elder Led Church', Brand and Norman (eds.), *Perspectives*, pp. 25–86; S. B. Waldron, 'Plural-elder Congregationalism', in Engle and Cowie (eds.), *Who Runs the Church?*, pp. 185–221 and J. R. White, 'The Plural-Elder-Led Church', in Brand and Norman (eds.), *Perspectives*, pp. 209–254; and J. L. Garrett Jr, 'The Congregation-led Church', in Brand and Norman (eds.), *Perspectives*, pp. 157–208.

[127] See Mark Dever, *Nine Marks of a Healthy Church* (Wheaton: Crossway, 2005), and *A Display of God's Glory: Basics of Church Structure: Deacons, Elders, Congregationalism and Membership* (Washington: IX Marks, 2001).

other two, where 'independence' is seen more as 'independence from the government'.[128]

The difficulty is when any one model claims too much. Episcopalians struggle to map their threefold order of bishops, priests and deacons onto the biblical data. Independency struggles with biblical interdependence. Calvin's claims for democratic elections go beyond the text. It might be better to adopt the level-headedness of Geoffrey Bromiley:

> The fact that there must be presbyterate does not mean that there has to be a particular Presbyterian structure; though the various kinds of Presbyterianism serve to emphasize this concern. The fact that there must be a diaconate does not mean that there has to be a particular Congregational structure; though some types of Congregationalism keep this element to the fore. The fact that there must be an episcopate does not mean that there has to be a particular Episcopalian rule and its interconnection with the ministry of the word.[129]

Healthy churches need biblically faithful elders/overseers and deacons, but there is flexibility about how put this into practice.

---

[128] See M. Williams, *Church after Christendom* (Carlisle: Paternoster, 2004), and N. Wright, *Free Church, Free State: The Positive Baptist Vision* (Milton Keynes: Authentic Media, 2005).

[129] G. W. Bromiley, *Christian Ministry* (Grand Rapids: Eerdmans, 1960), p. 81.

Romans 12:1–13
13. The church's gifts

Romans 12:1 marks a turn in Paul's letter. He wrote to produce 'the obedience of faith',[1] but to this point he has not pressed the applications;[2] from now on he addresses relationships. There were disagreements between Jewish believers, and between Gentile believers, and 'the strong' and 'the weak' of Romans 14 could be found in both camps. But that means we can apply this even when there are only Gentile believers in church, and over other relational matters as well.[3] He tells them twice to 'live in harmony with one another',[4] and writes eight separate sections on how they are to treat *one another*.[5] Our focus verses, 12:1–13, open with a call to individual commitment over how we use our own *bodies* (1), and then to corporate commitment as *one body* (4), the church.

1. Christians and their bodies (12:1–2)

Paul's summarizes Romans 1 – 11 in the phrase, *the mercies of God*, and it is *in view of*[6] those riches that he makes his *appeal*. His double goals are that our *sacrifice* is found *acceptable to God* (1), and his *will* is found *acceptable* to us (2).

a. Sacrifice your body (1)

God's expectations come above all others, and they must be right

[1] 1:5; see 2:7; 6:4, 17–19; 8:5–6.
[2] Although see 6:11–13 and 8:12–13.
[3] See D. Moo, *The Epistle to the Romans*, NICNT (Grand Rapids/Cambridge: Eerdmans, 1996), p. 745.
[4] Rom. 12:16; 15:5.
[5] Rom. 12:5, 10, 16; 13:8; 14:13, 19; 15:5, 7.
[6] NIV.

before our relationships with each other can be addressed. We are to *present* our whole beings to him as a *sacrifice*, explained in three adjectives: *living*, *holy* and *acceptable*.

A *living sacrifice* is vivid, because the word *sacrifice* (*thysia*) comes from the word 'to kill' (*thyō*). So we might translate it, 'a living death-offering'. The doves, lambs and bulls that were offered died in a moment – we are to die for a lifetime.

Sacrifices were God's rightful portion, and *holy* means 'set apart', or dedicated as God's personal property to do with as he wishes.[7] God says of every Christian, 'this one is mine, for my purpose', and no-one can argue. Not even the Christian.

The third adjective is also sacrificial, because a 'pleasing aroma' came from *acceptable* sacrifices.[8] Paul used this description of Christian obedience in general[9] and particular aspects of it.[10] What makes a sacrifice acceptable, then, is not cost or spontaneity, but continual obedience; that is what he expects us to offer.

This sacrificial life-style is *spiritual worship*. *Worship*, and its opposite, idolatry, are central to the diagnosis in Romans. Although God and his wisdom were clearly knowable, people 'did not honour him as God or give thanks to him',[11] and the entire destructive cycle of sin spun out from that. 'They exchanged the truth about God for a lie and worshipped and served the creature rather than the Creator, who is blessed forever. Amen!'[12] Romans 1 – 11 tells how God conquered that problem, so we may serve him without deserving his wrath. By faith in Christ we have been moved from idolatrous *worship* (*elatreusan*, 1:25) to true *worship* (*latreian*) here.

The word which qualifies *worship* is unusual.[13] It is to do with reason, which produced translations like 'reasonable';[14] unfortunately, that can mean something which is not too demanding. *Spiritual* is trying to capture that *worship* is internal and true rather than merely formal.[15] Perhaps it is best to think of opposites: just as *worship* is the opposite of idolatry, so this word is the opposite of 'futile . . . thinking', being 'fools', and 'exchang[ing] the truth

[7] Lev. 20:26.

[8] Exod. 29:18, 25, 41; Lev. 22:20, 29; Num. 15:7–14; Ps. 51:19.

[9] 2 Cor. 5:9; Eph. 5:10. See also Heb. 13:21.

[10] Giving money: Phil. 4:18. Obeying parents: Col. 3:20.

[11] Rom. 1:21.

[12] Rom. 1:25. Paul's primary reference is to Adam and Eve, echoed in both the history of Israel, and the general habits of the human heart.

[13] It is not in LXX, and in NT only in 1 Pet. 2:2. For translation options, see Moo, *Romans* 753.

[14] KJV.

[15] ESV, HCSB, NIV, NASB, etc.

about God for a lie'.[16] It means to live by God's truth, reason and wisdom, rather than sin's lies, irrationality and folly.[17]

b. Renew your mind and discern God's will (2a)

There are clear contrasts between the two patterns of behaviour, *do not be . . . but be*, and between the sinful *world* and the renewed *mind*. Leon Morris writes, 'Christians have been introduced into the life of the world to come; what a tragedy, then, if they conform to the perishing world they have left.'[18] So Paul writes a series of negative commands (*do not, never*) as well as positive instructions.[19]

God's will is his plan on the grand stage, the theme of Romans 1 – 11. Like an experienced traveller who boards a plane and immediately sets her watch by the time of her destination, rather than by any place on the route, Christians' values are set by where we are going rather than where we happen to be.[20]

That setting of the watch means that Paul understands day-to-day decisions within the overarching plan of God. At the opening of Romans, he reported that he has been praying 'that somehow by God's will I may now at last succeed in coming to you',[21] and he will close by asking them to pray 'that by God's will I may come to you with joy and be refreshed in your company'.[22] Paul did not know whether God was going to answer his prayers affirmatively, so he is not guessing what God's will is, or claiming to know it, or fearing that he might miss it. Rather, he humbly submits to God's will.[23]

There are three initial aspects to this. God's will is *good*, centred on a good and loving God; it is *acceptable*, a fitting thing to do; and it is *perfect*, it works towards the goal of Christ's kingdom. So when we make any decision, like Paul's wish to visit the Roman Christians, or a career choice, or finding a place to serve in church, we ask: is it *good* (would this violate any of God's commands? Is it an active step of obedience?); is it *acceptable* (is this a fitting thing to spend time

---

[16] Rom. 1:21–25.

[17] G. R. Osborne, *Romans*, IVPNTC (Downers Grove/Leicester: IVP, 2004), p. 320.

[18] L. Morris, *The Epistle to the Romans*, PNTC (Grand Rapids: Eerdmans and Leicester: IVP, 1998), p. 435.

[19] Rom. 12:3, 11, 14, 16, 19, 21.

[20] The verb *dokimazein* has a range of apt meanings. NIV's expanded *test and approve* covers several bases, and is 'a good solution to a difficult translation problem' (Morris, *Romans*, p. 436).

[21] Rom. 1:10.

[22] Rom. 15:32.

[23] A minor but complex problem lurks here, over whether the will of God is *good and acceptable and perfect* in God's eyes, or in ours. For a good description and conclusion, see Osborne, *Romans*, pp. 322–323.

and money on?); and is it *perfect* (would it actively encourage me or others in becoming more like Christ?).

But a fourth aspect is the turning point here. To *test and approve God's will* is that I not only have to dedicate my body (1), I need to serve the rest of the body (4). I have to take other Christians into account. I need the church.

2. Christians and the body (12:3–8)

The theme continues to be a renewed *mind*. One Greek word family (related to *phronein*, 'to think') appears four times in verse 3, and three times in verse 16:

> For by the grace given to me I say to everyone among you not to **think of himself more highly** (*hyperphronein*) than he ought to **think** (*phronein*), but **to think** (*phronein*) with **sober judgement** (*sōphronein*), each according to the measure of faith that God has assigned. (3)

> Be of the *same mind* (*phronein*) towards one another; do not be *haughty in mind* (*phronein*), but associate with the lowly. *Do not be wise* (*phronimos*) in your own estimation (12:16).[24]

a. Our body (3–5)

The idea of calling a group of people a 'body' was as common then as now, and Paul used it in various ways.[25] Here and in 1 Corinthians, it describes our differing and dependent roles in the local church, functioning like different limbs. In both letters 'body' introduces 'gifts', and in both 'love' is critical. Paul knows that what he is about to teach runs the risk of producing self-important, self-regarding Christians. So both letters address the issue relationally: Romans 12 is structured around body (3–5), gifts (6–8) and love (9–13); 1 Corinthians around gifts, body, love and gifts.[26]

Our selfish first question is always about ourselves: 'What are *my* gifts and how can *I* find a place to use them? If *you* don't let *me* use *my* gifts, then I'm leaving!' By contrast, Paul ties together each

---

[24] V. 3 from ESV and v. 16 from NASB. Leon Morris notes: 'I have made the break at the end of verse 16, but others prefer to make it at the end of verse 13. That is quite possible, and indeed the whole section is somewhat loosely structured' (*Romans*, p. 436).

[25] In Ephesians and Colossians it means the universal and single people of God, in Christ (Eph. 2:15; Col. 1:18).

[26] 1 Cor. 12:1–11; 12:12–31; 13:1–13; 14:1–25.

individual Christian (below in bold) with all the other Christians (in capitals):

> *For by the grace given to me I say to **every one** among YOU not to think of **yourself** more highly than **you** ought to think, but to think with sober judgement, **each** according to the measure of faith that God has assigned. For as in one body WE have MANY members, and the members do not all have the same function, so WE, though MANY, are one body in Christ, and **individually** members ONE OF ANOTHER.*

We must look at gifts relationally and not individually, because we only understand ourselves in relationship with others. Each of us is unique, but we belong to each other.

(i) It is wrong to have inflated ideas of ourselves (3a)
Paul begins with a warning: *I say to you . . . not to think of yourself more highly than you ought to think.*

The sociologist Jean Twenge suggests that today we are facing a 'narcissism epidemic' (in Greek myth, Narcissus fell in love with his reflection) where people are confident, entitled, assertive – but miserable because they believe they have a right to be perfect, and they are not.[27] Her work is not based on Christians, but neither does she exclude us, so we have to ask whether our faith makes us discernibly different from our culture. Richard Winter says Romans 12 is critical for avoiding perfectionism: 'As the Spirit of God renews our thinking patterns we begin to recognize two lies: first, that we have to be perfect to be accepted, and second, that we will be judged and evaluated by God in the way our culture assesses value – primarily on the basis of our performance or appearance.'[28] We are as likely as any first-century Christian to collude with a superficial and selfish culture, and fall in love with ourselves. So do not *think of yourself more highly than you ought to think.*

(ii) It is right to evaluate ourselves (3b)
It would be dreadful to be part of a church where the focus was on me rather than Jesus. Perhaps, because we live in a self-regarding culture, and potentially a self-regarding church, the risks of thinking about our gifts are too great.

Paul's response would be clear. Instructions to *love one another* and *serve the Lord* will not be missing (10, 11), but he still wants

---

[27] J. M. Twenge, *Generation Me* (New York: The Free Press, 2006); J. Twenge and W. K. Campbell, *The Narcissism Epidemic* (New York: The Free Press, 2009).

[28] R. Winter, *Perfecting Ourselves to Death* (Downers Grove: IVP, 2005), p. 161.

cool-headed self-understanding. *Think with sober judgement* is his phrase, the opposite of puffed-up arrogance.[29] For the Christian body to function, each part should know what it should be doing, and how it fits into the whole. We need self-knowledge, *according to the measure of faith that God has assigned*, which probably means that Christians are at different levels of maturity, faith and trust in God, and we should evaluate ourselves accordingly.[30]

(iii) As long as we do it in relationship with others (4)
Our self-evaluation is so we can serve others, because *in one body we have many members*. Other people have a say in the part we play in church. The fact that we enjoy singing does not mean other people enjoy our solos. But quieter people need to be affirmed that what they contribute is special in some way. And while putting similarly gifted people together fires them up, putting differently gifted people together can create vibrant new opportunities.

(iv) It is right to think about ourselves as unique (3)
Most churches seem to run quite well on Sundays with only a few people busy. Pastor/teachers do their work, along with the musicians. Administrators sort out welcomers and the coffee rota – and the rest of us are the audience. But *each* of us should *think with sober judgement* about our place, and that word *each*, is important.[31]

There are churches where training is focused on the preachers and study leaders. But Bible teaching is essential to a church because it is the way Christ gives, nourishes, guides all the other gifts. To paraphrase 1 Corinthians, if the whole body were the gift of teaching, where would the gift of mercy be? In other churches, a different mark of the Spirit's work is highlighted, but as with teaching we have to insist with Paul, *the members do not all have the same function*. We do *not* all have the same gifts, and we do *not* all have the same function in the body.[32]

---

[29] Thomas R. Schreiner, *Romans*, BECNT (Grand Rapids: Baker Academic, 1998), p. 651.

[30] 'As God has measured the measure of faith.' The question is whether that *faith* is objective (*the faith*) or subjective (*my faith*). Those who stress *faith* tend to favour an objective reading (e.g., Morris, *Romans*, p. 438; Moo, *Romans*, p. 761); those who stress *measure* tend to favour a subjective one (e.g., Schreiner, *Romans*, p. 652). I think vv. 4–8 fit the subjective reading, as we exercise our individual gifts fittingly. That gifts should be used in line with scriptural truth, is taught elsewhere.

[31] See 1 Pet. 4:10: '*Each of you* should use whatever gift he has received, to serve others.'

[32] See ch. 11.

(v) It is right to think of ourselves as belonging to each other (5)
This wonderful, healthy diversity, is because *we, though many, are one body in Christ.* Being *one body in Christ* sets us apart from any other human organization, no matter how united, valuable or caring. His concerns are our business. And we belong to each other because we are *individually members one of another.* That is a profound challenge to selfishness. I, as a hand, am a member of you, a foot. So to achieve our full potential as churches we must unleash our gifts together. One person's generosity needs another's administration; a third person's mercy needs the first person's generosity.

This will be hard to learn. Western culture sees dependence as immaturity, and maturity as becoming independent. Children leave home because of their mature independence. Christians, by contrast, should see maturity as *inter*dependence. In recognizing my gifts and yours, we both recognize what each of us contributes that the other does not. Together, our gifts are amplified.[33]

A book advising young adults on finding a career shows this starkly. In *Plugged In: The Generation Y Guide To Thriving At Work,* Tamara J. Erickson explains the cultural clashes that different generations in employment can produce. She encourages Gen Y readers (born between 1980–2000) to know their passions and contributions, and to make wise choices. Erickson describes their assumptions shrewdly, but disagreeing with the analysis of 'narcissism' we saw earlier, she writes directly to her readers:

> Most of you are jumping into the world with confidence and have a high level of self-esteem. Gen Y's as a whole are more willing to express their own ideas, bring new thinking to issues or problems, and critique the way things have always been done if they think they have a better way. As one of you expresses it, 'I've come to realize that the most significant characteristic of the Gen Y bird is that we are unapologetic. From how we look, to how spoiled we are, to what we want – even demand – of work, we *do* think we are special. And what ultimately makes us different is our willingness to talk about it, without much shame and with the expectation that somebody – our parents, our friends, our managers – will help us figure it all out.'[34]

Erickson views that as maturity. But in a church that attitude – whatever the generation of the person speaking – is immaturity. There is a gulf between considering ourselves as 'spoiled' and

[33] See B. Bugbee, D. Cousins and B. Hybels' course, *Network* (rev. ed., Grand Rapids: Zondervan, 2004).
[34] T. J. Erickson, *Plugged In* (Harvard: Harvard Business School Press, 2008), p. 52.

'special', and thinking we have being given gifts by Jesus, for his service and the benefit of others; not spoiled but an entrusted and accountable servant, not special, but a unique and interdependent part of one body.

That may be most clearly seen when we do not use our gifts, but serve anyway. Quietly emptying the bins because it needs doing. Often maturity means we just roll up our sleeves, and serve.

b. Our gifts (6–8)

So, *having gifts that differ according to the grace given to us* what are we supposed to do? English has to insert a phrase like, *let us use them*, to make sense of what follows. Before plunging into the list of gifts, we need to clear our minds.

(i) Gifts, spiritual gifts and grace

The writers of the New Testament never used the phrase 'spiritual gifts', despite our translators and editors. Here, Paul uses the single word *gifts*, once. In 1 Corinthians he uses *charisma*, meaning 'gift', and *pneumatikos*, 'a spiritual thing or person'.[35] So the phrase 'spiritual gifts' connects two ideas that Paul used separately. Secondly, the word *charisma* (*charismata*, the plural, gives us 'charismatic') is built from *charis*, 'grace'. And central to grace is the kindness of God, the focus on Jesus' death as the most important gift to us, standing in God's favour as the result of the gospel, and therefore the attitude we should have towards each other.

1 Corinthians also faces the worldliness of that church, and Paul sometimes writes ironically, or reinterprets their language. Is it quite coincidental that the first two *charismata* listed in 1 Corinthians are 'marriage' and 'singleness'?[36] It would certainly defuse any super-spirituality, because everyone has one of those gifts.

The word 'gift' keeps generosity in there, to highlight Christ who gives gifts, and others whom we serve with our gifts. But I think the phrase 'spiritual gifts' or 'charismatic gifts' is one we must drop, because it raises the idea of two categories of gifts, 'ordinary' ones (like generosity, leadership or marriage) and 'spiritual' ones that are somehow superior. No, all the gifts are grace-gifts, whether from the Father (here), the Son (Eph. 4) or the Holy Spirit (1 Cor. 12).

[35] *Charisma*: 1 Cor. 1:7; 7:7; 12:4, 9, 28, 30–31. *Pneumatikos*: 1 Cor. 2:13–15; 3:1; 9:11; 10:3–4; 12:1; 14:1, 37; 15:44, 46. Other terms include 'service' (1 Cor. 12:5); 'manifestation' (1 Cor. 12:7) and 'working' (1 Cor. 12:10).
[36] 1 Cor. 7:7, *charisma*.

(ii) Gifts, today?

Some would strongly disagree. Significant theologians argue strongly and competently that some (not all, they insist) New Testament gifts ceased late in the first century.[37] Vern Poythress summarized this view (often called cessationist) for others to interact with, so his is a good starting point.

Poythress is clear that 'the Spirit of God is at work today in a powerful, dynamic, supernatural, and direct way'.[38] That is important to hear, because the criticism is sometimes levelled that cessationists hardly believe in the Spirit's work today. No, writes Poythress, 'Not to experience the Spirit – in a vital, transforming, and thus powerful way – is not to have the Spirit at all.'[39] Of course the Spirit is at work. 'Nor', he continues, 'do I argue that miracles have ceased' – for why else would he pray for people to be healed, or circumstances to change?[40]

So what has ceased? Apostles. Ephesians 2:20 taught that they are foundational, and foundations are only built once. Alongside them stand prophets, also foundational and ceased.[41] Prophecy is listed in verse 6, so we shall deal with it shortly, but, from his definition, Poythress is clear: 'With this foundational element revelation completed, and so too their foundational role as witnesses, the apostles, and along with them, the prophets and other associated word gifts, pass from the life of the church.'[42] Those 'associated word gifts' include anything with revelatory content, such as tongues or interpretation. Poythress argues they *must* have ceased, *because* they are foundational, but he is equally certain that the Holy Spirit is powerfully at work in women and men today. He is suspicious about many claims to miracles today, but that is not the same as cessationism. Prayer for healing co-exists with a refusal to be gullible. But for Poythress, Paul's instructions on 'word gifts' have no direct relevance to any contemporary experience.

I find much to affirm in this: a strong understanding of the necessary work of the Spirit in every believer, confidence that God acts, and a trust in an infallible Scripture. I too believe that God has covenanted how he will behave, and no supposed new insights or ministries can

---

[37] See V. Poythress, *Perspectives on Pentecost* (Phillipsburg: P & R Publishing, 1979); R. B. Gaffin, 'A Cessationist View', in W. Grudem (ed.), *Are Miraculous Gifts for Today: Four Views* (Leicester: IVP, 1996), pp. 25–64; S. Ferguson, *The Holy Spirit* (Leicester: IVP, 1996). All three books are of their time, but remain significant. Gaffin's chapter is embedded within interacting viewpoints.

[38] Poythress, *Perspectives*, p. 26.

[39] Ibid., p. 41.

[40] Ibid.

[41] See ch. 11.

[42] Poythress, *Perspectives*, p. 44.

supersede that. He has bound himself. I strongly affirm the Ephesians 4:11 teaching on the irreplaceable and foundational role of the apostles and prophets, whose ministries cannot be replicated today.

But I am uneasy, because there is so much active encouragement, in those very Scriptures which superintend the church until Christ's return, to understand the Spirit's work in equipping members of the body with gifts for ministry. Some gifts may have ceased, but that is not a simple concept: we saw in chapter 11 that as the apostles cease so the gift of the evangelist comes into being; prophets cease so that pastor-teachers flourish continually.[43] Some 'word gifts' have ceased, in order for other 'word gifts' to exist all the time. And the place of pastor-teachers is to equip others.

That emphasis looks more biblically balanced to me. A church where the leading is done by those who have the gift of leadership, and where the teaching is done by those with the gift of teaching, would seem to me to be a church that is using those gifts in an appropriate way.

(iii) Gifts, how many?

One way to proceed would be to identify all the different biblical gifts, and try to map them so we could identify our own. Paul's lists, combined with 1 Peter 4:10–11 (the only other New Testament occurrence of the idea) look like this:

1 Corinthians 7:7	Romans 1:11	Ephesians 4:11
• Singleness	• An unspecified gift	• Apostles
• Marriage		• Prophets
	Romans 12	• Evangelists
1 Corinthians 12:8–11	• Prophecy	• Pastors-and-teachers
• Utterance of wisdom	• Service	
• Utterance of	• Teaching	**2 Timothy 1:6**
knowledge	• Exhorting	• An unspecified gift,
• Faith	• Generosity	presumably teaching
• Healing	• Leadership	but might be the
• Miracles	• Mercy	gospel itself.
• Prophecy	• Exhorting	
• Distinguish between		**1 Peter 4:11**
spirits		• Speaking
• Various kinds of		• Serving
tongues		
• The interpretation of		
tongues		

[43] Apostles having ceased, their authenticating signs have ceased too: 2 Cor. 12:12.

But translating the words does not mean we know what they were. 1 Corinthians 12:8 is translated by ESV as 'utterance of wisdom' and 'utterance of knowledge'; by NIV as 'message of wisdom' and 'message of knowledge'; and by NKJV as 'word of wisdom' and 'word of knowledge'. The first word involves some kind of speaking, but what distinguishes 'wisdom' and 'knowledge'? C. Peter Wagner is confident: 'The gift of wisdom is the special ability that God gives to certain members of the body of Christ to know the mind of the Holy Spirit in such a way as to receive insight into how given knowledge may best be applied to specific needs arising in the body of Christ.' Knowledge, by contrast, is 'the special ability that God gives to certain members of the body of Christ to discover, accumulate, analyze, and clarify information and ideas which are pertinent to the well-being of the body'.[44] But how does Wagner know? Nothing in the text draws those conclusions, and anyone who offers tight definitions has to import them. Another author defines knowledge as 'The special ability to master God's revealed truth in Scripture',[45] which is equally a stab in the dark. Gordon Fee, himself strongly in favour of the use of gifts, examined the problem thoroughly, and concluded that Paul's distinction 'is perhaps forever lost to us'.[46] We simply do not know.[47] That is the first sign that this subject is complex.

Even where we know what a gift is, and wish to map it on today's church, there are questions about the limits of such lists. For example, should we include other 'gifts' the Bible endorses, like music, song-writing, the creative arts or writing?[48] That expands any list considerably. But what about being a gifted warrior, sailor, lawyer or mourner?[49] And what about activities which find no mention in the Bible? Accountants, sound engineers, counsellors, youth workers and typists are all critical for many congregations. And what about those who use their gifts largely outside the church, like medics, film makers, apologists or software designers? Is it appropriate to talk about those gifts in the same way as tongues or teaching?

None of the biblical lists is designed as 'a list'. They are largely occasional descriptions of the *gifts that differ* among us (6). So any way of helping people to discover, grow and use their God-given

---

[44] C. P. Wagner, *Your Spiritual Gifts Can Help Your Church Grow* (Crowborough: Monarch/MARC Europe, 1985), p. 13. Typographical errors corrected.

[45] R. F. Houts, *Houts Inventory of Spiritual Gifts* (Pasadena: Charles E. Fuller Institute of Evangelism and Church Growth, 1985), p. 13.

[46] G. Fee, *God's Empowering Presence* (Carlisle: Paternoster, 1994), p. 168.

[47] It is tempting to add that the gift of wisdom would help here. Or knowledge.

[48] Among other passages, see for music (1 Chr. 16:41–42), songwriting (Ps. 45:1), the creative arts (Exod. 31:2–5), or writing (Eccl. 12:10).

[49] Warrior (Jer. 50:9), sailor (Ezek. 27:8), lawyer (Ezra 7:6), mourner (Amos 5:16).

gifts or abilities for the good of the church, must allow for considerable looseness at the edges. Many gifts appear to be simply an intensification of normal Christian obedience. Everyone is to be generous, but some have the gift of generosity (8, 13). Everyone teaches and evangelizes, but some have the gifts of teaching or evangelism.[50] 'Gifts' is not a boxed-in concept.

(iv) Christ's gifts

So we cannot compile a simple checklist, but since Paul uses each one to teach, we must take the seven in turn: four are introduced by *if*,[51] and with some overlap, the last five focus on the manner of *the one who* exercises the gift.[52]

Prophecy.[53] Some people in the earliest churches communicated direct words from God. Paul rates this gift of *prophecy* highly: in 1 Corinthians 12:28 'prophets' are second only to 'apostles', and in Ephesians 2:20 they are foundational alongside the apostles. They had a binding and final authority, and what they said still functions as Scripture today. John opened and closed Revelation by calling it an authoritative 'prophecy'.[54]

There seem also to have been those who had that or a similar gift, but without the same authority.[55] Apostles (and, presumably, prophets in that first sense) still have universal, final, and binding words, but these other prophets had local, sometimes personal, and apparently optional words,[56] and what they said was to be 'weighed' by the rest of the church.[57] In 1 Corinthians 12, Paul mentions prophecy, and then 'the ability to distinguish between spirits', which is presumably related; John lays down careful doctrinal tests.[58] These prophets' role enable the church to 'learn' and 'be encouraged',

---

[50] Teach (Col. 3:16); evangelize (Phil.1:5); teaching and evangelism as gifts (Eph. 4:11,12).

[51] *Eite.*

[52] Although 'why (Paul) changes . . . is not clear' (Moo, *Romans*, p. 767).

[53] The literature is large, strong, divergent – and occasionally strident. My position is close to M. Turner, *The Holy Spirit and Spiritual Gifts Then and Now* (Carlisle: Paternoster, 1996) or, because of the infallibility of Scripture, W. Grudem,*The Gift of Prophecy: In the New Testament and Today* (rev. ed., Memphis: Crossway, 2000); but note the care of Poythress, *Perspectives*.

[54] Rev. 1:3; 22:18.

[55] Acts 13:1; 19:6; 21:9.

[56] Local: Acts 11:27; 13:1–2. Personal: Acts 16:6–10; 18:10; 20:23. Optional: Acts 21:4, 10–14.

[57] 1 Cor. 14:29, and possibly 1 Thess. 5:19–22. This goes against John Frame's suggestion that NT prophets were identical in authority and role to OT prophets. J. Frame, *The Doctrine of the Word of God* (Phillipsburg: Presbyterian and Reformed, 2010), p. 91.

[58] 1 Cor. 12:10; 1 John 4:1–6.

and to experience 'upbuilding' and 'consolation'.[59] That sounds similar to what teachers or preachers to do, although they are distinguishable gifts.[60] Paul rates this gift highly: 'Pursue love and earnestly desire the spiritual gifts, especially that you may prophesy.'[61]

A fully biblical position must affirm both elements, and work with the complexity that follows. The years when the New Testament was being written were unique, and God gifted the church with apostles and prophets in that period, who could teach and write with full and final authority. It was one of those prophets who warned that there would not be any further prophecy of that kind:

> I warn everyone who hears the words of the prophecy of this book: if anyone adds to them, God will add to him the plagues described in this book, and if anyone takes away from the words of the book of this prophecy, God will take away his share in the tree of life and in the holy city, which are described in this book.[62]

That irreplaceable and finished work of prophecy makes it highly unwise to use a phrase like 'Thus says the Lord' to introduce any contemporary message other than a Bible reading.

But we can still expect the second group to exist, with no necessary claim to authority, and with a tentative spirit. Wayne Grudem calls this 'speaking merely human words to report something God brings to mind'.[63] The desire for a special status is real, so the New Testament warns about people who claim to be authoritative prophets but are actually false teachers in disguise; they are to be avoided.[64] Moses was even clearer:

> If a prophet or one who foretells by dreams, appears among you and announces to you a miraculous sign or wonder, and if the sign or wonder of which he has spoken takes place, and he says, 'Let us follow other gods' (gods you have not known) 'and let us worship them,' you must not listen to the words of that prophet

---

[59] 1 Cor. 14:31, 3.

[60] Calvin is nuanced on this: 'I am certain, in my own mind, that he means by prophets, not those endowed with the gift of foretelling, but those blessed with the unique gift of dealing with scripture, not only by interpreting it, but also by the wisdom they showed in making it fit the needs of the hour.' J. Calvin, *1 Corinthians*, transl., John W. Fraser, CNTC (Grand Rapids: Eerdmans, 1996 [1546]), p. 271.

[61] 1 Cor. 14:1. '*Spiritual gifts*' translates *pneumatika* – 'gift' has been imported into the translation although it is probably not far from Paul's thoughts.

[62] Rev. 22:18–19.

[63] Grudem, *Gift of Prophecy*, ch. 4.

[64] In Titus 1:12 it is a 'prophet' of the 'circumcision party' who must be rebuked, although translations do not always make this clear.

or dreamer. The LORD your God is testing you to find out whether you love him with all your heart and with all your soul.[65]

The test is not the accuracy of the prediction, but the orthodoxy of the teaching.

So the primarily rule of weighing any claimed prophecy will be to check its doctrine. Sounding biblical is not enough, because thousands of false prophets have fooled churches in that way. The prophecy must sit under Scripture, and cannot correct, supplement or in any way re-order Scripture's teaching.[66]

This is difficult in practice, because we tend to get more excited when someone says 'I have a word from the Lord', than when someone says, 'Please turn to Romans 6'. But the Bible is God's guaranteed, authoritative word, containing his binding promises and warnings. Perhaps one reason we are easily fooled by exciting (but false) prophets, is that we are not truly thrilled by God's word. After that, provided the claimed prophecy is doctrinally solid, the weighing process gives us the liberty to decide what we do with the prophecy.

Service. This is a general term, and the lesson is simple: whatever we do, and whether our culture or our church sees it as significant or low status, we are never more than servants.

That fights with our human capacity to place ourselves centre stage. Imagine the difference between saying to a newcomer, 'Hello, I'm a minister here at Riverside Church', and 'Hello, I'm a servant here at Riverside Church'. The first conveys importance, and probably a salary and a reserved place in the church car park, the second nothing of the sort. Yet 'minister' and 'servant' are identical in Greek: *diakonos*. We all serve. This is where narcissism dies, because *serving* always puts other person first.

Teaching. We have noticed *teachers* before,[67] but here the emphatic *the one who teaches in teaching* is double-edged. None of us, no matter how mature, passes beyond the need to be taught. We need to come to church spiritually prepared to praise and pray, enjoy fellowship and be encouraged, but we need to come expecting to be taught.

Those of us with this responsibility should see it as a service. So when we spend hours preparing, we must remember that this is one of serving other people. Teaching, like any other gift, is other-person centred. I know for myself how easy it is to use a pulpit or platform

---

[65] Deut. 13:1–3, NIV.

[66] Most commentators suggest *in proportion to faith* (NRSV) is most likely to be the faith of the person, and we should use our gifts in proportion to our spiritual maturity, *in proportion to our faith*.

[67] Acts 13:1; 1 Cor. 12:28–29; Eph. 4:11.

to stroke my own ego and enjoy the attention; but that must die for God to use us. My content must be faithful because lies about God damage people, and the truth brings life; not because I want people to think I am a good teacher, or because I secretly seek the approval of my peers. My concern for faithfulness should be because it is good for God's people that I am faithful. Does that mean we are stodgy? Certainly not! By all possible means we work to avoid being dull or irrelevant, because by becoming better teachers, we serve. If people say they are bored by us, or cannot understand us, we must assume it is probably our fault rather than theirs, and because we love them and long to serve them, we try even harder to avoid being boring. This is a serving role.

Second, because teaching is so critical, when we become entranced by architects' plans, balance sheets or political grandstanding we should force our attention back to our main work for which we are employed and gifted.

And third, because teaching and preaching often attracts introverts and bookish types, we should remember that just because teaching is our particular role, it is not our exclusive role. It does not exclude me from being a hospitable, servant-hearted, generous, prayerful, loving, merciful and willing Christian, who shows up gladly and is willing to stack chairs. Being a preacher does not make me important.

Exhortation. *Teaching* and *exhortation* belong together. This is the person who presses home the teaching to the point of unmissable application, who stirs people to adoration and actions, who helps them to see what to do.

Some people have both gifts. Paul was *the one who exhorts* (*parakalōn*) when he wrote, *I appeal* (*parakalō*) in verse 1, and he described himself to Timothy as 'a preacher and apostle and teacher'.[68] A church which welcomed *teaching* but never knew *exhortation* would be a dry place, where people understood the structure of a Bible book but never saw how it was supposed to change lives. And a church which encouraged *exhortation* without the foundation work of *teaching* would be full of superficial activity, but would never produce deep change because no-one would ever explain the 'why' and the 'because' of the gospel. But in a church where the teachers teach, and the exhorters get people out of their ruts by explaining how to put it into practice, lives are inevitably and irreversibly changed.

Contribution. Some people love giving; where other people are generous with their time and their talents, these people are generous with their treasure. 'Store up your treasure in heaven' seems to be

---

[68] 2 Tim. 1:11.

their life-verse.[69] 'You can't take it with you,' they laugh, 'but you can send it on ahead.' The word translated *generosity* means more than 'giving a lot'; it has the note of giving without strings attached.[70] This is another example of gifts not being used in a self-centred way, but being other-person focused.

Leadership.[71] We have seen that *teaching* and *leadership* are the required gift combination for pastor-teachers.[72] Here, though, they are distinguishable gifts. This person may never give a talk or guide a Bible study, but has the gift of setting directions and making things happen.

The trouble is that Christian leaders can get by on less than their best. Maybe it is because no-one actively supervises a self-starter, maybe they become weary, maybe the work seems ineffective and the results insubstantial. For whatever reason, most Christian leaders know that they are tempted to idleness.

When that happens, the church suffers, just as much as when the teachers don't teach and the generous become mean. Lazy leaders who don't challenge and inspire themselves to challenge and inspire others, hurt other people. Which is why they have constantly to heat up their gift to make sure they lead with passion, with enthusiasm, *with zeal*.

Mercy. The final item in this list takes us back to God's character. Paul grounded his appeal *in light of the mercies of God* (1), and now he addresses those who do *acts of mercy*. This is the only time he uses the word of the actions of people rather than God, and means a broad sweep, from individual acts of kindness, through a congregational decision to engage an issue together, to a national move to change unjust laws.

Here are the often unsung, unnoticed members of the church. Have a teaching gift and you are placed up front behind a microphone; be generous and you may receive public recognition. But an act of mercy like visiting in hospital, helping someone stay out of prison, or come off drugs, are hidden expressions of God's love. And they can be hard to keep on doing. People can need frequent and long-term help, and when they no longer need the mercy, someone else does. We can become ground down by the unending nature of the need, or grudging that there are not more resources or help. Paul

---

[69] Matt. 6:19–21.

[70] *Haplotēs* means both generosity (2 Cor. 8:2; 9:11, 13) and simplicity (2 Cor. 11:3; Eph. 6:5; Col. 3:22).

[71] There is a slight possibility that the previous financial reference means that Paul means the one who directs the financial affairs of the church, but the wider context makes that too specific in my view.

[72] See ch. 12.

noticed that too, which is why he says we should do these things *with cheerfulness.*

All the elements in this sequence have one important characteristic in common. I cannot exercise them on my own. They are not self-centred, but other-centred. They are not a gift to me, but they become a gift when I use them for someone else's benefit. Which is why Paul turns to *love.*[73]

c. Our love (9–13)

If we had studied 1 Corinthians 12 – 14 on gifts, we would have discovered the central, famous chapter 13 on love was placed there for a reason. The Corinthians, for all their giftedness, were a horrid church. Romans does not address the same poisoned relationships, but the issue of gifts again flows into the issue of love. These verses contain short, often disconnected, instructions about relationships, and are 'structured somewhat loosely'.[74]

The headline is that our *love* is to be *genuine*, or 'unhypocritical'.[75] In 13:10 Paul will argue that love sums up the entire Old Testament law so here he hardly needs to insist it exists. He assumes that we love each other, but says we must stop pretence in those relationships. Put as starkly as Paul, we must loathe anything evil, and glue ourselves to anything good.[76] To show that in practice, Paul gives ten little examples of genuine love, beginning and ending with words which sound alike: *philadelphia, brotherly love,* and *philoxenia, hospitality.*

Brotherly love was as countercultural in Paul's day as in ours, but he uses the words for love between siblings *(philadelphia)*, and that parents have for children *(philostorgoi)*. This was completely new, and revolutionary. Leon Morris quotes a literature survey, 'There are no examples of this more general use . . . outside the Christian writings.'[77] No one else had the idea that total strangers are as close to me as my blood family.

Outdo one another in showing honour seems to mean that we value each other highly, and show great respect (with *zeal*) for each other.[78]

---

[73] Some gifts tend to benefit the user. Paul identifies the gift of tongues in that way, which is why he prefers prophecy in a congregational setting, because that builds other people up (1 Cor. 14:1–5).

[74] Schreiner, *Romans,* p. 663.

[75] The word is *anypokritos* (2 Cor. 6:6; 1 Tim. 1:5; 2 Tim. 1:5; 1 Pet. 1:22; Jas 3:17). This phrase lacks a verb; it is almost a slogan, 'sincere love!'

[76] 'Glue' is Morris' word, *Romans,* p. 444.

[77] Morris, *Romans,* p. 444, fn. 63. *Philadelphia:* see 1 Thess. 4:9; Heb. 13:1; 1 Pet. 1:22; 2 Pet. 1:7. *Philostorgos* only occurs here in the NT.

[78] The phrase is difficult to translate, and all commentators wrestle with it.

And *be fervent* means something like, to bubble over or seethe.[79] So we must remember that we are not a club or a group of similar friends, but that as we love each other we actually *serve the Lord.*

Then come three snapshots of Christian optimism in difficult times. Looking forwards, we *rejoice in hope*; looking around, we are to *be patient in tribulation*; and looking upwards, we are *to be constant in prayer*, and it is the joy and hope of God's great future which enables us to be patient and constant in the present. Nothing erodes shallow optimism like brute facts, so our hope must cling to something deeper to keep us praying.[80]

Finally, we have practical instructions to make sure our *love* is *genuine*. First, *contribute to the needs of the saints*. In verse 8 Paul addressed those with the gift of generosity, but here is a responsibility we all share. We have already explored financial generosity,[81] but notice the word *needs*, which in the New Testament only ever refers to physical needs like food or shelter.[82] The words *saints* reinforces our particular responsibility for other Christians, although of course there are other right claims on our giving.[83]

Secondly, we are to be actively trying to be generous with our homes as we *seek to show hospitality*. It is so easy to shrink the idea of fellowship down to my little circle of friends, and to be nice to them because they will be nice to me in return. But welcoming strangers, being generous to people who cannot reciprocate, is an instruction that comes from the Lord Jesus himself.[84] I am still rebuked by the generosity of one family I know who, for years, cooked more food than they needed for Sunday lunch and actively invited strangers home each week.

4. Implementing gifts

When the first wave of 'spiritual gift surveys' became fashionable in the 1980s, the stress was almost only on identifying someone's gift. In the UK, David Pytches published *Come, Holy Spirit*, and in the States, C. Peter Wagner published the even more influential *Your Spiritual Gifts Can Help Your Church Grow.*[85] The Charles E. Fuller

[79] Paul could mean 'spirit' (i.e. in ourselves), or 'Spirit' (i.e. Holy Spirit), but neither translation would lead us into error.

[80] For *constant* prayer see Luke 18:1; Acts 1:14; 2:42; 6:6; Eph. 6:18; Col. 4:2; 1 Thess. 5:17; 1 Tim. 2:1.

[81] Ch. 7.

[82] *Chreia*. See Acts 6:3; 24:23; 28:10; Titus 3:14.

[83] Family: 1 Tim. 5:4, 8. Non-Christians: Gal. 6:10. See chs. 7, 12 and 16.

[84] Luke 14:12–14. See 1 Tim. 3:2; Titus 1:8; Heb. 13:2; 1 Pet. 4:9. See ch. 15.

[85] D. Pytches, *Come Holy Spirit* (London: Hodder & Stoughton, 1985); Wagner, *Spiritual Gifts.*

Institute of Evangelism and Church Growth, in Pasadena, California, where Wagner worked, published the 'Houts Inventory of Spiritual Gifts', 'Wagner-Modified Houts Questionnaire', 'Trenton Spiritual Gifts Analysis' and 'Wesley Spiritual Gifts Questionnaire' with subtle differences but the common core of looking at gifts alone.[86]

More recently, there have been several important modifications, as shown in 'Network', from Willow Creek Community Church, and 'S.H.A.P.E.' from Saddleback Community Church. The acronym S.H.A.P.E. shows the first modification: not only *S*piritual Gifts, but *H*eart (that is, passion – what someone loves to do), *A*bilities (things someone has learned to do, like speaking German or repairing an engine), *P*ersonality (extravert or introvert, for example), and *E*xperience, including spiritual maturity. All help identify where in church a gift might be used. A second modification is to have moved the issue of gifts outside a self-identifying 'charismatic' stream into a more central evangelical position. Thirdly, both require an implementation process to fit people into service, the lack of which left many people dissatisfied with earlier programmes. All three seem healthy developments to me.

Finally, just as having a gift does not mean having a right to exercise it, so having a gift does not remove the responsibility for improving it. King David set apart 288 men for service in the temple music, and the writer says all of them were 'trained and skilled in music for the LORD'.[87] That seems to capture a double emphasis that all musicians know: there is part of playing music which is hard-wired in some of us, but we still need to practice, practice, practice. So hospitable people learn new recipes, merciful people learn how to help strugglers, and good preachers study hard to learn the biblical languages.

Gifts, then, are an expression of the Lord Jesus' continuing love to his people; let us make sure we deploy them lovingly.

---

[86] Wesley and Trenton both in 1983, Houts in 1985 and Wagner-modified Houts in multiple editions. *Trenton Spiritual Gifts Analysis* (Pasadena: Charles E. Fuller Institute of Evangelism and Church Growth, 1983); *Wesley Spiritual Gifts Questionnaire* (Pasadena: Charles E. Fuller Institute of Evangelism and Church Growth, 1983); Houts, *Inventory*; C. P. Wagner, *Wagner-Modified Houts Questionnaire* (Pasadena: Charles E. Fuller Institute of Evangelism and Church Growth, 5th ed. 1989). Downloadable at <http://exchristian.net/images//wagner_modified_houts.pdf> and other sites.

[87] 1 Chr. 25:7.

1 Peter 2:9–12
14. The church's holiness

Christians are saved by grace not works, and motivated by grace not guilt. So we ought to be the most gracious people around. And since we have been saved from sin's power by grace, and motivated to change our sinful lives by grace, we ought to be clearly different from any other people. We live in a different kingdom. We are, as the King James Version quaintly translates a phrase we are about to study, 'a peculiar people' (9), owned by God as his treasure.

The reality is often different. An initial burst of enthusiastic change when we come to Christ is too easily followed by continued assimilation of our culture's values – except that we go to church on Sundays as well. Or our friends think we judge them by our weird moral code, one even we do not really adhere to in private. Perhaps, they hint, we fight on public moral battle grounds because we feel guilty, inadequate or threatened by cultural change. Hangers-on from a more superstitious age, intolerant and hypocritical, we are a very peculiar people indeed. And not very nice.

What does it mean to be different from a surrounding culture, when we use the same shops and watch the same TV shows? How do we avoid the trap of being 'Sunday' Christians? Is it possible to be a Christian without being a hypocrite?

1. What we were, what we are

1 Peter is concerned with being an authentic church in a hostile context. Peter draws on our identity as God's people, reaching far back into God's eternal purposes, and working it through to the homes and business of his day. Our section draws on three Old Testament passages: Exodus 19:5–6 and Isaiah 43:20–21 (LXX), and a medley of verses from Hosea. Together, they bind the church into the history of God's promises, and show us the long-term

reason for our existence. They recall that history, and place us within it.

God said to the Israelites, via Moses, 'You . . . shall be my treasured possession among all peoples, for all the earth is mine; and you shall be to me a kingdom of priests and a holy nation.'[1] This passage takes us to the exodus from Egypt, and once again to the assembly, or church, at Sinai. There God constituted the nation by covenant, and explained why he has saved them.

In Isaiah 43 we are taken to the second great saving event of the Old Testament: the exile in Babylon, and God's promise of redemption:

> Thus says the LORD,
>   who makes a way in the sea,
>   a path in the mighty waters,
> who brings forth chariot and horse,
>   army and warrior;
> they lie down, they cannot rise,
>   they are extinguished, quenched like a wick . . . :
> 'I will make a way in the wilderness
>   and rivers in the desert.
> The wild beasts will honour me,
>   the jackals and the ostriches,
> for I give water in the wilderness,
>   rivers in the desert,
> to give drink to my chosen people,
>   the people whom I formed for myself
> that they might declare my praise.'[2]

The language of 'the sea', 'chariots' and 'horse' reminds Isaiah's readers of the crossing of the Red Sea in Exodus, and promises something just as spectacular from God. Like their ancestors, they too will be fed and watered in a desert.

And in Hosea 2 we read:

> And in that day I will answer, declares the LORD, . . .
> And I will have mercy on No Mercy,
>   and I will say to Not My People, 'You are my people';
>   and he shall say, 'You are my God.'[3]

Hosea wrote during the troubled monarchy, when even Hezekiah's reforms could only slow down the inevitable progress of the two

[1] Exod. 19:4–6.
[2] Isa. 43:16–21.
[3] Hos. 2:21–23; see also Hos. 1:6, 9–10.

divorced and idolatrous nations into their respective exiles, Israel to Assyria, and Judah to Babylon.[4] Hosea promised a return to blessing, and inclusion for those who are currently not God's people.

As Peter lifts those passages and applies them to the church today, we see ourselves more clearly. First, Peter changes the tenses of those passages. Through Moses, God promised the Israelites that '*you shall be* to me a kingdom of priests . . . ',[5] Peter says that *you are a chosen race . . .* (9); for Isaiah, the blessings of being a people created to praise God lay the other side of Babylon, when 'The LORD will call you back',[6] but for Peter it was a present blessing, for God has *called* us; for Hosea there was simply the longed-for promise, '*I will say to Not my people, "You are my people"*', but for Peter, **Once you were not** a people, **but now you are** God's people; **once you had not received mercy, but now you have** received mercy (10). Those repeated contrasts, *once . . . but now, once . . . but now, were not . . . are, had not . . . have* explain how to understand the history of Israel as Christians, and how it is that the privileges and the responsibilities that were Israel's, now lie on the church's shoulders. It is now we who are God's *people* and who have to live *among the Gentiles* (12) as his *priests*. As Scot McKnight observes, 'There is no passage in the New Testament that more explicitly associates the Old Testament terms for Israel with the New Testament Church than this one.'[7] 'Church' is not God's alternative to a failed plan A. The church is what Israel was always promised it would become.

So 1 Peter 2:9–12 stands at a watershed. Almost everything in the first half of the letter has been leading up to 2:9–10, and almost everything in the second half flows out of 2:11–12. The letter begins as our section does, with an exploration of our rich blessings from God, and then turns to look at our tasks for God; in the first half we are distant from the world, in the second we are immersed in it; in the first we understand what it means to have *received mercy* from a kind Lord (10), and in the second what it means to 'receive a beating' from a cruel culture.[8] Both halves of our section share the same purpose, of bringing glory to God (9, 12).

2. Living in the presence of God (2:9–10)

Peter's foundation is the moment when God established his covenant with his people, which meant spelling out who he was, who they

---

[4] Hos. 1:1; 2 Chr. 29:1–31.
[5] Exod. 19:6.
[6] Isa. 54:6, NIV.
[7] S. McKnight, *1 Peter*, NIVAC (Grand Rapids: Zondervan, 1996), pp. 109–110.
[8] 1 Pet. 2:20, NIV.

therefore were, and what they were to be and to do. Their presence at Sinai was brief, and their possession of the land and God's presence among them was always a precarious relationship, dependent not on their flawed obedience, but on God's graciousness. Despite his repeated warnings, ultimately both the land and the temple lay abandoned.

a. A chosen race

Peter's first Old Testament quotation is from Isaiah. There Israel is repeatedly reminded that she has been chosen. The choice, or calling, or election, of Israel was a major part of her identity, going right back to the exodus story; it is language which Jesus feels comfortable using,[9] and which has been in Peter's mind since the opening of his letter 'to those who are elect exiles'.[10]

One chosen individual is particularly important in Isaiah, the mysterious suffering servant figure, who both represents Israel and yet substitutes for her.[11] This servant's focus would not be limited to Israel, however, because he 'will bring forth justice to the nations'.[12] Central to his being chosen by God, is that through his suffering he blesses the world.

Peter presents Jesus as this *chosen and precious* one.[13] He quotes Isaiah, with Jesus in mind, to say that God chose him with that purpose. But part of the servant's role is shared by Israel, who is also God's servant.[14] So if we take the focus slightly wider, from the individual servant and on to Israel the servant, we can see that her exile, and subsequent redemption, must also serve a purpose far greater than mere national restoration. It too will have global implications of blessing for all.

That helps in understanding the choice of Israel. It was not that God chose Israel so that the rest of the world could be ignored by him, but that Israel is chosen precisely because God is King of the world, and all the nations that live there, and he has a salvation plan for them. As Chris Wright has shown forcibly, *'Israel's election serves God's mission.* That is an utterly crucial point to grasp'.[15]

---

[9] Matt. 22:14; Mark 13:20, 22, 27; Luke 14:7; John 13:18; 15:16.

[10] 1 Pet. 1:1. Peter's focus is on 'corporate' election, or calling.

[11] Isa. 42:1; 45:4; 49:2.

[12] Isa. 42:1.

[13] 1 Pet. 2:4, 6.

[14] Isa. 44:1–5.

[15] C. Wright, *The Mission of God: Unlocking the Bible's Grand Narrative* (Nottingham: IVP, 2006), p. 257, emphasis original. Similarly, Jo Bailey Wells says 'What the reader is given is not a description of Israel in isolation, but in relation to the whole of God's earth' (J. B. Wells, *God's Holy People: A Theme in Biblical Theology*, JSOTSS 305 [Sheffield: Sheffield Academic Press, 2000], p. 49).

But Peter says that Christians are now God's *chosen race*. That must mean not only that the blessings and identity of being God's people flow over to us, but also that we too are chosen for that purpose, of our suffering bringing God's blessing to our neighbours. To understand that we need to move further along Peter's chain of descriptions.

b. A royal priesthood

Peter next draws from the exodus narrative that Israel was, and we are, *a royal priesthood*. Since God had emphasized that 'all the earth is mine'[16] we should probably think first of God's monarchy and his right to rule. They, and we, are 'a priesthood belonging to, and in the service of, the King'.[17]

Clearly then this meant something for the nation as a whole, rather than 'a kingdom which contains a priesthood', along the lines of the priesthood God provided in the chapters which follow. There were individual priests, like Jethro or Aaron,[18] and God was about to outline the pattern of ministry for the Levitical priesthood,[19] who offered sacrifices on behalf of Israel. This *royal priesthood* though is a national role for the entire nation, not a few. There is no expectation that they would intercede for the sins of the surrounding nations, or offer sacrifices for them.

What then do the priests of a global king do? John Durham says that the title in Exodus means 'Israel committed to the extension throughout the world of the ministry of Yahweh's presence'.[20] It would, of course be seriously anachronistic to think of that meaning Israel was, or should have been, committed to international evangelism and missionary work, and there is no evidence that they took it that way.[21] Nevertheless their existence as a holy nation was to be the next stage in God's plan to bring blessing to 'all the families of the earth' through the sons of Abraham.[22] Their purity and their purpose interlock.

There are several implications for us. First, 1 Peter 2:9 is rightly seen as one basis for the teaching of 'the priesthood of all believers',

---

[16] Exod. 19:5.

[17] A. M. Stibbs and A. F. Walls, *1 Peter*, TNTC (London: Tyndale Press, 1959), p. 103.

[18] Exod. 18:1; 19:22, 24.

[19] Exod. 28 – 29.

[20] John Durham, *Exodus*, WBC (Waco: Word, 1987), p. 263.

[21] E. Schnabel, *Early Christian Mission, vol. 1: Jesus and the Twelve* (Leicester: Apollos and Downers Grove: IVP, 2004), pp. 92–172 concludes, 'There was no missionary activity by Jews in the centuries before and in the first centuries after Jesus' and his followers' ministry, no organized attempts to convert gentiles to faith in Yahweh' (p. 172).

[22] Gen. 12:3

the idea that unlike the priesthood of Aaron and his sons, the death of Jesus has made access to God independent of any human agent other than himself. It is deeply unhelpful that some denominations, mine included, still refer to their church leaders as 'priests'. The justification for that is that the English word is not related to the sacrificial system at all, but derives from the medieval English transliteration of 'presbyter', elder. Linguistically that is true (and it is true for Spanish *presbitero*; French *prêtre*; Italian *prete*; and the German and Dutch *priester*), but we do not use words with all their historic roots intact. The English word 'priest' inevitably carries over the idea of sacrifice, access to a holy place, and spiritual privilege, all of which is deeply true if it relates to the blessings that flow to all Christians from the ministry of Jesus. But if it is used of any other person, then it is deeply antithetical to true Christian ministry, and antithetical to 1 Peter. We are all priests, not a select caste of us, and even though it is hallowed by tradition, our older denominations would do us a great service by stopping using the term altogether. Perhaps we should take the initiative.

Secondly, though, we should see that Peter uses this language not of individual Christians on their own, but of the church as a whole. This is the priesthood of all believers, not merely the priesthood of every believer. Our individual access to God is a glorious gift which Christ has won for us, but it is not quite what Peter has in mind here. This is language about the whole church.

Third, then, we should see that Peter uses this language to explain how a church relates to the world: priesthood is for the benefit of the others, committed to the expansion of the service of its King. Churches are to share the exodus commitment for the whole people of Israel, committed to 'the extension throughout the world of the ministry of (God's) presence'.[23] What that will mean is where Peter will conclude this section.

c. A holy nation

Third, we are a *holy nation*. As a whole they were owned by God, and that ownership was sealed at Sinai by a covenant of blood, just as the new kingdom of Jesus was sealed by his blood.[24] We belong to him, reflect his character and purpose. Although the two words *holy* and *nation* are common in the Old Testament, this critical moment is the only time they occur together.[25] As the people

[23] Durham, *Exodus*, p. 263.
[24] Exod. 24:1–8; Matt. 26:27.
[25] Deut. 7:6; 14:2; 26:18–19 are close in meaning, and also appear near the idea of a 'treasured possession'.

belonging to a holy God, they are to reflect his character to the sur-rounding nations, and be 'a display-people, a showcase to the world of how being in covenant with Yahweh changes a people'.[26]

Being 'owned' by the Lord Jesus Christ brought the first Chris-tians into direct conflict with the Roman state. Their royal lord was Jesus, not Caesar, their citizenship was in heaven, not in Rome. They were brought into a different relationship to God, each other and their world, and accusations of treason soon came thick and fast. The challenge to us is that our lifestyles, separately and together, must conform to God's holiness, not to our culture's acceptance. Just as Israel's new nationhood brought them closer to each other and to God, but simultaneously made them distinct from the nations even while they witnessed to it, so we must be willing to become outsiders from our culture's values, as we try to live out God's holy alternative.

d. An owned people

This fourth description is not a direct quotation from any one text, but a combination of Exodus 19:5, 'my treasured possession', and Isaiah 43:21, 'the people whom I formed for myself'. 'Treasured'[27] means 'the personal treasure of the monarch and his family',[28] and was used throughout the Old Testament to indicate how precious Israel was to God.[29] *People* marked Israel out as distinct from 'the nations'. Again the ideas of ownership and separation come through, this time with a sense of the value placed on the people by God. How much more is this true of the church, ransomed not with cheap silver or tacky gold, but at the cost of his own Son, purchased with his own blood (1 Pet. 1:18–19).

The force of that is two-edged. First, it should force us to value and treasure each other in the church. Backbiting and gossip, status-grabbing and power-wielding are quite inappropriate for us. We must force ourselves to remember that the other people in church are God's precious treasure, of infinite value and yet fragile. We abuse God's treasure at our peril, and that is even more so for God's accountable leaders.[30]

Secondly, it reminds us again of the church's role towards the world: the purpose of our being owned by God is that there are others, not yet believing in him, for whom Christ died, and whom

---

[26] Durham, *Exodus*, p. 263.
[27] Sĕgullâ.
[28] Wright, *Mission*, p. 256. Cf. 1 Chr. 29:3, Ezra 2:68.
[29] Deut. 7:6; 14:2; 26:18; Ps. 135:4; Mal. 3:17.
[30] Acts 20:18–35, the context for the 'precious blood' reference.

we were called to reach. That is where the Isaiah passage that Peter quotes is heading.

e. A people with a purpose (part one)

Here is the first of two purpose statements: God has done all the wonderful things *that you may declare the excellencies of him who called you out of darkness into his marvellous light* (9). The church has a purpose, which is to declare God's praises – but what are they, and who hears us?

The idea comes straight from Isaiah 43 'the people whom I formed for myself that they might declare my praise'. God rescued his people from Babylon to make his 'praise', his *excellencies* known.[31] That context is important, because Isaiah tells us they were to praise God not for his character (although his excellence is worthy of praise, of course) but for his deeds. They had been in 'darkness' in Babylonian exile,[32] but now they were to be released into the 'light'.[33] They were to praise God because he had rescued them; that is why God had 'called' Israel.[34] That work was to be accomplished by the wonderful and mysterious Servant figure, because the result of his work is that God's praises will be sung 'from the ends of the earth'.[35]

That is us. The Babylonian captivity of Israel is a picture or 'type' of the human captivity to sin and death. Peter takes the pictorial language and applies it to the reality of redemption: we were in *darkness*[36] but God has now *called us* into now in his wonderful *light*, and for Peter the language of 'calling' is an aspect of our redemption (1:15; 2:21; 3:9; 5:10). We have been called in order to declare his wonderful work of salvation. That is our purpose.

Who is to hear these words? Just as for Israel, the primary audience is not God, but the surrounding nations. The word translated *proclaim*[37] appears only here in the New Testament, and some have argued that its primary note is of praises expressed to God. But that does not fit either the close context here, nor Peter's more widely expressed concern for telling non-Christians about Christ (1:12, 25; 3:1; 4:17); nor does it fit the Isaiah material either. Just as there God told Israel, 'Fear not, for I have redeemed you, I have called you by

[31] Isa. 43:20–21.
[32] Isa. 42:7.
[33] Isa. 42:6.
[34] Isa. 43:1.
[35] Isa. 43:6.
[36] Cf. Acts 26:18; 2 Cor 4:6; Col. 1:12–13.
[37] *Exangelēte.*

name, you are mine',[38] with the express purpose that they would proclaim this event among 'all the nations . . . and the peoples',[39] so here God's *chosen* and *called people* are to *proclaim* his *excellencies* before the world. The next verse makes that crystal clear, as in combination with allusions to Hosea[40] Peter transfers the privileges and responsibility of being God's people from Israel on to the church: *Once you were not a people, but now you are God's people* (10).

What Peter has argued means that the church, by its very existence and character, is a demonstration in space and time, here and now, that the Lord Jesus means every one of his promises, and therefore that our life together should show that we believe them. Church is the place where God's promise to Abraham that 'in you all the families of the earth shall be blessed' is visibly kept.[41] But the existence of the church is not the gospel. It is the work of the Lord Jesus, not the work of the church, which transforms individual lives and whole societies, and it is the Lord Jesus, not the church, who will save us on judgment day. True, he has promised that he will work in and through his church, and there is no other organization or group to which he has made that, or indeed any other, promise. But the gospel creates the church, not the other way round, and although both are essential for us, we need to be clear about which is cause and which is effect.

So what have we seen about the purpose of the church in this section? If it is the purpose of the gospel to create the church (9a), what is the church for? The answer is a range of things, obviously, but here Peter has only one in mind. The church exists to make Jesus known, or as he puts it, God has done all this for you with the purpose *that you may proclaim the excellencies of him who called you out of darkness into his marvellous light* (9b). This has to be done with words (remember what we discovered about *proclaim the excellencies*), and by everyone (remember what we discovered about everyone being involved in the *priesthood*). In fact each of those three descriptions, *chosen people, royal priesthood* and *holy nation*, is an explicit expectation that everyone will be involved in telling non-Christians ('the nations') about Jesus. It is what each of us is here for.

It really is very simple. Evangelism is at the very centre of what we do. Some might say that God should be at the centre, but that is to confuse issues: it is God who insists that evangelism is central. Some might say that his word should be central, but it his word

---

[38] Isa. 43:1.
[39] Isa. 43:9.
[40] Hos. 1:6, 9; 2:1, 23.
[41] Gen. 12:3.

which insists on evangelism. Some might say it should be declaring his praises, but God insists that we should declare his praises to non-Christians. Some might say evangelism should be central for those who have the evangelist's gift, but just as with many other gifts (hospitality, generosity or teaching, for instance), what is a gift for some is still a responsibility for everyone. Peter is not being reductionist, and he fully understands that each of us is engaged in a range of daily activities, but – as he is about to demonstrate – those have evangelism at the centre as well.

3. Living in the presence of the nations (2:11–12)

a. Aliens and strangers

The context of both the Isaiah and Hosea passages was the Babylonian exile, and the transference of roles from Israel to the church is part of Peter's wider picture as well. He began his letter writing to God's 'elect exiles', and he will conclude by saying he is writing from 'Babylon'.[42] These are not map references of course, but a kind of spiritual history and geography lesson. As Karen Jobes has put it, 'Peter frames his letter in the motif of the historic Babylonian exile in order to identify his readers with the promises of deliverance'.[43] So both the letter's frame and its centre have the same emphasis. Even the word *beloved* (11) underlines it, because the emphasis is not on Peter's fondness for them, but God's deep love by which they have been called and chosen.

The two words combine to describe the status of Christians as foreigners. Some commentators suggest that Peter's first readers might have been expelled from Rome but whatever their temporary circumstances, Peter insists that being sojourners or temporary residents is a normal experience for them now they have a new Lord and a different home. In fact, physical exile is secondary, because they have become aliens due to their loyalty to Christ. It is a status that goes much further back even than Babylon, to Abraham who described himself as 'an alien and a stranger',[44] and it defines the correct position we believers must always have to our world. It may have two particular barbs as well. Foreigners are usually treated with distrust, especially if they retain some cultural distinctiveness, and that may lie behind the hostility Peter's readers were experiencing. The distinctiveness he has in mind, of course, is not of language, clothing or food, but of morality. Second, the reactions to this

---

[42] 1 Pet. 1:1; 5:13.
[43] Karen H. Jobes, *1 Peter*, BECNT (Grand Rapids: Baker Academic, 2005), p. 158.
[44] Gen. 23:4, NIV, identical in LXX. See Ps. 39:12.

pressure are either to form a closely-knit community which ignores the surrounding culture (and Peter has told us we are not to do that), or to disappear into it, and that is Peter's concern here. As Paul Achtemeier writes, this is 'not only a description of their present reality, it is also a description of their status they are to maintain, lest by abandoning that status, and reverting to their former values and customs, they estrange themselves from God'.[45]

Closeness to God and his people means separation from the world even while we live in it, just as Israel had to be loyal to God even while she lived in Babylon among the idolatrous Babylonians, and Abraham among the Hittites. Loyalty is sometimes hard, which is why Peter had to *urge* his readers to do it. In fact, he uses the same Greek word to summarize his entire letter, 'exhorting' his readers to 'stand firm'.[46] Our former homeland is not a thousand miles away, but around us everyday, on the television adverts and programmes, inside the covers of the novels and magazines, on the web and in our mail. No wonder we need to be *urged* to maintain our status as *foreigners and exiles.*[47]

Perhaps those of us who live in cities see the force of this language. In one sense all Christians are city dwellers, because we live in the heavenly Jerusalem, even if our physical home is small and rural – and that small village is itself 'Babylonian' in that it expresses idolatrous rebellion against God. But by giving the theological term 'Babylon' to the physical Rome, Peter is giving his readers the eyes with which to see their physical city. Simply because there are more people in a city, it experiences the highs and lows of the fallen grandeur of human beings with greater intensity. There are more people showing kindness, which is why the great teaching hospitals are located there, but there are many others wishing harm, which is why the drug barons and sex traffickers are there, which is why the police are there, and so on. Cities produce great art and architecture, much of which is beautiful even in its anti-Christian frame. Cities produce hideous corruption and violence, all of which serves God's plan despite itself. So although cities do not have a unique role in God's world, over against villages, towns or hamlets, they do act as a magnifying lens for the fallen image of God.

Churches which are placed in cities need to see their city through this lens. Being in a densely populated place, means more Christians to have fellowship with, and more non-Christians to reach. Those non-Christians are more likely to be those who will be influencers of others, because cities are centres of political, intellectual and

---

[45] P. J. Achtemeier, *1 Peter*, Hermeneia (Augsburg: Fortress, 1996), p. 175.
[46] 5:12, *parakalein*. See Rom 12:1; Eph. 4:1; Phil. 4:2; Phlm. 10.
[47] ESV consistently uses 'sojourner', but it is not a common noun.

artistic life. It is an obvious point that larger churches tend to be in places of larger populations, who may be more mobile, or may be more densely packed. Just as those cities influence the surrounding country, so the large churches exercise disproportionate influence on their surrounding culture, and on the surrounding churches. Most widely-used Christian resources have their origin in large urban churches, simply because those have the people to create them.

So being a city church is a wonderful opportunity and a terrible temptation. Babylon is a prostitute, a beast, the home of the antichrist which is a hell-made imitation of the New Jerusalem.[48] But it is a defeated enemy, from which God will rescue billions of his people.

b. Hostile desires

Peter's call does not mean they should form a closed community with no access to the pollution of non-Christians and their culture. That would be a dangerous misreading of the exile theme. No, the pollution is not external but internal, and comes not from non-Christians but continually[49] inside every believer. They are the *passions of the flesh, which war against your soul* (11).

That helps us to see one way in which Christians must be *foreigners and exiles* today. Ever since the rise of the Romantic movement in the eighteenth century, one of the most effective ways to challenge Christian morality has been to argue against the precise point of Peter. If something is experienced as a desire, it is said, and I enjoy acting upon it, that cannot then be an 'unnatural' or 'sinful' desire. The very fact that I want to do something is proof of the naturalness of the desire, and since Romanticism put forceful emphasis on the expression of our feelings, then any desire must be expressed. In fact, it is the very suppression of our desires which is unnatural and may cause us – so it is argued – emotional damage.

The argument is still found today, even in Christian circles, that the experience of something feeling good or enjoyable must mean that it is good. Pastors will frequently meet Christians who have committed adultery, and excuse themselves with the argument, 'But it feels so right'.

On the contrary, says Peter, our *passions* are 'continually waging war'[50] against *our soul*, and the word, *strateuō* is a military word which Paul and James also use to describe sin's assault.[51] This is

---

[48] Rev. 17.
[49] The present tense means '*continually* keep away from sinful desires', Wayne Grudem, *1 Peter*, TNTC (Leicester: IVP and Grand Rapids: Eerdmans, 1988), p. 115.
[50] Grudem, *1 Peter*, p. 115.
[51] Rom. 7:23; Jas 4:1. See 1 Cor. 9:7; 2 Tim. 2:4.

critical as we try to be distinct from our culture where it differs from us over whether certain feelings, usually sexual ones, may be expressed. We need to be clear that feelings are by themselves not sufficient ground to say something is permissible (and clearly even Shelley did not feel that over incest), but we must also be clear that we are not exempt from these battles. Because these desires are inside us, we must always be clear that there is no-one (Jesus apart) who ever experienced desires as God intended, that no one (Jesus apart) is as sexually normal as God intended. If we are to be distinct it is because we realize the danger from which we have been rescued, and from which others can also be rescued.

c. Hostile people

Peter now moves from the 'negative and private' to the 'positive and public'.[52] Just like the exiled Jews, we are *aliens and strangers* who *live . . . among the Gentiles*; or rather, if we translate the phrase more naturally as 'among the nations',[53] we tap into the rich root that Israel was always to live an exemplary life in the eyes of her neighbours. As God had said at the nation's formation, 'Observe [my laws] carefully, for this will show your wisdom and understanding *to the nations*, who will hear about all these decrees and say, "Surely this great nation is a wise and understanding people".'[54] The phrase 'the nations' came to mean 'the rest of the world' and therefore 'the Gentiles',[55] and it is the flip-side of the way Peter consistently describes Christians by the titles that belong to Israel.

So how are we to behave? Peter consistently describes our ambition as a *good* life,[56] meaning one that continually commends Christ in all circumstances. In other words, 'The proclamation of God's excellencies must be undergirded by "excellent behaviour".'[57] This is all-round discipleship, which Peter later spells out in detail for particular groups.

The reason for spelling it out is that not all non-Christians are friendly, and in fact a number of Christians in the church Peter was writing to were under assault. Scot McKnight summarizes it: 'Foolish

[52] Stibbs and Walls, *1 Peter*, p. 106.

[53] *En tois ethnesin.*

[54] Deut. 4:6, NIV, emphasis added.

[55] 1 Pet. 4:3.

[56] 2:15–16, 20; 3:1–2, 6, 13, 16. Peter also here uses *anastrophē*, meaning 'behaviour', which again appears in 1:15 of all Christians, 3:1–2 of wives married to non-Christian husbands, and 3:16 of suffering Christians.

[57] A. Köstenberger and P. O'Brien, *Salvation to the Ends of the Earth: A Biblical Theology of Mission*, NSBT (Leicester: Apollos and Downers Grove: IVP, 2001), pp. 239–240.

men have said ignorant things (2:15), slaves were being mistreated (2:18–21), spouses were probably turning against one another (3:1–7), and believes were being insulted unfairly and persecuted (3:9, 13–17; 4:12–16).'[58] More than that, and hurting far more, was that such people, even good, intelligent people, were starting to *speak against* the believers *as evildoers*. That is, their mere faith as Christians was a bad thing. Perhaps then, as in many oppressive regimes since, the accusation was that they were politically disloyal; today, certainly in the West, the accusation is more that we are culturally disloyal, refusing to move with society's undercurrents. Whichever it might be Peter warns us to accept that the misunderstanding and misrepresentation is to be expected. He also tells us how to respond: we are to *keep your conduct among the Gentiles honourable* that people *may see your good deeds*. Once again, in line with Israel's task, we are to be visibly distinct. As Jesus put it, in words that Peter may be consciously reflecting on, 'Let your light shine before others, so that they may see your good deeds and give glory to your Father who is in heaven'.[59]

d. A people with a purpose (part two)

What a beautiful balance, we might think: words to *proclaim the excellencies* of God to a watching world, and actions to demonstrate his worth. Except that Peter does not quite say that. Our actions have a purpose, that our neighbours *may see [our] good deeds and glorify God on the day of visitation* (12).[60]

That *day* is undoubtedly the day of Christ's return, which has been a consistent promise throughout Peter's letter.[61] The more difficult question is what it means for those who watch the Christians to *glorify God* on that day. Some argue that this a belated realization that Christians were right after all, and that God has vindicated them,[62] and it is undoubtedly the case that that day will be one of judgment as well as salvation. But the language of 'giving glory' does not work that way. Wayne Grudem calculates that there are sixty-one uses of the word in the New Testament, and they always mean freely giving God glory, not being forced to do so. Tom Schreiner summarizes it very clearly, 'Typically in the New Testament people

[58] McKnight, *1 Peter*, p. 127.

[59] Matt. 5:16.

[60] Another example of the *episkopos* word-group meaning 'to visit'. See ch. 12.

[61] 1:5, 7, 13; 4:5, 7, 13, 17b; 5:1, 4. Grudem's translation 'on a day when God visits' (*1 Peter*, p. 116) has not won support, probably because of the eschatological emphasis of 1 Peter.

[62] McKnight, *1 Peter*, p. 128.

glorify God or give him glory by believing ... Conversely those who refuse to believe do not glorify God.'[63]

Now if the purpose of our *good lives* is that our neighbours *glorify God*, and if the only people who do that are Christians, then it is clear that something has happened to our neighbours. They have become Christians too. Our actions have had an evangelistic impact, and given a plausibility to what we say (3:1–2). Our words and our deeds do indeed go together, but they are not the same kinds of things, and even our best actions do not get us out of our responsibility to speak for Christ.

This, then, is the justification for churches to be involved in acts of compassion and mercy in a despairing world. Churches should be running soup kitchens and collecting clothes for street families, it is right that we rebuild homes after tornadoes and get medical help for kids with HIV/AIDS. These are good things in themselves, but they lead to something even better. It is foolish to play evangelism and acts of compassion off against one another, as if they were competing tasks and a church which has paid attention to one automatically means it must have compromised on the other. They are both commanded by God, and they are both to be done. The language we use about this is important, and so I think it is unhelpful to talk of finding a point of 'balance' between the two. That immediately sets the two tasks up as rivals, with even the slightest move in one direction being potentially destabilizing to the other. Anyone who has been involved with setting a church budget, or planning a year of a church's activities knows how paralyzing such thinking is. No, both are to be done, for connected but not identical reasons.

4. Church

Three elements of Peter's argument have a particularly sharp edge, whenever there is persistent temptation for the church to think or act in conformity with a surrounding culture.

The first is that the church is *holy*. Not 'ought to be holy', but 'is holy'. God has, by a decisive act, created us to be his own people, and declared us to be *a holy nation*. That language of being owned by God and being distinct from our culture and its values needs to become increasingly embedded in our thinking about ourselves. God has made this claim of ownership over no-one else on the planet, and given this character to no other institution. We belong, unreservedly, to him.

---

[63] Thomas R. Schreiner, *I, II Peter and Jude*, NAC 37 (Nashville: B&H Publishing Group, 2003), p. 124.

The second is that this *holy* church has members with *passions of the flesh*. They *wage war* on us, and we are to *abstain from* them. So when we speak out to our world on moral matters, especially sexual ones, we need to get our message right. Pretending we do not have such desires is not only unbiblical, it is implausible. Our friends simply do not believe we are not tempted to commit adultery or to lie, and they are right not to believe us. Of course we are tempted, sometimes very strongly, and our best leaders are included in that. No-one should be vilified for their temptations. But it is not the nature of the temptation which is important. Rather, it is the nature of our response. Flirting with temptation, dancing on its edge, or even celebrating it as part of the way God has made us, is dangerously self-deluding. Rather we must identify such *passions of the flesh*, accept God's description of them, and respond obediently. We can never speak to the world or to each other without remembering that we, too, are tempted.

The third element is that this *holy* church is a place where people change. Watch again what Peter has told us He has told us that we are *foreigners in* our world, and so we will believe and want to behave differently. Having identified what our particular *passions of the flesh* are, we will take a life-long decision to continue to *abstain from* them, which means an ongoing and life-long commitment. This does not take us into an airless ghetto, but rather to live *good lives among* our non-Christian family and friends with the goal that they too, having seen the way we have changed in order to obey Jesus, come to believe in him. This will be in marked contrast to those who tell us that people cannot change, because under the sound and in the power of the gospel we do. And even if it is a struggle, and there are lapses back and old temptations are strong, we should remember that whatever we did last night, we are members of *a chosen race, a royal priesthood, a holy nation, a people for his own possession, that you may proclaim the excellencies of him who called you out of darkness into his marvellous light* (9).

If we pull this together it can help us into one contemporary dilemma on evangelism: do people belong to church before they believe in Christ, or believe before they belong? And where does their behaviour fit in? It is quite clearly true, socially speaking, that people tend to hang around Christians quite a lot before they commit to Christ themselves. People can come to church for many years, watching and listening, before the gospel penny drops. In terms of making friends, turning up to events, and feeling part of things, people identify that they frequently felt they belonged long before they believed. But theologically speaking, the reverse is true. Membership of the great heavenly church is only open to those who are in Christ, and the only way in is through faith in him. From God's perspective of his assembled people, believing must precede belonging. So the answer to the question 'which comes first?' depends on what is meant by the question: often, both can be right answers.

What can never come first is 'behave'. The public perception of Christians is that we are basically concerned with a few moral issues on which we are primly self-righteous, which fits with the idea of religion as something that people 'do'. On that model, becoming a Christian means, 'stop behaving like that, and start behaving like us', which is obviously a disastrous distance from the gospel, which is nothing about what we 'do', and everything about what God has 'done'. Because people, including Christians, like to think we can get right with God by doing good things, we flatter our inbuilt, sinful tendency to raise behaviour into the entry criterion for the gospel. But true change comes as a result of the gospel, not as the gateway to it.

Churches which put 'behave' before 'believe and belong' will never take the risk of dealing with the sin that has wrecked people's lives. Instead, they will instil a pattern of prudish social conformity which is external, superficial and hypocritical. Ultimately it denies the gospel, because they act as if some people are too badly caught in sin to be reached by grace, and others are too good to need it.

Churches which put 'believe and belong' before 'behave' will be much messier places, confronting difficult questions. A church puts on a weekend away as part of its evangelism course, and an unmarried couple who have been happily living together for many years, and have three children, want to come and expect to share a bedroom. They are not yet Christians – how do we expect them to behave before they believe and belong? A woman has been coming to church for several months, not yet converted but really interested – can she help out on the welcome team, or the sound desk? You need to work it out.

2 and 3 John
15. The church's boundaries

Why should you trust this book? Perhaps you bought it on a whim, or because your pastor recommended it. Maybe you are discussing it in your home group, or at an elders' meeting. But why should you trust me? How do you know you could let me preach, or run a small group?

The question of boundaries, and where we set them in our churches, is explored in 2 and 3 John. Together, they teach about two opposite dangers: gullibility and defensiveness. One danger is being too generous, the other too suspicious. The letters work together, and speak to each other's concerns.

These early churches were often small groups in villages, larger in the towns, scattered over large provinces, and connected by the infra-structure of the Roman Empire. So frequent visitors brought news and prayer, and some were travelling preachers. The pattern was efficient, and well used.[1] Churches received information and teaching, and in return provided hospitality against the dangers of travel, and the nature of the inns.[2] But hospitality from an elder gives more than a bed – it gives credibility.[3] A preacher staying with an elder gains the elder's approval on both the person and the message. And that underlies these letters.

A group of *deceivers* (2 John 7) had left John's church, and were roving Asia Minor, becoming parasites on healthy churches and evan-gelizing for their deviant doctrines. John wrote a sharp letter to slam the door on such a dangerous person: *do not receive him into your house or give him any greeting* (10). In 3 John, by contrast, one

[1] Rom. 16 and Col. 4:7–17.

[2] J. R. W. Stott, *The Epistles of John*, TNTC (London: Tyndale Press, 1964), pp. 198–199.

[3] Hospitality as a virtue: Rom. 12:13; Heb. 13:2; 1 Pet. 4:9. Necessity: Acts 16:15; 28:7; Rom. 16:23. Leadership requirement: 1 Tim. 3:2; Titus 1:8.

power-hungry individual had seized control of a congregation, and refused authorized Christian teachers access to the members. Even John was barred, and the man concerned *does not acknowledge our authority* (9). John wrote to prise the door open. So John faced two opposite issues, in close congregations.[4] The dilemma is sharp. Thomas Johnson observes, 'Note that what Gaius is commended for doing in 3 John, the Elder commands "the elect lady" not to do in 2 John 10–11 . . . Both factions are sending itinerant teachers, and the churches must be discerning. That is why in 1 John 4:1–2 the Elder urges the churches to test the prophets . . . and provides for them the test.'[5]

1. Walking (2 John 1–6)

The halves of this letter match like a butterfly's wings, joined by *for* in verse 7. The first half raises issues that the second throws into clearer, if deadly, perspective.

John wrote to a church, with the affectionate title of *the elect lady and her children*. It is an unusual description, but the way John moves from singular (5) to plural (6, 8, 10, 12) shows he is addressing a congregation, or cluster of congregations, each symbolized as an individual woman. He repeats the image to describe his own church in verse 13 (*The children of your elect sister greet you*).[6]

God's people were described with various female images in the Old Testament: a virgin daughter, a beautiful woman, a queen, a bride, a prostitute, an adulteress, a mother and a widow.[7] In the New Testament, the church in both its cosmic and local expressions is described similarly,[8] the dominant image being a bride with Christ as the bridegroom.[9] And in a beautiful way, the title *Lady* (*kyria*) connects any church with her 'Lord' (*kyrios*), which is how John records Jesus being constantly addressed.[10]

Christians are described as *children*, both as members of that congregation (1) and also towards John (4). Christians are part of a

---

[4] 'It is no doubt best to view these letters as coming from the same approximate time period and addressing the same general crisis in the church', G. M. Burge, 'John, Letters of', *DLNTD*, pp. 587–599.

[5] T. Johnson, *1, 2, and 3 John*, NIBC (Peabody: Hendrickson, 1993), p. 171.

[6] Compare how Israel is the sister of Judah in Ezek. 16:46; 23:4.

[7] A virgin daughter, in obedience, a daughter of Zion (Isa. 52:2), but in idolatry, a daughter of Babylon (Isa. 47:1); a beautiful woman (Ezek. 16:7); a queen (Ezek. 16:13–14); a bride (Isa. 62:5); a prostitute (Ezek. 16:15); an adulteress (Ezek. 16:32); a mother (Isa. 54:1–3); a widow (Isa. 54:4; Lam. 1:1).

[8] Cosmically: Eph. 5:22–33; Rev. 21:9. Locally, this verse is a good example.

[9] John 3:29; 2 Cor. 11:2; Gal. 4:25–26; Eph. 5:22–32; Rev. 18 – 19 (the anti-church Babylon is female too).

[10] John 4:11, 15, 19, 49; 5:7; 6:34, 68; 9:36, 38; 11:3, 12, 39; 12:21.

network of God's people who belong to each other, and so Calvin strongly reinforced it: 'To those whom [God] is a Father, the church must also be a mother.'[11] But, we must immediately notice, John is talking about a local congregation having this motherly role. Describing a denomination in these terms is far from John's thought, as is describing a cathedral as the 'mother church'. It is quite possible the Jerusalem church once tried to claim this title, and Paul opposed them. The only originating mother church is the heavenly one: 'The Jerusalem above is free, and she is our mother.'[12]

John introduces himself as *the elder*; and 2 and 3 John are the only New Testament letters to come from a titled rather than a named person. It is also unusual because the New Testament refers to elders in the plural.[13] To write as *the elder* gives a different meaning for the word, and perhaps the solution lies with seeing the easy way John and Paul refer to their fatherly roles towards churches they planted.[14] 'Elder' describes a relationship, and may be why Peter also uses it.[15] Underlining it would certainly make sense when John's authority is being ignored.

a. Truth

The letter is subtly repetitive, bringing truths into ever-changing patterns. Tracing through 2 John shows the first half contains five repetitions of *love*[16] *and truth*,[17] and a fourfold repetition of *commands*.[18] There is a repeated picture of *walking* (*we walk . . . you walk*, 6) expanded into *walking in the truth* (4), and *walk according to his commands* (6).[19] It is the familiar biblical image that we 'must walk in the same way in which [Jesus] walked'.[20]

Christian *truth* is intimately related to Christian *love*. John wrote to people *whom I love in truth* (1),[21] and he loves *all who know the truth* (1). This is a personal relationship with truth *that abides in us*

[11] *Institutes* 4.1.1; and before Calvin see Cyprian, *De Unitate* 6.
[12] Gal. 4:26.
[13] See ch. 12.
[14] See 1 Cor. 4:14; Gal. 4:19; Phil. 2:22.
[15] 1 Pet. 5:1.
[16] Vv. 1, 3, 5, 6 (twice).
[17] Vv. 1 (twice), 2, 3, 4.
[18] Vv. 4, 5, 6 (twice).
[19] See too 1 John 1:6; 2:6, 11; 3 John 3, 4, etc.
[20] 1 John 2:6. E.g. Pss 1, 119; Mark 7:5; Acts 21:21; Rom. 14:15; Eph. 5:2, 8; Col. 4:5, etc.
[21] The definite article is missing, so it could be 'love truly'. But most modern commentators and translations agree that 'In Johannine thought, one can only love "truly" or "genuinely" if one abides in *the* truth', M. M. Thompson, *1–3 John*, IVPNTC (Downers Grove: IVP, 1992), p. 151.

and will be with us forever (2), and of course John means Jesus, who said, 'I am the way, and *the truth* and the life'.[22] John is saying, positively, that knowing Jesus guarantees true knowledge of God, and that, negatively, we cannot say we know Jesus and simultaneously deny key truths about him, nor walk in disobedience to him. John concludes verse 3 as he began in verse 1: all God's blessings come to us through *Jesus Christ in truth **and** love*.

This church, having grasped that wonderful *truth* about *love*, was a source of *great joy* to John (4). He was *overjoyed*[23] to have heard news of a wonderful fellowship of growing, loving Christians.

b. Love

Having found some of the church *walking in the truth, just as the Father commanded* (4, NIV) he tells them that that the Father's *command is that you walk in love* (6, NIV). 'Walking in love' sounds good, and indeed, if we are not careful, it can sound like the exact opposite of what we have just seen; *truth* may be cold and hard, but *love* can be warm and soft-edged. That would misunderstand John, and we need to learn from the way he uses words. Just as he gave *truth* a particular meaning, so too with *love*.

We begin with God. 1 John says 'God is love',[24] partnering the statement that Jesus is *the truth*. Both *truth* and *love* are God's eternal and perfect character, so *truth* without *love* would become a tyrannous idol, and *love* without *truth* a blasphemous lie.

John's relationship with the church shows that love: *the chosen lady and her children whom I love in truth* (1). That *love* is real, because it involves living people whom he knows. Leaving *love* at the level of theory would mean we never worried about the people who irritate or hurt us – or whom we insult or slander. But because John *loves* people he knows, he cannot avoid the realities of relationships. It does not stop there, however, because he also loves *all who know the truth* (1). Here are people he does not know, but because of their shared love for God, he already loves them. Notice too that it is the Father's *command . . . that you walk in love* (6). It is impossible to command a feeling, but it is possible to command an action, and it is practical acts of service and hospitality (12) which show whether we do *love* each other.

In the second century, the Christian philosopher Aristides wrote to the emperor Hadrian, saying that Christians,

---

[22] John 14:6.
[23] NRSV.
[24] 4:16.

love one another. They never fail to help widows, they save orphans from those who would hurt them. If they have something they give freely to the man who has nothing; if they see a stranger they take him home, and are happy as though he were a real brother. They don't consider themselves brothers in the usual sense, but brothers instead through the Spirit, in God.[25]

c. Obedience

The kaleidoscope turns, and John's third theme comes into view. *And this is love, that we walk in obedience to his commandments* (6, NIV).

The Western twenty-first century thinks that rules – especially religious rules – are an expression of legalism, hypocrisy and repression. Love is better seen in self-expression. The tension between what someone ought to do, and what they feel like doing, should be resolved in the direction of their feelings.

But John disagrees. Love, for him, is expressed in obedience, not just to one single *commandment* (5), but to all the *commandments* (6).[26] He learnt this from Jesus, who said 'If you love me you will keep my commandments', and 'If anyone loves me he will keep my word . . . Whoever does not love me does not keep my words'.[27] Just as love and truth are intertwined, so are love and obedience.

Again, the first Christians took this to heart. The second century apologist Justin showed how love and obedience mingled:

> Those who once rejoiced in fornicating now delight in continence alone; those who made use of magic arts have dedicated themselves to the good and unbegotten God; we who once took pleasure in the means of increasing our wealth and property now bring what we have into a common fund and share with everyone we need; we who hated and killed one another and would not associate with men of different tribes because of (their different) customs, now after the manifestation of Christ live together and pray for our enemies and try to persuade those who unjustly hate us, so that they, living according to the fair command of Christ, may share with us the good hope of receiving the same things from God the Master of all.[28]

---

[25] Quoted by B. Milne, *Dynamic Diversity: The New Humanity Church for Today and Tomorrow* (Nottingham: IVP, 2006), pp. 53–54.

[26] *Entolēn* (5); *entolas* (6).

[27] John 14:15, 23–24. See too John 15:10, 12 and 14, and Rom. 13:8–10.

[28] C. Richardson (ed.), *Early Christian Fathers* (Philadelphia: Westminster, 1970), pp. 249–250, cited Milne, *Dynamic Diversity*, pp. 53–54.

So God does not speak with two voices, one stern, saying 'Obey me', and the other soft, saying 'Love me'. He delights to sees us walking in love, truth and obedience. And having held those elements so firmly together, John now shows the danger of forcing them apart.

2. The church that loves too much (2 John 7–13)

Can a church love too much? History is littered with the bickering, splintering, petty jealousies, feuds, and even murders of believers who evidently show they love too little. How could we love too much?

It happens, says John, when we separate love from truth and obedience, and then emphasize love at their expense, using one to drown out the others. We can hear echoes of the voices that so concerned him in almost any church today. 'I can't believe that God takes small matters so seriously.' 'It's doctrine that divides, but love which unites.' 'Surely Christianity is about loving people, not beating each other over the head with Bible verses.' John says that those voices express false views of truth, love and obedience.

These verses build on contrasts: between believers in *truth* (4) and *deceivers* (7), between *some* (4) and *many* (7), and between those who *walk in love* (6) and those who *run ahead* (9).[29] One truth runs throughout: true love does not love deception.

a. True love does not love deception (7–9)

Swirling around John's churches is deceptive teaching from those who *do not confess the coming of Jesus Christ in the flesh* (7). Whether that questioned the physicality of Jesus' first or last *coming* – or even his glorified incarnation in heaven – need not concern us, because each is a key Christian belief. But their radical position is apparently quite modest. They do not actively deny truth, or openly affirm revisionism; rather, more gently, they *do not confess* something. They have, as they might put it, questions. And rather than taking their questions to a more certain Christian friend, *many* of them *have gone out into the world.*[30] *Gone out* could mean they have left church, but verse 10 shows they have simply moved from one church to others, as missionaries for their error. John is quite sharp: he calls them, twice in this one verse, *deceivers*. That is, they are spreading non-truth, anti-truth, the opposite of truth. It looks as though their questions are not honest questions at all, but a deceptive strategy to win churches to their shrivelled message.

[29] NIV.
[30] Like Judas, John 13:27, 30.

The effect is tragic, for in wandering so far from core Christianity, yet still demanding that churches welcome them, they require a church to say that Christ's incarnation or return is secondary. That is shocking, but perhaps explains John's other term for them: *antichrist*. He had used it in his first letter for one individual but also, as here, numerous opponents of the gospel.[31]

So John's readership is being infested with aggressive, anti-Christian teachers, but the church is so nice that it welcomes and looks after them (10–11). John's warning is stark: *Watch yourselves, so that you may not lose what we have worked for* (8).[32] Their salvation may be secure, but they risk never having Jesus say, 'Well done, good and faithful servant'.[33] And they risk it by being too nice.

John prescribes a double test. First, he says, *Watch yourselves* (8). We need continually to check that we remain in the teaching of Christ. We must be honest with ourselves, because one of our temptations will be to see our wandering away as a form of progress, dressed up as being 'the avant-garde'. John uses the language of movement here, contrasting a steady reliable *walk* with a dangerous running ahead (9), indeed, progressing out of the good path rather than making progress in it, and progressing so far that we leave God behind (such a person *does not have God*).[34] One way we might fool ourselves is to talk of where we have come from, and our 'evangelical roots', as if they guaranteed safety as we progress on our spiritual journey. But that is as foolish as the captain of a ship thinking he is safe in a storm at sea because the harbour he left was calm. No, the question here is not about the safety of the place of origin, but the safety of the path we are currently on; or as John puts it, the continual danger is that someone *does not abide in the teaching of Christ* (9). That has been John's concern since verse 2, where he wrote of *the truth that abides in us and will be with us for ever*.

The second element of the test is to examine those who teach us: *Everyone who goes on ahead and does not abide in the teaching of Christ, does not have God. Whoever abides in the teaching has both the Father and the Son* (9). John underlines twice that the test is theological: *the teaching . . . the teaching*; so we need to be intimately familiar with the teaching of Christ, both his words and the words

---

[31] 1 John 2:18.

[32] The text might read *ha eirgasasthe* ('what *you* have worked for') or *ha eirgasametha* ('what *we* have worked for'). NIV, NRSV and ESV, with most commentators, opt for 'we'.

[33] Matt. 25:21. See 1 Cor. 3:11–15; 1 Tim. 4:15–16, or the repeated warnings in Hebrews.

[34] *Run ahead* translates *proagōn*, 'to walk ahead of those going slowly' (*BGD*, p. 702).

about him.[35] Those who engage in theological revision may do so in a sophisticated way, and the churches need a well-thought response. And even when their denial is crude, a careful rejoinder must show why it is wrong, and what is the alternative.

True love does not love theological deception. Deception imperils the spiritual state of individuals and churches, leading us away from Christ and the safe path of discipleship. What are we to do about it?

b. True love does not love deceivers (10)

John now raises the stakes. Added to truths which might be hard to say (7, 9), now he has actions which it will be hard to take. Put simply, love has limits. This is no hypothetical example: John sees a church he loves including and embracing someone who injects spiritual poison. So he is emphatic, that *if anyone comes to* them with a different message to John's they must *not receive him into your house or give him any greeting*. Remember, too, that the question here is not so much warning against inviting a Mormon indoors for a chat, but of elders endorsing these strangers and their alien gospel, in church.

Welcoming a false teacher seems to gain a prized Christian virtue: fellowship. John uses that word *koinōnia* in verse 11, as well as in his description of our foundational 'fellowship . . . with the Father and with his Son, Jesus Christ'.[36] But here it has an edge: *whoever greets him takes part in* (has fellowship with, *koinōnei*) *his wicked work*. It is the wrong kind of fellowship! We become guilty because we have tolerated the error.[37] Even worse, although we might appear to have gained fellowship with a Christian, we have lost fellowship with God, because having fellowship with a false teacher means ceasing to walk in either obedience or love.

Tolerating false teachers and false teaching looks loving, but actually violates both truth and love. John insists we should not give them or it any encouragement, so we need to obey his advice and *watch* (8). I am always grateful when a student Christian Union asks me to sign a doctrinal basis before I speak at their meetings. It is safe, both for them and for me. Church members should encourage their pastors to explain complex doctrinal issues, because false teaching is itself often complex, subtle and devious. Those of us who are older need to beware mellowing as we mature. Of course it is right to grow in love and fellowship, and people do grow out of hard and exclusive

[35] This phrase could mean either, but v. 7 makes 'teaching about Christ' most probable.
[36] 1 John 1:3.
[37] See too the tolerance of the church in Thyatira (Rev. 2:20).

contexts, but it is important not to grow tired of the need for vigilance. Notice John's insistence that not everyone who says he is a Christian, is a Christian. There are key words in this section: *deceiver* (twice), *antichrist, does not have God, do not receive him into your house or give him any greeting*. A charitable reading of someone's intentions is not always the right one. And those of us who are movers and shakers, who have a bias towards action and like to live life at the leading edge, need to recall that not all new ideas are true ideas, that innovation is not necessarily the Spirit's work, and progress is sometimes progress out of the gospel. We must *walk* (4, 6) not *run* (9).[38]

c. True love (12–13)

So 2 John teaches our churches to walk in truth (4), but there is a wrong kind of teaching (7); to walk in obedience (6), but there is a wrong kind of progress (9); and to walk in love (6), but there is a wrong kind of fellowship (11). By contrast, his final words are gentle, breathing an inclusive love to match the exclusive love which has gone before. The Christians are to show love for those they know, like John (12) and those they do not, like the brothers associated with John (13). There should be no automatic suspicion of unknown Christians, because the test is not 'we do not know you', but 'such a person does not know God' (9). The love we should show is explained more in 3 John.

3. The church that loves too little (3 John)

3 John is brief (in Greek, it is the shortest New Testament letter), but it carries a critical lesson. It shows how a church can turn into a cult. Like several New Testament letters, it is written to an individual, but with a community impact.[39]

There are three main characters in this letter: Gaius (1), the person to whom John wrote; Diotrephes (9), who caused the crisis; and Demetrius (12), who was about to arrive. John finds here a positive and a negative example, and a test for the first readers.

Behind them lies a domineering church leadership refusing to welcome visiting Christian workers, *the brothers* (5, 10).[40] The history is simple but fierce. John had written to the church (9), presumably a letter of commendation, either in advance of the brothers' visit, or to accompany them as a proof of orthodoxy. Diotrephes

---

[38] NIV.
[39] Phlm., 1 and 2 Tim. and Titus.
[40] 1 Cor. 16:19–20; Gal. 1:2; Eph. 6:23–24; Phil. 1:14; 4:21–22; Col. 1:2; 4:15.

banned them, and shredded John's letter. John is now trying again, writing to a senior Christian, probably not a member of that church, to commend those brothers in general, and one particular brother, Demetrius, who is coming to defuse the problem. John seems to say, if you welcome him you are welcoming me, and the problem is resolved; refuse him and you refuse me, and the problem is unresolved. So although there is little explicit theology in 3 John, there is active theology in what it was designed to achieve. Only in this letter does John use the word *church*, and he does so three times (6, 9, 10).

We can take the three principal characters in turn, and behind them stands a larger cast (*my children, friends*, 4, 15).

a. Gaius: a wonderful example of true love (1–8)

The letter is written to *the beloved Gaius, whom I love in the truth* (1). Love is so important to John that he mentions it three times in the first eleven words. Parts of their friendship are personal, such as John's concern for Gaius' physical and spiritual health (2), but others are to do with the church, and it is those we must explore.

The first characteristic of true love is that Gaius is committed to walking together in the truth (3–4): *For I rejoiced greatly when the brothers came and testified to your **truth**, as indeed you are **walking in the truth**. I have no greater joy than to hear that my children are **walking in the truth**.* As in 2 John, there is progress, but no new truth. As an apostle, and one of the authorized witnesses of that truth (1 John 1:2–3), what delighted John was that Gaius was correctly related to their teaching. It is a mark of Christian maturing that we delight in increasing obedience to the apostles' teaching.

The second characteristic of true love is that Gaius is committed to working together for the truth (5–8). Gaius is commended for his *efforts for the brothers*, and even though they were *strangers* he showed *love*, and *support, send[ing] them on their journey in a manner worthy of God*. He took delight in evangelism, world mission, and the growth of the church, at some personal cost.

Gaius, then, is a model of a healthy Christian life: he loves God's truth and God's servants, for the sake of his church and the world. He is a shining contrast to the disaster about to unfold.

b. Diotrephes: a terrible denial of true love (9–10)

That disaster is summarized in one awful phrase: *Diotrephes, who likes to put himself first*. One heart polluted and tyrannized the entire congregation. *Diotrephes, who likes to put himself first, does not acknowledge our authority.* And not content with that, *he refuses to welcome the brothers, and also stops those who want to and puts them out of the church.* It shows the critical importance of the heart of the pastor, and how destructive it is to have someone with 'the loving-to-be-first-among-them' spirit,[41] even in the little power plays of the elders' meetings.

There are two signs of what had gone wrong. They are identical to those strengths we have already seen in Gaius, but this time they are negative.

Diotrephes was committed to neither love nor truth. He refused to submit to the Apostle's authority: *I have written something to the church, but Diotrephes, who likes to put himself first, does not acknowledge our authority* (9). The verb behind *does not acknowledge*, is in the present tense, implying a settled antagonism towards John and his co-workers. Diotrephes, whose unusual name means, ironically, 'God-nurtured',[42] is so blatant that we might think him too extreme to be a real warning for us – until we remember his background as someone who had been in a good relationship with John, and leading a church that had also been in a good relationship with John. If Diotrephes could do this, any one of us could.

The second sign of the denial of true love is that Diotrephes was not committed to working together for world mission, and here it is that attitude to *the brothers* who *have gone out* (7a) which is critical. They worked with the explicit support of the apostle, but Diotrephes was undermining both. Verses 9–10 describe, first, a wilful ignoring of the apostle's influence, and then malicious gossip (*wicked nonsense*), particularly against John. Anyone familiar with churches can testify that this is not an unfamiliar pattern, nor is it unusual for even mature leaders to feel an inner smugness at the failings of others. Growing out of that gossip was an isolationist stance: *he refuses to welcome the brothers.* And the final step in creating a cult was building a ring-fence around it by making personal loyalty to Diotrephes the key test of membership. He excluded the brothers, and so anyone who welcomed them was in turn expelled by him. *He stops those who want to [welcome the brothers] and puts them out of the church,* where the phrase *put out* translates a word John used to describe Jesus being *thrown out* of the synagogue.[43] That hints at physical intimidation. This is persecution of Christians at the hands of a church.

---

[41] Johnson, *1, 2, and 3 John*, p. 176, translating *philoprōteuōn*. He adds Mark 10:42–45 as a contrast.

[42] Raymond E. Brown, *The Epistles of John*, AC 30 (Yale: Yale University Press, 1983), p. 716.

[43] *Ekballein*, John 9:34–35.

Abusing power is a principal temptation facing Christian leaders. They see the need for clear direction, tight programmes, solid priorities, firm planning and high commitment, and they see them so clearly that the centre of loyalty slides away from Christ and onto themselves. Doing that, they discover a dangerous truth: as Diotrephes had discovered, it works. And so they start to make it a tactic to say, work my way or not at all. Or, like Diotrephes, only people I approve of are welcome here. Remember, this is not a doctrinal test – *the brothers* were warmly commended by an apostle, so there is no question of theological error. This is a pure power-play as a church wraps itself around a leader, against everyone else, and turns into a cult. No doubt as Diotrephes portrayed it, the issues were those of boundary truths and brotherly love, but John sees to the dark heart. Would he see the dark heart of our churches? Would he see the dark heart of our leadership practices? Or, as he puts it to the first person in this letter, will Gaius join the cult or not? John sets him a test to find out.

c. Demetrius: a costly test of true love (11–15)

Demetrius has a reputation for commitment to (or by) *the truth* before *everyone*, including John (*we also add our testimony*), and was quite probably the bearer of this letter.[44] In which case, his reception is an important moment, as we can see from verse 11. John sets it up with care: there exists what is *good* and what is *evil*; someone who *does good*, and someone who *does evil*; the former *is from God*, the latter *has not seen God*. It is clear which group contains Diotrephes, with his malice, gossip, isolationism and bullying. It is also clear which group contains Demetrius, commended both by *the truth*, and by Christians around the world. The question is, which group will Gaius be in? Demetrius is the test: will Gaius side with him, John, and the worldwide church (earning the hatred and exclusion of Diotrephes), or will he side with his local friends in their local cult, winning local approval but global shame? If Gaius welcomes Demetrius, he will be excommunicated by Diotrephes. If he refuses to welcome him, he will be cut off from John. Demetrius is a costly test, because giving the right answer, and welcoming him, will lose Gaius his friends. This is a sober moment, and Howard Marshall notices that the structure of *evil . . . good . . . good . . . evil* 'suggests that the primary force is one

---

[44] 'Third John . . . is a commendation for Gaius and a letter of recommendation for Demetrius' (J. L. Sumney, 'Adversaries', *DLNTD*, p. 24–34). The fourth-century *Apostolic Constitutions* 7.46.9 claimed that John appointed Demetrius the bishop of Philadelphia.

of warning'.[45] If 2 John asks whether we would exclude someone for the sake of the gospel, 3 John asks whether we would be willing to be cut off for the sake of the gospel.

So the climax is charged. John tests Gaius to *greet the friends, every one of them.* That is, in the context where Diotrephes will have nothing to do with John or his associates, Gaius is to prove his loyalty to John by seeking out each spiritual pariah in turn. Even more pointedly, John promises an urgent personal visit *soon* – will Gaius extend to him the *support* which *the brothers* have been denied, and which ugly pattern Diotrephes still withholds?

Many Bible passages expect us to stand for truth in the face of error, but 3 John contains a different challenge, which is to make a stand for love in the face of error. We have travelled far enough with John to hear him say that truth and love come so intimately entwined that he draws parallel conclusions. Perhaps we could imagine hearing ourselves say, 'This church is doctrinally in error; I shall leave.' But could we ever imagine hearing ourselves say, 'This church is relationally in error; I shall leave'? That twin standard, of truth and love, is the one John calls us to.

4. Boundaries

a. Inclusion

John gives four stages for how to treat Christian workers from other churches. First, we extend hospitality. In the phrase, *we ought . . . to support* (8), *we* is emphasized, and *support* means 'to receive amicably with support and protection'.[46] That is more than just a bed for the night. At the very least, then, we need to become churches which are open to others, and where our fundamental stance is to be inclusive.

So we must identify the invisible boundaries we put in place, which ensure that we exclude fellow Christians without the right accent, background, connections, status, friendships, experience, or whatever. I am fairly relaxed, and am happy in a 'jeans and T-shirt' church, but my parents are not; and I dislike body piercing and tattoos, especially when they are combined. I prefer to sing in English rather than Latin, and to a band rather than an organ, but I must not allow those prejudices to build walls.

So, how do we react to today's culture? A friend told me that he feared being part of a 'Mary Poppins church', which was 'practically

[45] I. Howard Marshall, *The Epistles of John*, NICNT (Grand Rapids: Eerdmans, 1978), p. 92.
[46] TDNT 4.15. The word is *hypolambanein*.

perfect in every way', pretending that there are not real people with messy lives. John Burke puts the challenge well:

> Think about it this way, if you are reaching the average person under forty, more than likely, one out of every three women you interact with will have had an abortion. One or even two out of six women you talk to will have been sexually molested. More than six out of ten people you speak to will think living together before marriage is the wisest way to prevent divorce, and five out of those ten will already have lived with someone. Most will have been sexually active, and the thought of waiting until marriage will sound totally foreign and will need explaining. Most men will have struggled with pornography or serious problems with lust. One in five to ten people will struggle with substance abuse. At least one in five and as high as two out of five people who come to your church will smoke.[47]

It is sinful to put border patrols around our churches such that both Christians and non-Christians have to pretend to be better than they are in order to hear the gospel and live it out.

But the word 'inclusive' is loaded, because it has come to mean, in many older denominations, an agenda for the inclusion and acceptance of certain ideas and lifestyles which Christians have traditionally seen as wrong. We shall need to return to that, because John's inclusiveness is not unqualified.

Then, when the workers move on, we *send them on their journey*, giving supplies for the next leg of their travel. The word is 'a technical term for missionary support in the early church'.[48] We do more than wave farewell.

Thirdly, the workers were *accepting nothing from the Gentiles* (7), assuming that financial support would be both generous and continual. Christians were expected to pay the costs of evangelism fully, so that non-Christians hear for free. And fourth, in consequence, the supporters become *fellow workers* with the truth.[49] In letters dealing with the boundaries of the church, John has redrawn the map, and shown that those who actively support are just as much workers.

Any Christian who travels is struck by the imbalance of resources. Inside a wealthy bubble are books, conferences, ideas and facilities

---

[47] J. Burke, *No Perfect People Allowed* (Grand Rapids: Zondervan, 2008), p. 45.

[48] Colin G. Kruse, *The Letters of John*, PNTC (Grand Rapids: Eerdmans and Leicester: Apollos, 2000), p. 223.

[49] ESV, translating *synergoi*. See too, being fellow sufferers (2 Tim. 1:8) and fellow contenders (Phil. 1:27).

that are way beyond the means of Christians elsewhere. The bubble does not quite end where we expect, so while Christians in the UK look at American mega-churches with incredulity, Christians in continental Europe and the old Eastern bloc do the same to the British ones. But those of us inside the bubble have the responsibility (and we know this) of equalizing the imbalance where we can. By the same token, though, outside the bubble of wealth there exist earnest prayer, deep fellowship, courageous witness and a passion for Christ, and there is an imbalance of those resources too. All of us need to tackle this, so that whether in our giving, praying, or time commitments, we grasp being *fellow workers* across the world.

b. Reconciliation

In dealing with Diotrephes, John faced a relational error rather than an explicit heresy, so his strategy aimed to rebuild relationships.[50] First, John sent a letter which Diotrephes binned. It is unlikely to have been 1 John, because that contains no commendation of the brothers, so most probably the note is lost.[51] Then John sent emissaries, who were shunned. Now, he sends a second letter (3 John) with another emissary (Demetrius), and involves Gaius as someone who has not been involved so far. As Gary Burge says, 'Gaius becomes a point of reference that gives John pastoral objectivity in this remote congregation.'[52] And finally, John promises a personal visit, to *bring up what* [Diotrephes] *is doing* (10), in contrast to the good things that Gaius is *doing* (5).[53]

John works hard at rebuilding relationships with the church, even if Diotrephes is not yet within his grasp, because he is caught in a pattern of *evil* behaviour (11). John uses a battery of methods (letters, representatives, an intermediary, a third person, a visit) to effect a restoration.

Christians are engaged in work that matters at church, and our passion can be misplaced onto trivia which we then inflate into being die-on-the-hill gospel certainties. I know Christians who did not talk for twenty years because of a disagreement about cleaning, which is funny but tragic at the same time. John would want that sorted out.

---

[50] Cf. G. Burge, *Letters of John*, NIVAC (Grand Rapids: Zondervan, 1996), pp. 251–254.

[51] Both 2 and 3 John were brief enough to have been written on one piece of papyrus, the *paper* of 2 John 12.

[52] Burge, *Letters*, p. 252.

[53] NIV.

But John's concern is focused on Diotrephes and his sinful love of power; a concern about which any church member or leader can tell you a dozen stories. Christians in denominational churches should work to ensure that their structures promote proper account-ability and stop ego-trips; those of us in independent congregations must ensure all our leaders are surrounded by people who will speak truthfully to them, and challenge them if necessary. And it might be right, as John writes to Gaius here, for other churches to get involved in sorting out the tangled lines of relationships.

c. Exclusion

Inclusion and reconciliation have been mentioned so strongly, that the exclusion in 2 John can jar. It is not unusual for commen-tators to disagree with John completely on this point. Raymond Brown even suggested that 2 John was so strong that it backfired on the elder, and in 3 John he was getting a taste of his own medicine.[54] The Ephesians had been warned to expect interfering wolves, and Diotrephes was being a defensive pastor.[55] Is not John acting in defiance of Jesus, who said, 'For if you love those who love you, what reward do you have? Do not even the tax collectors do the same? And if you greet only your brothers, what more are you doing than others? Do not even the Gentiles do the same?'[56]

But this is a false view of what John is writing. He is rightly known for his emphasis on love: the verb (*agapaō*) occurs thirty-one times, the noun (*agapē*) twenty-one times[57] – and yet that is in striking contrast with his reaction to errorists. We should notice, first, that his stance is not that we 'hate' the false teachers. 'Hate' comes five times in 1 John (although not at all in 2 or 3 John), but it demon-strates either the hypocrisy of the errorists, that they 'hate' people while claiming to 'love God', or that those who hate while claiming to love are 'murderers' and 'liars'.[58] The fifth occurrence is when the world 'hates us'.[59] 1 John uses strong language of his opponents: they are antichrist (4:3), deny truth (2:22), children of the devil (3:10), false prophets (4:1), idolatrous (5:21), and even that some should not be prayed for (5:16–17). But at no stage does he suggest that our heart should hate.

[54] Brown, *Epistles*, p. 693.
[55] Acts 20:29.
[56] Matt. 5:46–47.
[57] See Kruse, *Letters*, p. 229.
[58] 1 John 2:9, 11; 3:15; 4:20.
[59] 1 John 3:13.

Here is John Stott in debate with the views of C. H. Dodd.

We must 'find a way', [Dodd] writes, 'of living with those whose convictions differ from our own upon the most fundamental matters'. But of course! In the case of a private individual who denies Jesus Christ, it is enough to look to ourselves . . . lest we embrace his error, and seek to win him to the truth; but in the case of someone officially sanctioned to teach his error to others, we must reject not only it but him.[60]

That last phrase is surely the key. In 2 John the issue is not a private opinion, but an attempt to recruit people into error. It is that attempt which must be blocked, by refusing the hospitality which would give public endorsement to their views.

One cutting edge of this idea lies in our relationships within and across our denominational boundaries, in a culture where religious disagreement is seen as a cause of manifest evil, and tolerance as an ultimate good. Although the worldwide ecumenical movement in the World Council of Churches may be less vibrant than it was in the 1960s, the same issues have now shifted to local and national level, and they still affect many denominations. So Stott's comment from the 60s is still relevant, when he explains that because 'Christian love is founded upon Christian truth, we shall never increase the love which exists between us by diminishing the truth which we hold in common. In the contemporary movement towards Church unity we must beware of compromising the very truth on which alone true love and unity depend'.[61] Discussions between churches perpetually raise the spectre of elevating love and diluting truth.

So our task in our discussion with each other, is to discover how much of our disagreements are within the emphases of acceptable Christian orthodoxy, or where we disagree over a core matter. This is obviously where the great guides from the past can help us, because the Bible's teaching over the Trinity and the incarnation were laid out in the creeds, and over the cross, the Bible and the church at the Reformation. But those cannot be the only boundaries, otherwise we would have to say that they are answering the only possible errors. So we must proceed with thoughtful care, because it is always possible that we are facing new questions, or that our traditions and ideas are wrong. Is the age of baptism a church-dividing matter? May we pray with a Muslim? Is it ever permissible to bless non-marital sex? Are those three questions equally serious? There is a seductiveness and

[60] Stott, *Epistles*, p. 213.
[61] Ibid., p. 203.

security to giving a quick, safe answer, but there is also a seductiveness in engaging in long and pleasant conversations with those with whom we are in serious disagreement.[62] We can flatter ourselves that we are being sophisticated, when we are actually being lulled into accepting an error because we like the errorist. My personal rule has been that whenever I have been engaged in that kind of dialogue, I have some limit, such as that I will not partake in the Lord's Supper, or share a meal.[63] Whether as a sign to other people or only to me, it is a way of marking out that while I am not cutting myself off from discussions with whom I disagree, I will not let any of us think that my disagreement is lessened by my willingness to discuss.

[62] Defining a core matter is, of course, the heart of the problem. I would suggest that a core belief is one where *non*-belief of it threatens salvation. In that way, the age of baptism is not a core belief, but I would include both the exclusiveness of prayer through Christ, and persistent engagement in sexual immorality.

[63] 1 Cor. 5:11.

Acts 11:19 – 20:38
16. The church's future

Church planting has moved from being hardly discussed twenty years ago, to the front of many churches' plans. Ed Stetzer and Warren Bird find that 'An important shift happened in recent years. After decades of net decline, more U.S. churches are being started each year (approximately 4,000) than are being closed each year (approximately 3,500)',[1] and a 2007 article in *Christianity Today* concluded, 'Today church planting is the default mode for evangelism'.[2] David Garrison surveyed church planting globally, and concluded 'God is doing something extraordinary *in our day*. As he draws a lost world to himself Church Planting Movements appear to be the *way* he is doing it. What began as a small trickle of reports a few years ago has now grown into a steady stream of previously unreached people groups pouring into God's kingdom.'[3]

This has produced a new way of describing churches, with a new question. The new description is that churches are to be 'missional'.[4] The question is, 'What exactly is the mission of the church?'

It is in Acts, and especially in the great spread of work from Antioch, that we have the biblical answer. Antioch governs the second half of Acts as Jerusalem governs the first, and the picture of church life from Acts 2 is complemented by chapter 13. It results,

[1] E. Stezter and W. Bird, *Viral Churches: Helping Church Planters become Movement Makers* (San Francisco: Jossey-Bass, 2010), p. 1.

[2] T. Stafford, 'Go and Plant Churches of All Peoples: Crusades and Personal Witnessing Are No Longer the Cutting Edge of Evangelism', *Christianity Today* (Sept 2007), vol. 51, p. 9.

[3] D. Garrison, *Church Planting Movements* (Midlothian: WIGTake Resources, 2004), p. 16.

[4] The concept emerged in C. Van Engen, *God's Missionary People* (Grand Rapids: Baker, 1991), but the headline occurred with D. L. Guder and L. Barrett (eds.), *Missional Church* (Grand Rapids: Eerdmans, 1998).

not with churches having been planted, but with church-planting churches having been planted. 'Church planting' is our summary phrase, not a biblical one, because the biblical language of 'planting' deals with evangelism, not starting new congregations.[5] Moreover, many contemporary patterns (like grafting people into a struggling congregation, or sending a team of families) do not find biblical witness. Instead, evangelists 'established' or 'strengthened' churches and then moved on.[6] But we do use non-biblical words to summarize biblical themes, and church planting is a good name for the pattern where a church so has mission on its heart that it reproduces itself.

Luke's narrative shows a typically careful literary strategy that teaches how to plant, and I share Ben Witherington's conclusion that 'Luke is intending to present a lasting model of what a universalistic Christian mission ought to look like.'[7]

1. The place: Antioch (11:19–30)

Antioch was one of the five major cities of the Roman empire, and this section of Acts also dwells on Caesarea, Ephesus and Rome, with Paul spending extended time in each.[8] With around half a million people, and a diplomatic, cultural and commercial centre, it described itself on its coins as 'Antioch, metropolis, sacred, and inviolable, and autonomous, and sovereign, and Capital of the East'.[9] Like any metropolis it had wonderful culture alongside vice and violence, and the Roman satirist, Juvenal, compared it to a foul sewer.[10] It had five walled, racial districts: Greek, Syrian, Jewish, Latin and African.[11] Perhaps the large Jewish population made it a natural place for the Jewish Christians expelled from Jerusalem after Stephen's death (8:1) to continue their preaching here (8:4), but *to no-one except Jews* (11:19).

At some point, though, a few anonymous, faith-filled believers took a decision which made history. Spontaneously, some of the evangelists *began to speak to Greeks also*, with the same *good news*

[5] 1 Cor. 3:6.

[6] 1 Thess. 3:2.

[7] B. Witherington, *The Acts of the Apostles* (Grand Rapids: Eerdmans and Carlisle: Paternoster, 1998), p. 373.

[8] The missing city is Alexandria, home of Apollos (18:24).

[9] Witherington, *Acts*, p. 366. For background on Antioch see M. Green, *Evangelism in the Early Church* (rev. ed., Eastbourne: Kingsway, 2003), pp. 162–164.

[10] D. J. Williams, *Acts*, NIBC (Peabody: Hendrickson and Carlisle: Paternoster, 1990), p. 203.

[11] R. Bakke, *A Theology as Big as the City* (London: Monarch and Downers Grove: IVP, 1997), pp. 145–146.

about the Lord Jesus, and with the same result that *a great number of people believed and turned to the Lord* (11:20–21).[12]

a. Antioch was a genuine church

The result was a *church* (11:26), and Luke intends that to startle us. So far only one body has been called a *church*, which was in Jerusalem.[13] This is now the second. No doubt other groups existed, but Luke deliberately takes the word that he reserved for one exclusively Jewish entity (11:22) and applies it to a quite new phenomenon. It was so new that non-believers did not have a name for something which involved Jews who had stopped being Jews (but were not Gentiles) and Gentiles who had stopped being pagans (but had not become Jews). They coined, *Christians*, meaning 'people who are always talking about *Christos*, the Christ-people',[14] and possibly 'Christ's slaves'.[15] But Luke knows only one name for an entity which bridges racial boundaries with the gospel – *the church.*

b. Antioch was a similar church

Luke underlines the similarities between the *church* in Jerusalem and the *church* in Antioch. The Antioch congregation traced its roots to Jerusalem (11:19), sharing their habits of being devoted to teaching (11:26), and prayer (13:2) and concern for the poor. When the prophets announced a *famine* in Jerusalem (11:28), the Christians immediately arranged a collection. Acts changes direction: to this point everything has flowed out of Jerusalem, but now something flows back. Antioch is a proper church, standing independently of Jerusalem. So we should avoid thinking of Jerusalem as the 'mother church' and Antioch as the 'daughter'. That implies a senior/junior relationship which Acts does not show.[16]

c. Antioch was a validated church

Curious, the Jerusalem *church* sent Barnabas to investigate (11:22). He is another comparison between the two, because he typified

---

[12] NIV.

[13] Acts 5:11; 8:1, 3; 9:31.

[14] F. F. Bruce, *The Book of the Acts*, NICNT (rev. ed., Grand Rapids: Eerdmans, 1988), p. 228.

[15] *Christian* is only used by non-believers in the New Testament (here, Acts 26:28 and 1 Pet. 4:16).

[16] 'Mother church' was quite possibly a title the Jerusalem church wanted to use about itself, but which Paul firmly resisted. Gal. 4:26.

generosity in Jerusalem (4:36–37). Perhaps because he came from Cyprus he would understand the Antioch scene better than someone who had only known Jerusalem, and certainly he would be trusted by those innovative evangelists who also came from Cyprus (11:20).[17] He was *a good man* (11:24).[18] But above all, the Jerusalem church sent someone whom they nicknamed 'Son of Encouragement', which was a sure sign that although they were curious, they did not intend to block it. True to his name (*paraklēsiōs*, 'encouragement') Barnabas *encouraged* (*parekalei*) *them* that what they were doing was true to the gospel.

d. Antioch was an inevitable church

Judaism had little interest in winning converts,[19] but now these Christian missionaries flooded across the racial barrier, fulfilling Israel's mission to the Gentiles.[20] 'Christianity had never been more itself, more consistently with Jesus and more evidently en route to its own future' than at this critical moment.[21] Barnabas seems to prove this too, being *full of the Holy Spirit and faith* it was almost guaranteed he would endorse the *great many* conversions (11:24).[22]

e. Antioch was a turning-point church

Their decision still defines the stance that any Christian takes to any non-Christian. From this moment on, Christians 'sought out converts to Christianity from any people group all over the Roman empire . . . and beyond'.[23] Individuals had been converted (8:26–40; 10:1–48), but never before had there been an open, frequent, determined and successful attempt to reach Gentiles with the gospel, and incorporate them as equal members. David Gooding is right to call this 'an immeasurably important advance of the gospel to an altogether new level',[24] and if this alone were all they achieved, Antioch would

---

[17] R. N. Longenecker, *The Acts of the Apostles*, in EBC 9, *John, Acts* (Grand Rapids: Zondervan, 1981), p. 401.

[18] Acts 9:36; 23:1.

[19] See S. McKnight, 'Gentiles, Gentile Mission' (*DLNTD*, pp. 388–394) especially p. 389; and E. Schnabel *Early Christian Mission, vol. 2: Paul and the Early Church* (Leicester: Apollos and Downers Grove: IVP, 2004), pp. 92–173.

[20] 1:6–8; 2:39; 3:17–26; 15:14–18; 26:23; 28:23.

[21] B. F. Meyer, *The Early Christians* (Wilmington: Michael Glazier Inc.,1980), p. 206, who sees this step as automatically leading to world mission.

[22] Witherington, *Acts*, p. 370.

[23] McKnight, 'Gentiles', p. 388.

[24] D. Gooding, *True to the Faith: A Fresh Approach to the Book of Acts* (London: Hodder and Stoughton 1990), p. 188.

deserve an honoured status. This was indeed 'a quantum leap forward in gentile evangelization'.[25] But this was only the start.

f. Antioch was a unique church

Luke has already introduced Paul[26] as a significant figure, because God had said, 'he is a chosen instrument of mine to carry my name before the Gentiles and kings and the children of Israel'.[27] But he remained in the shadows until the Jerusalem church recognized that 'to the Gentiles also God has granted repentance that leads to life'.[28] Then he is reintroduced, initially as a gifted teacher and evangelist recruited to work alongside Barnabas,[29] and then taking the famine gift to Jerusalem (11:26, 30). But Paul is God's *chosen instrument*, and the uniqueness of the Antioch church lies in the extraordinary nature of one of its leaders. Luke reintroduces the enlarged team on the way back to Antioch: *Barnabas and Saul returned from Jerusalem when they had completed their service, bringing with them John, whose other name was Mark* (12:25), and they return to what was possibly the most influential prayer meeting in the history of world mission.

The church's leadership was remarkable (13:1). *Barnabas*, whom we have met; *Simeon who was called Niger* (probably meaning he was black); *Lucius* from *Cyrene* in modern day Libya, maybe one of the Cyreneans who with the Cretans had first evangelized Gentiles (11:20); *Menean*, the childhood foster-brother[30] of Herod, who had possibly been posted to Antioch to fulfil Herod's prestigious building plans;[31] and the intelligent and talented Paul. If nothing else, this church would be known for its staff team.[32] Here is a church learning, evangelizing, praying together, where its leadership reflects the ethnic and cultural mix of the city, and where commitment to the poor is a high concern, and 'a better model for city churches cannot be found than this church at Antioch'.[33]

[25] R. Reymond, *Paul – Missionary Theologian: A Survey of his Missionary Labours and Theology* (Ross-shire: Mentor 2000), p. 99.

[26] At this point still called 'Saul', only becoming 'Paul' at 13:9.

[27] Acts 9:15.

[28] Acts 11:18.

[29] The word *look for* (*anazēteō*) implies Barnabas head-hunted him.

[30] So G. Twelftree, *People of the Spirit* (London: SPCK, 2009), p. 113.

[31] So Witherington, *Acts*, p. 367.

[32] G. Appel, '"Do It Again, God! Do It Again!" Planned Pregnancies: Churches Planting Churches', in T. Jones (ed.), *Church Planting from the Ground Up* (Joplin: College Press Publishing, 2004), p. 29.

[33] R. S. Greenway and T. M. Monsma, *Cities: Mission's New Frontier* (Grand Rapids: Baker, 1989), p. 14 fn. 4.

They were *worshipping, praying* and *fasting*. The doubly empha-sized *fasting* (13:2, 3) implies that something was on their hearts where they wanted God's guidance. Arthur Glasser sees the matter clearly: 'It is impossible to speak of this church without using super-latives. It was noteworthy as a true cosmopolitan, most evangelistic, well-taught, and outwardly generous company of the Lord's people. And yet, in Acts 13:1–5, the church is described as burdened, and on its knees.'[34]

In context, the most likely matter is the Gentile outreach. For all their gifting and abilities they knew that the only way this mission work could be accomplished was on their knees. Later they produced strategies, and used their gifts, but first they fast, worship and pray. This is the only occasion the New Testament uses the word *worship* for anything like the kind of Christian meeting we hold, though the word was common for the work of priests and Levites in the temple.[35] Paul used temple language for his apostolic ministry to the Gentiles,[36] for other Christians supporting that ministry,[37] and financial generosity across the Jew/Gentile divide.[38] In line with that, the Antioch leaders strain every spiritual muscle to focus on the issue of the Gentiles. What was to be done?

The answer was the most costly they could imagine: God told them to disband the team, and send Saul and Barnabas away *for the work to which I have called them* (13:2). Remarkably, they did it. Ajith Fernando sees the challenge: 'This is typical of churches that have a missionary vision, churches whose main aim is more than survival or maintenance. Missions is so important to them that they willingly take steps that may seem harmful to the church in order for the missionary program to thrive.'[39]

g. Antioch was a base church

Antioch became the first church to engage in world mission, on purpose.[40] This is the centre of Luke's theme, to 'present Paul as the first to inaugurate a deliberate policy for direct appeal to the Gentiles'.[41] It has been called 'The Antioch effect – going deliberately

---

[34] A. F. Glasser, 'The Apostle Paul and the Missionary Task', in R. D. Winter and S. C. Hawthorne, *Perspectives on the World Christian Movement* (3rd ed., Pasadena: William Carey Library and Carlisle: Paternoster, 1999), p. 129.

[35] See ch. 8.

[36] Rom. 15:16.

[37] Phil. 2:17, 25, 30.

[38] Rom. 15:27; 2 Cor. 9:12.

[39] A. Fernando, *Acts*, NIVAC (Grand Rapids: Zondervan, 1998), p. 377.

[40] Witherington, *Acts*, p. 390.

[41] Longenecker, *Acts*, p. 401.

to all Peoples'.[42] Each of Paul's three church-planting journeys, a combined distance of some 10,000 miles,[43] have Antioch as the sending and receiving centre, and although other cities are given more prominence in terms of the length of time Paul spent there, Antioch is the hub.

h. Antioch was a model church

It was here that Paul learnt to reach Gentiles, nurture them, establish this new phenomenon of a Jew/Gentile church, and to plant more. As Robert Greenway noted, 'A great deal of what we have come to recognise as the Pauline strategy of church planting (and the theology that accompanies it) can be traced back to his early experience with the vibrant young church in Antioch.'[44]

That is a critical observation. If Antioch was a template for the churches Paul planted, then even though we are not apostles, it is a template for the churches to which we belong. So if Antioch's vision was to be a church-planting church, and we see that in Paul's ministry, we should expect to have it in our church's heart as well. Paul was not content to convert individuals, or to build them into churches, but to be true to his task, *they must be church-planting churches*. Ed Stetzer and Warren Bird have adapted a famous Peter Wagner quotation to make this point: '"The single most effective method-ology under heaven is planting new churches" *who in turn reproduce themselves*.'[45] If we read Acts rightly, we have Luke's church-planting manual.

i. The inevitable happens: Sergius Paulus at Paphos (13:4–12)

Paul's team continued with Jewish evangelism in numerous *syna-gogues* (13:5), but meeting the proconsul on Cyprus, Sergius Paulus, marked 'a new policy – the legitimacy of a direct approach to and full acceptance of Gentiles apart from any distinctive Jewish stance'.[46] Without this brave moment, evangelism would always be limited to the well-meaning crowd around a synagogue. They were

[42] J. M. Terry, E. Smith and J. Anderson (eds.), *Missiology: An Introduction to the Foundations, History and Strategies of World Missions* (Nashville: Broadman and Holman, 1998), p. 80.

[43] R. F. Hock, *The Social Context of Paul's Ministry* (Philadelphia: Fortress, 1980), p. 27.

[44] Greenway and Monsma, *Cities*, p. 36. See too Terry, Smith and Anderson, *Missiology*, pp. 470–471.

[45] Stetzer and Bird, *Viral Churches*, p. 16, their italics. See C. P. Wagner *Church Planting for a Greater Harvest* (Ventura: Regal, 1990), p. 11.

[46] Longenecker, *Acts*, p. 420.

only a few miles from home, but they had made the greatest leap forward in Christian mission.

2. The principles (13:1 – 20:38)

The next eight chapters cover three journeys, although Luke's emphasis is less on the miles Paul travelled than on the length of stay in particular places. Here are developing concepts which are clearly central for Luke's theology and practice of church planting. The first is the theme of Acts itself, and the basic justification for evangelism.

a. Every nation under heaven

Luke opens his book with two markers. The first is the risen Jesus addressing his disciples: 'You will receive power when the Holy Spirit has come upon you; and you will be my witnesses in Jerusalem and in all Judea and Samaria, and to the ends of the earth.'[47] That gives a pattern to their mission, and shows that the entire planet is to be reached. The second comes at Pentecost, when Luke notes 'that there were staying in Jerusalem God-fearing Jews from every nation under heaven'.[48] That echoes numerous prophecies about God gathering his disobedient and scattered people in order to forgive and restore them.[49]

The context is Jesus' ascension into heaven (1:9–11), where Stephen later 'gazed into heaven and saw the glory of God, and Jesus standing at the right hand of God. And he said, "Behold, I see the heavens opened, and the Son of Man standing at the right hand of God."'[50] Heaven is where Jesus rules from. What does the phrase 'under heaven' add to 'every nation'? It says that every nation on earth is under heaven's rule, under Jesus' lordship. Nowhere is off limits for the gospel. Everyone, everywhere must hear.

b. The gospel

Luke recounts the gospel with considerable literary care. His practice is to lay out a first example, and then by increasingly brief repetition show that this was an embedded habit,[51] so Pisidian Antioch

---

[47] Acts 1:8.
[48] Acts 2:5, NIV.
[49] Lev. 26:27–45; Deut. 4:25–31 and especially 30:4–5. Neh. 1:8–9 and Jer. 31:8 both draw on this hope.
[50] Acts 7:55–56.
[51] See C. Green, *The Word of His Grace* (Leicester: IVP, 2005), pp. 22–25, and pp. 54–60.

284

(13:16–41) is the first occasion for Paul's evangelistic speaking to Jews and Gentiles, and is the pattern for what follows.

First, Paul summarizes God's covenant: God sent a *Saviour Jesus as he promised* (13:23), repeating that this is *the message of this salvation* (13:26). The core facts are that Jesus lived, was crucified, died, rose, was seen, and ascended to heaven, with a warning about the consequences of rejecting him (13:27–41). How is this a message of *salvation?* Because *through Jesus the forgiveness of sins is proclaimed to you. Through him everyone who believes is set free from every sin, a justification you were not able to obtain under the law of Moses* (13:38–39).[52] *Forgiveness of sins, salvation* and *justification* are introduced as overlapping blessings that anyone who *believes* receives from God. Paul calls this *the good news* (13:32) for the rest of the journey (14:7, 15, 21).

So the message to both Jews and Gentiles is titled *the word of God/ the Lord; salvation* offered in the synagogue (13:26) will now go to the Gentiles through Paul and Barnabas; both Jews and Gentiles must *believe* (13:38); and in addition to *salvation, justification* and *forgiveness,* both believing Jews and believing Gentiles experience the blessings of *eternal life. Gentiles* are mentioned three times in these verses, as God had promised.[53]

c. Communication

The Antioch team spoke formally (17:19–34) and informally (14:1–7); on other people's premises (14:1) or their own (19:9–10); in households (18:7), with small groups (16:13), and with individuals (16:14). They used detailed exposition (13:32–41) and broad-brush summaries (14:15–17), careful Bible studies (17:11) and close debate (17:17), fierce confrontation with the thought-world of the day (17:22–31) and careful instruction for new Christians (14:22) and established leaders (20:18–35).

Not only did they *preach* (14:7),[54] they *reasoned* (17:2),[55] urged (13:43), discussed (19:9), *refuted* and proved (18:28), dialogued (20:7, 9), testified (18:5; 20:24) and discoursed.[56] The words obviously overlap, so when Paul was in Thessalonica, he

---

[52] NIV. Both *dikaiōthēnai* and *dikaioutai* belong to the 'justification' word-group, but the first phrase probably means 'freed from' (cf. Rom. 6:7). HCSB translates both as '*justified*', which captures the repetition but loses the idea of 'freedom'; ESV translates both as '*freed*', losing the idea of 'justification'.

[53] Isa. 49:6.

[54] 14: 21, 25; 15:21, 35; etc.

[55] 17:17; 18:4, 19.

[56] 24:25.

went in, as was his custom, and on three Sabbath days he *reasoned* with them from the Scriptures, *explaining* and *proving* that it was necessary for the Christ to suffer and to rise from the dead, and saying, 'This Jesus, whom I *proclaim* to you, is the Christ.' And some of them were *persuaded* (17:2–4).

And in Corinth,

he *reasoned* in the synagogue every Sabbath, and tried to *persuade* Jews and Greeks. When Silas and Timothy arrived from Macedonia, Paul was *occupied with the word*, testifying to the Jews that the Christ was Jesus . . . And he stayed a year and six months, *teaching the word of God* among them (18:4–5, 11).

Three challenges to our contemporary practice emerge. First, they used a range of speaking styles and methods, deliberately aiming to engage their hearers and challenging them to respond, and almost daring them not to. Secondly, the focus is not on 'telling my story of how Jesus changed my life' but telling his story. Thirdly, they engage intellectually with their culture, proving the truth of the gospel and the *ignorance* of any alternative (17:30).

d. Strategy, surprises and the Spirit

Paul knew *the work* to which God had called him (13:2; 14:26; 15:38), which was to *bring salvation to the ends of the earth* (13:47),[57] with a particular energy on pioneer work.[58] Not even a prophecy or the pleading of his friends could distract him.[59] His commitment resulted in churches planted in over fifty towns.[60] That suggests careful planning,[61] and in the mind of one high-profile non-Christian opponent 'an aggressive expansion of the repulsive superstition'.[62]

The work was God's – *Set apart for me Barnabas and Saul for the work to which I have called them* (13:2) – and Luke records his interventions.[63] But Paul's flexibility can also be seen,[64] as when he tells the Corinthians

---

[57] See Schnabel, *Paul*, p. 1295.
[58] Gal. 2:7; Rom. 15:14–21.
[59] Acts 21:10–14.
[60] E. Schnabel, 'Mission, Early Non-Pauline', *DLNTD*, pp. 757–758.
[61] Rom. 15:19.
[62] Pliny, quoted in Schnabel, 'Mission', p. 752.
[63] The Lord Jesus (18:9; 23:11), the Spirit (13:2; 15:28; 16:6) and the Spirit of Jesus (16:7). See 8:26, 29, 39; 10:19.
[64] Rom. 1:10–11, 13; Gal. 4:13; 1 Cor. 16:8–9; 2 Cor. 12:12–22.

I will visit you after passing through Macedonia, for I intend to pass through Macedonia, and perhaps I will stay with you or even spend the winter, so that you may help me on my journey, wherever I go. For I do not want to see you now just in passing. I hope to spend some time with you, if the Lord permits. But I will stay in Ephesus until Pentecost, for a wide door for effective work has opened to me, and there are many adversaries.[65]

Even with his divine mandate, he did not confuse his plans with God's.

e. Strategic cities

Of the major cities of the Roman Empire, Paul spent fifteen out of twenty-five years in five of them, and without being anachronistic we can see similarities to today's urban world. Large concentrations of people mean large concentrations of sin, violence and idolatry, but also large concentrations of God's common grace, in security, the arts and compassion.[66]

What accounts for 'the urban emphasis in Acts'?[67] I am not myself persuaded that cities have any redemptive purpose,[68] and although city dwellers may be more open to new ideas, and new churches may best reach emerging cultures there, that is not where Luke dwells.[69] Instead, he seems to have two reasons.

First, cities contain more people. Cities where Rome ruled shared a culture, commerce was vibrant, and there was often a sizeable Jewish population. Those all required people, and the early Christians used each of those connections. Tim Keller, describing his experience in Manhattan, says, 'The only way to increase the number and percentage of Christians in a city is to plant thousands of new churches'.[70]

But secondly, the missionary Roland Allen noticed that these cities were gateways to their provinces.[71] They were not the only large

[65] 1 Cor. 16:5–9.
[66] See especially Greenway and Monsma, *Cities*; Harvie M. Conn and Manuel Ortiz, *Urban Ministry: The Kingdom, the City & the People of God* (Downers Grove: IVP Academic, 2010), and T. Keller, *Center Church* (Grand Rapids: Zondervan, 2012).
[67] Conn and Ortiz, *Urban Ministry*, p. 127.
[68] See Conn and Ortiz, *Urban Ministry*.
[69] See D. Tidball, 'Social Setting of Mission Churches', *DPL*, pp. 883–892, following W. Meeks, *The First Urban Christians* (London: SCM, 1983).
[70] Stetzer and Bird, *Viral Churches*, p. 68.
[71] R. Allen, *Missionary Methods: St. Paul's or Ours?* (repr. Grand Rapids: Eerdmans, 1997 [1927]), p. 16. For a contemporary reappraisal of Allen, see R. L. Plummer and J. M. Terry (eds.), *Paul's Missionary Methods: In His Time and Ours* (Downers Grove: IVP Academic and Nottingham: IVP, 2012).

cities, and Paul visited small towns too, but nevertheless these were strategic. Allen suggested Paul made them strategic by what he did, but David Lim observes that 'Paul chose to set up churches in only a couple of urban centres in each province . . . to serve as outreach centres in their respective regions.'[72] So Luke focuses on cities: 'the *city* of Joppa' (11:5), *Lystra and Derbe, cities of Lycaonia* (14:6), *the city of Thyatira* (16:14) and 'the *city* of Lasea' (27:8),[73] but as the keys to their provinces. Paul, based in Ephesus (19:1) influenced *almost all of Asia* (19:26).[74] Just as Paul is not content with converting people but builds them into a church, so he is not content unless the church he has planted is itself planting churches. He stayed in Ephesus, and never met the churches of Colossae, Laodicea, Hierapolis, Smyrna, Pergamum, Thyatira, Sardis or Philadelphia, all of which were planted in the province, arguably from Ephesus, at that time. Ephesus caught the Antioch vision.

Today's mega-cities are global carriers of culture, and intentional church planting there would be a key to reaching far beyond their geographical footprint and into their intellectual provinces. Not only are non-Christians gathered there, but they are the non-Christians who influence most other non-Christians. Cities remain strategic for church planting.

f. Strategic places

Philippi shows that the missionaries normally worked with intelligent care.

> So, setting sail from Troas, we made a direct voyage to Samothrace, and the following day to Neapolis, and from there to Philippi, which is a leading city of the district of Macedonia and a Roman colony. We remained in this city some days. And on the Sabbath day we went outside the gate to the riverside, where we supposed there was a place of prayer, and we sat down and spoke to the women who had come together. One who heard us was a woman named Lydia, from the city of Thyatira, a seller of purple goods, who was a worshipper of God. The Lord opened her heart to pay attention to what was said by Paul (16:11–14).

The team knew when (the *Sabbath*, at *the time of prayer*) and where (*by the river*, where Jews gathered when there was no synagogue)

---

[72] D. S. Lim, 'Evangelism in the Early Church', *DLNTD*, p. 355; Allen, *Missionary Methods*, pp. 13–17.

[73] Conn and Ortiz, *Urban Ministry*, p. 128.

[74] 19:10, 22, 26f; 20:4, 16, 18; 21:27; 24:19; 27:2.

their audience would meet, and they intentionally made contact and began talking about Christ. It is almost a model in evangelistic training – which is what Luke intends. No human cleverness can produce a convert, so it is only when *the Lord opened her heart* that Lydia believed, but nevertheless, Paul and his companions made thoughtful decisions and acted on them.

But where would they meet Gentiles? The only example Luke gives is in Athens: Paul *reasoned in the synagogue with the Jews and the devout persons, and in the marketplace every day with those who happened to be there* (17:17). Here again are thoughtfulness, and seizing opportunities.

g. Race

Of all the literature on mission and church planting, the most controversial remains Donald McGavran's. Based on his work as a missionary in India, and observing conversions among different racial, class and caste groups, he concluded 'People like to become Christians without crossing racial, linguistic or class barriers',[75] an insight often called the Homogeneous Unit Principle (HUP). McGavran arouses strong feelings. For David Bosch, McGavran's approach 'robs the gospel of its ethical thrust', because it focused exclusively on evangelism and allows racism to remain unchecked.[76] C. Peter Wagner, probably McGavran's most vocal supporter, strongly disagrees that HUP is either 'racist or classist', claiming that HUP 'is a serious attempt to respect the dignity of individuals and the social units to which they belong, and to encourage their decisions for Christ to be religious decisions rather than social decisions'.[77]

I live in London, and these issues are live for us. There is an extraordinary racial and cultural mix which it shares with a handful of other cities in the world, not just because of its size, but its diversity. Beijing is double the size, but mono-cultural. In London, the world's nations meet, and Christians rub shoulders with people whom our ancestors would have taken decades to contact. We can meet non-Christians from Beijing and talk openly about Christ.

[75] D. A. McGavran, *Understanding Church Growth* (rev. ed., Grand Rapids: Eerdmans, 1980), p. 163.

[76] This is his summary of a broader disagreement with McGavran. D. Bosch, *Transforming Mission: Paradigm Shifts in Theology of Mission* (New York: Orbis, 1991), p. 382.

[77] C. P. Wagner, 'Homogeneous Unit Principle', in S. Moreau (ed.), *Evangelical Dictionary of World Missions* (Grand Rapids: Baker, 2000), p. 455. See J. R. W. Stott (ed.), *Making Christ Known: Historic Documents from the Lausanne Movement 1974-1989* (Carlisle: Paternoster, 1996), pp. 57–72.

Yet such multicultural cities are often places of heightened tension, and frequently of violence. Central to the vision of the Antioch church was that Jews and Gentiles belong together to Christ, and the mixed-race nature of their leadership demonstrated that commitment. As Daniel Hays puts it,

> As a pattern of true discipleship, Luke reminds the Church today that the gospel demands that we forsake our inherited culturally driven racial prejudices, and accept all people – especially those different from us – as integral parts of the Church. The demolishing of racial barriers within the Church is a task in which the Spirit leads us. I would also suggest that the inverse is true: flourishing racial prejudice within a church is probably indicative of the Spirit's absence.[78]

London typifies the questions surrounding McGavran's observations. Large groups of people hardly speak English at all, or at least cannot function in it. Central London hospitals offer multilingual translators, and some streets have bilingual road signs. The Mayor of London's website works in twenty-six, mutually incomprehensible, languages. If our ministry happens only in English, hundreds of thousands of people in the city where I live will never hear the gospel. That is a genuinely racist choice.

In addition, Paul worked within *households*,[79] and Ajith Fernando notices that in Sri Lanka, in contrast with the individualized West, decisions to come to Christ are often family decisions.[80] This seems to bear out another part of HUP, at least in some societies.

We must insist, and model, that racism is always wrong. The gospel requires us to be inclusive, as the Jerusalem church finally had to admit (15:12–21); that the heavenly assembly contains people 'from every nation under heaven';[81] and that the gospel imperative requires us to cross every cultural barrier for people to hear, respond, be reconciled, be built up, and be members of planting churches. Cities show this at its starkest, because to be true churches there requires us to be both indigenous and cosmopolitan at the same time, as Antioch showed. Issues of culture, and especially language, are complex, but the duty to overcome them is ours.

---

[78] J. D. Hays, *From Every People and Nation*, NSBT (Leicester: Apollos and Downers Grove: IVP, 2003), p. 179.

[79] Acts 11:14; 16:15, 31; 18:8.

[80] Fernando, *Acts*, p. 451.

[81] Acts 2:5.

h. Prayer and fasting

The challenge to cross-cultural church planting came while the Antioch church was *praying, worshipping* and *fasting* (13:2–3). We have already noticed the importance of prayer,[82] but here Luke's point is surely that they were so earnestly seeking God's help and guidance, because of the awesome significance of the Gentile response. As Arthur Glasser says, 'What was needed now was a structured way of extending the knowledge of Christ, one which would surmount all the barriers, whether geographic, linguistic, cultural, ethnic, sociological, or economic. So they fasted and prayed.'[83] John Piper is even clearer: 'They were fasting to seek the leading of the Holy Spirit in the direction of the mission . . . [It] changed the course of history. It is almost impossible to overstate the historical importance of that moment in the history of the world.'[84]

That is strong, but surely right. Without that praying church, there would have been no organized attempts to reach out beyond the synagogues and nail the claims of Christ to every door in the world. Prayer is in David Wells' phrase, 'rebelling against the status quo',[85] and if the status quo is a world population heading towards seven billion, of whom two-thirds are unbelievers, then we know what to pray for, because we know the answers to Antioch's prayers. Teams of planters.

i. The supernatural

This mission team saw God do extraordinary things in their work as a result of their fervent prayer.[86] They were amazed at *all that God had done with them* (14:27), but yet the most important miracle remains conversion. Elymas the sorcerer was blinded by God for his opposition to the gospel, and Luke records that *the proconsul believed, when he saw what had occurred, for he was astonished at the teaching of the Lord* (13:12). Amazing as the miracle was, it was the *teaching* which converted him. The team grasps that, because on their return *they declared all that God had done with them, and how he had opened a door of faith to the Gentiles* (14:27). We should pray for the miracle of conversion.

[82] See above p. 282 and ch. 2.
[83] Glasser, 'Apostle Paul', p. 129.
[84] J. Piper, *A Hunger for God* (Leicester: IVP, 1997), pp. 104, 107.
[85] D. Wells, 'Prayer: Rebelling Against the Status Quo', in Winter and Hawthorne, *Perspectives*, p. 142.
[86] 14:3; 15:12; 19:11.

Some of these extraordinary events are markers of the Gentile conversions having God's blessing. In Acts the words *signs* or *wonders* are a specific category of miracles, marking the birth of the church.[87] They run from Acts 2 to 15, and once the Jerusalem Council heard Paul and Barnabas relate *what signs and wonders God had done through them among the Gentiles* (15:12), the phrase disappears from the story. The final boundary has been crossed. We should expect God to act, but to call that a sign or a wonder is to misuse the term.

j. Finance

Money is handled consistently with what we have seen elsewhere.[88] Christians demonstrate generosity to believers in need (11:27–30; 12:25). Second, non-Christians are not to pay to hear the gospel, so Paul set to work in the smelly business of making tents (18:3; 20:34–35).[89] 'Tent-maker' is used in mission circles for someone whose work gives entry to an otherwise closed country,[90] but for Paul it was a necessary way of paying for food and lodging, and possibly for the hire of a meeting room (19:9).[91] So, thirdly, Christians pay for non-Christians to hear the gospel, and when Silas and Timothy arrived with money collected from the Macedonian churches,[92] *Paul devoted himself exclusively to preaching, testifying to the Jews that Jesus was the Christ* (18:5).[93] We can imagine his relief.

k. Teams

A constantly changing list of names accompanies Paul, with around a hundred men and women coming and going.[94] Eight were particularly prominent: Barnabas, Timothy, Luke, Aquila and Priscilla, Silas, Titus and Tychicus, and they were probably being trained as well as used. 'Messengers of the churches'[95] maintained the links. Once again, Christian leadership is plural rather than singular.

---

[87] 2:19, 22, 43; 4:30; 5:12; 6:8; 7:36; 8:6, 13; 14:3; 15:12.

[88] See ch. 17.

[89] P. Barnett, 'Tentmaking', *DPL*, p. 926; Hock, *Social Context*, p. 67. 1 Cor. 4:12; 9:1–18; 2 Cor. 6:5; 11:23–27; 1 Thess. 2:9; 2 Thess. 3:8.

[90] So both T. Yamamori, 'Tent-making Mission', in Moreau, *Dictionary*, p. 939, and R. Siemens 'Tentmakers Needed', in Winter and Hawthorne, *Perspectives*, p. 736.

[91] The western text of Acts says Paul had the hall from 11am to 4pm – 'off peak'.

[92] Phil. 4:14–18.

[93] NIV.

[94] Schnabel, *Paul*, p. 1426; A. Köstenberger, 'Women in the Pauline Mission', in Peter Bolt and Mark Thompson, *The Gospel to the Nations: Perspectives on Paul's Mission* (Leicester: Apollos, 2000), p. 225.

[95] 2 Cor. 8:23.

Antioch continues to care for those whom they sent, and we should similarly maintain strong connections with those who work cross-culturally, by prayer, finance and personal contact. Every church should be actively involved in supporting world mission.

Antioch also teaches that church planting may take our best people away. Ed Stetzer says,

> Few church planters have been blessed by the sponsorship of an Antioch congregation, a church that willingly sponsors new churches. Very few churches volunteer, as Antioch, to send the *best* of their leaders and to contribute *significant* sums of money for the establishment of new congregations. The Antioch church did just these things.[96]

l. Responsible and strategic leadership

The plant was not established until senior Christians were in charge. Paul and Barnabas *appointed elders for them in every church,* and *with prayer and fasting they committed them to the Lord in whom they had believed* (14:23). The characteristics of those leaders are spelt out in Acts 20.

In addition to local leadership, some had a wider responsibility. The repeated model here is Timothy, a gifted young Christian brought to Paul's attention by the church, and taken under his wing (16:1–3). Timothy spent time with Paul, being taught and tried out (16:4 – 17:13), then was given responsibility of his own (17:14 – 18:5). Further deployments occurred continually (19:22; 20:4).[97] The pattern is repeated with Silas, who was recruited (15:22), taught and trained in association with Paul and subsequently deployed (17:14).[98]

So part of the role of the local church is to identify future gospel workers. And those workers need to have the best training they can, with the best theological minds combined with the best evangelists, preachers and church planters.

m. Size

The early Christians met in homes, which were available, practical and inconspicuous, and on four occasions the New Testament talks about 'house churches'.[99] Perhaps, as both Lydia's household and

[96] Ed Stetzer, *Planting New Churches in a Postmodern Age* (B&H Academic, 2003), pp. 45–46.
[97] Phil. 2:19; 1 Thess. 3:2; 1 Cor. 4:17; 16:10; 1 and 2 Timothy.
[98] 2 Cor. 1:19; 1 Thess. 1:1; 2 Thess. 1:1. The pattern can be traced with Titus as well.
[99] Rom. 16:5; 1 Cor. 16:19; Phlm. 2; Col. 4:15.

the Philippian gaoler's household found, the conversion of the leader meant profound changes for everyone (16:15, 33–34). Writing from Singapore, Chua Wee Hian says that 'At times it is difficult for individualistic Westerners to realize that in many "face to face" cultures, religious decisions are made corporately. The individual in that particular type of society would be branded as a "traitor" and treated as an outcast if he were to embrace a new religious belief'.[100] That would be an excellent reason for the normal use of houses for meetings.[101]

In six cities Luke emphasizes the large numbers who responded.[102] Without idolizing large churches and dismissing small ones, we must face Luke's challenge. Perhaps they copied the Jerusalem pattern and used larger buildings as well as homes, or only held their very large meetings occasionally, or squashed really close. Luke implies Paul copied the Jerusalem church, teaching *publicly and from house to house*.[103] These were not necessarily tiny groups of people.

n. Ambition and God's sovereignty

This expansion did not happen by accident, and Luke identifies the connection between the activity of church planting and the determination of the church planter. Elsewhere Paul talks of his *ambition* to work new areas,[104] and this section shows that ambition in action. Paul's unswerving nature is shown when he *resolved* (literally, 'he resolved in (the) s/Spirit) *to go to Jerusalem*, and *'I must also see Rome'* (19:21). Church-planting churches must have equivalent determination.

But Paul's determination is irrelevant without God's sovereignty. One the big scale, God *opened a door of faith to the Gentiles* (14:27); on the small scale, he *opened [Lydia's] heart to pay attention to what was said* (16:14). God is in control, and is the true evangelist. Repentance is his gift too: he granted 'repentance to Israel and forgiveness of sins',[105] and *to the Gentiles also God has granted repentance that leads to life* (11:18). When the Christians preached, *as many as were appointed for eternal life believed* (13:48).

---

[100] Chua Wee Hian, 'Evangelization of Whole Families', in Winter and Hawthorne, *Perspectives*, pp. 613–616, p. 614.

[101] Chrys Caragounis (quoted by Schnabel, *Paul*, p. 1459) suggested they may have rented large halls.

[102] Antioch: 11:21, 24, 26; 15:35; Iconium: 14:1; Derbe: 14:21; Corinth: 17:4; 18:8, 10; Berea: 17:12; Ephesus: 19:26.

[103] Acts 20:20, emphasis added.

[104] Rom. 15:20; Gal. 2:7.

[105] Acts 5:31.

o. Interdependence

Antioch welcomed the team back to report on *the work* (13:2; 14:27), and they then reported to Jerusalem (15:3, 12; 21:19), a habit that others shared too (11:5–17; 12:17). This is nothing like a denomination, with controlling boards and committees; those are later inventions. Nevertheless, Paul recognizes that major decisions like the requirements on the Gentiles should be made by an authorized and authorizing group. Churches who value independence should see that there is room here for something mutual, almost an accountability structure; those who value denominations should see how light are the relationships between Antioch and Jerusalem.

p. Suffering and opposition

Suffering is normal. Paul revisited those church plants, *encouraging them to continue in the faith, and saying that through many tribulations we must enter the kingdom of God* (14:21–22). We might not call that an encouraging message, and our courses for new Christians rarely highlight it. But it is normal, so being forewarned is, indeed, *en-couraging* – it puts courage in us. This the only time Luke tells us what Paul taught new churches, but he indicates it was repeated in other places. This is what follow-up ought to look like.

That makes suffering normal for church planting. Gentiles accepted the gospel, but Paul still goes to the synagogue first (13:5) even when it gets unpleasant. In Pisidian Antioch:

> *the word of the Lord was spreading throughout the whole region. But the Jews . . . stirred up persecution against Paul and Barnabas, and drove them out of their district. But they shook off the dust from their feet against them and went to Iconium.* And what do the missionaries to the Gentiles do there? They *entered together into the Jewish synagogue and spoke in such a way that a great number of both Jews and Greeks believed* (13:49 – 14:1).

> *When an attempt was made by both Gentiles and Jews, with their rulers, to mistreat them and to stone them [they] fled to Lystra and Derbe . . . and there they continued to preach the gospel* (14:5–7).

> *But at Lystra Jews came from Antioch and Iconium, and . . . stoned Paul and dragged him out of the city, supposing that he was dead. But when the disciples gathered about him, he rose up and entered the city, and on the next day he went on with Barnabas to Derbe* (14:19–10).

It is in those very churches, in Lystra, Iconium and Antioch, that Paul had insisted *We must go through many hardships to enter the kingdom of God* (14:21–22).[106]

3. The process

Can we order this list into a sequence? If so, it is very simple. Michael Green says 'neither the strategy nor the tactics of the first Christians were particularly remarkable. What was remarkable was their conviction, their passion, and their determination to act as Christ's embassy to a rebel world, whatever the consequences'.[107] Tim Keller says that Paul 'had a rather simple, two-fold strategy. First, he went to the largest city of the region . . . and second, he planted churches in each city'.[108]

These churches were expected to be church-planting churches, and the priorities of Acts 13 are as normative as Acts 2. Tim Chester and Steve Timmis are surely right to observe that 'at present church planting carries a certain mystique. Church planters are portrayed as a unique kind of rugged pioneer. But we need to create a culture in which transplanting is normal. Every church should be aiming to transplant and raise up church planters'.[109]

May God change our hearts so that we pray and fast, give and go, passionate for God to 'Do it again, God! Do it again!'[110]

---

[106] NIV.

[107] Green, *Evangelism*, p. 23.

[108] Timothy J. Keller and J. Allen Thompson, *Church Planting Manual* (New York: Redeemer Church Planting Center, 2002), p. 27. See too Greenway and Monsma, *Cities*, p. 21.

[109] T. Chester and S. Timmis, *Total Church* (Nottingham: IVP, 2007), p. 95.

[110] Appel, 'Do It Again', p. 27.

Putting it all together: Part two[1]
How churches organize themselves

Of all the books which have influenced pastors in the last twenty years, none has been as significant as *The Purpose Driven Church* by Rick Warren.[2] It summarizes his ministry at Saddleback Community Church, and has attracted praise and loathing in almost equal measure. His central diagram overlays the core purposes of a church on the bases of a baseball diamond, with critically placed classes to help people grow. When I was a pastor we used it to help us clarify what we were trying to do, and no other book had the explanatory simplicity of Warren's.

Nevertheless, having lived with it for a number of years, several thoughts have dared me to tweak it. British people do not, on the whole, play baseball. They see only a diamond. I tried various equivalents, but since most other sports involve either two ends or goals, or a race with one end, they did not seem to be flexible enough to work. I needed an alternative.

I also became aware of a missing element. Warren has five; the central one is magnifying God, and then comes in sequence membership (what it means to be part of a church); maturity (growing as a Christian); ministry (where and how to serve with your gifts); and mission (covering both evangelism and social action). Our church leadership spent one summer covering a huge board with sticky notes, making sure we identified every part of our church's life, and that everything justified its existence.[3]

It was enormously valuable, but one conversation we had did not fit. We were keen to plant, and I had Warren's notes from his *Purpose*

[1] For Part One, see p. 176.

[2] Rick Warren, *The Purpose-Driven Church: Growth Without Compromising Your Message and Mission* (Grand Rapids; Zondervan, 1995).

[3] Emmanuel Church, Tolworth, in south-west London, deserves particular thanks for patience as we reinvented ourselves.

Driven Church Planting conference in my study. But it troubled us that such a significant element was not on the diamond. We also knew that planting would require more leaders, and they did not appear either.

In writing this book, the chapter that has most surprised me has been the previous one, and it has suggested a small modification.

First, using Warren's sequence of the letter 'M', I identified the missing topic as 'multiplication'. That has two elements: planting, as Acts has shown, and developing good leadership, from chapter 11. Paul told Timothy, 'And the things you have heard me say in the presence of many witnesses entrust to reliable people who will also be qualified to teach others'.[4] He is to equip many people for teaching roles in the congregation. This verse is not about the careful passing of ministry from one generation to the next, like a relay baton; it is about the explosive multiplication of ministry in the habits of a training church.[5]

With that extra 'M' in the sequence I have tipped Warren's diamond and added a roof, to give a child's drawing of a house, adding my word to his:

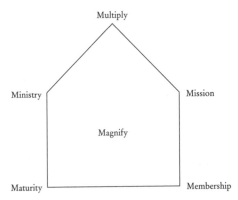

This gives me wider cultural references than baseball, although in many parts of the world this shape of house is as alien as a baseball diamond. It includes that missing element. But the greatest advantage is the ease with which biblical references to the church as God's house find a place.

[4] 2 Tim. 2:2, NIV.
[5] See (despite the title) C. Marshall, *Passing the Baton: A Handbook for Ministry Apprenticeship* (Sydney: Matthias Media, 2009), and C. Marshall and T. Payne, *The Trellis and the Vine: The Ministry Mind-Shift that Changes Everything* (Sydney: Matthias Media, 2009).

Revelation 21:1 – 22:5
17. The church for eternity

We began with a dream, and a nightmare. The dream was of a captivatingly perfect church, utterly devoted to fulfilling its God-given purposes. The nightmare was of a self-centred and corrupt institution, obsessed with its own interests and survival. We have now seen that both are true. One family comes home from church, exhilarated by the teaching, the praying, the singing and the fellowship, while another comes home from the same church in tears because of the unaddressed realities of torn relationships and painful lives. The good news is that the Bible recognizes both, and holds out hope of change. The last staging post in our journey is the description of the bride of Christ at the end of Revelation, but first we need to recall two obvious but important truths about Revelation: its structure and its symbols.

1. The description of the bride

a. Structure

Revelation begins with letters to seven churches in chapters 2 – 3, and ends with the bride of Christ in chapters 21 – 22. In between are multiple descriptions of the church. The imperfections, sufferings and sin of the present churches are finally resolved, but we must remember that the wonderful description of the church at the end of the book is not yet true, although we all want it to be. The letters at the beginning describe the church as it is, and for those who despair about that, the picture at the end tells it will not always be that way. The picture at the end tells us what the church will be like, but for those who fantasize about that, the letters at the beginning remind us of currently reality. We need to bear both ends of the book in mind at the same time.

Once again the task is to understand the present church in the light of the future, as we live under the New Covenant but still in the old creation. Churches that fail to grasp the change the gospel brings will be indistinguishable from the surrounding culture. Rather than the gospel, they offer a religious substitute which talks sufficiently spiritual language to mean they still look like a church, although actually they have nothing of value. When we find ourselves tempted to keep our church the way we like it, contoured to pamper our prejudices and sooth our sin, we should repent. John Stott rightly wrote that '[O]ur static, inflexible, self-centred structures are "heretical structures" because they embody a heretical doctrine of the church'.[1]

By contrast, other churches face constant problems of reality. They can be exciting, visionary places, full of fun and energy, but they will be artificial. People have to pretend that they do not sin, struggle, nor doubt, and leaders have to pretend that they are too spiritually advanced to need oversight. Occasionally they have to manufacture a religious experience to shrink some of the gap between promise and reality. Some people maintain the façade for many years, others live in guilt-ridden dependence, but many leave, exhausted and cynical.

Those errors are related. One promises too little and the other too much, but both erroneously release the tension caused by a proper biblical understanding of when we live, which says that though we are *no longer* what we once were, we are *not yet* what we will one day be, but we are *now* living demonstrations of the power of Christ to forgive and change us. Churches who understand this know that they will have to deal with sin and love of sin, but there is always forgiveness, restoration, love and permanent opportunities for change, and they have passion to share that liberating news and to live it out. Showing how the tensions in the churches at the opening of Revelation are answered by the closing vision, G. K. Beale draws the contrasts as shown in the table opposite.

b. Symbols

Revelation's symbols have deep Old Testament roots,[2] describing spiritual realities in ways that are frequently breath-taking. To enhance that, some are described in more than one way, to make more than one point. So when John glimpses the reigning Lord Jesus,

[1] J. R. W. Stott. *The Living Church* (Nottingham: IVP, 2007), p. 58.
[2] Themes from Genesis, Isaiah and Ezekiel are important in what follows.

The present churches:	The future church will:
Contain false prophets (2:2)	Be built on twelve true apostles (21:14)
Contain false Israel (2:9; 3:9)	Contain only members of the tribes of true Israel (21:12)
Dwell where Satan has his throne (2:13)	Dwell where God has his throne (22:1)
Contain some who are dead (3:1)	Contain only those whose names are written in the Lamb's book of life (21:27)
Are flickering lampstands (1:20; 2:5)	Have God and the Lamb as their only light (21:23–24; 22:5)
Contain idolatrous impurity (2:14–15, 20) and liars (2:9; 3:9)	Be pure and truthful (21:8, 27)
Are persecuted, hoping in God's promises to overcomers (2:8–10, 13)	Reign as overcomers who inherit those promises (2:7 = 22:2; 2:17 = 22:4; 3:5 = 21:27; 3:12 = 2:10 and 22:4; 3:21 = 22:1 and 22:5)[3]

one of the elders said to me, 'Weep no more; behold, the Lion of the tribe of Judah, the Root of David, has conquered, so that he can open the scroll and its seven seals.' And between the throne and the four living creatures and among the elders I saw a Lamb standing, as though it had been slain, with seven horns and with seven eyes, which are the seven spirits of God sent out into all the earth.[4]

We are supposed to contrast the invitation ('behold, the Lion') with the vision ('I saw a Lamb'). Which is Jesus? He is both: he is our reigning Lord and our crucified sacrifice. Or consider the number of believers. According to Revelation 7:4–8, there are 144,000 of them, carefully listed by tribe. But in the next verse, John says, 'After this I looked, and behold, a great multitude that no one could number, from every nation, from all tribes and peoples and languages'.[5] Is this a second group, a countless crowd in contrast to the counted crowd? Surely not: it is the same reality described from two angles. One describes the spiritual ancestry and perfection of the Old Testament promises in the gospel, the other the international evangelistic effectiveness of the gospel; both produce the church.

[3] G. K. Beale, *The Book of Revelation*, NIGTC (Grand Rapids: Eerdmans and Carlisle: Paternoster, 1999), p. 134.
[4] Rev. 5:5–6.
[5] Rev. 7:9.

That multiple perspective applies in the final chapters as well. John saw *a holy city . . . prepared as a bride* (21:2), which is hard to picture in our minds. Even more clearly,

> *Then came one of the seven angels who had the seven bowls full of the seven last plagues and spoke to me, saying, 'Come, I will show you* **the Bride,** *the wife of the Lamb.' And he carried me away in the Spirit to a great, high mountain, and showed me* **the holy city** *Jerusalem coming down out of heaven from God* (21:9–10).

Again, we are to contrast the invitation (*Come, I will show you the Bride*) with the vision (he *showed me the holy city*). Neither is a new image, but we must hold them together: the city is not where the bride will live; rather, the city is the bride. Together, they describe the church.

That double description of the city-bride has a dreadful counter-image in Revelation, in a world actively rebelling against God. The pure bride of the Lamb is contrasted with a decadent prostitute (17:1–18), and faithful Jerusalem with idolatrous Babylon (18:1–24). But by the end that city-whore has gone, having been judged and punished. Only the city-bride is left, ravishingly beautiful in the spotlight.

2. Living the perfect life (21:1–4)

Our first glimpse of the city-bride is stunning. The temporary first creation has been swept away, and instead, the eternal new creation is introduced, into which descends *the holy city, new Jerusalem* (2).[6] God has been preparing his people, his *bride* for this day, and a wonderful day it will be.

a. People in God's presence

From Eden onwards, every promise of God's presence has drawn us forwards, while reminding us we are not fully there. God had consistently promised that he would dwell with us,[7] and in Jesus he did, for a season.[8] By faith, we are fully in God's presence now,[9] but on this day no visible or spiritual barrier has to be taken into account.

---

[6] See also Rev. 21:10; 22:19. For the holy city, see Isa. 48:2, and the new name, Isa. 62:1–2.
[7] E.g. Exod. 25:8; Lev. 26:12; Ezek. 37:26–28; Zech. 2:10–11.
[8] John 1:14.
[9] Rev. 13:6; 15:5.

b. Many peoples in God's presence

We have seen that the covenant with Abraham and his descendants was always intended to have saving implications for the rest of us, too.[10] Zechariah's hope for the Gentiles was in Jerusalem terms: 'Sing and rejoice, O daughter of Zion, for behold, I come and I will dwell in your midst, declares the LORD. And many nations shall join themselves to the LORD in that day, and shall be my people.'[11] Gentiles are openly included in the eternal, unbreakable covenant so that we will always belong to him. That is what was written into the creeds, when in 381 the Council of Constantinople asserted 'We believe in (the) one, holy, catholic and apostolic church'. The word 'catholic' simply means 'all-inclusive'.[12] This multi-racial, multi-cultural gathering is what God always intended his church to be, and it is daily moving in that direction.[13]

c. Painless people in God's presence

Revelation is brutally honest about the struggles of God's people, beaten by persecutors, standing by gravesides, ripped apart by false teachers, and in love with their world. Every Christian, and every pastor, knows what it is to weep. But all those tragedies will one day *have passed away* (4),[14] and there will be no *death, mourning, crying, pain* or *tears* (4). The only people weeping then will be those who have refused Christ.[15]

d. . . . but not yet

We rightly long for that day, and the realities of our daily life show why. Pastors often dream of a clear diary, an empty desk and some free time to think, but the reality is that fallen people cause work. To avoid becoming irritable about this, we should remember that Paul saw himself as accountable for the problems in the Corinthian church, and even interprets them in those same wedding-day terms:

[10] Gen. 12:1–3; 17:2–8; Ezek. 47:22–23; Gal. 3:16. See ch. 3.

[11] Zech. 2:10–11. See Isa. 19:25.

[12] *Kath' holou* (thoroughly, completely) is used once in the New Testament (Acts 4:18), although not of the church. It appears first referring to the church in Ignatius: 'Wherever the bishop appears, there let the congregation be; just as *wherever Jesus Christ is, there is the Catholic church*. It is not permissible to baptize or hold a love feast without the bishop' (*Smyrn.* 8:1–2); Ignatius died c. 110.

[13] See P. Jenkins, *The Next Christendom: The Coming of Global Christianity* (3rd ed., Oxford: Oxford University Press, 2012).

[14] Isa. 65:16–17.

[15] Rev. 18:2–8, 15, 19. See too Matt. 8:12.

'I feel a divine jealousy for you, for I betrothed you to one husband, to present you as a pure virgin to Christ.'[16]

Those of us responsible for church discipline should remember these perspectives. First, every church is made up of repentant, saved sinners, including us, so there are no grounds for perfectionism. Second, serious sin should be dealt with, privately or publicly, as appropriate for the seriousness of the sin and the seniority of the sinner.[17] And third, the ultimate goal is not the removal of the sinner, but his or her repentance and restoration. This is a levelling task, because all who discipline are subject to the same temptations,[18] and we are warned explicitly about the risks of unintended cruelty.[19] The great goal is that all of our church's members take part in this new creation.

3. Enjoying the perfect victory (21:5–8)

This is only the second time that Revelation has reported God's speech, so this is of great importance.[20] On both occasions God has called himself *the Alpha and the Omega*, the first and final letters of the Greek alphabet, *the beginning and the end* (6).[21] As at the first creation, God speaks, and simply by his *trustworthy and true* words from the *throne* (5) he brings a new world into being.[22] As the omnipotent ruler whose words have total power, all he has to say is *'It is done!'* (6) – or more literally, 'They are done' – because the word is plural, referring back to all the prophecies and covenant promises he has made. God will keep his word. But what has he created by his speech?

a. The victorious life

Thirst is a biblical metaphor for our continuous dependence on God. In my part of the world water is easily available, but one desert visit without enough water, and one visit to a drought-stricken country, were enough to make me still thankful for it. How much more for the *living water* that Jesus promised will be available in abundance. It is a summary picture of all God's kindnesses keeping us eternally alive,

---

[16] 2 Cor. 11:2.

[17] Private/public: Matt. 18:15–20. Seriousness of sin: 1 Cor. 5:1–2; 2 Cor. 6:14 – 7:1. Seniority of sinner: 1 Tim. 5:20.

[18] Gal. 6:1–2.

[19] 2 Cor. 2:5–6.

[20] See Rev. 1:8.

[21] Jesus also calls himself *Alpha and Omega* in 22:13, consistent with sharing God's throne.

[22] Gen 1:1 – 2:3. On a new creation, see Rom. 8:21; 2 Cor. 5:17.

of salvation *without payment*, by grace. So Revelation ends with this wonderful invitation: 'And let the one who is thirsty come; let the one who desires take the water of life without price.'[23] This is for every Christian who endures pressure to the end, or – in the phrase used to each of the seven churches in turn – to 'the one who conquers'.[24]

b. The second death

By contrast with the vast crowd who conquer and live forever, is another crowd of cowards, who compromise, and die. Theirs is a gruesome list of sins, but it is not random. It identifies the temptations that God's people will face, and then contrasts what Christians might be doing with what they should be doing. However true these words might be about our culture, they are meant as warnings about us.

The *cowardly* and *faithless*[25] (8) are those who do not *fear God* enough to endure suffering or humiliation.[26] *The detestable, murderers, the sexually immoral* and *sorcerers* in Revelation are those who take part in the depraved idolatry of whore-Babylon,[27] engage in sexual immorality,[28] and kill Christians.[29] Finally, *all liars* turns the focus back onto the church, and the danger of tolerating 'false apostles', 'teachers' and 'prophets',[30] and even false churches.[31] Being courageous and victorious in such times will be hard; but those times are the only times when we will live.

Ultimately, God is the victorious judge over his rebellious subjects, and in contrast to those who inherit God's blessing, *their portion will be in the lake that burns with fire and sulphur, which is the second death* (8). This destiny is the fate of those who oppose God,[32] and it is consistent with the many passages which affirm serious warnings for professing Christians who defy God.[33]

c. . . . but not yet

Christians die daily. Tyrannical governments and vigilante terrorists murder in an on-going bloodbath, and Revelation tells us that the

[23] 22:17.
[24] Rev. 2:7, 11, 17, 26; 3:5, 12, 21.
[25] 'Cowardly' is not mentioned elsewhere; for 'faith', see 2:13, 19; 13:10; 14:12.
[26] Rev. 11:11; 14:7; 15:4; 19:5.
[27] Rev. 2:14, 20; 13:13–15; 18:23.
[28] Rev. 22:15.
[29] Rev. 2:9, 13; 3:9; 6:11; 13:10.
[30] Rev. 2:2, 14, 20.
[31] Rev. 3:9.
[32] Rev. 19:20; 20:10, 14 (twice), 15.
[33] 1 Cor. 6:9–10; Gal. 5:21; Eph. 5:5; Col. 3:6; 1 Pet. 4:5. See too Rom. 1:32.

prayer of the heavenly martyrs is 'O Sovereign Lord, holy and true, how long before you will judge and avenge our blood on those who dwell on the earth?'[34] One Christian leader I know never leaves his house without ensuring that his wife knows where his will is kept. I asked another, publicly, 'Do you expect to die?' 'Yes', he said.[35] What are we to do?

First, we should pray. Hebrews reminds us to 'remember those who are in prison, as though in prison with them'.[36] I tremble at the thought of my reactions in such circumstances and how I would stand, but the Bible gives sufferers repeated guidance:

> Yes, and I will rejoice, for I know that through your prayers and the help of the Spirit of Jesus Christ this will turn out for my deliverance, as it is my eager expectation and hope that I will not be at all ashamed, but that with full courage now as always Christ will be honoured in my body, whether by life or by death.[37]

Second, we should work for their protection and care. Paul was grateful for those who found him in prison, and kept him fed and clothed, but beyond that he longed for even one person willing to stand publicly with him at his various court appearances, whatever the personal cost.[38] We must offer practical and political support where we can.

Third, those of us at liberty should realize it is we, not the persecuted ones, who are unusual. Jesus clearly predicted the persecution of believers by the world:

> If the world hates you, know that it has hated me before it hated you. If you were of the world, the world would love you as its own; but because you are not of the world, but I chose you out of the world, therefore the world hates you. Remember the word that I said to you: 'A servant is not greater than his master.' If they persecuted me, they will also persecute you. If they kept my word, they will also keep yours.[39]

There should be no shallow promises or glib optimism in our churches.

---

[34] Rev. 6:10.

[35] As I write he has not yet been killed, but throughout the writing of this book the news from his country has been the almost daily murder of Christians.

[36] Heb. 13:3.

[37] Phil. 1:18–20. See Eph. 6:18–20; Col. 4:3–4.

[38] Phlm. throughout; 2 Tim. 1:16–18; 4:9–18.

[39] John 15:18–20.

Fourth, we should discern pressure points in our country, and be willing to be as courageous in our turn. We may not all face a bullet or a machete, although some of us will, but we might face opposition, hostility and resistance. Alternatively, we might find the temptations of money, sexual immorality or idolatry more alluring. As Peter warns us,

> Beloved, do not be surprised at the fiery trial when it comes upon you to test you, as though something strange were happening to you. But rejoice insofar as you share Christ's sufferings, that you may also rejoice and be glad when his glory is revealed. If you are insulted for the name of Christ, you are blessed, because the Spirit of glory and of God rests upon you. But let none of you suffer as a murderer or a thief or an evildoer or as a meddler. Yet if anyone suffers as a Christian, let him not be ashamed, but let him glorify God in that name.[40]

We should not get too comfortable in our air-conditioned houses with well-stocked fridges and expensive toys. It is those who have suffered who are the real victors. The martyrs are the ones who have conquered.

4. Celebrating the perfect church (21:9–27)

Now we see the city-bride, and from this point on the 'city' dominates. But for one last time, hear that the church is *the Bride, the wife of the Lamb* (9). God had described himself as Israel's promised 'husband'[41] and encouraged them to look to when they would be 'married'.[42] His love was a counterpoint to their unfaithfulness, and God called them serial adulterers, even threatening divorce.[43] Yet he still promises that one day the marriage will take place. What a privilege to be raised from the gutter to the throne because he loves us.

But we need to turn to the city imagery. John is on *a great, high mountain*, giving him a clear view but, because this is the work of *the Spirit* (10), he shares the prophetic perspective of other great mountain-top meetings.[44] Each element is described with material from a number of biblical authors, principally Isaiah and Ezekiel,

---

[40] 1 Pet. 4:12–14.
[41] Isa. 54:5.
[42] Hos. 2:19–20; Isa. 62:4–5.
[43] Hos. 2:1–13.
[44] Exod. 19; Deut. 34:1–4; Ps. 48:1–3; Ezek. 40:2.

'collapsing temple, city and land into one end-time picture of the one reality of God's communion with his people'.[45]

a. The exterior of the city (9–14)

As the *holy city Jerusalem* descends *out of heaven*, it is gorgeous, sharing God's stunning glory.[46] It glitters *like a most rare jewel*, which John names *jasper* (11). That is a form of quartz which comes in many colours, but is always opaque; the clarity and transparency of this heavenly jasper shows how pure the new church will be. Earlier he had described God's glory as like jasper,[47] so we are supposed to see this city sharing God's splendour.

Around the city stretches a square *wall, with twelve gates* (three on each side, 13) each attended by an *angel*, who stands for a tribe of Israel (13). God had promised the full restoration of *the twelve tribes*,[48] and here their names are *inscribed*, carved eternally into those gates. So the wall shows the continuity and completion of God's promises to Abraham, and where the angels once barred us from God's presence,[49] now they welcome us in.

There are twelve gates, twelve angels and twelve tribes, and each gate has its own foundation: *the wall of the city had twelve foundations, and on them were the twelve names of the twelve apostles of the Lamb* (14). Paul identified the apostles as the foundation stones of the church,[50] but this is even more wonderful: the apostles are also the foundation stones for Israel's completion. God has not abandoned his people, nor has he a separate plan for them outside the gospel. The same gospel he has promised from eternity will save both Jews and Gentiles.

b. The size and symmetry of the city (15–17)

Two other men watched an angel measuring: Zechariah saw one measure Jerusalem, and Ezekiel watched one measure the new temple.[51] But as those two ideas combine, the scale of this new city dwarfs anything seen before. The way God keeps his promises seems always to be wonderfully greater than we initially think.

---

[45] Beale, *Revelation*, p. 1061.
[46] Isa. 60:1, 2, 19.
[47] Rev. 4:3.
[48] Isa. 49:5–6; 56:1–8; 60:3–7; 66:18–23; Jer. 31:10; Ezek. 34 – 37; Zeph. 3:20; Zech. 8:7–8.
[49] Gen. 3:24; 1 Kgs 6:29–35; 2 Chr. 3:7.
[50] Eph. 2:20.
[51] Zech. 2:1–2; Ezek. 40 – 41.

This city is a gigantic cube, each of its twelve sides being about fourteen hundred miles in length. By comparison, Babylon and Alexandria were only nine miles in circumference, and Mount Everest is a mere six miles high – this new Jerusalem is taller than two hundred and fifty Everests. Measuring seven million feet in each direction, it is about two thousand times larger than even Ezekiel dared to believe.[52] But it is not the size but the symbolism we are to notice: the new Jerusalem is not measured in miles or metres but in *stadia*, and we do not need to know how long those were to understand the significance of the number *12,000* (16). Here is another number twelve, this time written large. And a cube having twelve edges gives the number which symbolized the totality of God's people in Revelation 7:4: 144,000. By comparison, the wall is ludicrously small, but then this is a city without enemies.

The city is a cube, the shape of the Holy of Holies, God's dwelling place in Solomon's temple.[53] But that was a mere thirty feet in each direction, and even the insignificant wall of this new dwelling place overshadows that. The great God will dwell with his people.

So God does not have a small plan for his people. Church leaders sometimes talk about 'church growth' as if God's plan were fulfilled when a congregation doubles, or triples in size. Acts showed spectacular numerical growth of the church, and individual change as the church grows one life at a time. But from a new creation perspective, nothing but this unimaginably vast plan will do.

c. The splendour of the city (18–21)

It is almost pointless to give the details of these blindingly fabulous building materials, wildly beyond price and wildly beyond human experience. Here is *jasper* again, and *pure gold*, so pure it is transparent, *pearls* so vast that just one can be a city gate hundreds of feet high, and a dazzling setting of every kind of jewel. The meaning is clear: God's bride has been dressed with a splendour that only God could arrange.

There is one significant background passage to this. The high priests in the tabernacle and temple wore a square jewelled breastplate with twelve jewels, each one representing a tribe.[54] There is no correlation between the two jewel lists, partly because there was no standard terminology for minerals, but the number twelve is again present in both. This is not a picture of mere wealth or splendour, but of the privilege of being part of God's people, and once again, the

---

[52] Ezekiel measured Jerusalem at 18,000 cubits; John's Jerusalem is 12,000 stadia.
[53] 1 Kgs 6:15–22; 2 Chr. 3:8–14.
[54] Exod. 28, especially v. 16.

fulfilment dwarfs the promise, just as God had promised.[55] The priests in the temple walked on gold, but here every believer does that, and even the gold is better.[56]

Our proper destiny should put the contemporary world into some clearer perspective. What we see around us is the tattiness of doomed Babylon, and the fake love of the prostitute. How foolish of us, then, to allow our churches to fall in love with this world, to ape its values, flinch at its mockery and fear its rebukes. Encouraging each other in Bible studies, praying together and reaching out to the lost can look insignificant besides the empire-building of the great companies and governments that appear in the news, and many pastors feel that they are wasting their talents in doing something hardly anyone notices. We should take courage. This vision is our true home, and one day we shall live there.

d. The spiritual reality of the city (22–27)

John pauses, surprised. Of all the things he could see, one appeared to be missing – *I saw no temple.* But of course, the city does not need one, because *its temple is the Lord God and the Lamb* (22). Even the temple in Jerusalem was nothing more than a symbol representing the presence of God among his people, but this city will experience God's presence in its full, sinless love.

(i) Glory streams out
God's glorious presence is so strong that there is no need for either *sun or moon.* Even better, God does not rise or set, wax or wane, nor will he hide behind cloud. He had promised this constancy to Isaiah, who wrote that after Israel returned from exile,

> The sun shall be no more
> your light by day,
> nor for brightness shall the moon
> give you light;
> but the LORD will be your everlasting light,
> and your God will be your glory.
> Your sun shall no more go down,
> nor your moon withdraw itself;
> for the LORD will be your everlasting light,
> and your days of mourning shall be ended.[57]

[55] Hag. 2:9; Jer. 3:16–17.
[56] 1 Kgs 6:30. See R. H. Mounce, *Revelation*, NICNT (Grand Rapids: Eerdmans, 1997), p. 383.
[57] Isa. 60:19–20.

But once again the ways God keeps his promises transcends what the people might have dared to hope, because the new Jerusalem's eternal *lamp is the Lamb*, the sacrifice (23).[58] God's glory shines out through the cross.

Even more wonderfully, the *nations* who were outside the covenant and rejoiced in the humiliation of Israel will now *walk* by that same *light* (24). Earlier in that same chapter Isaiah had foreseen this too, and told Israel,

> Arise, shine, for your light has come,
>   and the glory of the LORD has risen upon you.
> For behold, darkness shall cover the earth,
>   and thick darkness the peoples;
> but the LORD will arise upon you,
>   and his glory will be seen upon you.
> And nations shall come to your light,
>   and kings to the brightness of your rising.[59]

If we look for a consistent timeline within Revelation we might think the nations had a conflicting role, or that it was a puzzle that they should still exist outside the New Jerusalem and needing to be drawn in. But because Revelation deals in overlapping symbolism we know that this is describing the present as well, and all over the world women and men are daily being drawn into the heavenly assembly which will one day be revealed as the New Jerusalem.

(ii) Glory streams in
Between those two passages, Isaiah wrote more about the Gentiles and their rulers:

> Your gates shall be open continually;
>   day and night they shall not be shut,
> that people may bring to you the wealth of the nations,
>   with their kings led in procession.[60]

Israel having been humiliated, looted, and led into captivity by Gentile armies, it is entirely natural that God's victory leads to a complete reversal of that experience, with trophies from around the world flooding into Isaiah's vision of the renewed Jerusalem. But Isaiah, with the other prophets, knew that this was not forced tribute nor pillaged loot, but the glad tribute of people who had been (as

[58] Ps. 132:17b.
[59] Isa. 60:1–3.
[60] Isa. 60:11.

we would say) converted. In Isaiah's remarkable vision, he foresaw that God's enemies would 'know the LORD' and 'worship with sacrifice and offering, and they will make vows to the LORD and perform them'.[61] So too in Revelation, *kings*, who to this point have led the rebellion and taken their treasure to Babylon,[62] even from those *nations* who have so persecuted Christians,[63] will lead their people in delighted worship of God, bringing their *glory* (twice) and *honour*.

We should not be misled by this triumphant inclusion into a triumphant universalism. John is clear that sin will still be banished (*nothing unclean will ever enter it*), as will be unrepentant sinners (*nor will anyone who does what is detestable or false*). The basis for entry is still only for *those who are written in the Lamb's book of life* (27).[64] But nor should we allow our current cultural marginalization to mislead us into negativity or withdrawal into a sub-cultural niche. The church of God has an unimaginably wonderful future ahead of it and in God's loving wisdom he has even promised that those who are currently at the forefront of opposition to him may be included among those who adore him for eternity. The leaders of the nations where Christians do not dare meet, the politicians who collude in the secularization of public discussion, and the aggressive anti-theists who mock the gospel, each has the possibility of belonging in the New Jerusalem.

e. . . . but not yet

Christians have a number of views about the church, but they seem to fall into two groups, for quite understandable reasons. Members and leaders of larger churches tend to be positive and optimistic, even running the risk of confusing their plans with God's, or confusing their numerical growth with spiritual growth. Members and leaders of smaller churches, and denominational officers (whose denominations are mostly made up of those smaller churches) tend to be pessimistic, sometimes acting as if the only possible future is to dwindle, or compromise with a hostile culture.

Neither view is biblical, and both are criticized in different ways by Scripture, but at this point it is the negative view which is in John's mind. Drawing the wagons in a circle or managing decline are inconceivable. He does not take a position midway between optimism and

[61] Isa. 19:19–25; see Jer. 3:17; Zech. 2:11; 8:22–23.
[62] Rev. 6:15; 11:2, 18; 18:3–9; 19:19 (1:5 and 21:24 are exceptions to the hostility of the kings).
[63] Rev. 5:9–10.
[64] Rev. 20:11–15.

312

pessimism, but leans completely towards a right optimism. Our little part of the world may be hostile and scathing, but across the globe the gospel is hourly bearing more fruit, and it will increasingly do so. We do not need to trim our teaching because it is currently unfashionable, for that would be to teach what is *false*, and such false teachers have no place in the New Jerusalem, nor lower God's standards, because that would be to affirm *what is detestable* to him (27). Instead, the gospel remains wonderfully true, and our duty as churches is to hold it out with confidence, so that today's unbelievers will hear, understand and respond in faith. We may live at a time when that does not seem to happen, but that would be worryingly unusual.

5. Perfect worship (22:1–5)

Finally, John is taken into the city, to see the central *river of the water of life . . . flowing from the throne of God and of the Lamb.*[65] Here is the answer to our 'thirst' in 21:6. A river flowing through the city centre is a commonplace in many countries, including Babylon and Rome, but not for Jerusalem. Perched high, it had no equivalent for the Seine, the Thames or the Potomac, and it was dependent on wells and streams. How odd, then, for the psalmist to say, 'There is a river whose streams make glad the city of God'.[66] A tourist would scratch her head and wonder where it could possibly be. Ezekiel contains an even odder vision, because he foresaw a temple with a stream flowing out of the altar, through its entrance and down the steps, that swelled until it became deep enough to swim in.[67]

It is, once again, a symbol, this time of eternal life itself. The garden where Adam and Eve rebelled contained both the tree of life and a river,[68] and now this garden-city contains an eternal *river . . . of life*, and an eternal *tree of life*.[69] Anything associated with that rebellion, anything *accursed*, is removed.[70] The river will give life for eternity, and the tree's fruit will give healing for eternity. Solomon's temple contained crafted fruit and flowers, but even though their carved splendour lasted for centuries, that was a momentary flash compared this eternal garden.[71]

[65] They share a throne in 3:21.
[66] Ps. 46:4.
[67] Ezek. 47:1–12; Joel 3:18; Zech. 14:8.
[68] Gen. 2:9–10.
[69] Isa. 35:6–9.
[70] E.g. Gen. 3:14; Zech. 14:11.
[71] 1 Kgs 6:18, 29, 32, 35; 7:18. See too Ezek. 47:12.

Because this city has God as its own temple, there will be no more veils, curtains, walls, sacrifices, barriers or priests.[72] There will be no more occasional visions for a privileged few.[73] Gone will be the difficulty of describing the indescribable.[74] Gone too will be waiting, longing faith.[75] Because there all his people will have the most intimate, privileged and sinless blessing possible: *They will see his face.*[76] High priests, they carry God's *name on their foreheads,*[77] forever (4). They will be an eternal priesthood. David was promised a Son who would reign for ever, and he does,[78] and so all who are in him *will reign for ever and ever* (5).[79] They will be eternal kings.

And there they *will worship him.* At last, in the visible presence of God, we will engage in the task, the privilege, the duty, the right, the wonderful, eternal pleasure of enjoying his love together in utterly captivated *worship.* On that day, and from then on, forever, there will truly be 'glory in the church'.[80] God has indeed commanded, 'Assemble the people before me, to hear my words, so that they may learn to revere me.'[81] So our prayer and praises will echo back for eternity: 'Let the assembled peoples gather round you, while you sit enthroned over them on high.'[82]

---

[72] Exod. 33:20; see John 1:18; 1 John 4:12.

[73] Gen. 32:30; Exod. 24:2–11; 33:11; Num. 12:8; Deut. 4:12; Judg. 13:22; Isa. 6:1.

[74] Ezek. 1:1–28; notice his repeated description that what he saw was 'like' something else.

[75] Ps. 42:2.

[76] Face-to-face meetings with God were associated with his blessing: e.g. Num. 6:25; Pss 17:15; 31:16; Job 19:25–27; Matt. 5:8; 1 Cor. 13:12; 2 Cor. 3:18; 1 John 3:2.

[77] Num. 6:25–27.

[78] 2 Sam. 7:13, Pss 21:4; 16:8–11 is quoted by Peter about Jesus' monarchy, Acts 2:30–36.

[79] Dan. 7:18, 27; 1 Cor. 6:2.

[80] Eph. 3:21.

[81] Deut. 4:10, NIV.

[82] Ps. 7:7, NIV.

Study and action guide

HOW TO USE THIS GUIDE

This study and action guide aims to help you get to the heart of the book, and challenge you to apply what you learn to your own life, and to your church. The questions are for use by individuals or by small groups of Christians meeting, perhaps for an hour or two each week, to study, discuss and pray together. They have also been designed to be used by a church's leadership groups. When time is limited, the leader should decide beforehand which questions are most appropriate for the group to discuss during the meeting and which should perhaps be left for group members to work through by themselves or in smaller groups during the week.

PREVIEW. Use the guide and the contents pages as a map to become familiar with what you are about to read, your 'journey' through the book.

READ. Look up the Bible passages as well as the text.

ANSWER. As you read look for the answers to the questions in the guide.

DISCUSS. Even if you are studying on your own try to find another person to share your thoughts with.

REVIEW. Use the guide as a tool to remind you what you have learned. The best way of retaining what you learn is to write it down in a notebook or journal.

APPLY. Translate what you have learned into your attitudes and actions, considering your relationship with God, your personal life, your family life, but especially to your thinking and actions in your church life.

1. Introducing the church (pp. 13–18)

1 What makes the difference between being gathered and being scattered by God (pp. 13–14)?

'Church – a group of vibrant, loving, risk-everything people who are passionately committed to living out the values of God's word and looking forward to the new creation – that is a plan worthy of God himself.' (p. 14)

---

2 Do you have any responsibility for the state of your church (p. 14)?
3 What are the 'cheap solutions' you might be tempted by (p. 15)?
4 What are the strengths and weaknesses of the two sets of diagrams (p. 16)?
5 What does Chris Green mean by 'Mission only exists because church doesn't' (p. 16)?

'The church ... may be evidence, proof, plausibility, manifestation, physical or cultural expression of the gospel, but it is not the gospel.' (p. 17)

---

6 How will you guard against becoming so enthusiastic about the church that you confuse it with the gospel (p. 17)?

Ephesians
2. The church from eternity to Eden (pp. 19–39)

1 Why will there always be believers?
2 What has happened to make the Lord Jesus Christ the most important person in the cosmos (pp. 20–22)?
3 Why has God done this (p. 22)?
4 What does it mean that we are Christ's body from a heavenly perspective? How might we misunderstand the idea (pp. 24–25)?
5 How is the church a demonstration of God's wisdom (p. 25)?
6 How does the temple appear in God's plan today (p. 28)?
7 Why is this a day to be optimistic about the church (p. 30)?

'We are so closely identified with Christ, that in caring for us it is almost as though he is caring for himself.' (p. 32)

---

8 Is it possible to talk of a pastor as the 'head' of a congregation (p. 34)?
9 Why should we understand the word 'church' to mean 'gathering' (pp. 34–36)?

Genesis 17:1–27; Galatians 3:15–29; Colossians 2:11–18
3. The church from Eden to exodus (pp. 40–59)

1 What are the significant patterns for church that flow on from Eden (p. 40)?
2 What are the clues that help you see Genesis 17 as a climax (p. 41)?
3 What is the significance of each element of the covenant promise (pp. 42–43)?
4 How are Christians inheritors of the promise to Abraham (pp. 44–45)?

'We are what God meant, when he told Abraham to count the stars.' (p. 45)

---

5 Why is setting your watch by the wrong time zone so damaging (pp. 45–46)?
6 What are the three lessons about baptism that Galatians 3:15–29 teaches (pp. 46–48)?
7 In what ways has the cross overcome the three barriers (pp. 48–52)?
8 Why is circumcision of importance to Christians (pp. 52–54)?
9 What are the five aspects of Christ's victory in Colossians 2:11–18 (pp. 54–57)?
10 How does Paul relate circumcision to baptism (pp. 57–58)?

'Every Christian was spiritually circumcised, but not at their baptism. Nor was it at their conversion. No, you were spiritually circumcised in Christ, with Christ, on the cross.' (p. 58)

Thinking it through

11 How could you improve your church's theology and practice of baptism?

Exodus 19; Hebrews 12:18–29
4. The church from exodus to exile (pp. 60–77)

1 What are the main differences between worshipping God and worshipping the golden calf (pp. 61–65)? How might people get true and alternative worship confused (p. 65)?
2 How confident are you that what you do in church is what God wants? How do you know what he wants (p. 66)?

3 What are the seven marks of the Sinai meeting (p. 67)?
4 What are the seven marks of the heavenly meeting (p. 68)?

'The awe, wonder, transcendence and mystery that we crave is not produced by candles, medieval architecture, Latin chants and incense; nor by echoing the emotional impact of a contemporary music festival, such as Glastonbury or Burning Man. Instead, it is produced by the gospel, by the awareness that, by faith, we participate in this heavenly assembly.' (p. 72)

---

5 Why does Chris Green say, 'we must deliberately refuse to do anything which might seem to produce an "effect"' (p. 72)?
6 What is the fundamental similarity between Sinai and today (p. 72)? Does your church's life reflect that (p. 73)?
7 What is 'acceptable worship' today (pp. 74–77)?

'We use the word "worship" routinely and easily. "Let's have a time of worship." "John's going to lead us in worship." "We have our worship service at 6.30." "I worship at Highlands Community Church." Here is the radical thought. No New Testament writer wrote those sentences, or anything like them. In fact, they might not have understood what we are talking about.' (p. 74)

---

8 How different is the way Chris Green uses the word 'worship' from how you use the word (p. 77)?

Thinking it through

9 How could you help your church pay better attention to God speaking through Scripture?
10 How could you remember the awe that comes from thinking about the heavenly assembly?

Matthew 16:13–20
5. The church from exile to eternity (pp. 78–94)

'In reaching today's non-Christians, discipling them and developing them into godly leaders for the future, we must recognize that the "church" culture erects an almost insurmountable barrier in the way.' (p. 79)

---

1 How culturally shaped do you think your church is (pp. 78–82)? Make a list of things you do which are cultural expressions, old or new.
2 What are the pressures surrounding this crisis of clarifying Jesus' identity (pp. 81–82)?
3 How would Jesus' various hearers have understood the title, 'Christ' (p. 83)?
4 How would Jesus' various hearers have understood the title, 'Son of God' (pp. 83–84)?

'Throughout this section Peter seems constantly to confess more than he realizes.' (p. 85)

---

5 What are the five viable options for understanding the word 'rock' (pp. 86–89)? Do you agree with Chris Green's choice (p. 89)? Why?
6 How will the gates of hell not prevail against the church (pp. 90–92)?
7 What are the keys to the kingdom of heaven (p. 92)?
8 What could Jesus mean by 'binding' and 'loosing' (pp. 92–93)?
9 What are the three characteristics Chris Green identifies in a church built on Peter (p. 94)?

Thinking it through

10 Make a list of your church's characteristics that reflect the kind of church Jesus did intend to start.

Acts 2:41–47
6. The church's life (pp. 95–110)

1 How would you know if your church shared the early church's commitment to the apostles' teaching (pp. 96–97)?
2 What is the connection between fellowship and finance (pp. 97–99)?
3 What habits does your church have to encourage people to eat together (pp. 100–101)?

'Although the book is frequently called "The Acts of the Apostles", it really is "The Acts of God", and although he is sovereign and generates his own acts, he responds to the prayers of his people, and his people know that.' (p. 102)

---

4 What were the different circumstances in which the early church prayed (p. 101)?

5 What was the double pattern of their meeting? What were the benefits of that pattern (pp. 102–104)?

6 Why was it appropriate for God to bless this church with 'signs and wonders' (p. 104)?

7 What is the evidence for the growth in the number of Christians (pp. 107–108)?

8 What is the evidence for the growth in the number of congregations (p. 109)?

'If growth is natural, we do not ourselves produce it, but our spiritual inattention and love of congregational habits can cause it to be stifled.' (p. 109)

---

9 Do you agree with Chris Green that numerical growth is natural? What might inhibit it (p. 109)?

10 Why has Luke withheld using the term 'church' until this point (p. 109)?

Thinking it through

11 What is the greatest challenge to your church from the pattern in Acts 2?

2 Corinthians 8 and 9
7. The church's compassion (pp. 111–129)

1 What are the three groups Chris Green says we should give to? Does your personal giving mirror them (pp. 112–114)?

'God can, has done, and will again achieve his saving purposes without publishers, conference centres, and seminaries, but he has promised he will never do it without a church' (p. 115)

---

2 What are the three aspects of the giving of the Macedonian churches that Paul commends (pp. 115–116)?

3 How are they a contrast to the Corinthians, and to us (p. 116)?

4 Chris Green says, 'The Lord Jesus models grace leading to generosity'. How is that expanded in this section of Corinthians (p. 117)?

5 What would 'equality' look like in your church' (pp. 118–119)?

6 What lessons could your church learn from how Paul handles the collection (pp. 119–121)?

7 Do you plan your giving (p. 121)?

8 What are the elements of sowing and reaping generously? How do your motivations need to change (pp. 121–124)?

9 How does Paul reassure the Corinthians that they can trust God as he calls on them to be generous (pp. 124–125)?

Additional note: tithing

10 What are the three ways that we move from Old Testament elements to the contemporary church? Can you think of more examples than Chris Green gives (p. 126)?

11 Chris Green has argued for his own position that tithing is no longer binding. Do you agree, and if not, why not (p. 128)?

Thinking it through

12 What is the principal lesson you think your church can learn from Paul's attitude to money?

1 Corinthians 11:17–34
8. The church's meal (pp. 130–147)

'The householder was a generous host, but only to his friends; by contrast, Paul wants them to pay attention to the meal where the Lord Jesus is the host.' (p. 132)

---

1 Think carefully – does your church play 'status games' like the Corinthians (p. 131)?

'Jesus was acting out with the bread what was about to happen to his body on the cross.' (p. 134)

---

2 What are the differences and similarities between the Lord's Supper and the Passover that Chris Green identifies? Can you think of more (p. 135)?

3 When your church holds a Lord's Supper, is the cross central, or something else (p. 136)?

4 How would you answer the two questions which should trouble a sensitive Christian (p. 137)?

5 How might you reassure a scrupulous Christian who feared to take the bread and wine (p. 138)?

6 How would you disturb the conscience of those who should hold back (pp. 138–140)?

7 What does it mean to say that the Lord's Supper is a 'symbol' (pp. 141–143)?

8 Does the way your church handles the Lord's Supper allow enough room for the horizontal elements of the Lord's Supper (pp. 143–146)?

Thinking it through

9 What recommendations might you make to your church's leadership about how the Lord's Supper might be better held?

Colossians 3:15–17
9. The church's praise (pp. 148–162)

1 What are the three areas that Paul wants the Colossians to 'resolve' to address (pp. 149–152)? What actions should they be taking?

'Put simply, relationships between Christians are so important, that they put a potential question mark against anything that divides them.' (p. 150)

---

2 What does your church do ensure the word of God 'dwells' in your teaching? How would it be noticed and corrected if it slipped (pp. 153–154)?

3 Do the songs you sing match the full biblical range Chris Green describes? Which are missing, or muted (p. 155)?

'Paul . . . does not want the Colossians to sing nonsense.' (p. 156)

---

4 How powerfully does music (as opposed to words) move you (p. 157)? Can you think of occasions where you have sung nonsense? How can you guard against that?

5 What are the six benefits of singing that Chris Green identifies (pp. 158–160)?

6 Does your daily life reflect that same gratitude (p. 161)? What could you do to help yourself be grateful, both in word and in deed?

Thinking it through

7 Think through all the different elements that happen when you go to church, from how you travel to church to what you talk about afterwards. How could you ensure that the word of God dwells in all those areas?

Ephesians 4:1–6
10. The church's unity (pp. 163–179)

1 What are the five tests for the relationships in your local church (pp. 165–167)? Which do you think you would find the most challenging?

2 Why is it so important to start from the truth that unity has already been achieved (p. 167)?

'Whatever God has done, this is his supreme masterpiece.' (p. 168)

---

3 What are the seven aspects of Christian unity that Paul lists (pp. 168–173)? How is each one related to the gospel?

4 How is each one related to the Jew/Gentile division being overcome?

5 Chris Green describes 'three major changes in the Christian landscape' (p. 173) Do you agree? Have you seen others?

Putting it all together, part one

6 In terms of the diagram on p. 176, what are the strengths and weaknesses of each of the four aspects?

7 Which aspect does your church most seem to stress?

Thinking it through

8 Do your relationships in your local church demonstrate the unity that Christ has already won? How might you work to improve that?

9 How does your church relate to others in your local area? Are there are some relationships which are easier than others? Why? Do you need to strengthen some boundaries, or knock them down?

10 If your church is part of a denomination, do you put primacy on relating to churches within the denomination? Can you explain why?

Ephesians 4:7–16
11. The church's maturity (pp. 180–196)

1 Read Psalm 68 right through. How does that describe Jesus (p. 181)?

2 What is the relationship between 'grace' and 'a gift' (p. 181)?

3 What are the groups of people that Paul describes (pp. 181–187)? What do they have in common? Why does Ephesians 2:5 mean that some can be described as a 'foundation'?

4 Which of the styles of being an 'evangelist' most aptly describes you (pp. 183–185)? How can you build on that in your relationships? If you are studying in a group, compare your different styles. How might they be used in arranging an evangelistic event for your group? If you are in a leadership role in your church, how can you enable the members to discover their styles and deploy them?

5 How do the words 'shepherd' and 'teacher' explain each other (pp. 185–187)?

6 How do evangelists and shepherd-teachers equip the saints and build up the body (pp. 188–192)?

7 What are the six contrasts between churches where those people do their work, and ones where they neglect it (pp. 192–193)?

Additional note: APEPT

8 If you are familiar with the work of Frost and Hirsch, what do you make of Chris Green's critique (pp. 194–196)?

Thinking it through

9 Who, in your church, would you put in the 'shepherd and teacher' category?

10 Can you see any promising people whom you could encourage to grow into that role?

11 Who, in your church, would you put in the various aspects of the 'evangelist' category?

12 Can you see any promising people whom you could encourage to grow into that role?

1 Timothy 3:1–13; 5:1–25
12. The church's servants (pp. 197–222)

1 Why does Chris Green emphasize that 'Jesus has the only essential ministry for the church' (p. 198)? How does that relate to the ideas of 'service' and 'oversight'?

2 Why does he say we need to rethink the ideas of 'clergy' and 'laity' (pp. 199–200)?

3 What are the arguments for thinking that 'overseers' and 'elders' are the same group (p. 200)?

4 Should a Christian leader have ambition (p. 201)?

5 From the list of characteristics of an elder, which do you think is most demanding today (pp. 202–207)?

6 Why is 'able to teach' highlighted by Paul (p. 207)?

7 What are the similarities and differences between the list for deacons and the one for elders (pp. 210–211)?

8 How generous is your church towards those who work hard at teaching (p. 213)? How could you take that further?

9 How does your church manage to hold its leaders to account without making them vulnerable to gossip (pp. 214–215)?

10 What are the biblical meanings of calling (pp. 216–217)? Would you use the phrase 'a call to ministry'?

11 What is the contribution to the contemporary debate of these passages? Chris Green has suggested that while both men and women were allowed to be deacons, the role of elder was restricted to men. Do you agree, from these passages?

12 What are the qualifications for being an apostle (p. 219)? Could such people exist today?

13 What biblical language does your church use to describe people and structures? Which of the three models of church government does it most identify with (pp. 220–221)? Does it use biblical language biblically?

Thinking it through

14 Can you identify anyone in your church who needs to be encouraged to develop their roles in church in the light of what you have seen in this section? Does this apply directly to you?

Romans 12:1–13
13. The church's gifts (pp. 223–241)

1 What does it mean to 'sacrifice your body' (p. 224)? What are the three adjectives which qualify that? Which is the hardest one for you at the moment?

2 What does it mean to 'renew your mind' (p. 225)? Where do you find it hardest to think differently to our surrounding culture?

3 What does it mean to 'discern God's will' (p. 225)? Do you have a major decision to make, either as an individual or as a church? How does Paul teach us to make such decisions?

4 How does your Bible translate all the words related to *phronein* in vv. 3 and 16 (p. 226)? What do they have in common?

'We must look at gifts relationally and not individually, because we only understand ourselves in relationship with others. Each of us is unique, but we belong to each other.' (p. 227)

---

5 Jean Twenge talks about the 'narcissism epidemic' (p. 227). Do you see evidence of that in your church?

6 What might stop you from giving a correct evaluation of your contribution to the body (pp. 227–228)?

7 Why does Chris Green not like the phrase, 'spiritual gifts' (p. 230)?

8 How would you react to someone who argued that the gifts listed in the New Testament have all ceased (p. 231)?

9 How would you react to someone who argued that the gifts listed in the New Testament all continue (pp. 231–232)?

10 Would you put sound engineers, medics, songwriters or soldiers on your list of gifts (p. 233)? Why/why not?

11 From the list of gifts in Romans 12, which do you see in yourself, your small group or your church (pp. 232–238)? Does it matter if any are not present? What other gifts do you see present?

12 Why do you think Romans 12, like 1 Corinthians 13, puts so much emphasis on love (p. 239)?

Thinking it through

13 Does your church have a clear policy of helping people identify their gifts and find a place to serve? If not, what might a sensible one look like? If you do have one, how could you stop a culture of narcissism ruling the issue?

1 Peter 2:9–12
14. The church's holiness (pp. 242–258)

1 How does Peter adapt each of the three Old Testament passages he quotes to show their fulfilment in Christians today (pp. 242–244)?

'"Church" is not God's alternative to a failed plan A. The church is what Israel was always promised it would become.' (p. 244)

---

2 Why did God choose Israel? Why did he choose the church (p. 245)?

3 What was Israel's role as a 'royal priesthood'? What does Chris Green say are the three implications for us (pp. 246–247)?
4 How is the church a 'holy nation' (p. 247)?
5 How does the idea of being 'owned' by God change the way we relate to each other, and to those outside the church (p. 248)?
6 What does Chris Green say is the point of church (p. 249)?
7 How is where you live like Babylon (pp. 251–253)?
8 Where do you see the fight taking place internally (p. 253)?
9 Do you encounter, or see, hostility towards Christians today (p. 255)? Which persecuted Christians do you regularly pray for?
10 What does Chris Green identify as the three elements with sharp edges for us (pp. 256–257)?
11 Is your church a safe place for Christians to admit they struggle with sin? Who knows about your struggles?
12 How do you resolve the question about the right order of believing, belonging and behaviour (p. 258)?

Thinking it through

13 Chris Green ends this chapter with a series of practical and pastoral questions. How would you resolve them in your church?

2 and 3 John
15. The church's boundaries (pp. 259–276)

1 What does 'walk in truth' mean (p. 261)?
2 What does 'walk in love' mean (p. 262)?
3 What does 'walk in obedience' mean (p. 263)?
4 How are those three ideas related (p. 264)?
5 What are the two things that true love does not love (pp. 264–267)? Which of these is the greatest temptation for your church?
6 How do the two halves of 2 John fit together (p. 267)?
7 What lessons should we learn from Gaius (p. 268)?
8 What are the two warning signs we should be alert to from Diotrephes (p. 269)?

'Abusing power is a principal temptation facing Christian leaders. They see the need for clear direction, tight programmes, solid priorities, firm planning and high commitment, and they see them so clearly that the centre of loyalty slides away from Christ and onto themselves. Doing that, they discover a dangerous truth: as Diotrephes had discovered, it works.' (p. 270)

---

9 How is Demetrius a costly test for the church John is writing to (p. 270)?
10 What are the four stages for treating Christian workers well (pp. 271–272)?
11 Is there any context where you need to pursue reconciliation in relationships (p. 273)? How could you take action from 3 John?
12 Can you think of examples in contemporary church life, where disagreements between congregations or denominations are so serious that they merit exclusion (p. 274)?

Thinking it through

13 Where are the pressure points for your church to love too much, or too little? Which is the greater danger for you?

Acts 11:19 – 20:38
16. The church's future (pp. 277–298)

1 What are the eight features of the Antioch church that Chris Green lists before Sergius Paulus' conversion (pp. 279–283)?
2 Which features are ones that you think should challenge your church?
3 Why is nowhere 'off limits' for the gospel (p. 284)?
4 What core elements make up the gospel (p. 285)? What would you say to the suggestion that it must vary from place to place?
5 What words does Luke use for the range of speaking tasks the missionaries engaged in (pp. 285–286)? What are the three conclusions Chris Green draws from them?
6 How did Paul coordinate his plans with God's (p. 286)?
7 Does your country have strategic cities (pp. 287–288)? Why are they strategic? Do you know what is happening in church planting for each of them?
8 What was Paul's careful evangelistic plan in Philippi (p. 289)?
9 Is the Homogeneous Unit Principle a key to evangelistic effectiveness or a denial of the gospel (pp. 289–290)?
10 Why did the Antioch church fast (p. 291)?
11 Why does Chris Green suggest that miracles continue, but not signs and wonders (pp. 291–292)?
12 What are the three lessons about money (p. 292)?
13 Why are teams necessary for church planting (p. 292)?
14 Does your church have one leader, or several? How is Paul's training of Timothy an example for us to copy (p. 293)?

15 What are the strengths and weaknesses of small and large churches (p. 294)?
16 Is your church ambitious for something (p. 294)?
17 How does your church express its complete dependence on God's sovereignty?
18 How does Paul intend the churches he plants to relate to each other (p. 295)?
19 Why is suffering integral to church planting (p. 295)?
20 Would the process map on contemporary church planting (p. 296)? What might need to be added?

Putting it all together, part two (pp. 297–298)

(This is probably a separate study task, and a leadership team could copy Chris Green's example and spend substantial time on it)

21 Chris Green invites us to find biblical references on the theme of 'house' or 'building' for his diagram (p. 298). What would you suggest?
22 Chris Green describes how his church's leadership thought through its core activities. How do your church's activities map onto his or Rick Warren's diagrams?

Thinking it through:

23 Does your church have a plan to plant? How could you encourage that to happen?

Revelation 21:1 – 22:5
17. The church for eternity (pp. 299–214)

1 How does the structure of Revelation help us to contrast the present and the future (pp. 299–300)? What were the two errors simultaneously present?
2 What are the characteristics of our future life (pp. 302–304)?
3 What are the practical implications of that for church leaders, especially as they exercise discipline (p. 304)?
4 What are the two destinies of humankind (pp. 304–305)?
5 How does that explain the present reality of suffering for our faith? What does Chris Green suggest that those of us at liberty should do (pp. 306–307)?

'But by the end that city-whore has gone, having been judged and punished. Only the city-bride is left, ravishingly beautiful in the spotlight.' (p. 302)

6 How does John excite us about our future glory (pp. 308–310)?
7 How does glory stream out from the future temple (p. 310)?
8 How does glory stream into it (p. 311)?
9 Are you disappointed in your current church? How might this vision correct your understanding?

Thinking it through

10 Chris Green has repeatedly said, ' . . . but not yet'. Do you think your church thinks too much, or too little, about its future glory?

The Bible Speaks Today: Old Testament series

The Message of Genesis 1 – 11
The dawn of creation
David Atkinson

The Message of Genesis 12 – 50
From Abraham to Joseph
Joyce G. Baldwin

The Message of Exodus
The days of our pilgrimage
Alec Motyer

The Message of Leviticus
Free to be holy
Derek Tidball

The Message of Numbers
Journey to the promised land
Raymond Brown

The Message of Deuteronomy
Not by bread alone
Raymond Brown

The Message of Judges
Grace abounding
Michael Wilcock

The Message of Ruth
The wings of refuge
David Atkinson

The Message of Samuel
*Personalities, potential, politics
and power*
Mary Evans

The Message of Kings
God is present
John W. Olley

The Message of Chronicles
One church, one faith, one Lord
Michael Wilcock

**The Message of Ezra and
Haggai**
Building for God
Robert Fyall

The Message of Nehemiah
God's servant in a time of change
Raymond Brown

The Message of Esther
God present but unseen
David G. Firth

The Message of Job
Suffering and grace
David Atkinson

**The Message of Psalms
1 – 72**
Songs for the people of God
Michael Wilcock

**The Message of Psalms
73 – 150**
Songs for the people of God
Michael Wilcock

The Message of Proverbs
Wisdom for life
David Atkinson

The Message of Ecclesiastes
*A time to mourn, and a time to
dance*
Derek Kidner

**The Message of the Song of
Songs**
The lyrics of love
Tom Gledhill

The Message of Isaiah
On eagles' wings
Barry Webb

The Bible Speaks Today: New Testament series

The Message of the Sermon on the Mount (Matthew5– 7)
Christian counter-culture
John Stott

The Message of Matthew
The kingdom of heaven
Michael Green

The Message of Mark
The mystery of faith
Donald English

The Message of Luke
The Saviour of the world
Michael Wilcock

The Message of John
Here is your King!
Bruce Milne

The Message of Acts
To the ends of the earth
John Stott

The Message of Romans
God's good news for the world
John Stott

The Message of 1 Corinthians
Life in the local church
David Prior

The Message of 2 Corinthians
Power in weakness
Paul Barnett

The Message of Galatians
Only one way
John Stott

The Message of Ephesians
God's new society
John Stott

The Message of Philippians
Jesus our Joy
Alec Motyer

The Message of Colossians and Philemon
Fullness and freedom
Dick Lucas

The Message of Thessalonians
Preparing for the coming King
John Stott

The Message of 1 Timothy and Titus
The life of the local church
John Stott

The Message of 2 Timothy
Guard the gospel
John Stott

The Message of Hebrews
Christ above all
Raymond Brown

The Message of James
The tests of faith
Alec Motyer

The Message of 1 Peter
The way of the cross
Edmund Clowney

The Message of 2 Peter and Jude
The promise of his coming
Dick Lucas and Christopher Green

The Message of John's Letters
Living in the love of God
David Jackman

The Message of Revelation
I saw heaven opened
Michael Wilcock